SICKNESS UNTO DEATH

I

story by: hikaru asada
art by: takahiro seguchi

D0036125

SICKNESS UNTO DEATH 1

CONTENTS

VERTICAL.

As long as man is human,
there is a despair he will never
fully comprehend.

That despair is a sickness unto death.

From *Sickness Unto Death*
by Søren Kierkegaard

Chapter 1 Emiru

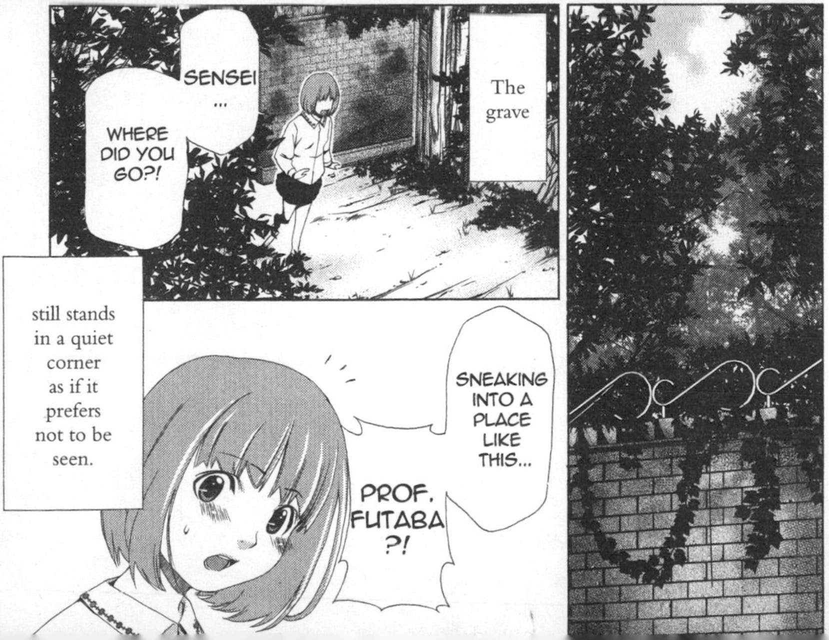
The grave
SENSEI ... WHERE DID YOU GO?!
still stands in a quiet corner as if it prefers not to be seen.
SNEAKING INTO A PLACE LIKE THIS...
PROF. FUTABA?!

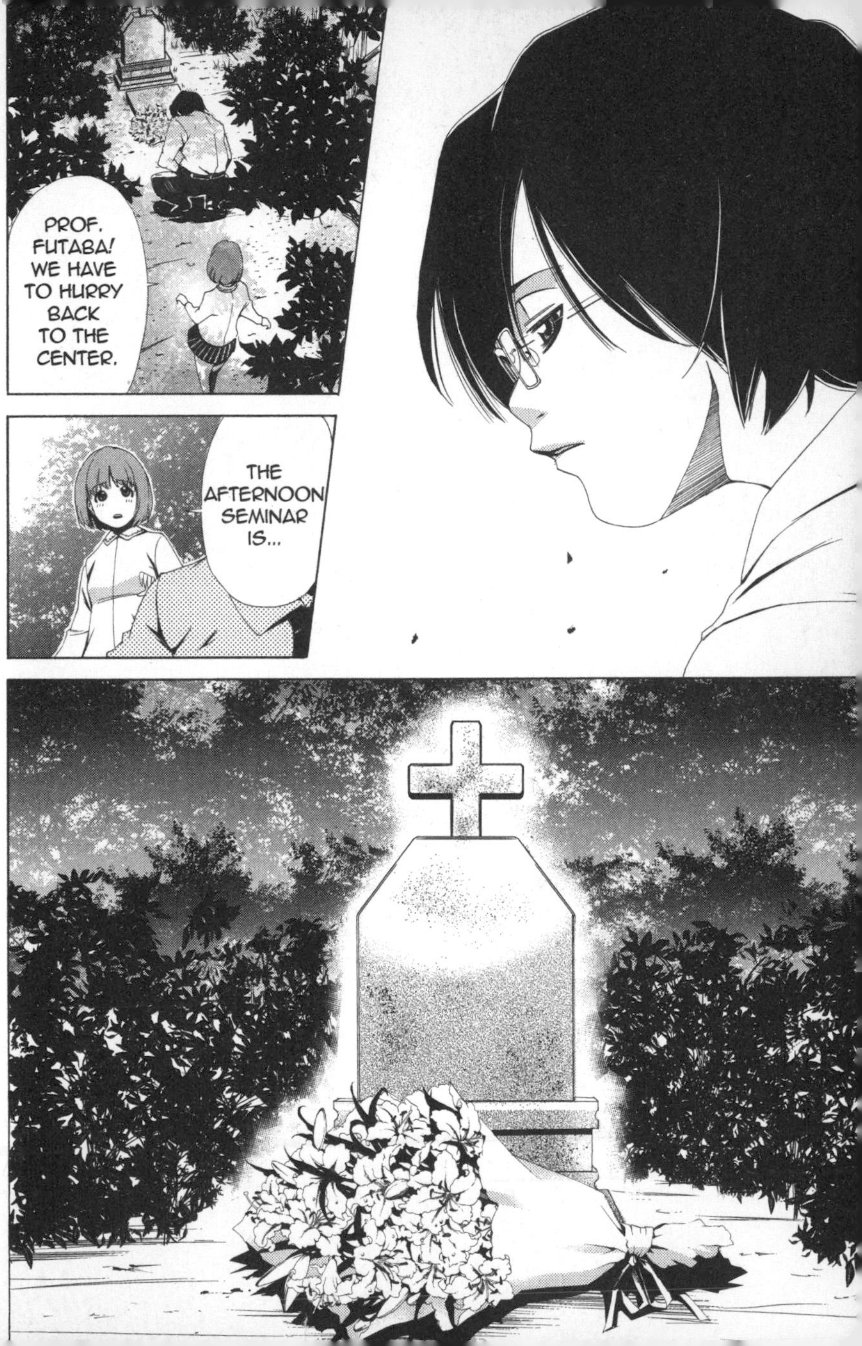
PROF. FUTABA! WE HAVE TO HURRY BACK TO THE CENTER.
THE AFTERNOON SEMINAR IS...

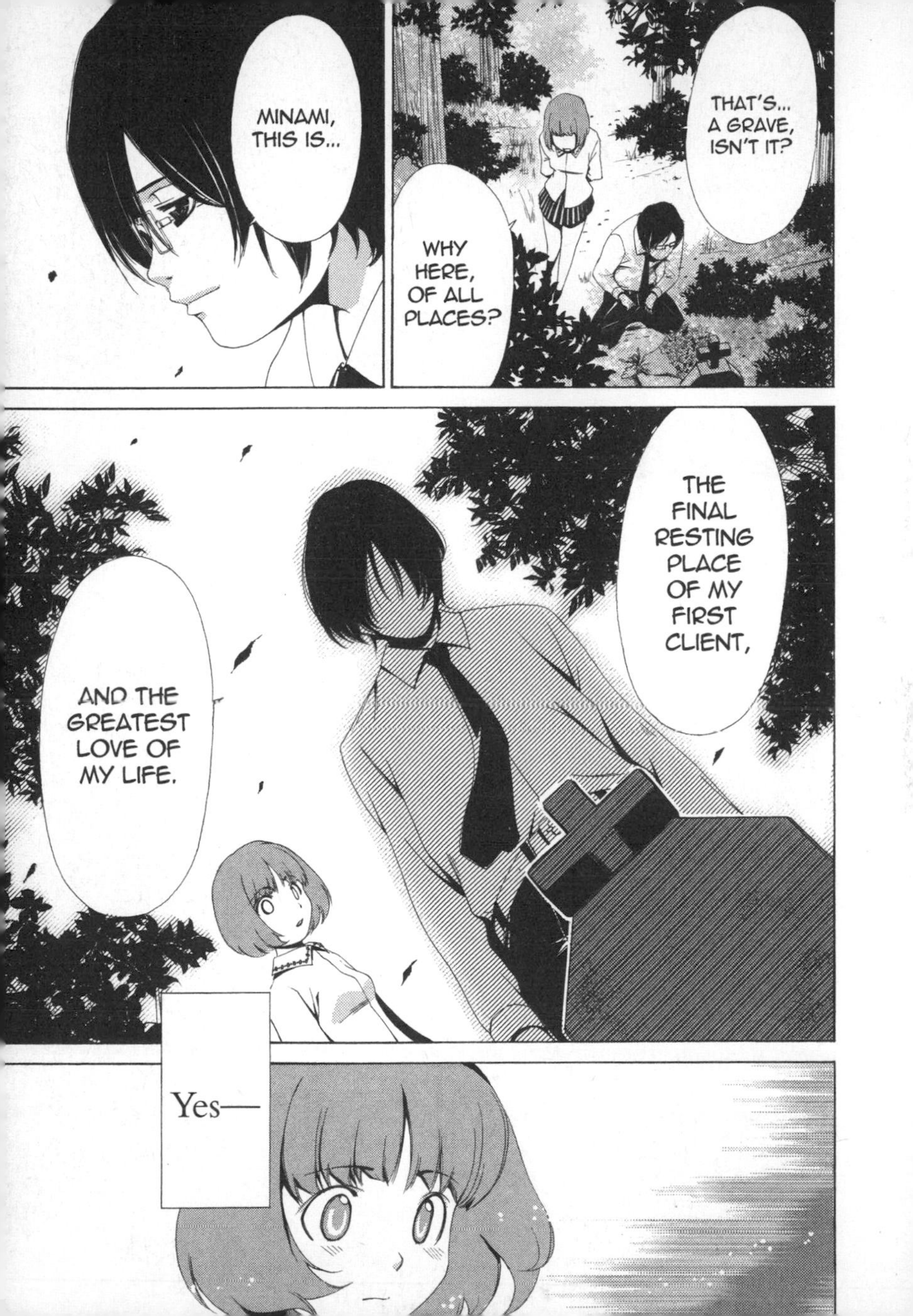
THAT'S... A GRAVE, ISN'T IT?
WHY HERE, OF ALL PLACES?
MINAMI, THIS IS...
THE FINAL RESTING PLACE OF MY FIRST CLIENT,
AND THE GREATEST LOVE OF MY LIFE.
Yes—

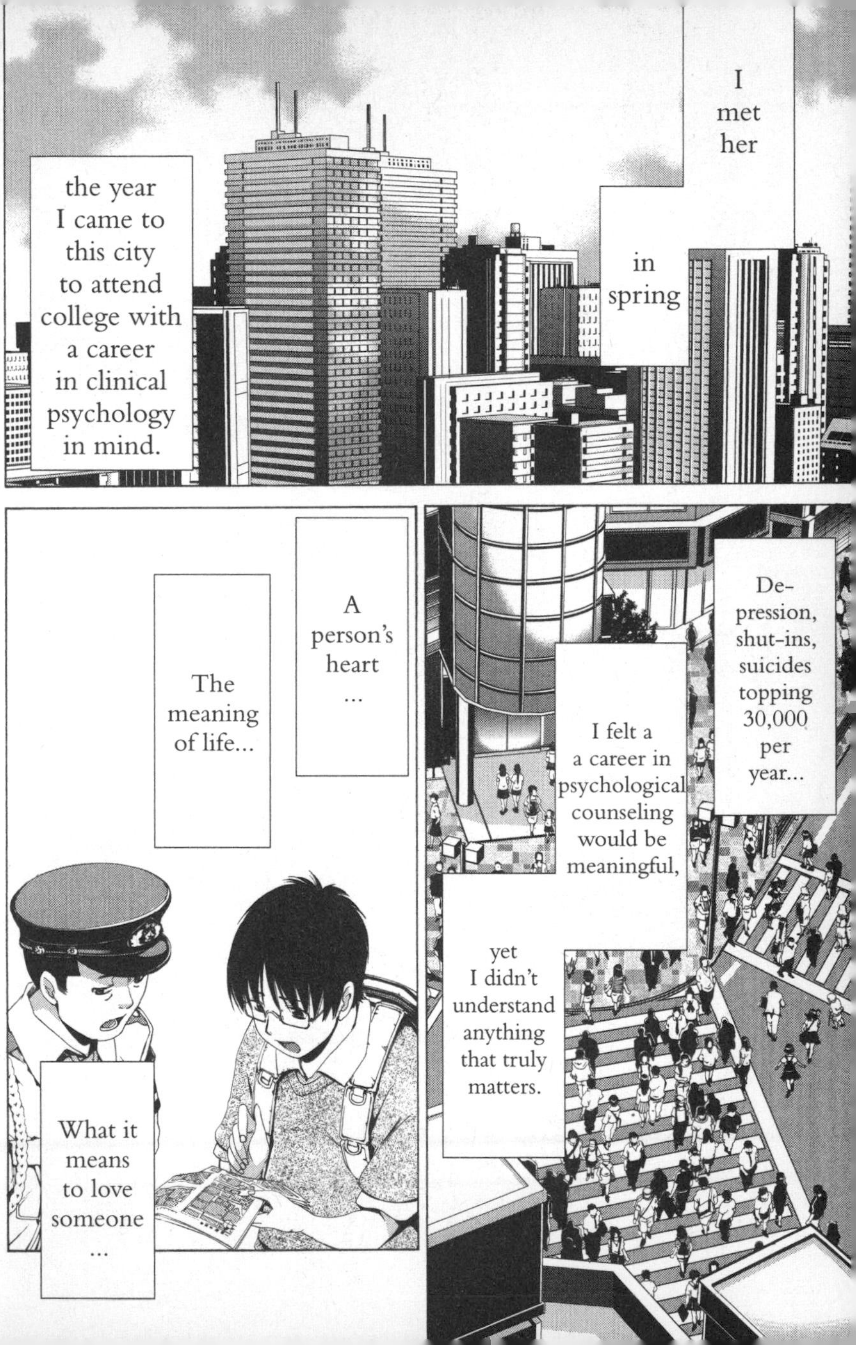
I met her
in spring
the year I came to this city to attend college with a career in clinical psychology in mind.
De-pression, shut-ins, suicides topping 30,000 per year...
I felt a a career in psychological counseling would be meaningful,
yet I didn't understand anything that truly matters.
A person's heart ...
The meaning of life...
What it means to love someone ...

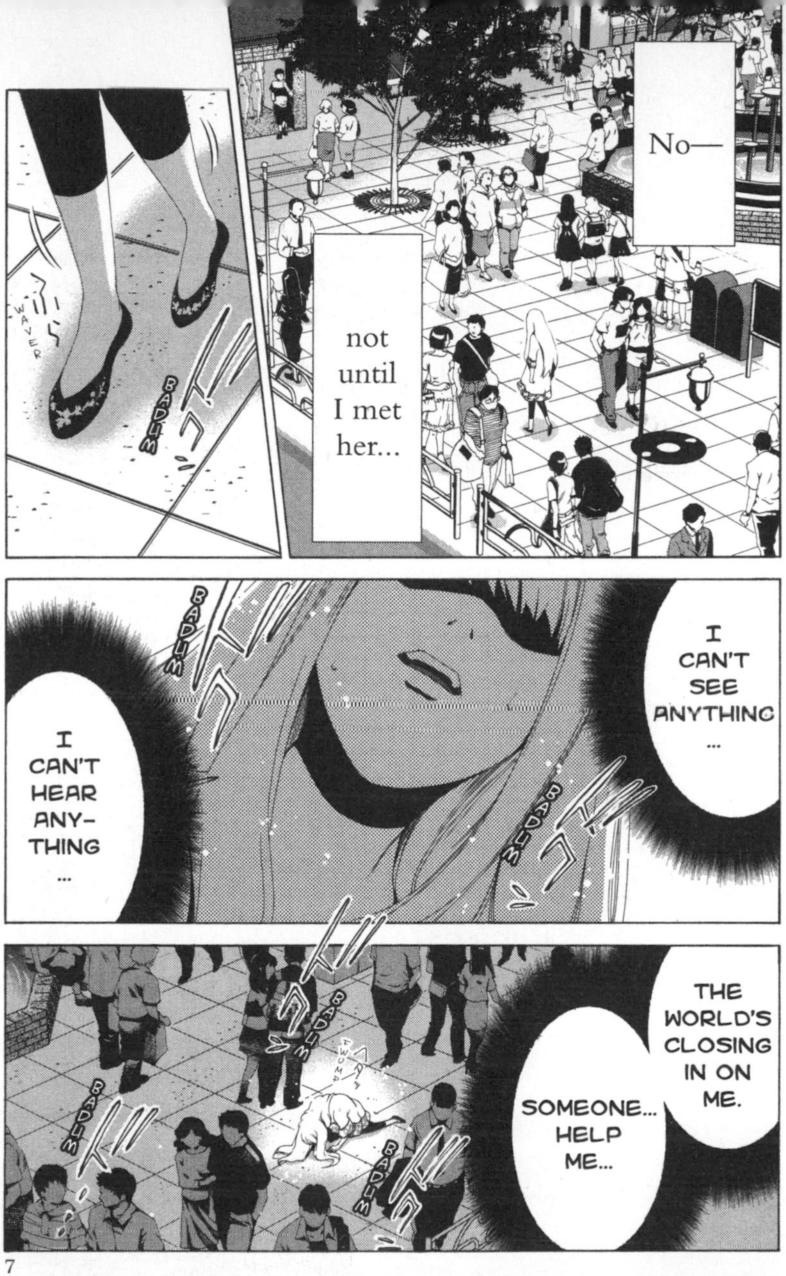
No—
not until I met her...
WAVER
BADUM
I CAN'T SEE ANYTHING...
BADUM
I CAN'T HEAR ANYTHING...
BADUM
THE WORLD'S CLOSING IN ON ME.
SOMEONE... HELP ME...
BADUM
FWUMP
BADUM
BADUM

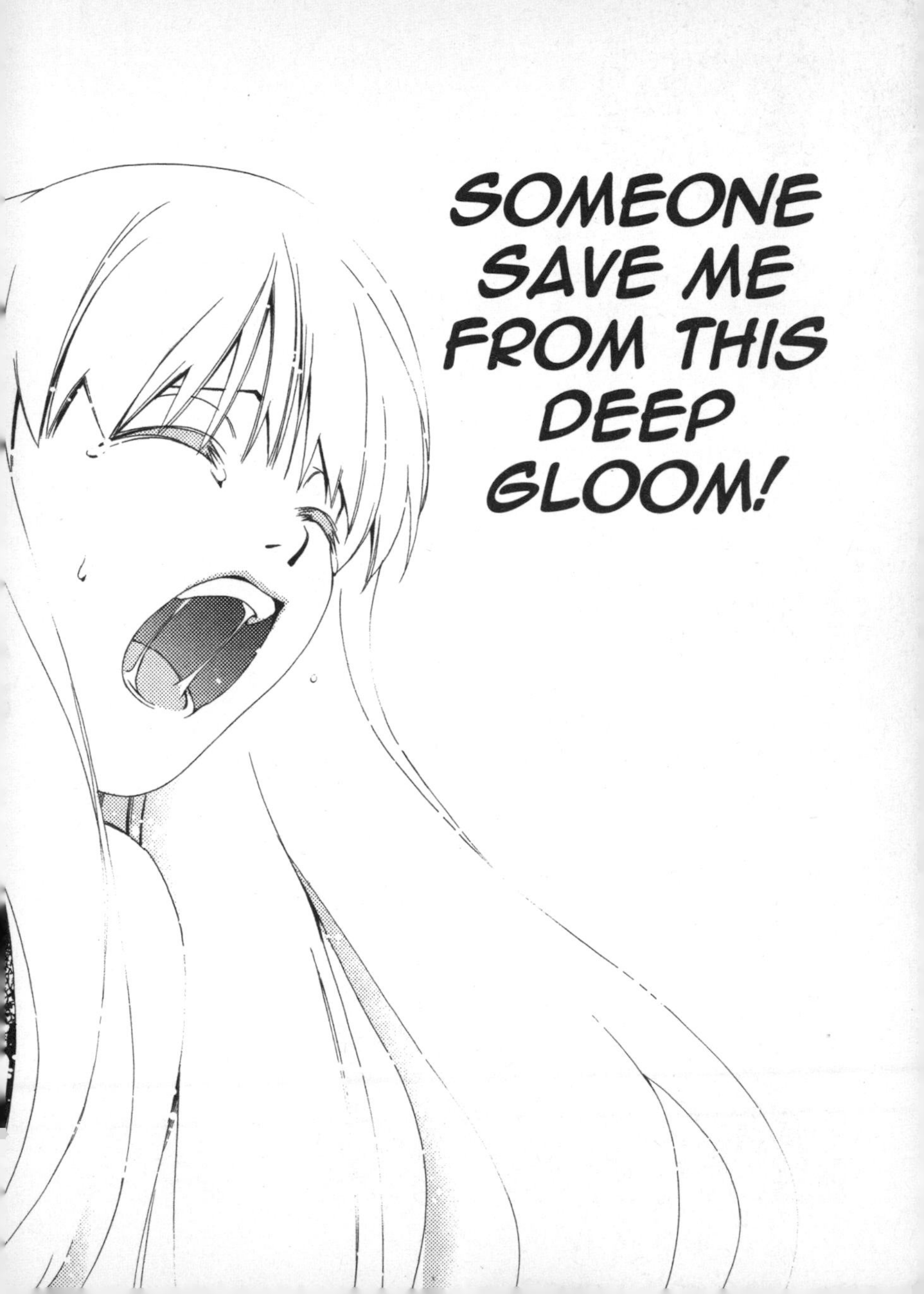
SOMEONE SAVE ME FROM THIS DEEP GLOOM!

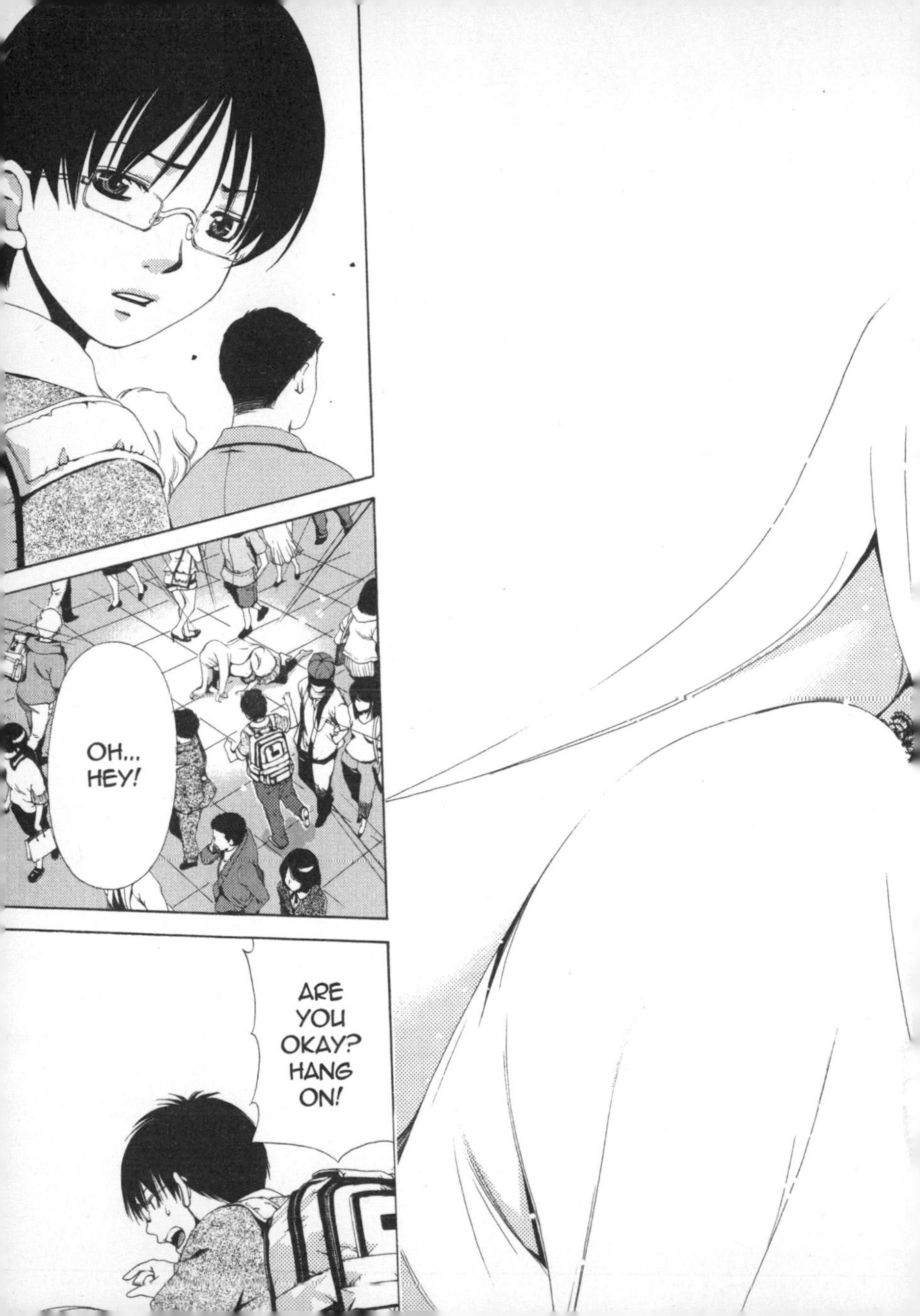
OH... HEY!
ARE YOU OKAY? HANG ON!

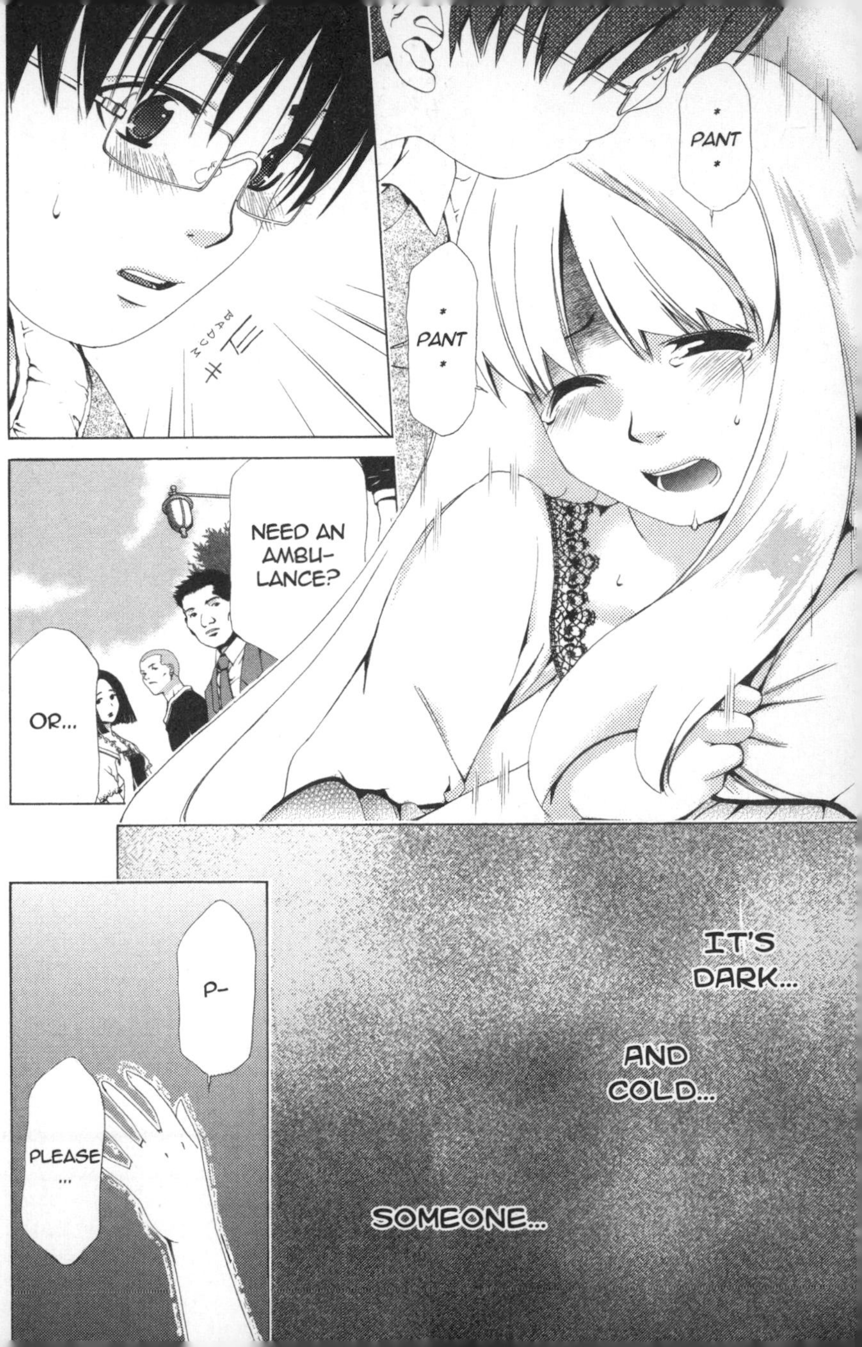
* PANT *
* PANT *
BADUM
NEED AN AMBU-LANCE?
OR...
IT'S DARK...
AND COLD...
SOMEONE...
P-
PLEASE ...

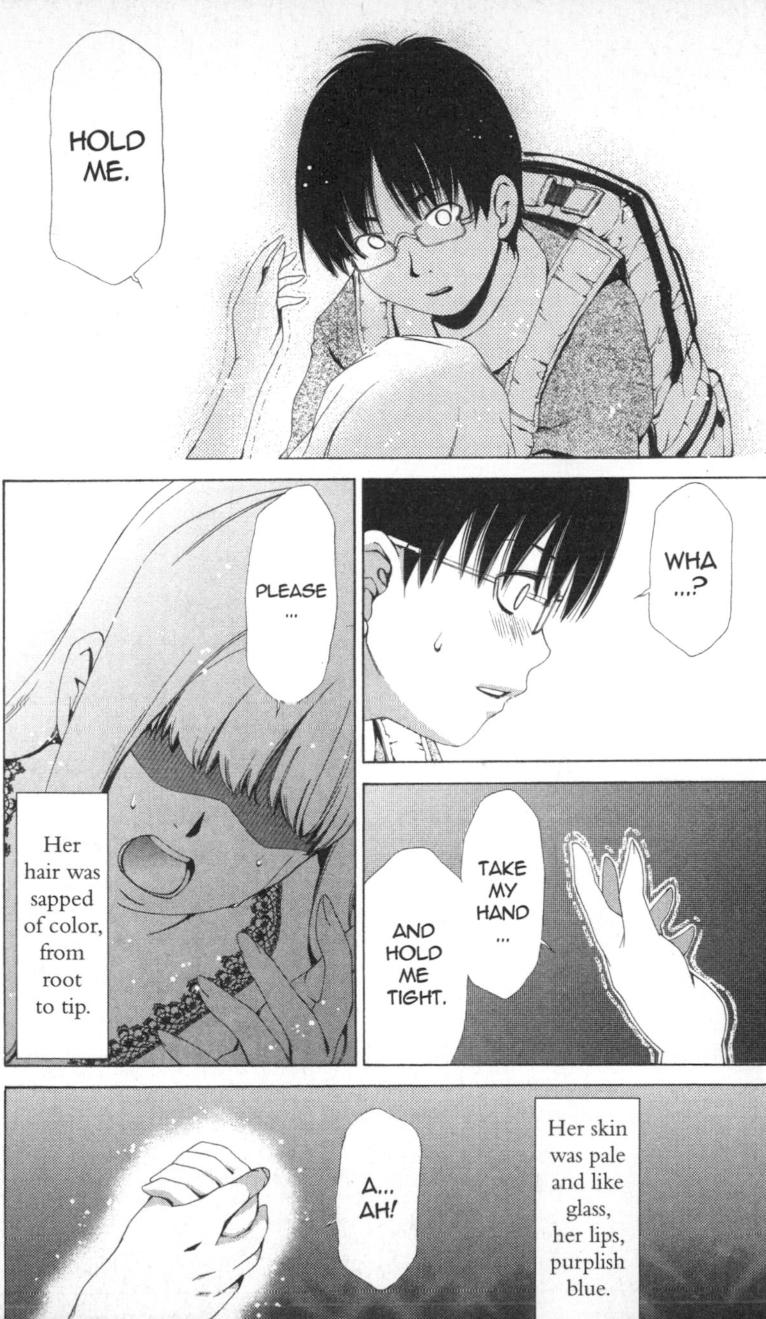
HOLD ME.
WHA ...?
TAKE MY HAND ...
AND HOLD ME TIGHT.
PLEASE ...
Her hair was sapped of color, from root to tip.
Her skin was pale and like glass, her lips, purplish blue.
A... AH!

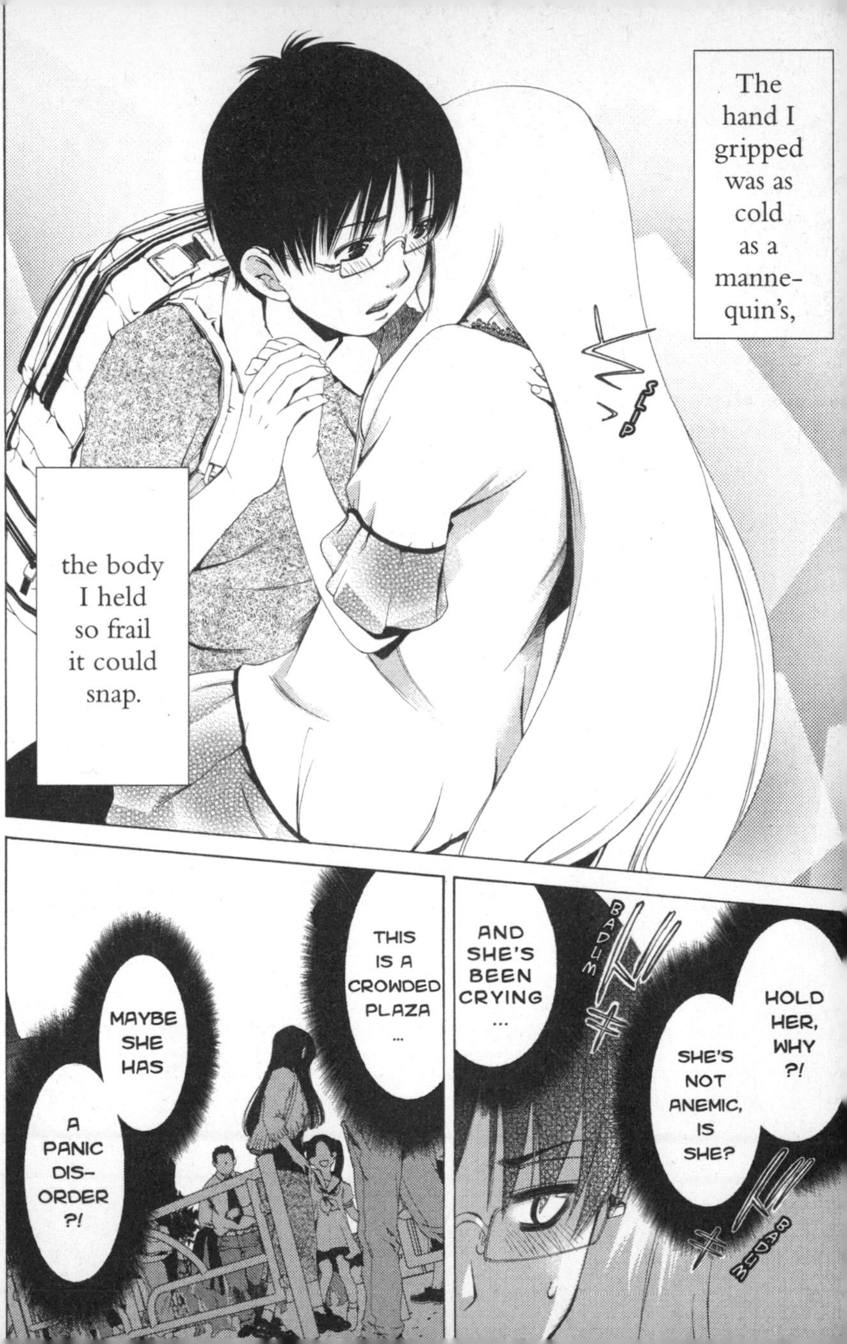
The hand I gripped was as cold as a manne-quin's,
SLIP
the body I held so frail it could snap.
BADUM
HOLD HER, WHY?!
SHE'S NOT ANEMIC, IS SHE?
BADUM
AND SHE'S BEEN CRYING ...
THIS IS A CROWDED PLAZA ...
MAYBE SHE HAS
A PANIC DIS-ORDER ?!

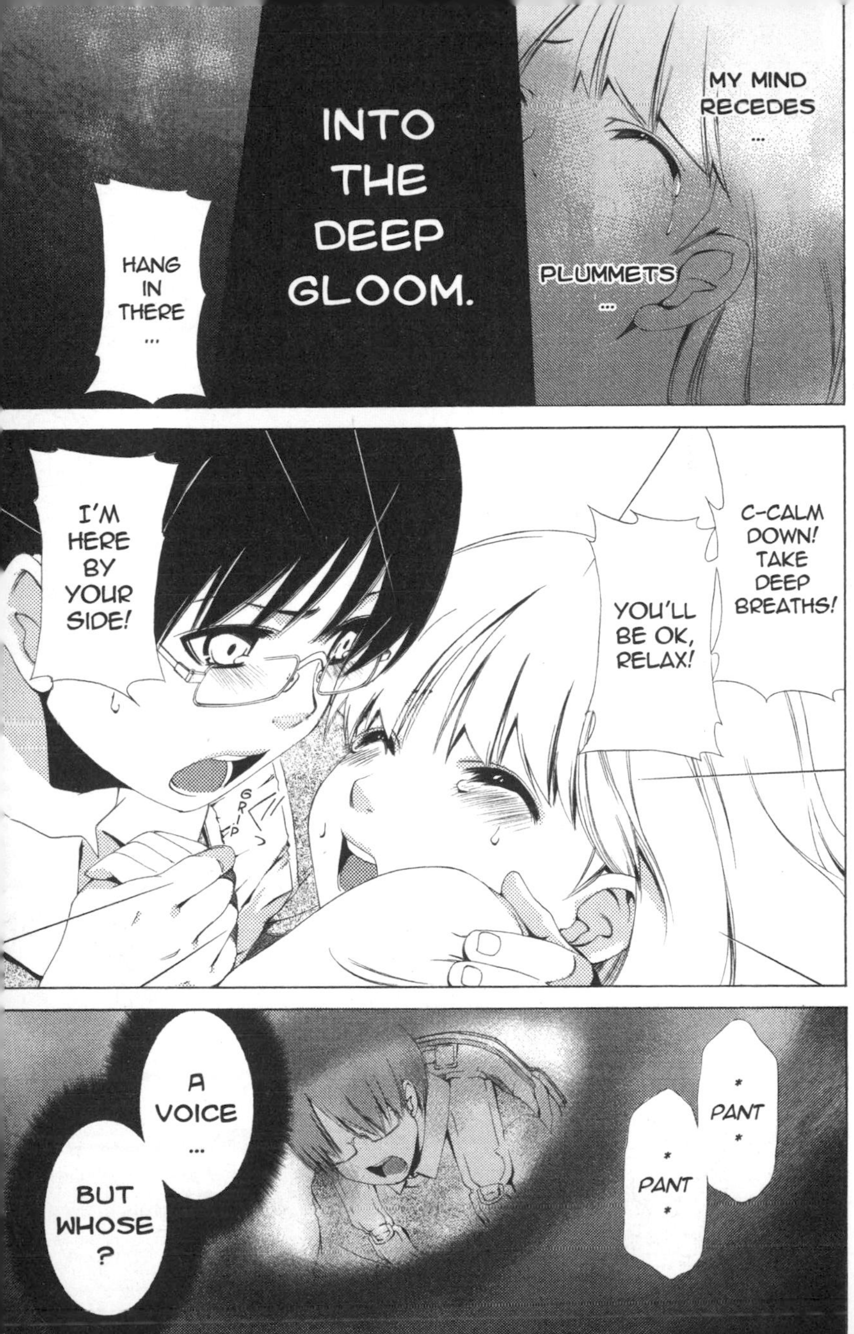
MY MIND RECEDES ...
PLUMMETS ...
INTO THE DEEP GLOOM.
HANG IN THERE ...
C-CALM DOWN! TAKE DEEP BREATHS!
YOU'LL BE OK, RELAX!
I'M HERE BY YOUR SIDE!
GRIP
* PANT *
* PANT *
A VOICE ...
BUT WHOSE ?

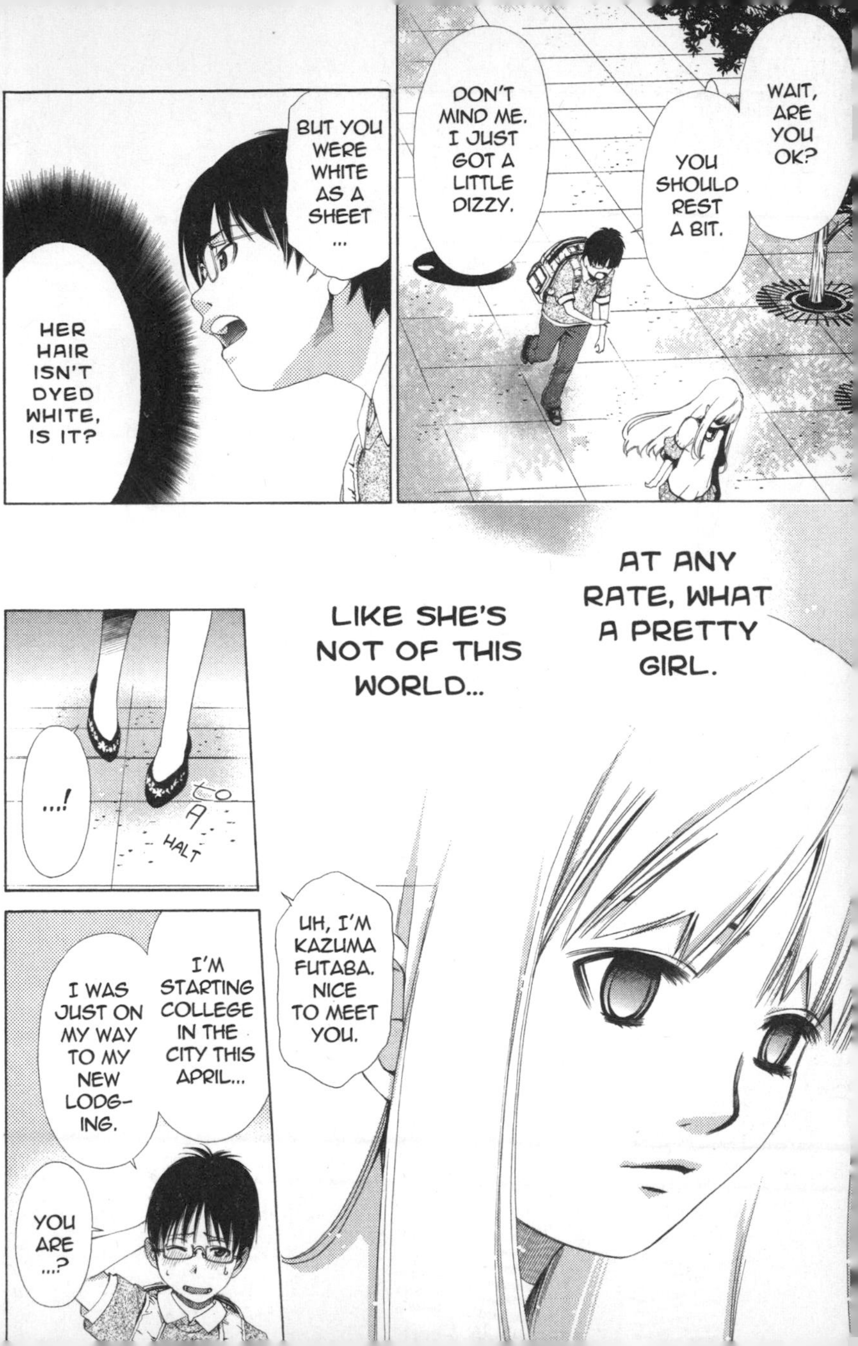
WAIT, ARE YOU OK?
YOU SHOULD REST A BIT.
DON'T MIND ME. I JUST GOT A LITTLE DIZZY.
BUT YOU WERE WHITE AS A SHEET ...
HER HAIR ISN'T DYED WHITE, IS IT?
AT ANY RATE, WHAT A PRETTY GIRL.
LIKE SHE'S NOT OF THIS WORLD...
...!
TO A HALT
UH, I'M KAZUMA FUTABA. NICE TO MEET YOU.
I'M STARTING COLLEGE IN THE CITY THIS APRIL...
I WAS JUST ON MY WAY TO MY NEW LODG-ING.
YOU ARE ...?

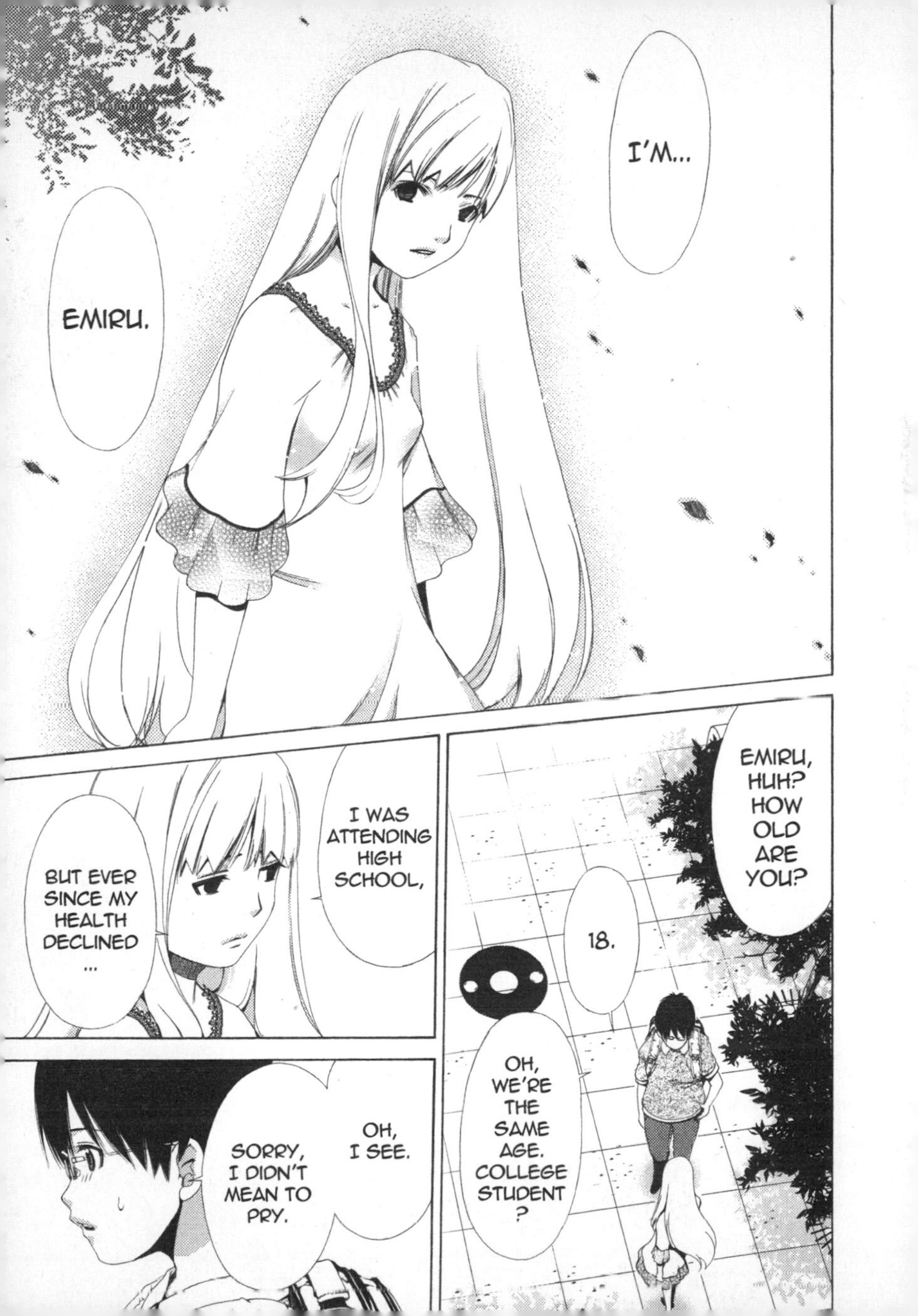
I'M...
EMIRU.
EMIRU, HUH? HOW OLD ARE YOU?
18.
OH, WE'RE THE SAME AGE. COLLEGE STUDENT?
I WAS ATTENDING HIGH SCHOOL,
BUT EVER SINCE MY HEALTH DECLINED ...
OH, I SEE.
SORRY, I DIDN'T MEAN TO PRY.

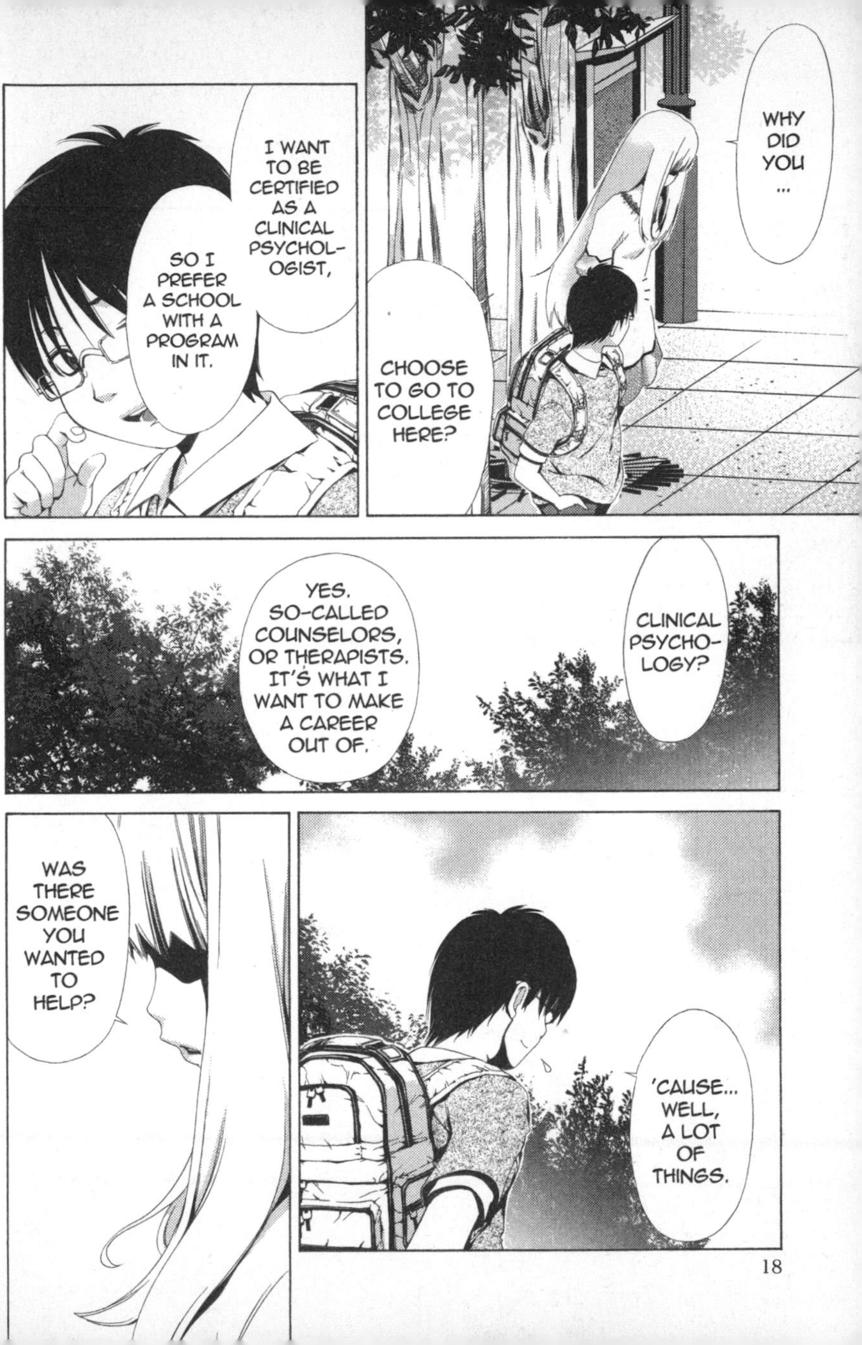
WHY DID YOU ...
CHOOSE TO GO TO COLLEGE HERE?
I WANT TO BE CERTIFIED AS A CLINICAL PSYCHOL-OGIST,
SO I PREFER A SCHOOL WITH A PROGRAM IN IT.
CLINICAL PSYCHO-LOGY?
YES. SO-CALLED COUNSELORS, OR THERAPISTS. IT'S WHAT I WANT TO MAKE A CAREER OUT OF.
'CAUSE... WELL, A LOT OF THINGS.
WAS THERE SOMEONE YOU WANTED TO HELP?

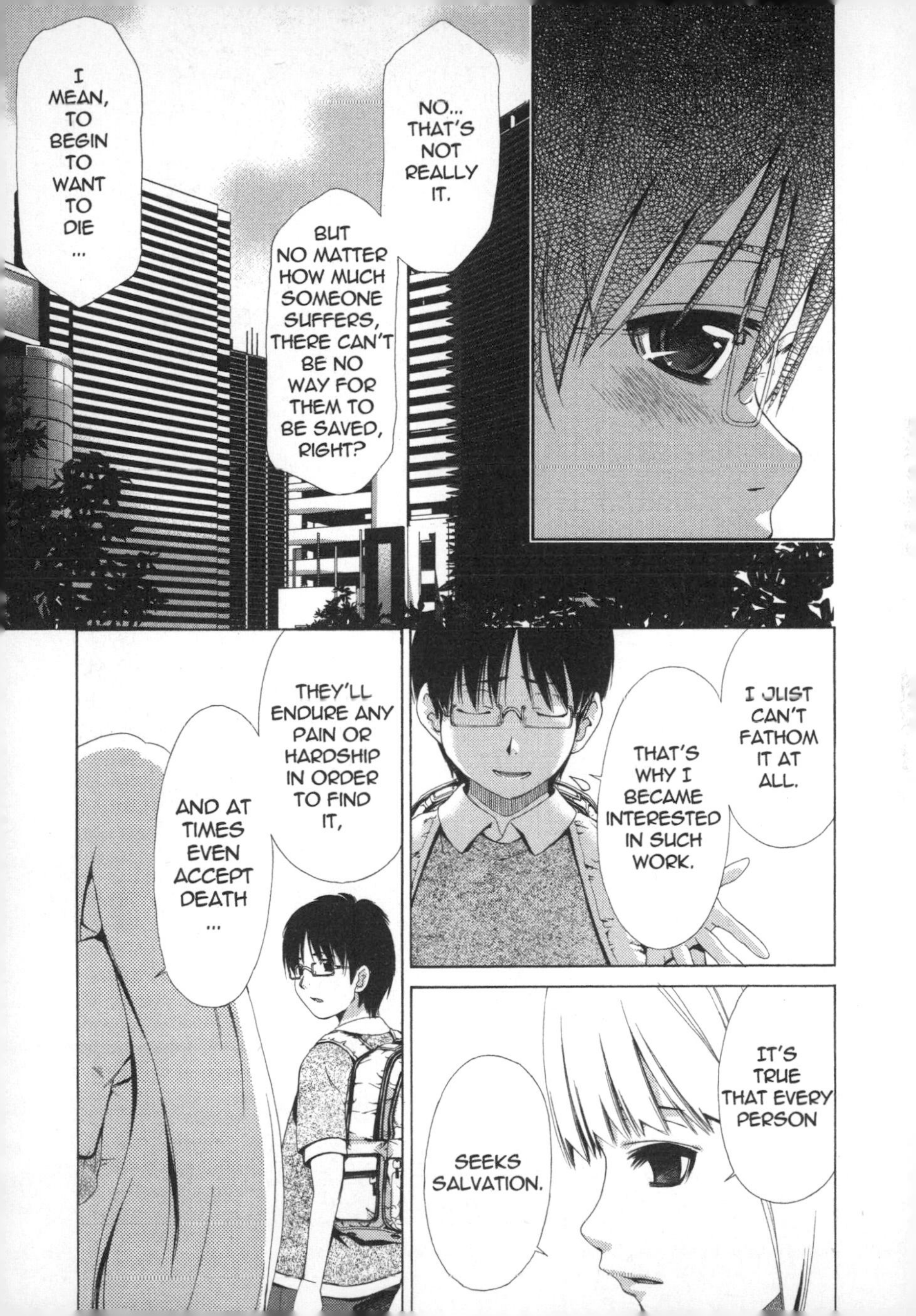
NO... THAT'S NOT REALLY IT.
BUT NO MATTER HOW MUCH SOMEONE SUFFERS, THERE CAN'T BE NO WAY FOR THEM TO BE SAVED, RIGHT?
I MEAN, TO BEGIN TO WANT TO DIE ...
I JUST CAN'T FATHOM IT AT ALL.
THAT'S WHY I BECAME INTERESTED IN SUCH WORK.
IT'S TRUE THAT EVERY PERSON
SEEKS SALVATION.
THEY'LL ENDURE ANY PAIN OR HARDSHIP IN ORDER TO FIND IT,
AND AT TIMES EVEN ACCEPT DEATH ...

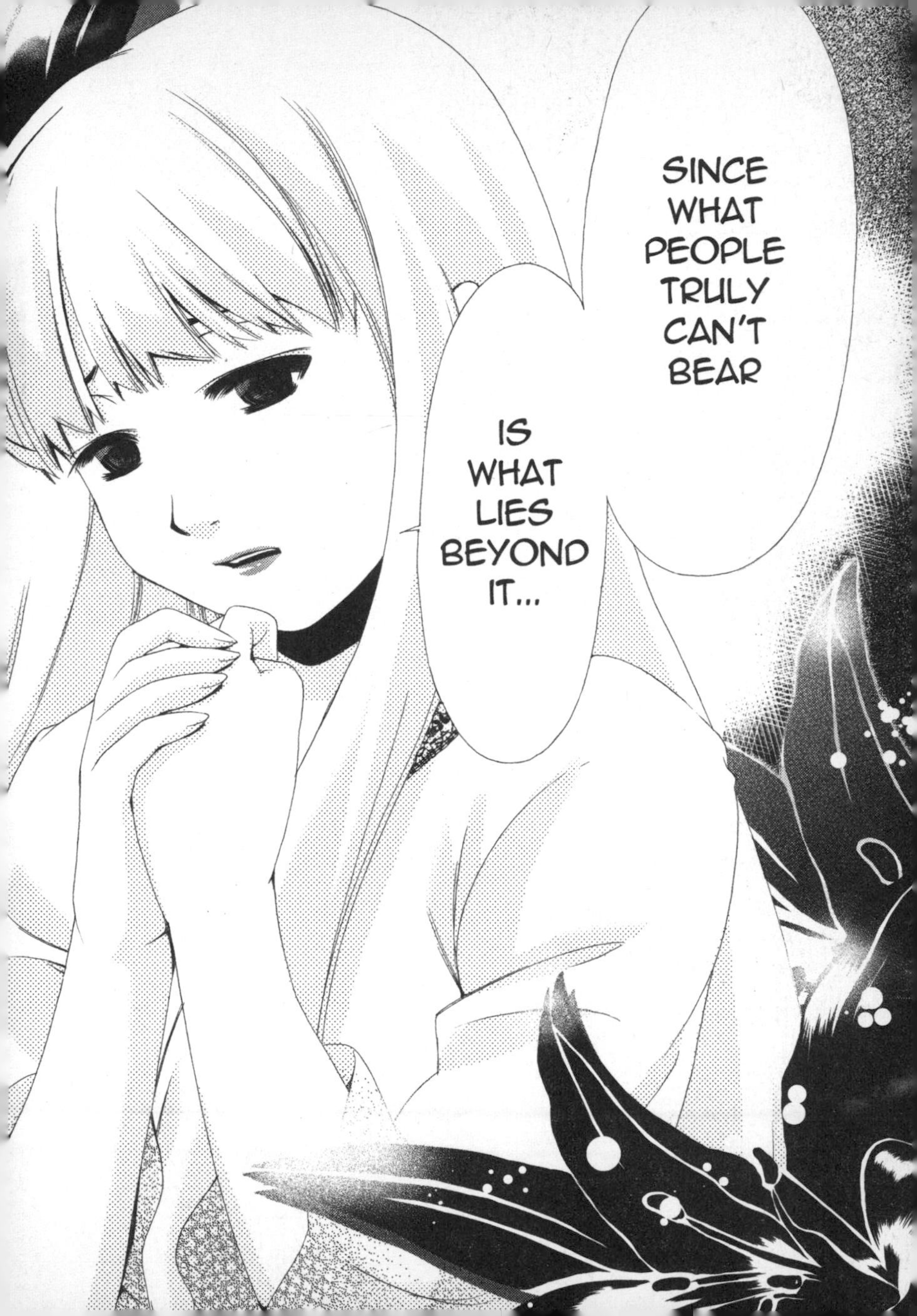
SINCE WHAT PEOPLE TRULY CAN'T BEAR
IS WHAT LIES BEYOND IT...

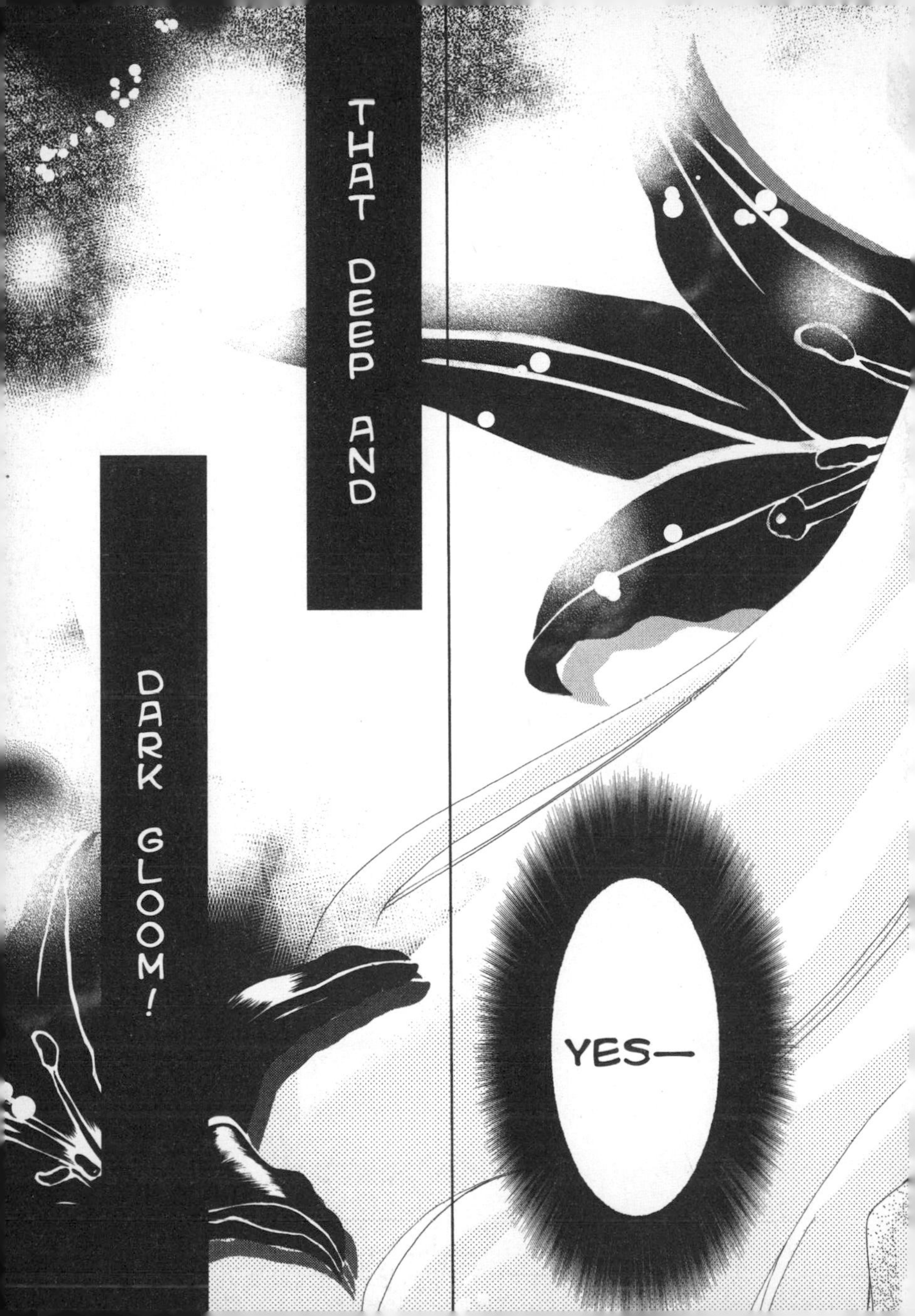
YES—
THAT DEEP AND
DARK GLOOM!

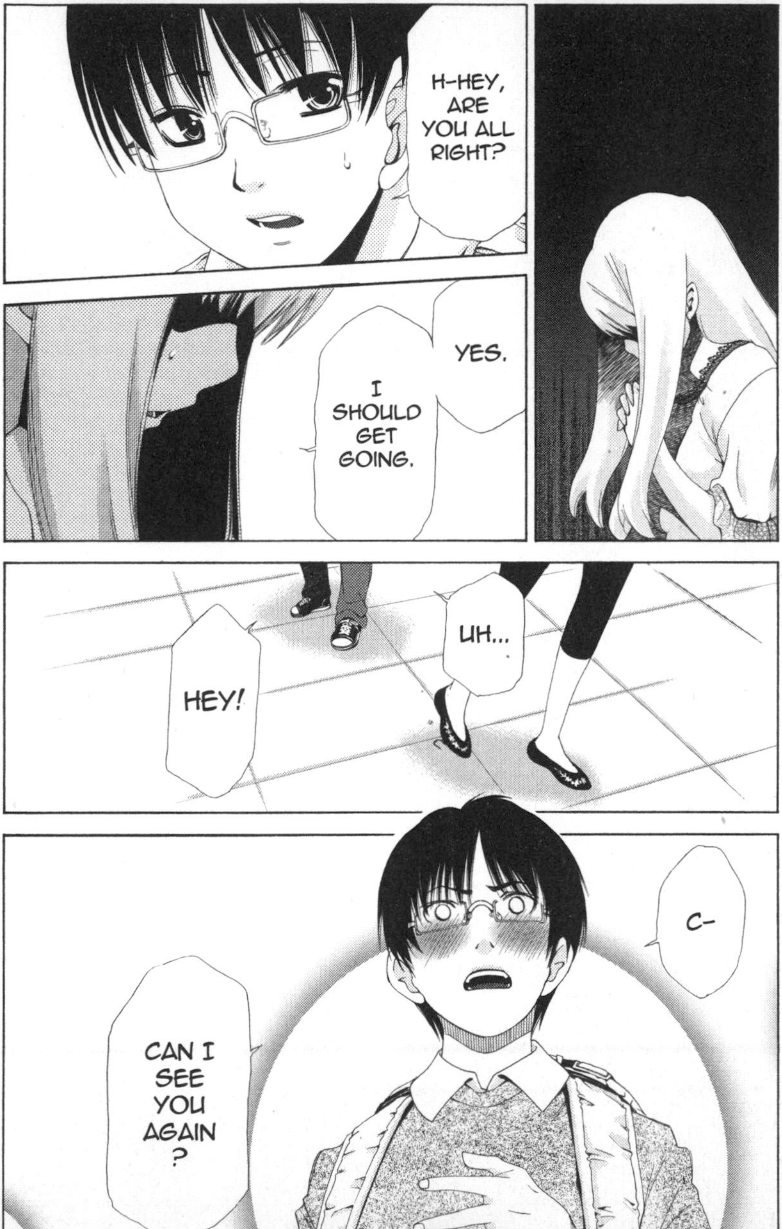
H-HEY, ARE YOU ALL RIGHT?
YES.
I SHOULD GET GOING.
UH...
HEY!
C-
CAN I SEE YOU AGAIN?

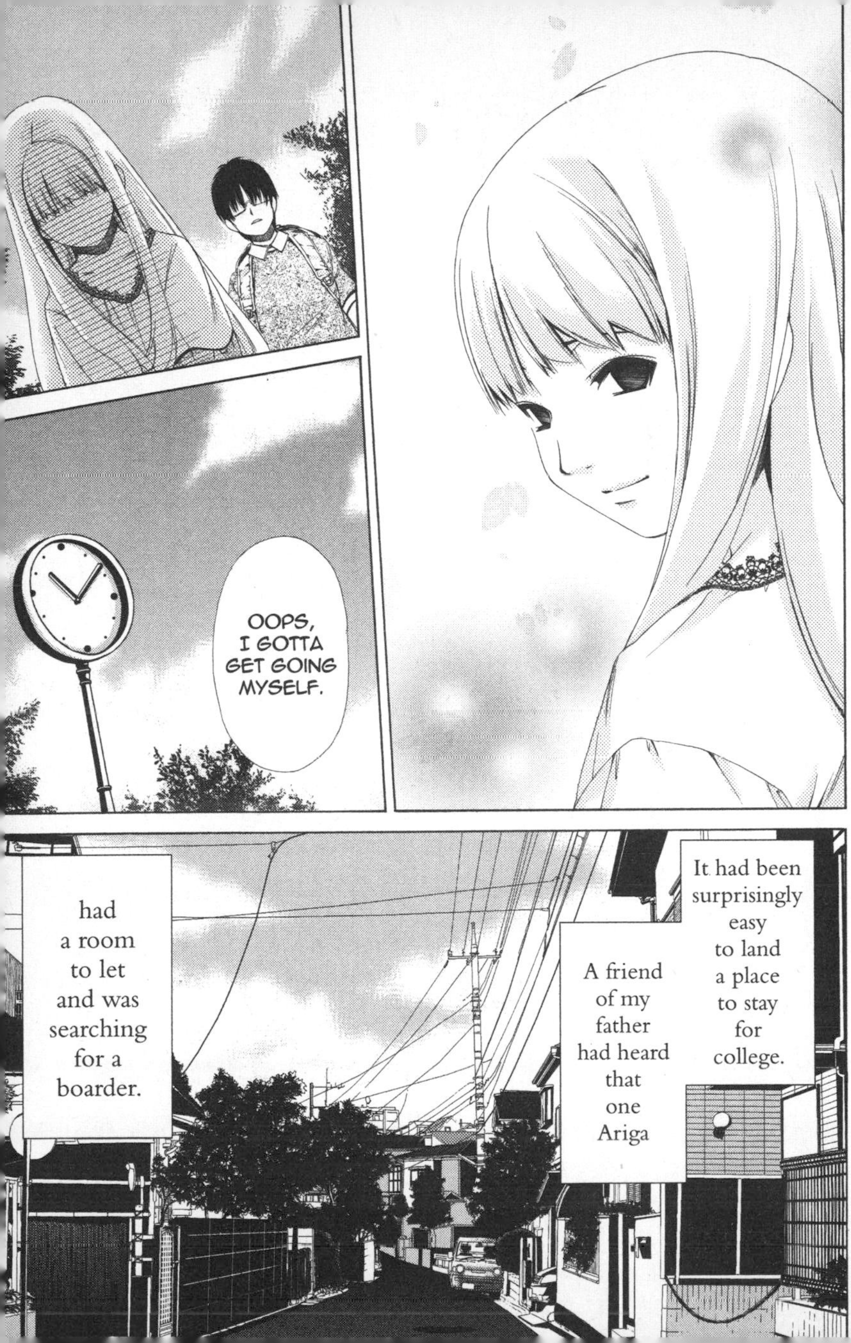
OOPS, I GOTTA GET GOING MYSELF.
It had been surprisingly easy to land a place to stay for college.
A friend of my father had heard that one Ariga
had a room to let and was searching for a boarder.

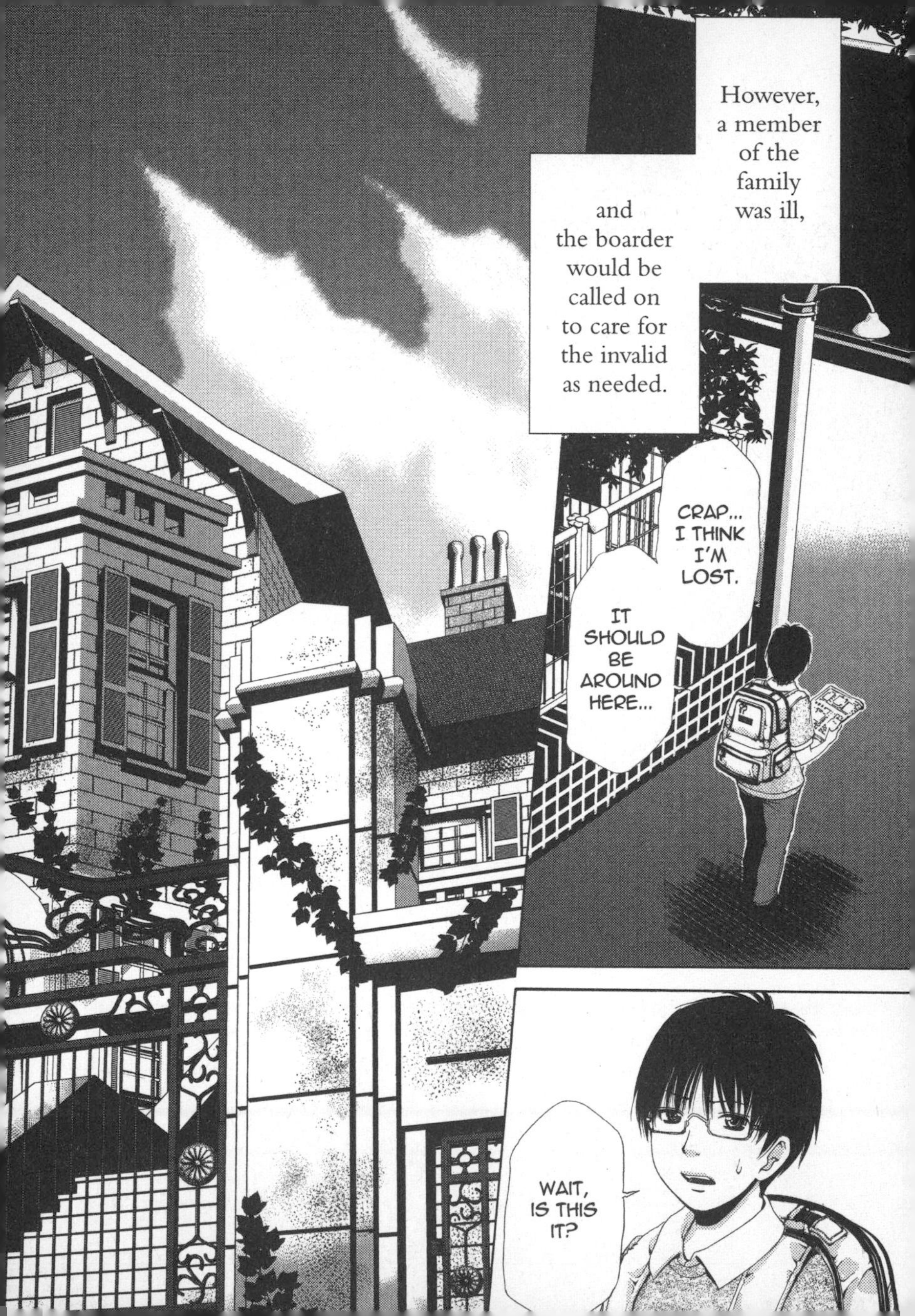
However, a member of the family was ill,
and the boarder would be called on to care for the invalid as needed.
CRAP... I THINK I'M LOST.
IT SHOULD BE AROUND HERE...
WAIT, IS THIS IT?

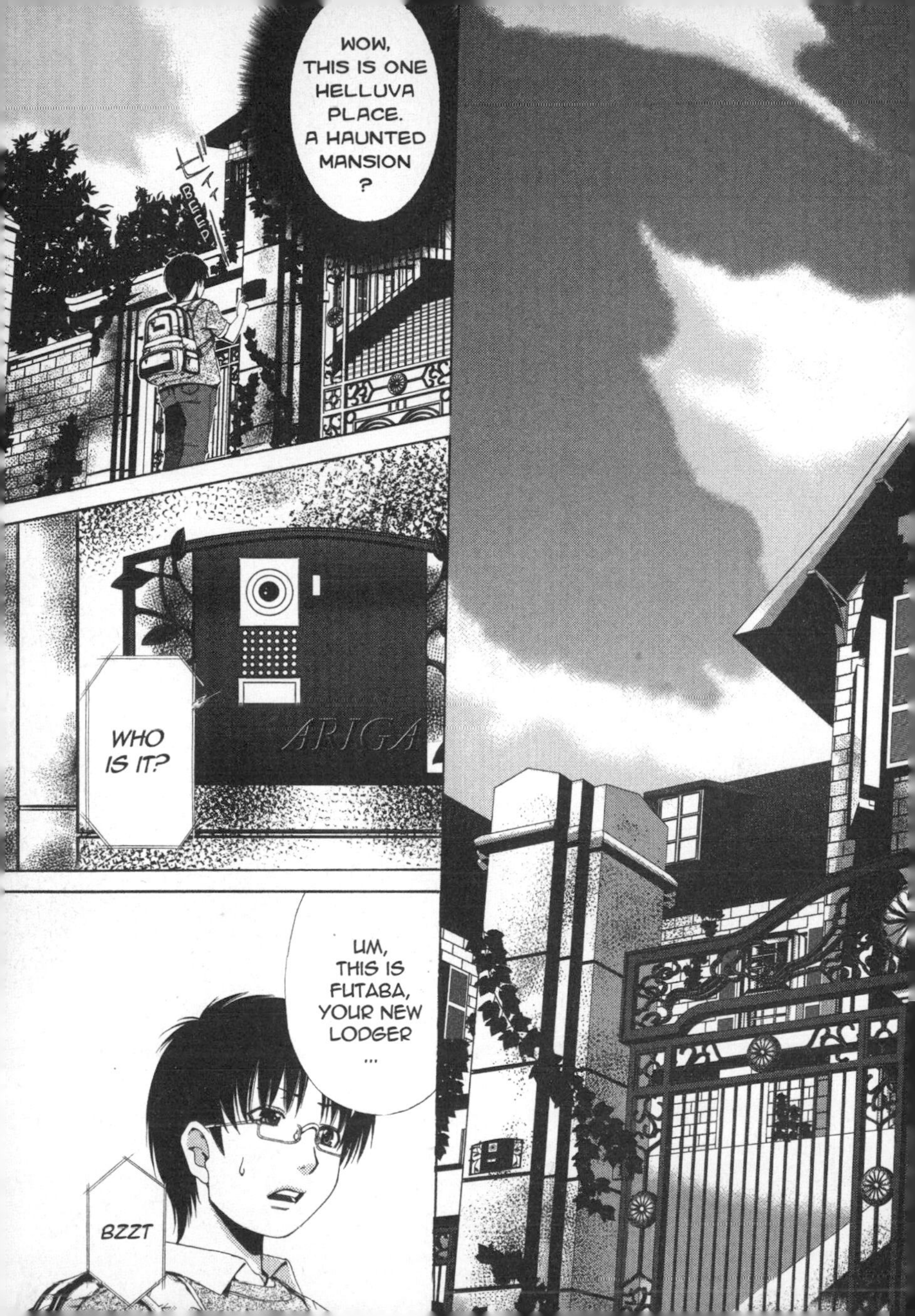
WOW, THIS IS ONE HELLUVA PLACE. A HAUNTED MANSION ?
BEEP
WHO IS IT?
ARIGA
UM, THIS IS FUTABA, YOUR NEW LODGER ...
BZZT

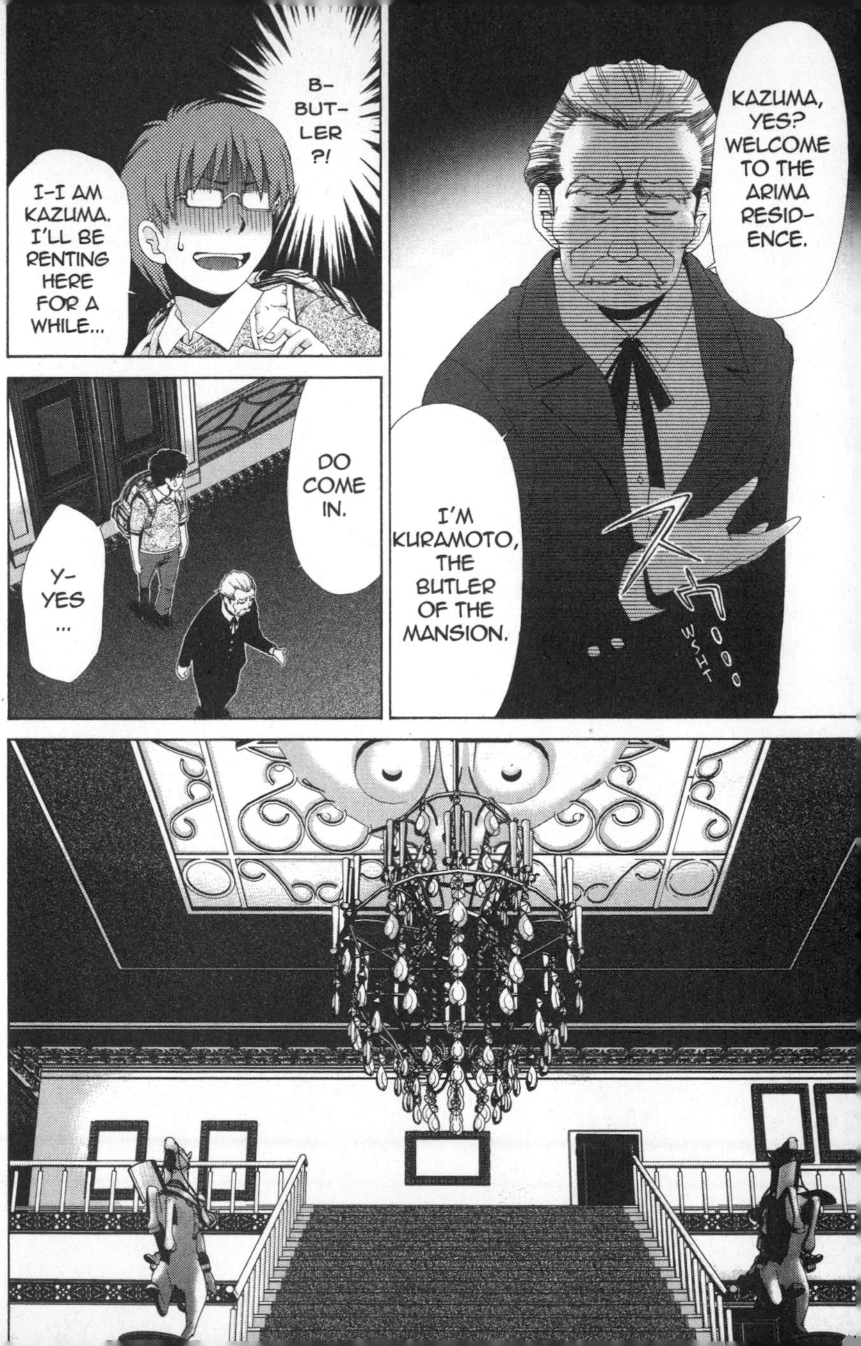
KAZUMA, YES? WELCOME TO THE ARIMA RESIDENCE.
I'M KURAMOTO, THE BUTLER OF THE MANSION.
B-BUT-LER?!
I-I AM KAZUMA. I'LL BE RENTING HERE FOR A WHILE...
DO COME IN.
Y-YES ...

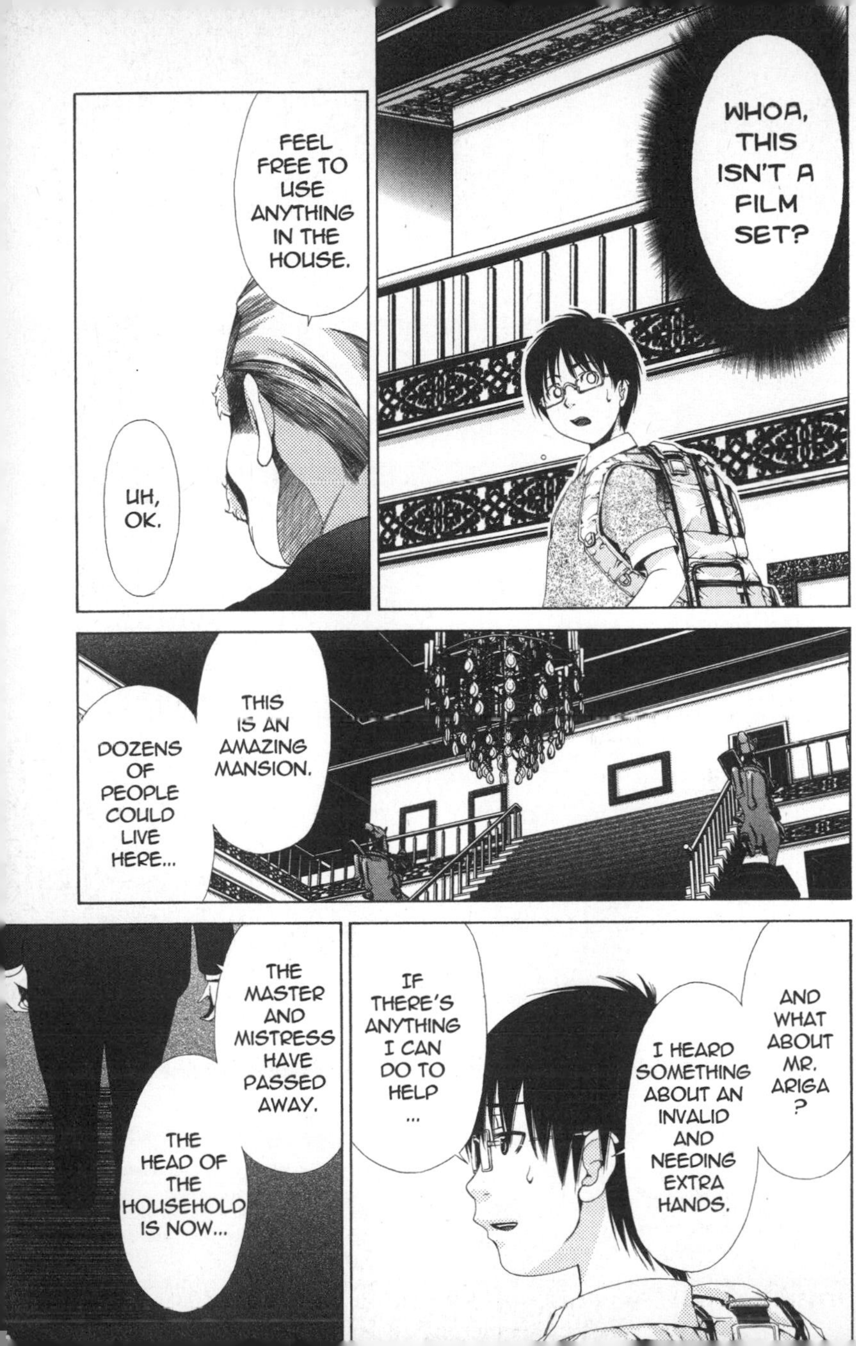
WHOA, THIS ISN'T A FILM SET?
FEEL FREE TO USE ANYTHING IN THE HOUSE.
UH, OK.
THIS IS AN AMAZING MANSION.
DOZENS OF PEOPLE COULD LIVE HERE...
AND WHAT ABOUT MR. ARIGA?
I HEARD SOMETHING ABOUT AN INVALID AND NEEDING EXTRA HANDS.
IF THERE'S ANYTHING I CAN DO TO HELP ...
THE MASTER AND MISTRESS HAVE PASSED AWAY.
THE HEAD OF THE HOUSEHOLD IS NOW...

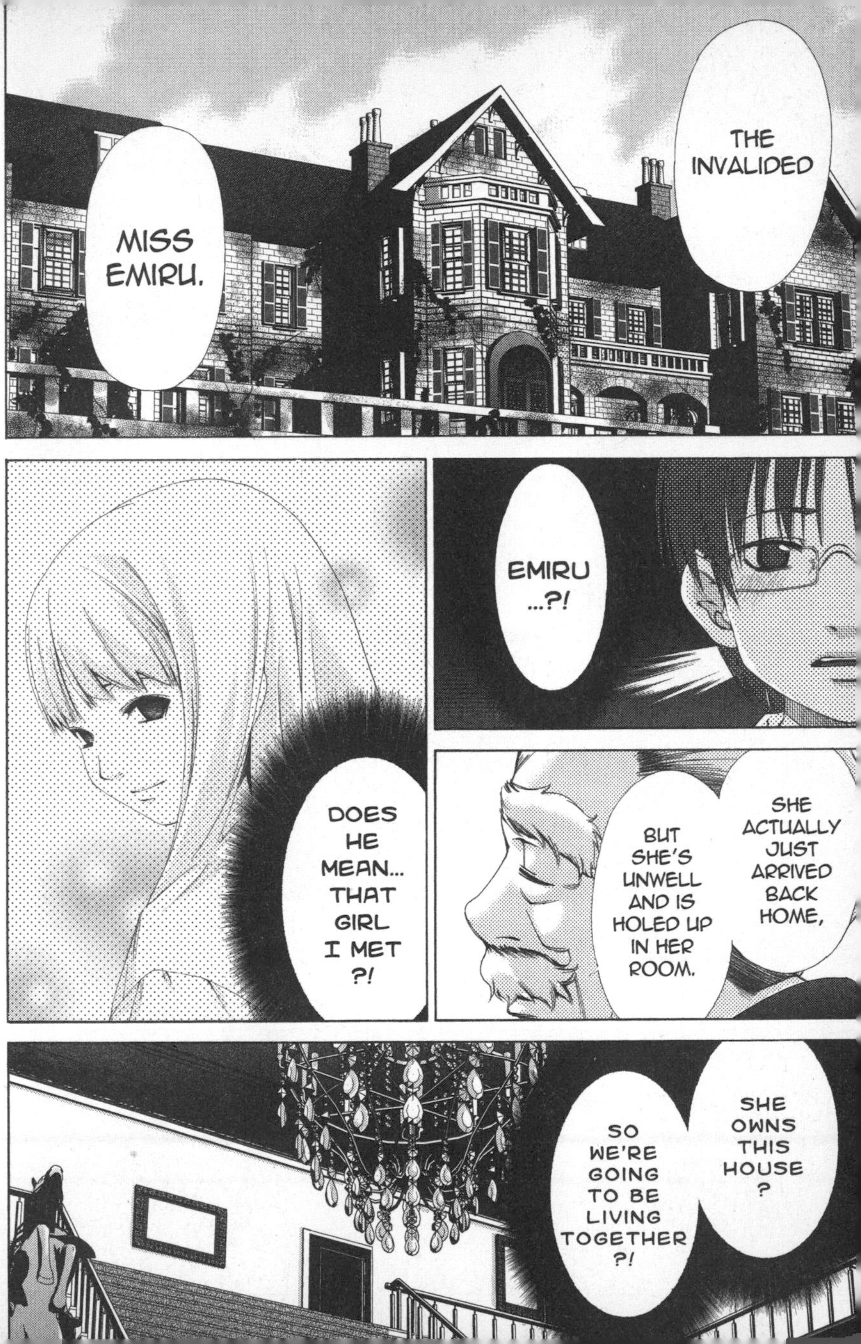
THE INVALIDED
MISS EMIRU.
EMIRU ...?!
SHE ACTUALLY JUST ARRIVED BACK HOME,
BUT SHE'S UNWELL AND IS HOLED UP IN HER ROOM.
DOES HE MEAN... THAT GIRL I MET ?!
SHE OWNS THIS HOUSE ?
SO WE'RE GOING TO BE LIVING TOGETHER ?!

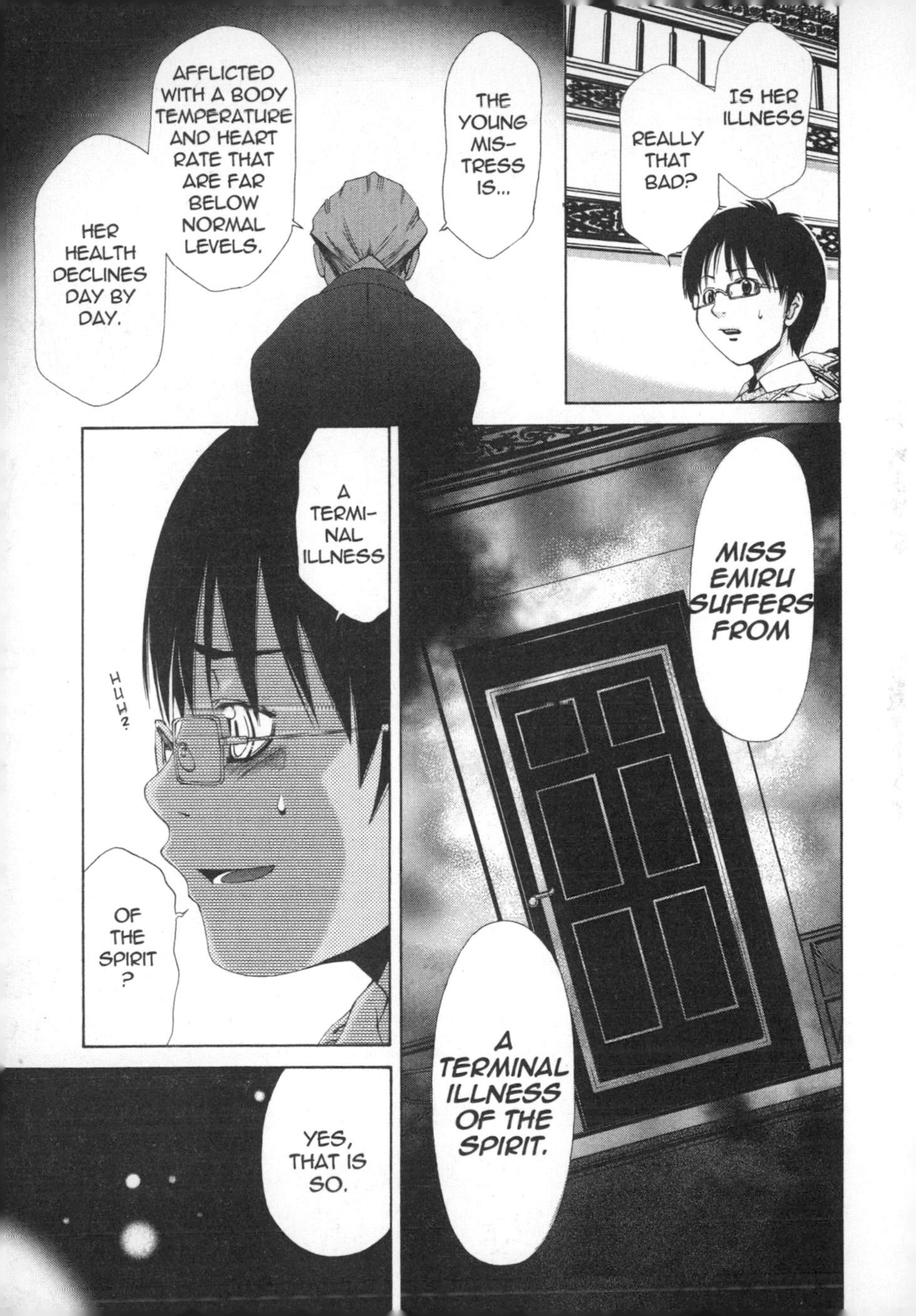
IS HER ILLNESS
REALLY THAT BAD?
THE YOUNG MISTRESS IS...
AFFLICTED WITH A BODY TEMPERATURE AND HEART RATE THAT ARE FAR BELOW NORMAL LEVELS.
HER HEALTH DECLINES DAY BY DAY.
MISS EMIRU SUFFERS FROM
A TERMINAL ILLNESS OF THE SPIRIT.
A TERMINAL ILLNESS
HUH?
OF THE SPIRIT?
YES, THAT IS SO.

FROM DESPAIR!!

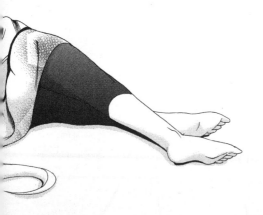

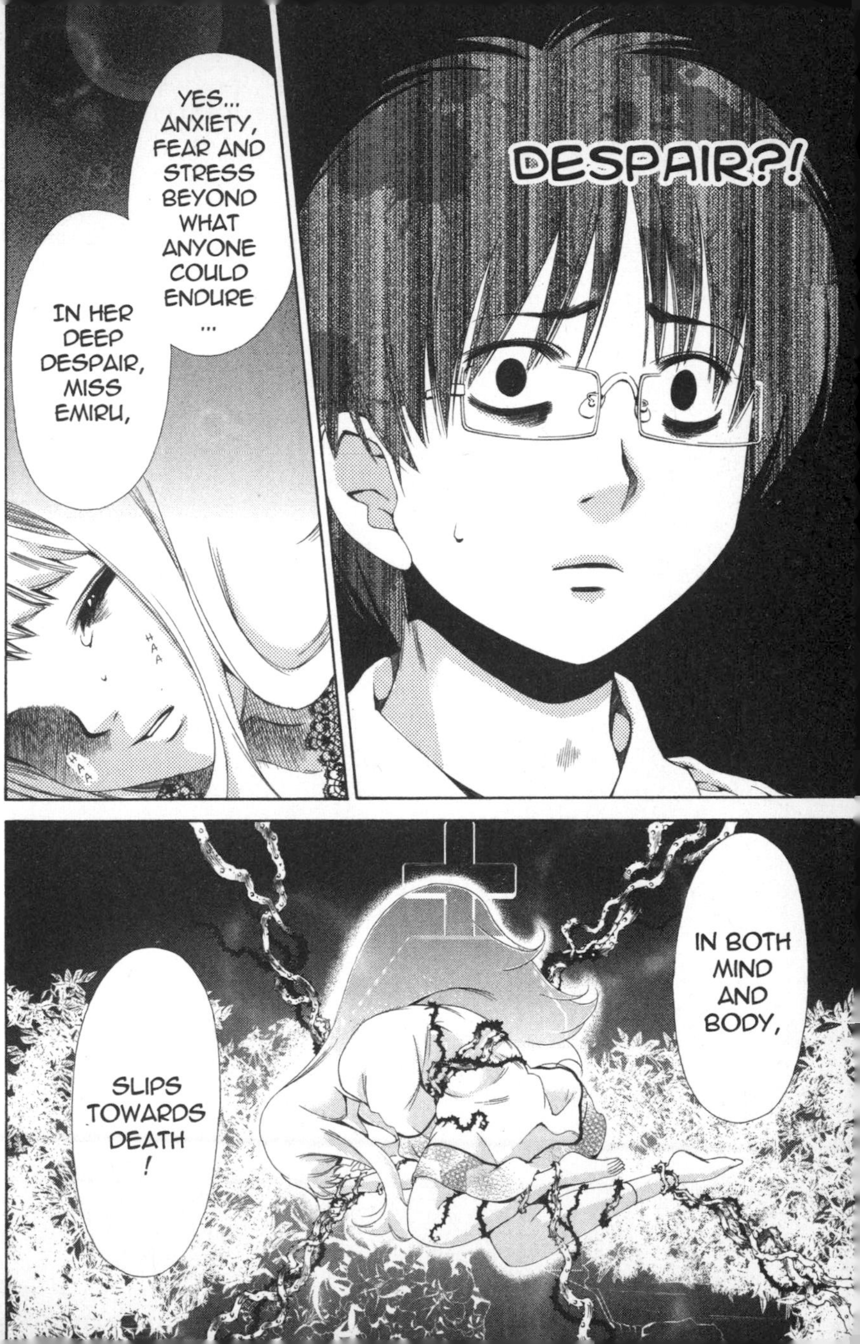
DESPAIR?!
YES... ANXIETY, FEAR AND STRESS BEYOND WHAT ANYONE COULD ENDURE ...
IN HER DEEP DESPAIR, MISS EMIRU,
HAA
HAA
IN BOTH MIND AND BODY,
SLIPS TOWARDS DEATH !

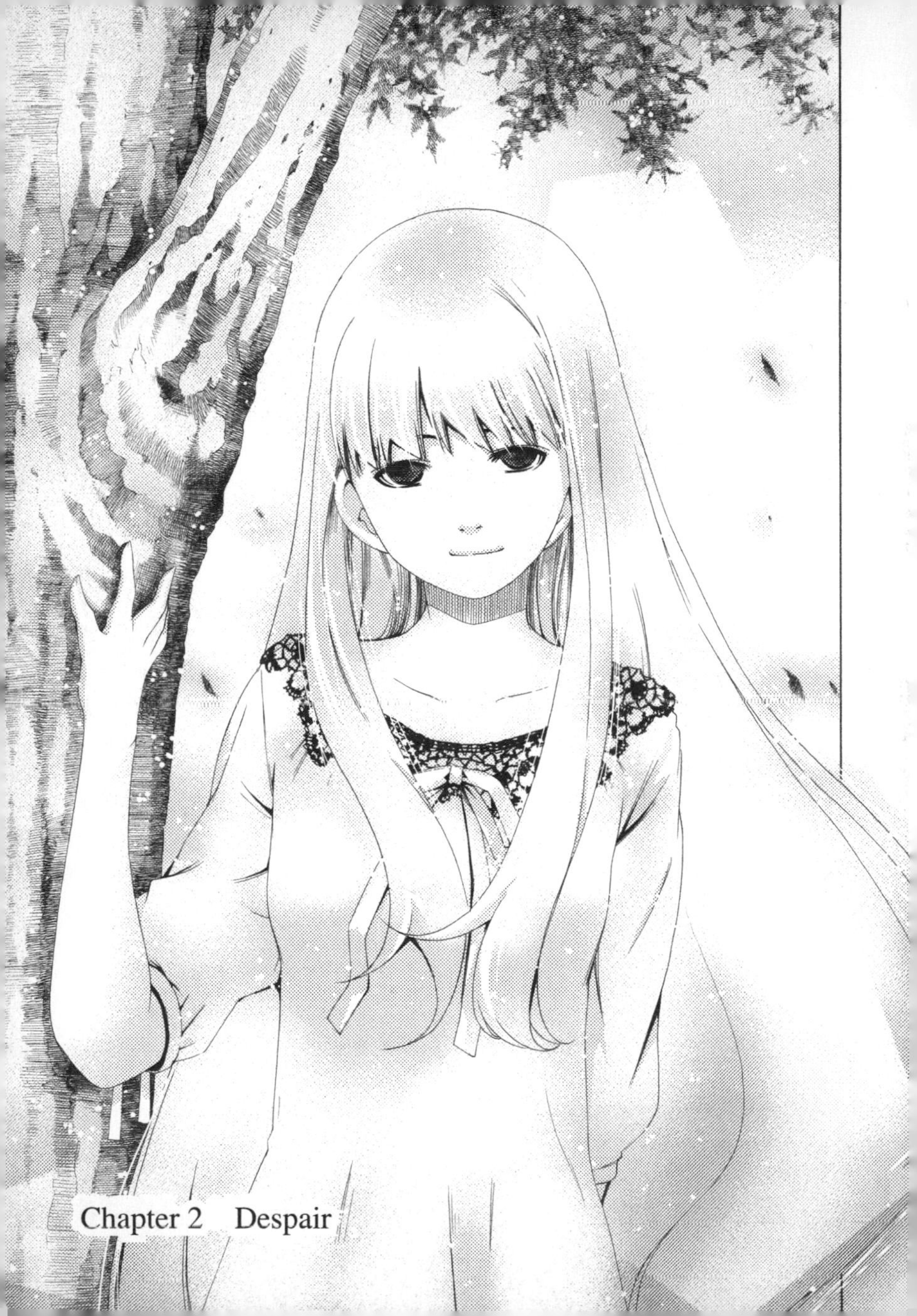

Chapter 2 Despair

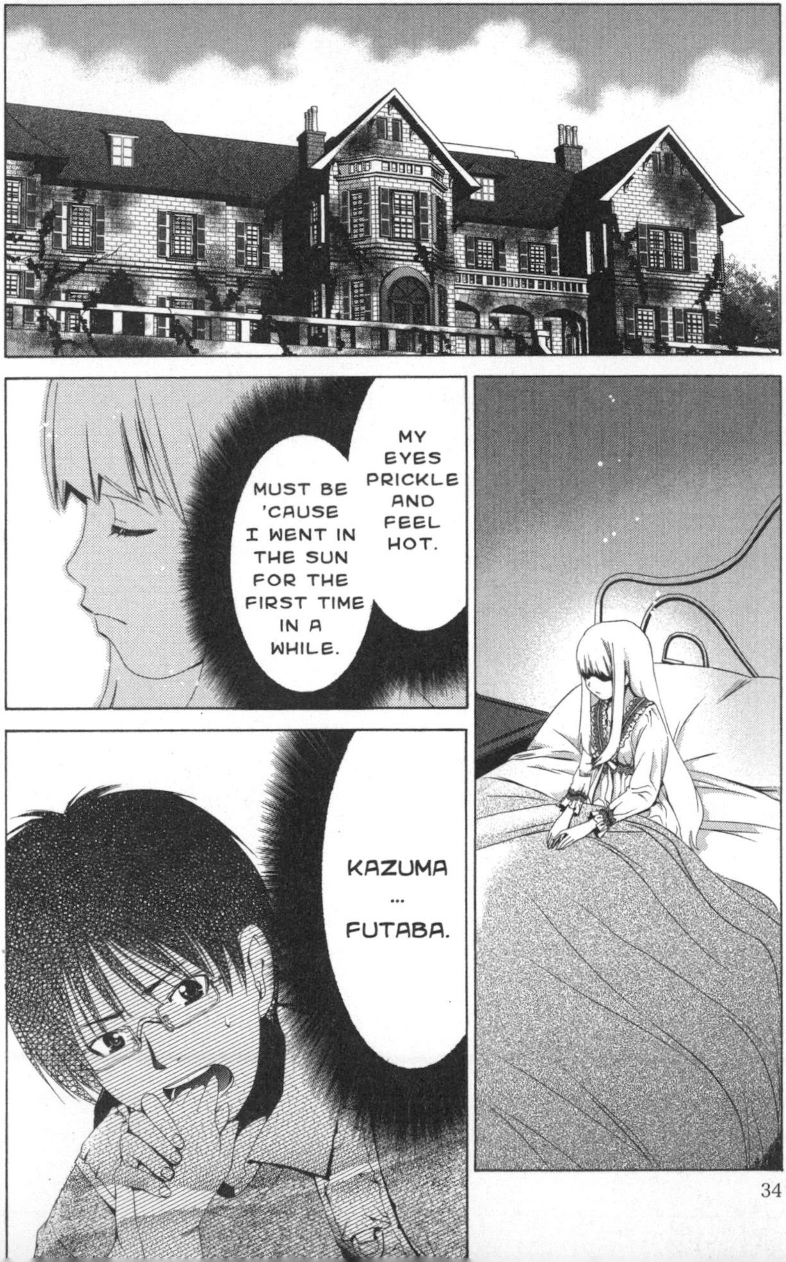
MY EYES PRICKLE AND FEEL HOT.
MUST BE 'CAUSE I WENT IN THE SUN FOR THE FIRST TIME IN A WHILE.
KAZUMA ... FUTABA.

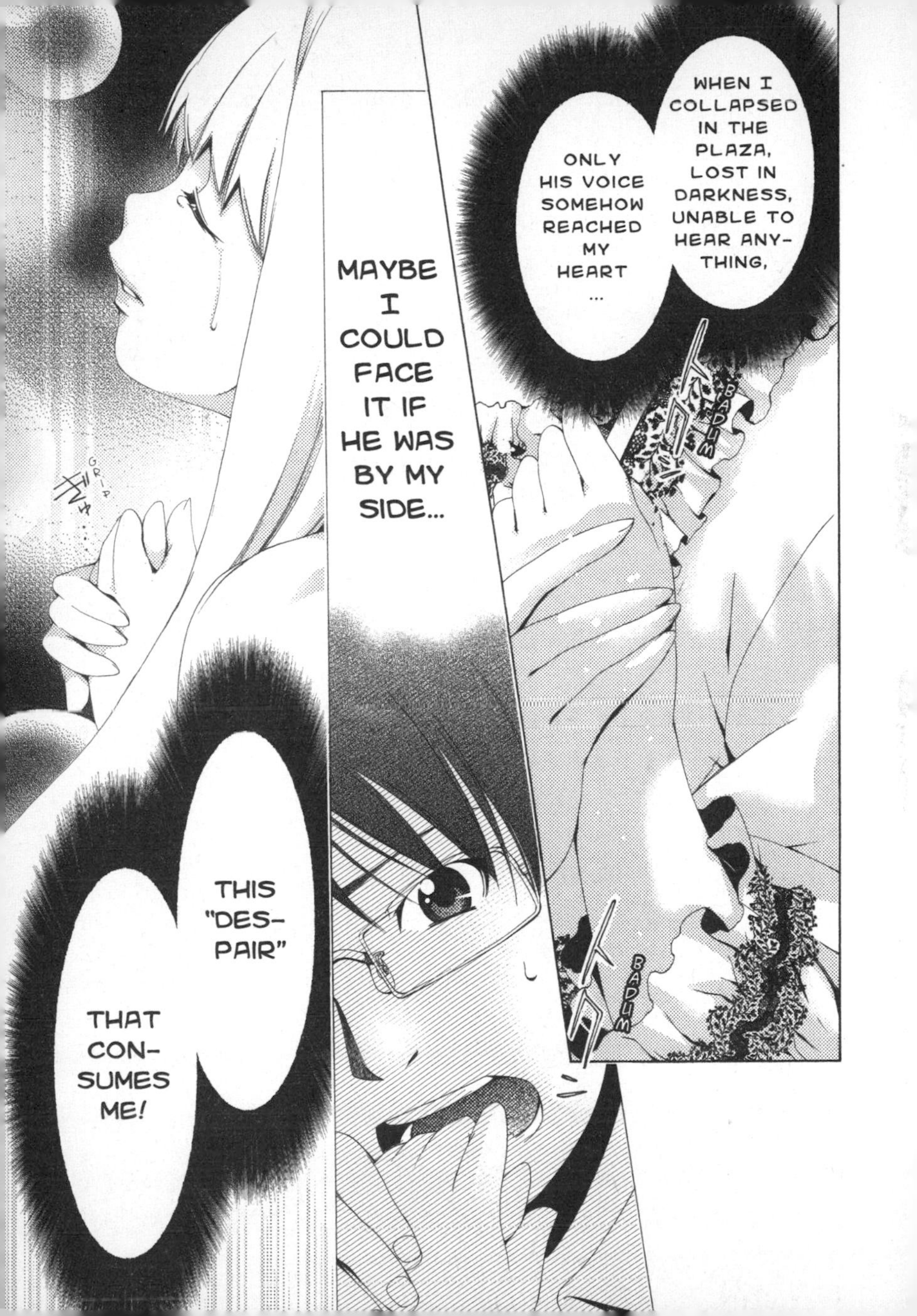
WHEN I COLLAPSED IN THE PLAZA, LOST IN DARKNESS, UNABLE TO HEAR ANYTHING,
ONLY HIS VOICE SOMEHOW REACHED MY HEART ...
BADUM
BADUM
MAYBE I COULD FACE IT IF HE WAS BY MY SIDE...
GRIP
THIS "DESPAIR"
THAT CONSUMES ME!

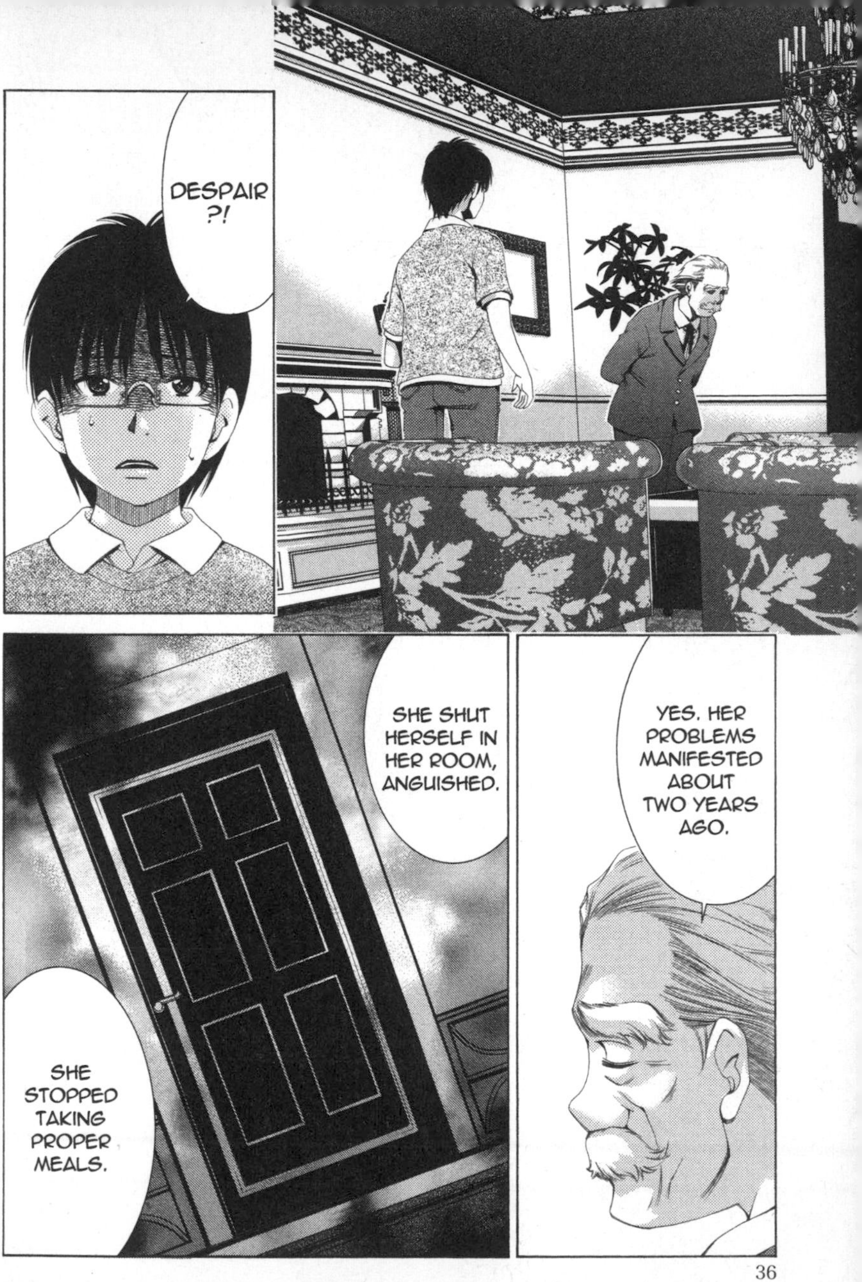
DESPAIR ?!
YES. HER PROBLEMS MANIFESTED ABOUT TWO YEARS AGO.
SHE SHUT HERSELF IN HER ROOM, ANGUISHED.
SHE STOPPED TAKING PROPER MEALS.

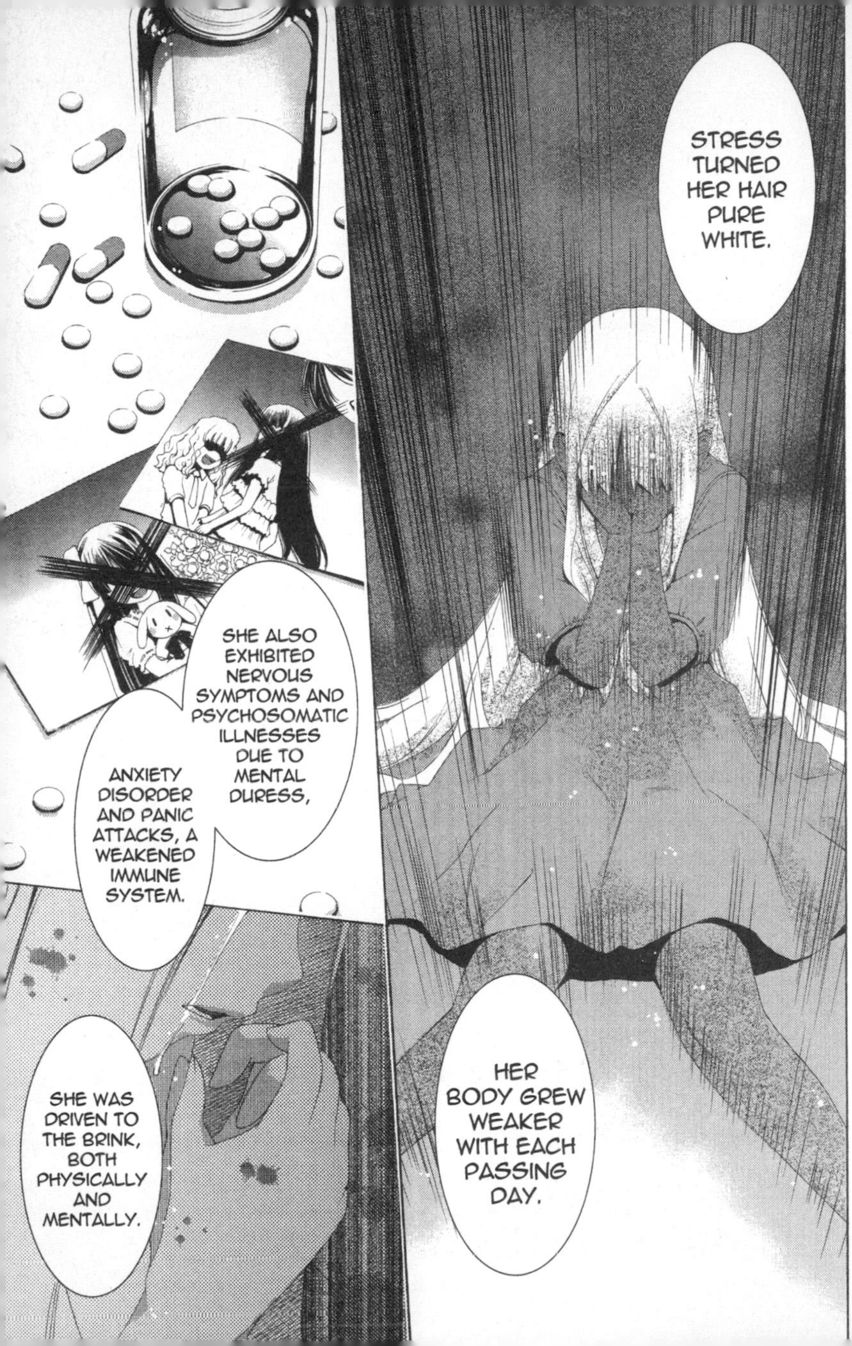
STRESS TURNED HER HAIR PURE WHITE.
HER BODY GREW WEAKER WITH EACH PASSING DAY.
SHE ALSO EXHIBITED NERVOUS SYMPTOMS AND PSYCHOSOMATIC ILLNESSES DUE TO MENTAL DURESS,
ANXIETY DISORDER AND PANIC ATTACKS, A WEAKENED IMMUNE SYSTEM.
SHE WAS DRIVEN TO THE BRINK, BOTH PHYSICALLY AND MENTALLY.

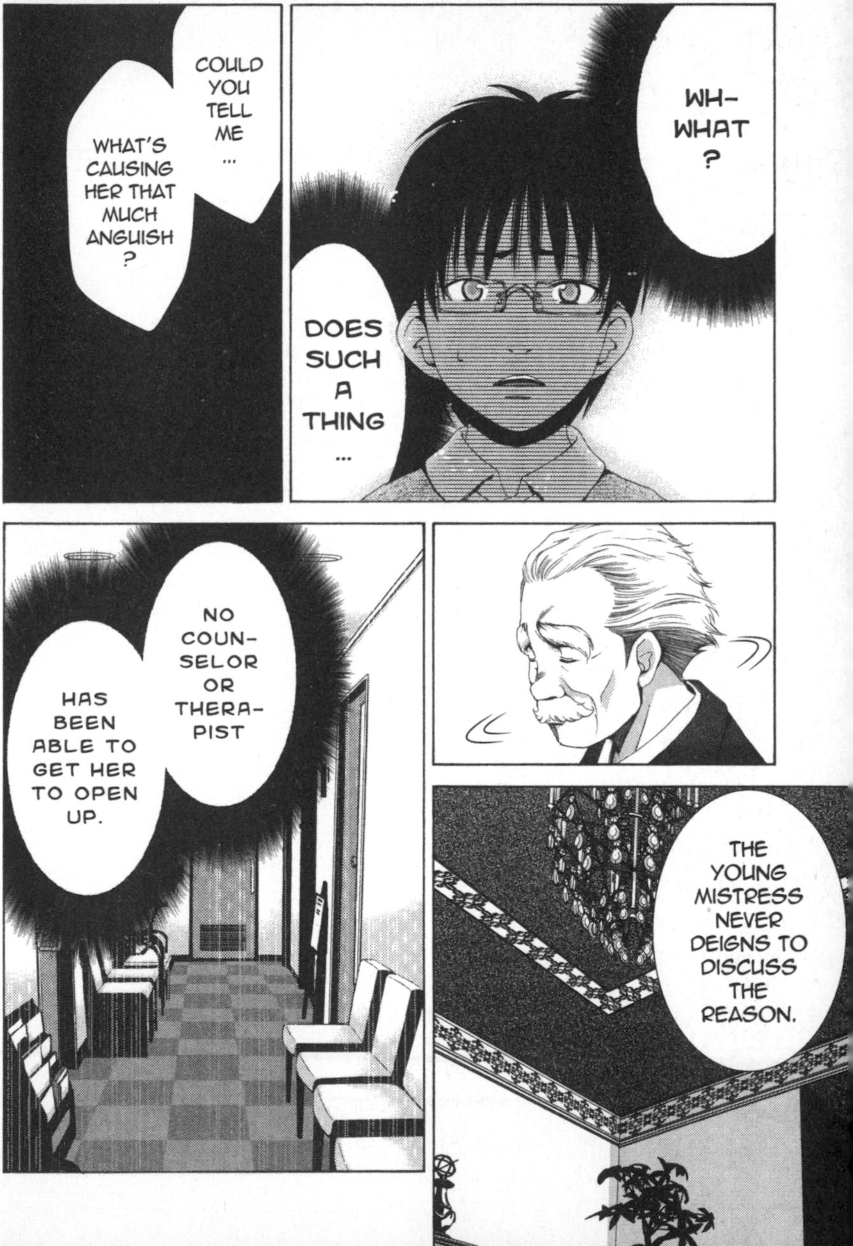
WH-WHAT?
DOES SUCH A THING...
COULD YOU TELL ME...
WHAT'S CAUSING HER THAT MUCH ANGUISH?
THE YOUNG MISTRESS NEVER DEIGNS TO DISCUSS THE REASON.
NO COUNSELOR OR THERAPIST
HAS BEEN ABLE TO GET HER TO OPEN UP.

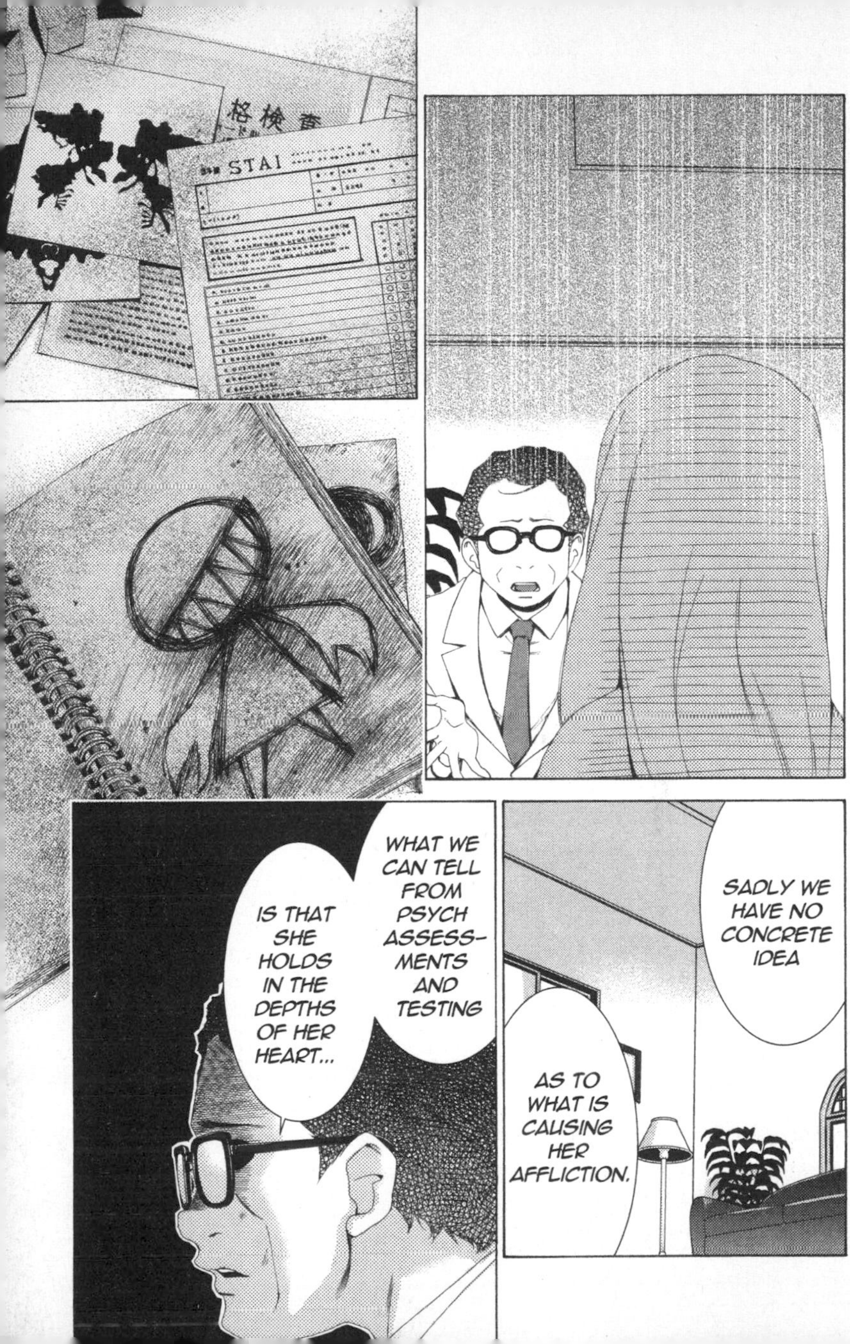

格検査
STAI
SADLY WE HAVE NO CONCRETE IDEA
AS TO WHAT IS CAUSING HER AFFLICTION.
WHAT WE CAN TELL FROM PSYCH ASSESSMENTS AND TESTING
IS THAT SHE HOLDS IN THE DEPTHS OF HER HEART...

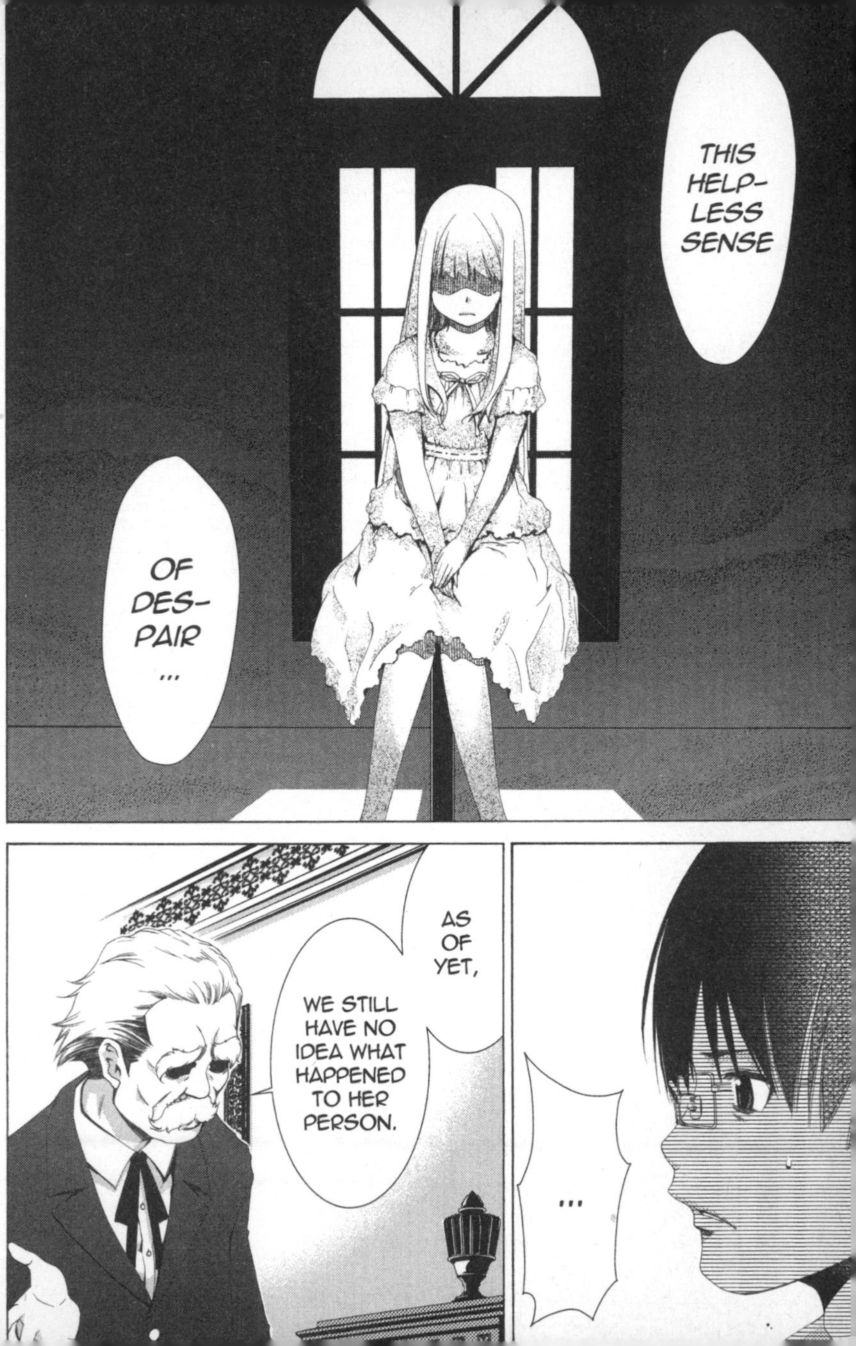
THIS HELP-LESS SENSE
OF DES-PAIR ...
...
AS OF YET,
WE STILL HAVE NO IDEA WHAT HAPPENED TO HER PERSON.

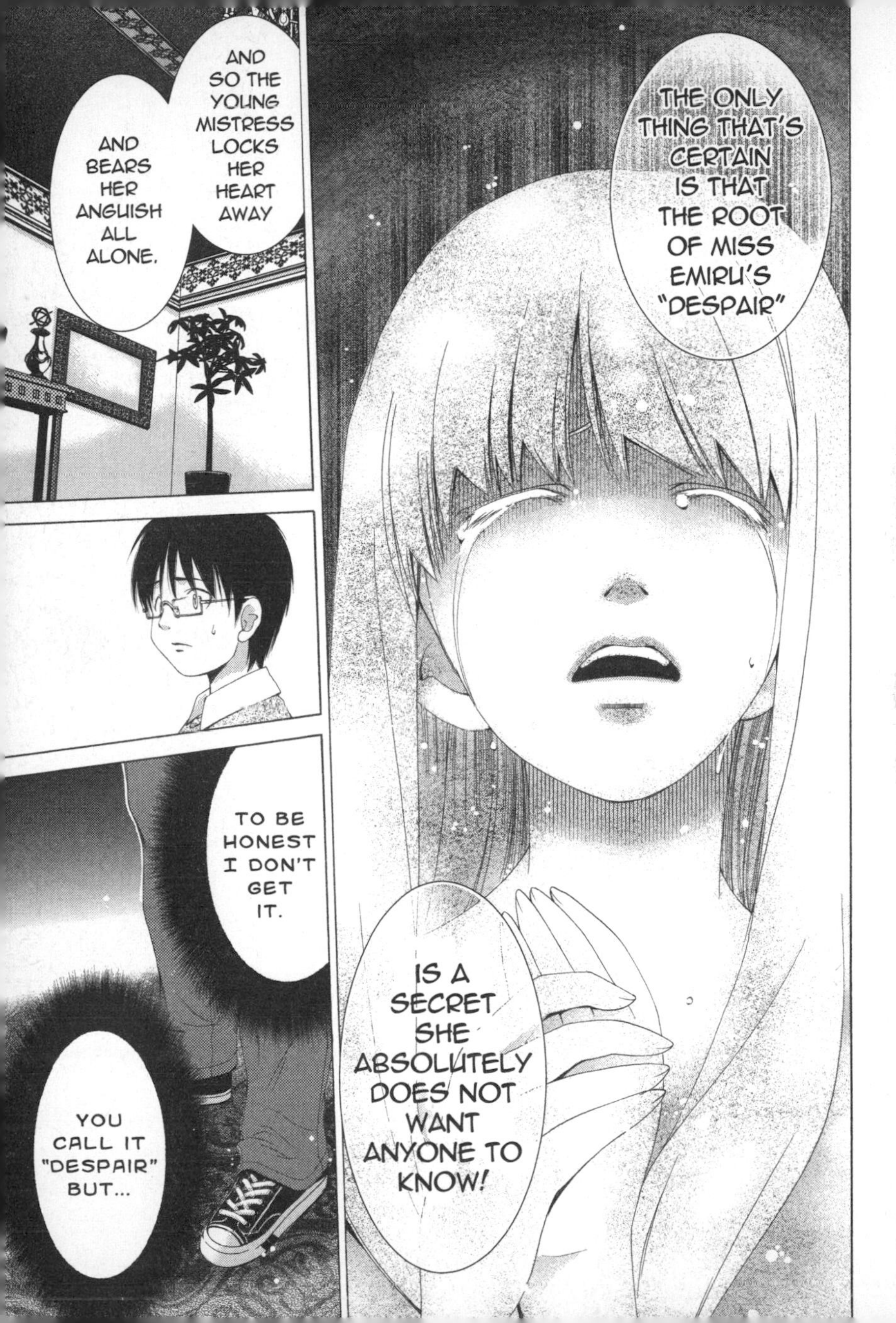
THE ONLY THING THAT'S CERTAIN IS THAT THE ROOT OF MISS EMIRU'S "DESPAIR"
IS A SECRET SHE ABSOLUTELY DOES NOT WANT ANYONE TO KNOW!
AND SO THE YOUNG MISTRESS LOCKS HER HEART AWAY
AND BEARS HER ANGUISH ALL ALONE.
TO BE HONEST I DON'T GET IT.
YOU CALL IT "DESPAIR" BUT...

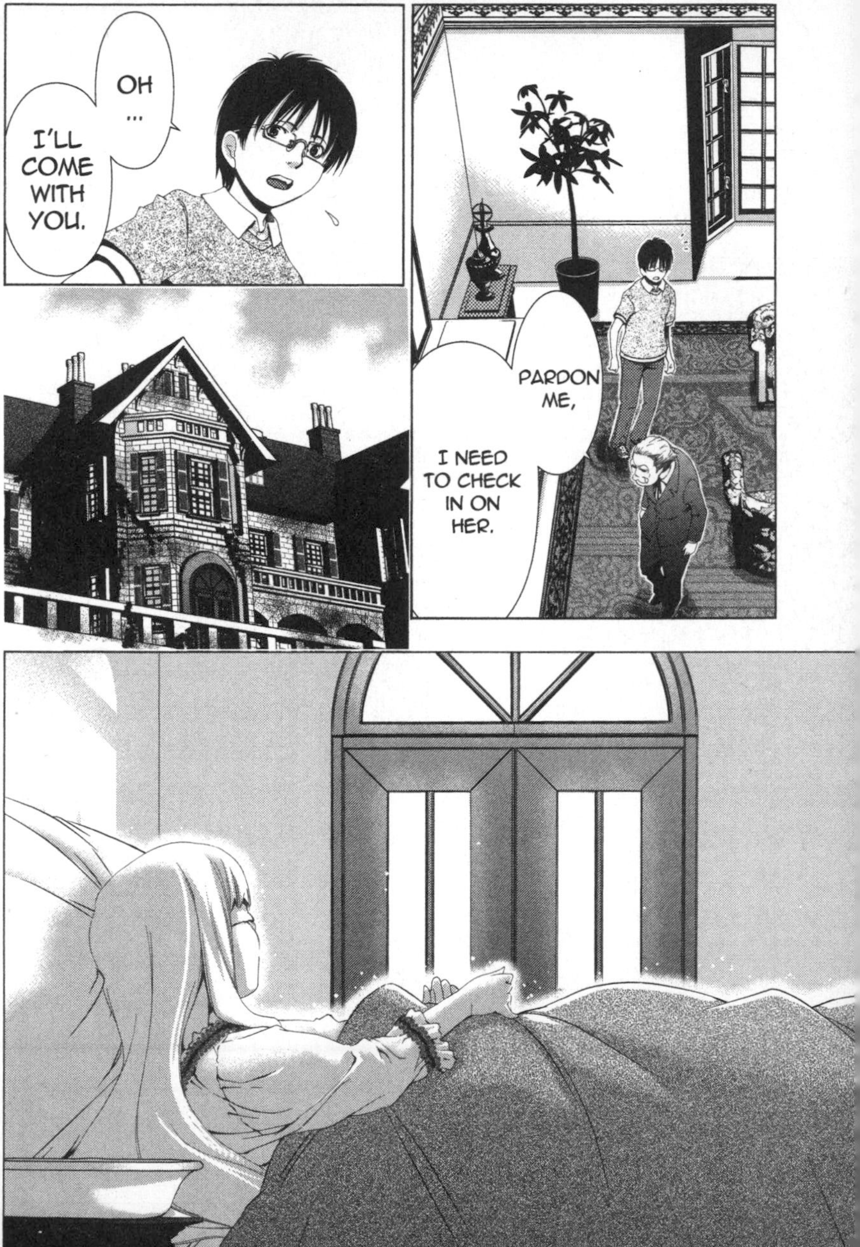
PARDON ME,
I NEED TO CHECK IN ON HER.
OH ...
I'LL COME WITH YOU.

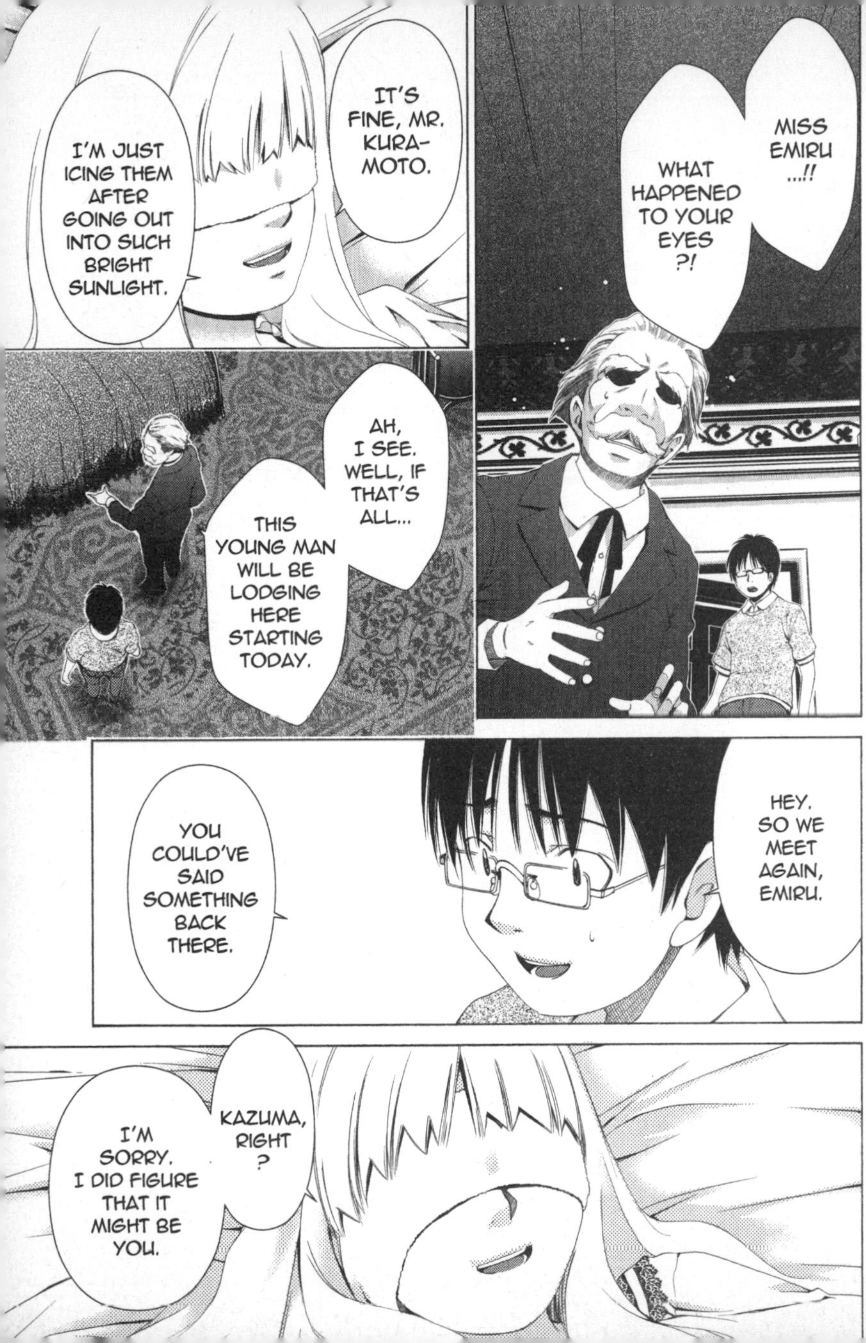
MISS EMIRU ...!!
WHAT HAPPENED TO YOUR EYES ?!
IT'S FINE, MR. KURA-MOTO.
I'M JUST ICING THEM AFTER GOING OUT INTO SUCH BRIGHT SUNLIGHT.
AH, I SEE. WELL, IF THAT'S ALL...
THIS YOUNG MAN WILL BE LODGING HERE STARTING TODAY.
HEY. SO WE MEET AGAIN, EMIRU.
YOU COULD'VE SAID SOMETHING BACK THERE.
KAZUMA, RIGHT ?
I'M SORRY. I DID FIGURE THAT IT MIGHT BE YOU.

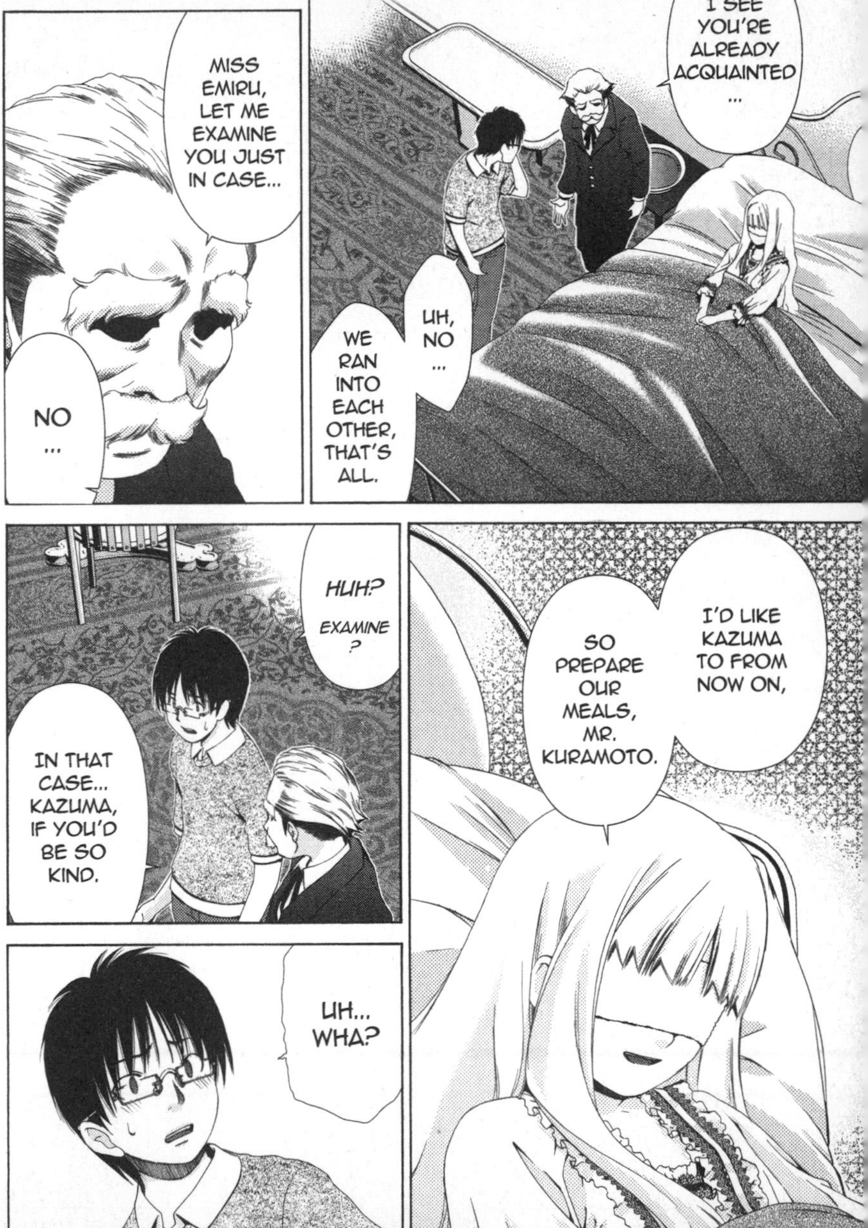
I SEE YOU'RE ALREADY ACQUAINTED ...
UH, NO ...
WE RAN INTO EACH OTHER, THAT'S ALL.
MISS EMIRU, LET ME EXAMINE YOU JUST IN CASE...
NO ...
I'D LIKE KAZUMA TO FROM NOW ON,
SO PREPARE OUR MEALS, MR. KURAMOTO.
HUH? EXAMINE ?
IN THAT CASE... KAZUMA, IF YOU'D BE SO KIND.
UH... WHA?

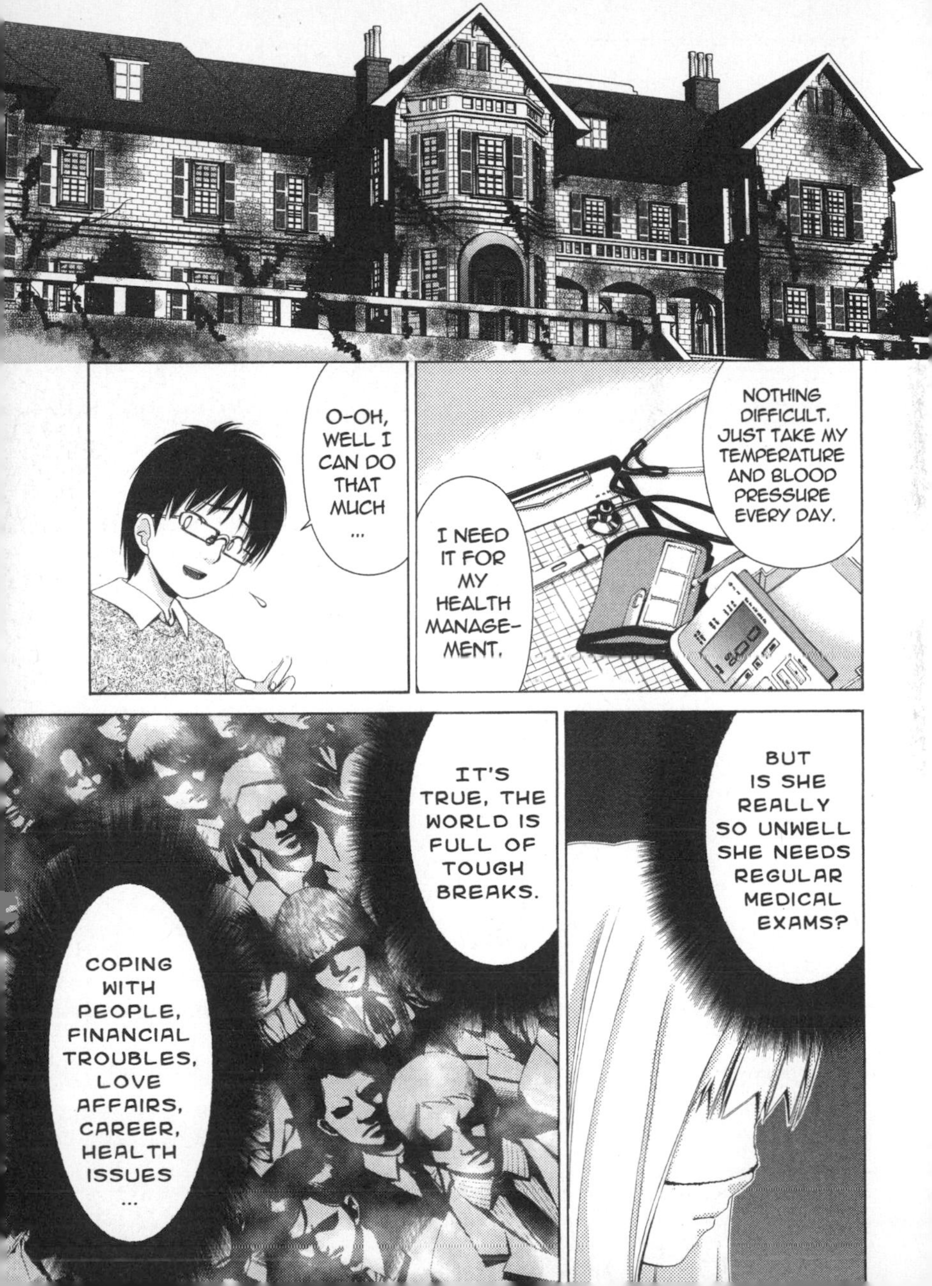
NOTHING DIFFICULT. JUST TAKE MY TEMPERATURE AND BLOOD PRESSURE EVERY DAY.
I NEED IT FOR MY HEALTH MANAGE-MENT.
O-OH, WELL I CAN DO THAT MUCH ...
BUT IS SHE REALLY SO UNWELL SHE NEEDS REGULAR MEDICAL EXAMS?
IT'S TRUE, THE WORLD IS FULL OF TOUGH BREAKS.
COPING WITH PEOPLE, FINANCIAL TROUBLES, LOVE AFFAIRS, CAREER, HEALTH ISSUES ...

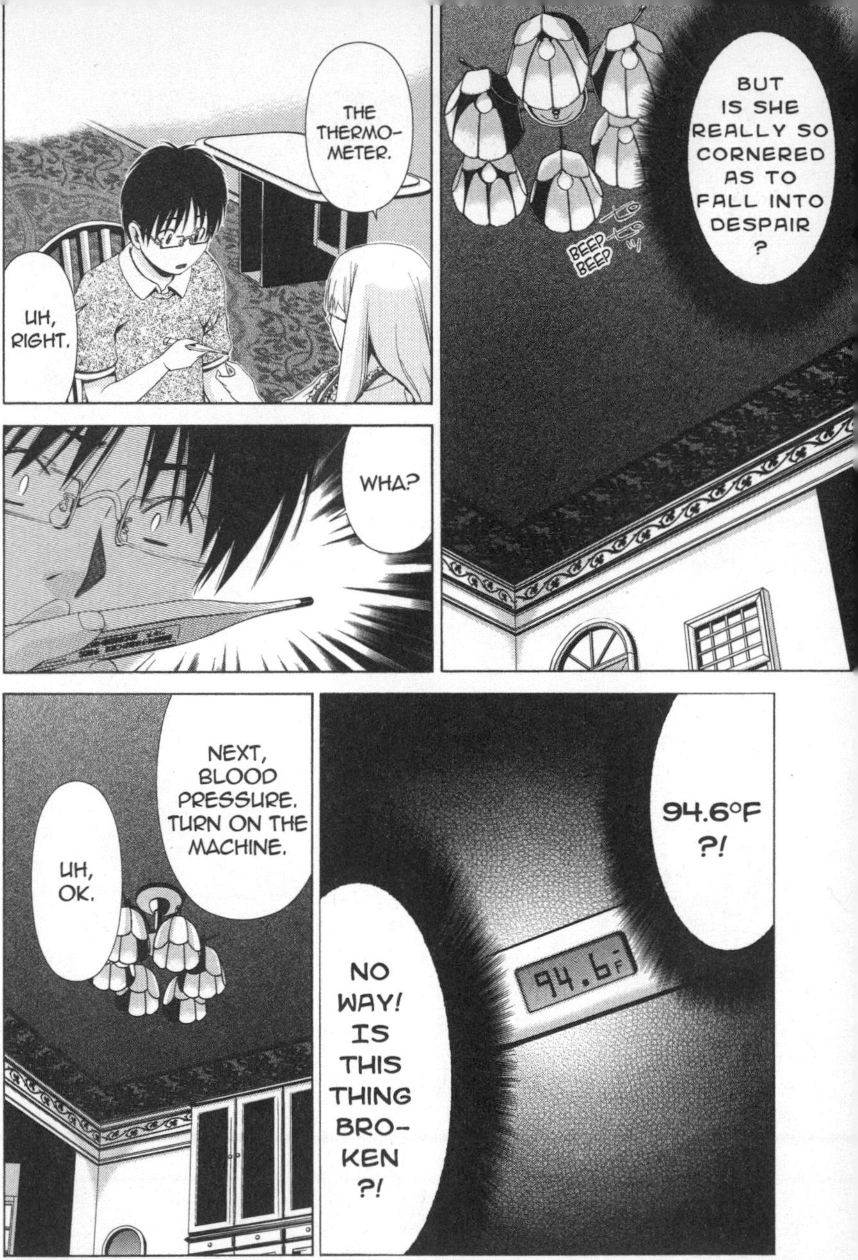

BUT IS SHE REALLY SO CORNERED AS TO FALL INTO DESPAIR ?
BEEP BEEP
THE THERMO-METER.
UH, RIGHT.
WHA?
94.6°F ?!
NO WAY! IS THIS THING BRO-KEN ?!
94.6F
NEXT, BLOOD PRESSURE. TURN ON THE MACHINE.
UH, OK.

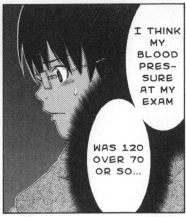

I THINK MY BLOOD PRESSURE AT MY EXAM

WAS 120 OVER 70 OR SO...

WH-WHAT'S UP WITH THIS GIRL?

HIGH OF

80?

LOW OF 43 ...?!

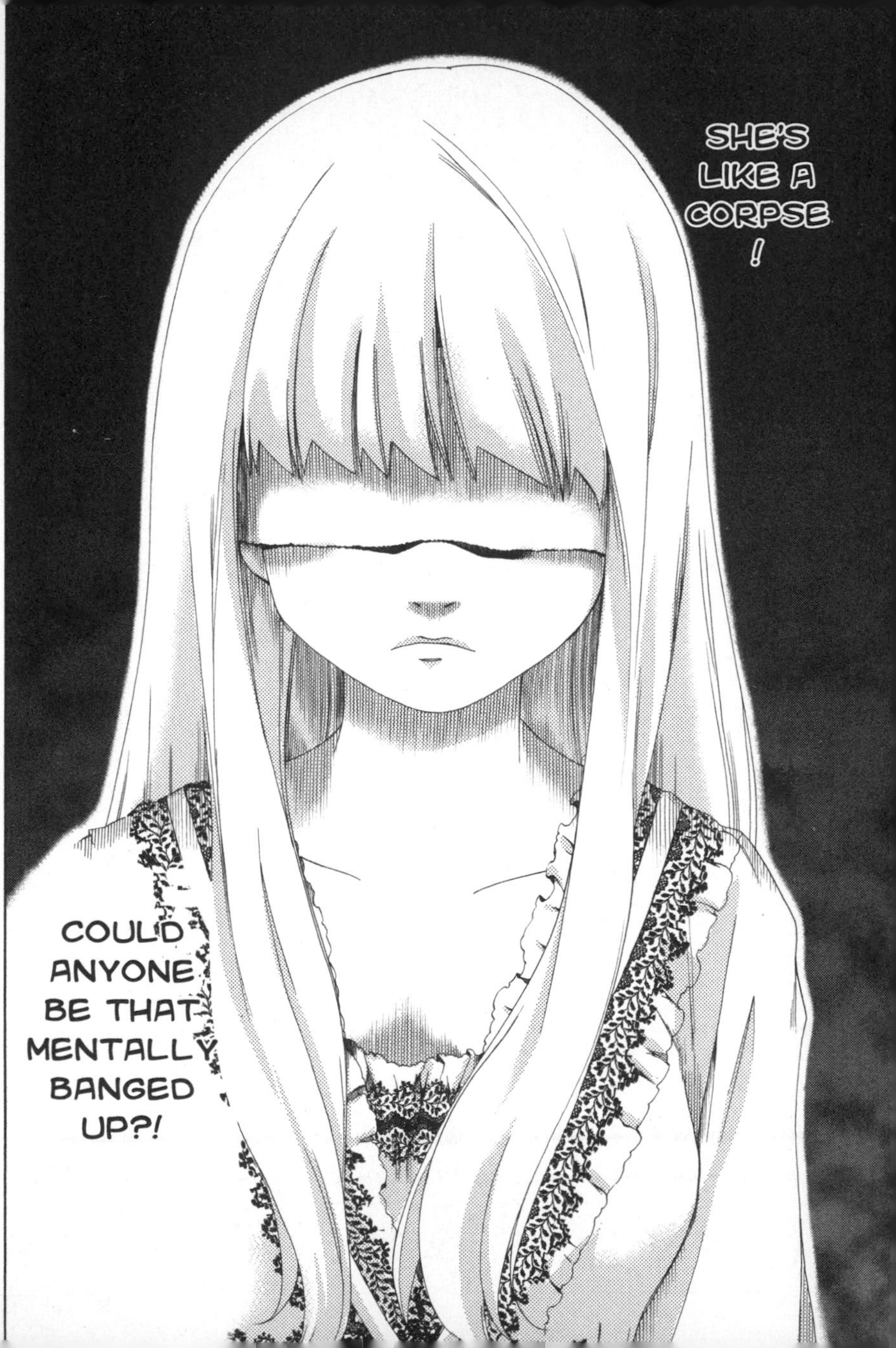
SHE'S LIKE A CORPSE!
COULD ANYONE BE THAT MENTALLY BANGED UP?!

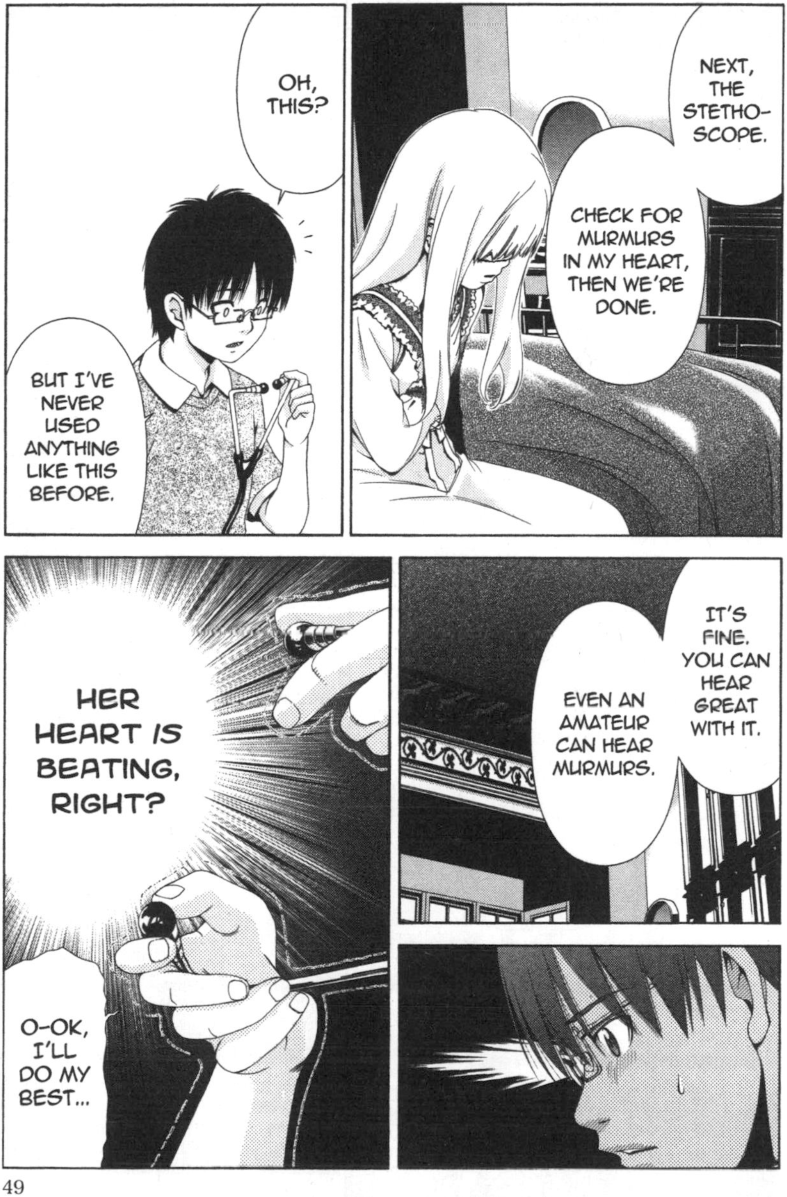
NEXT, THE STETHO-SCOPE.
CHECK FOR MURMURS IN MY HEART, THEN WE'RE DONE.
OH, THIS?
BUT I'VE NEVER USED ANYTHING LIKE THIS BEFORE.
IT'S FINE. YOU CAN HEAR GREAT WITH IT.
EVEN AN AMATEUR CAN HEAR MURMURS.
HER HEART *IS* BEATING, RIGHT?
O-OK, I'LL DO MY BEST...

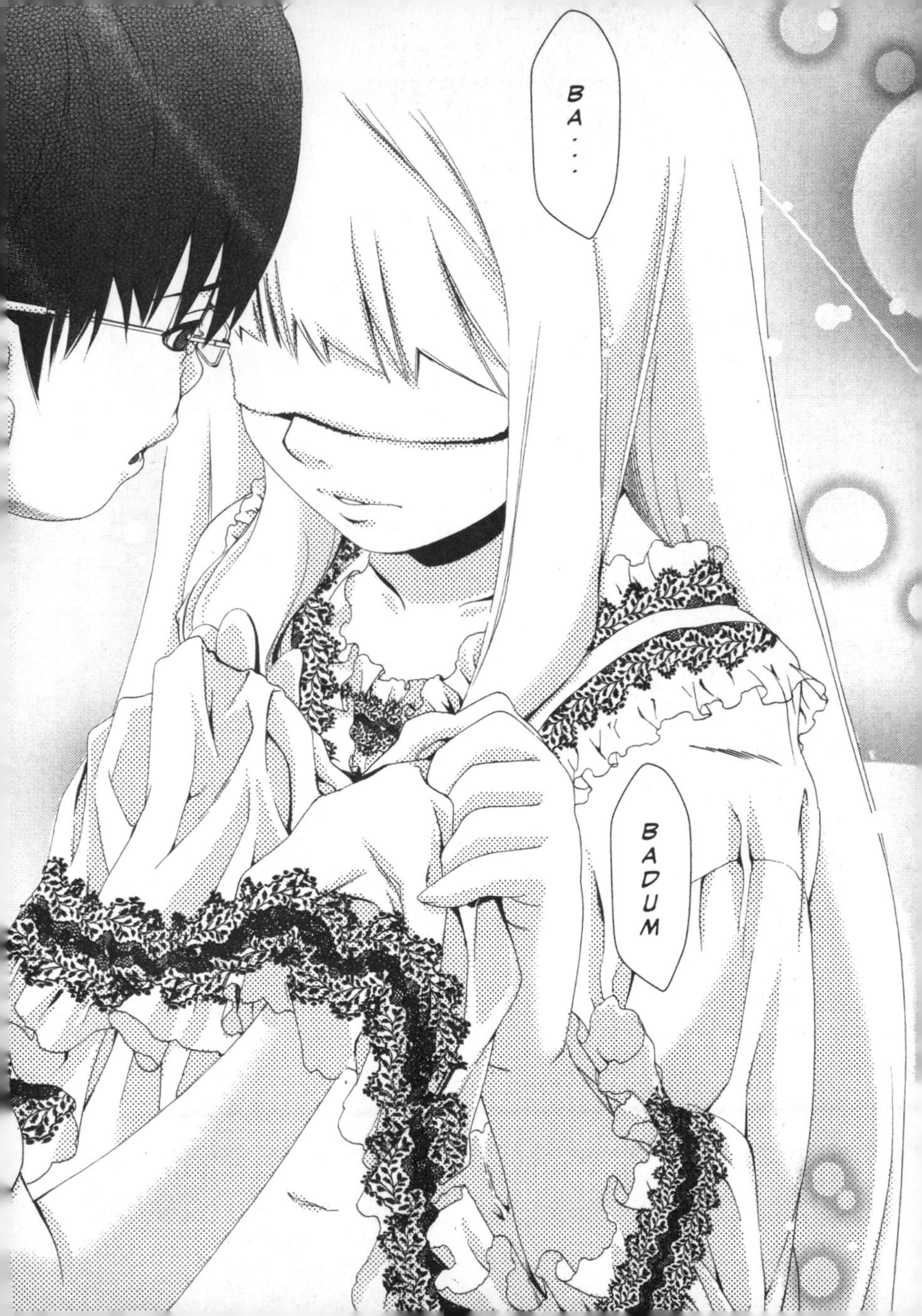
BA...
BADUM

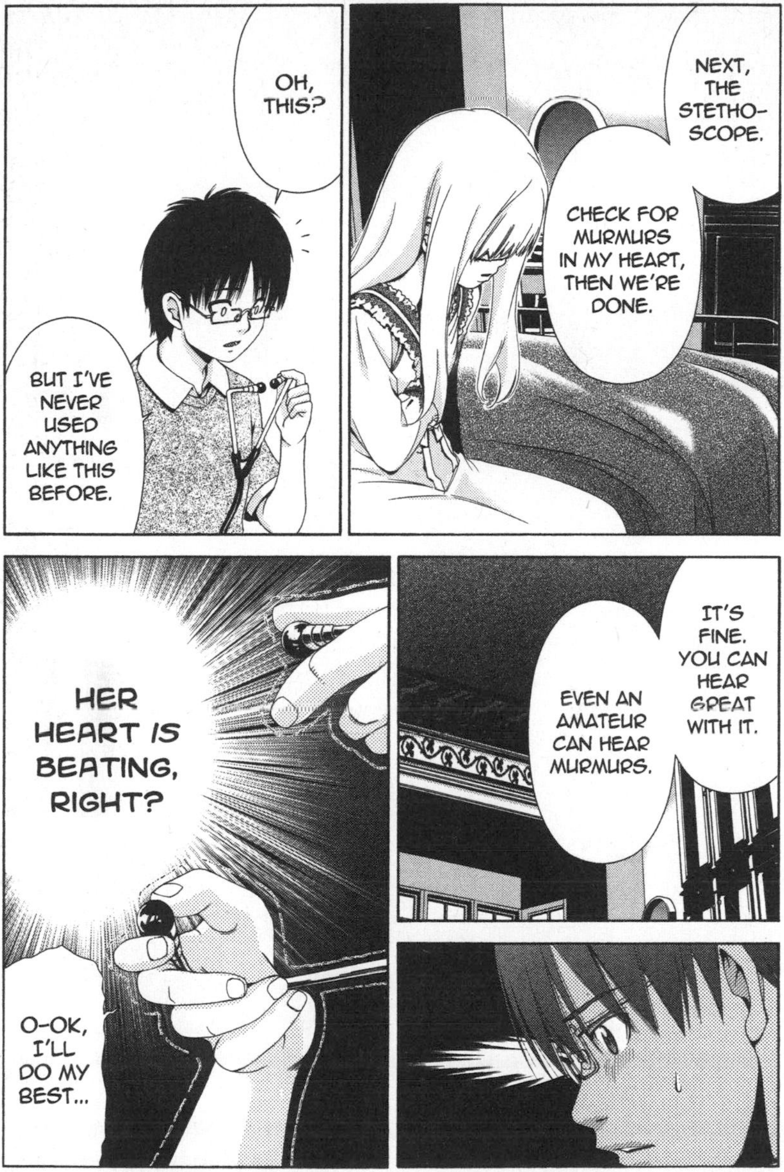
NEXT, THE STETHO-SCOPE.
CHECK FOR MURMURS IN MY HEART, THEN WE'RE DONE.
OH, THIS?
BUT I'VE NEVER USED ANYTHING LIKE THIS BEFORE.
IT'S FINE. YOU CAN HEAR GREAT WITH IT.
EVEN AN AMATEUR CAN HEAR MURMURS.
HER HEART IS BEATING, RIGHT?
O-OK, I'LL DO MY BEST...

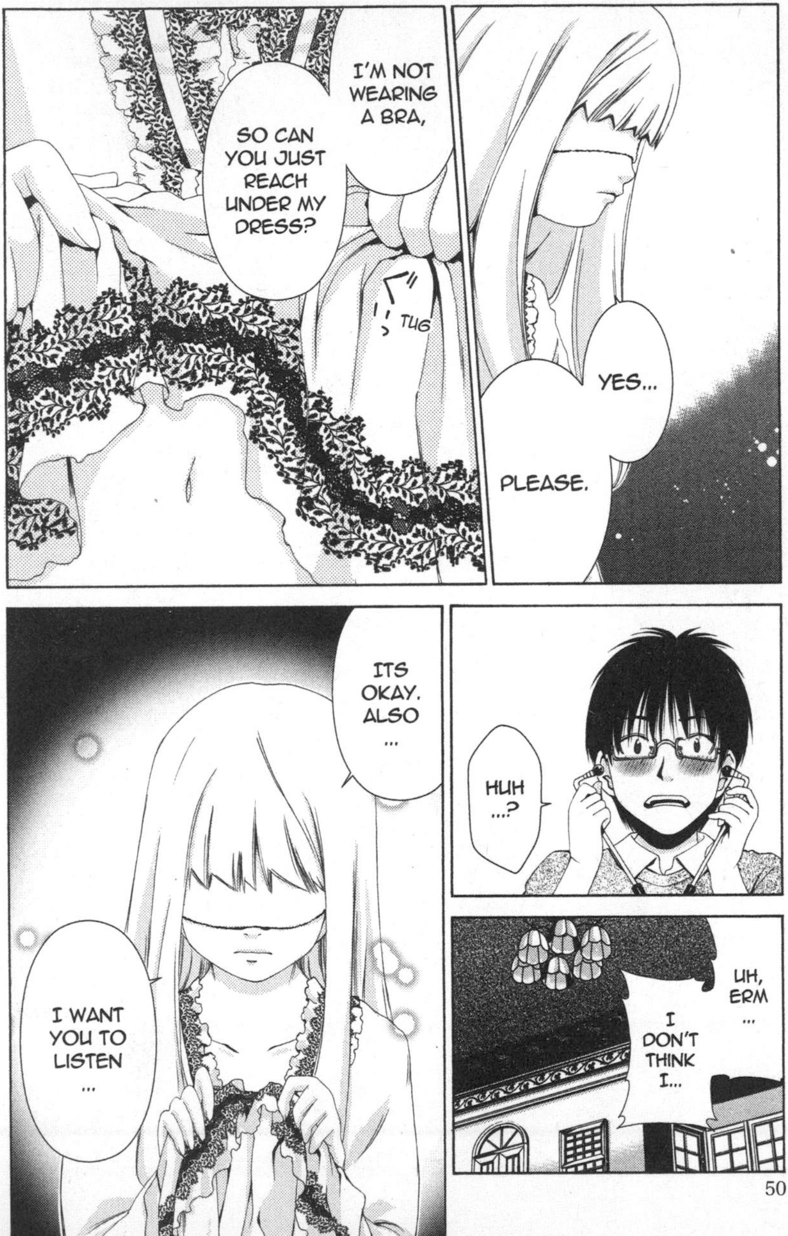
YES...
PLEASE.
I'M NOT WEARING A BRA,
SO CAN YOU JUST REACH UNDER MY DRESS?
TUG
HUH ...?
UH, ERM ...
I DON'T THINK I...
ITS OKAY. ALSO ...
I WANT YOU TO LISTEN ...

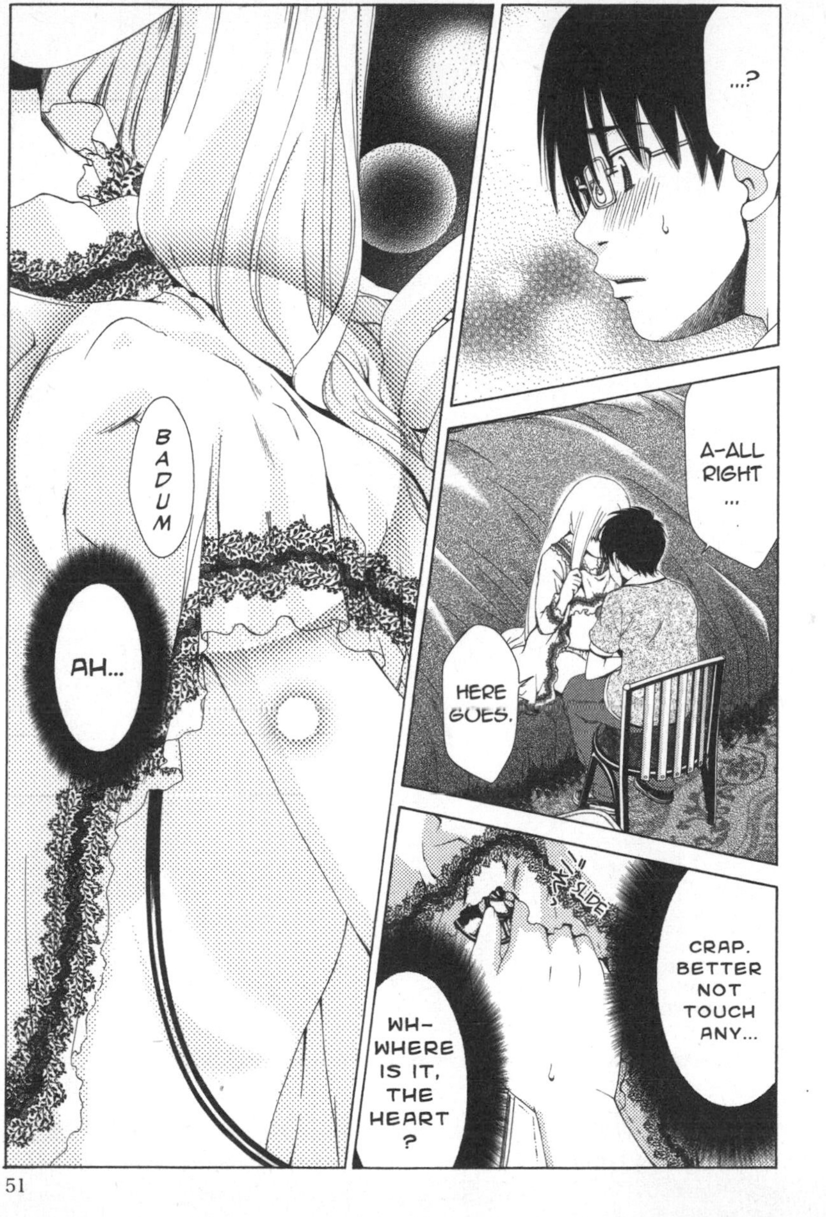
...?
A-ALL RIGHT ...
HERE GOES.
CRAP. BETTER NOT TOUCH ANY...
SLIDE
WH-WHERE IS IT, THE HEART?
BADUM
AH...

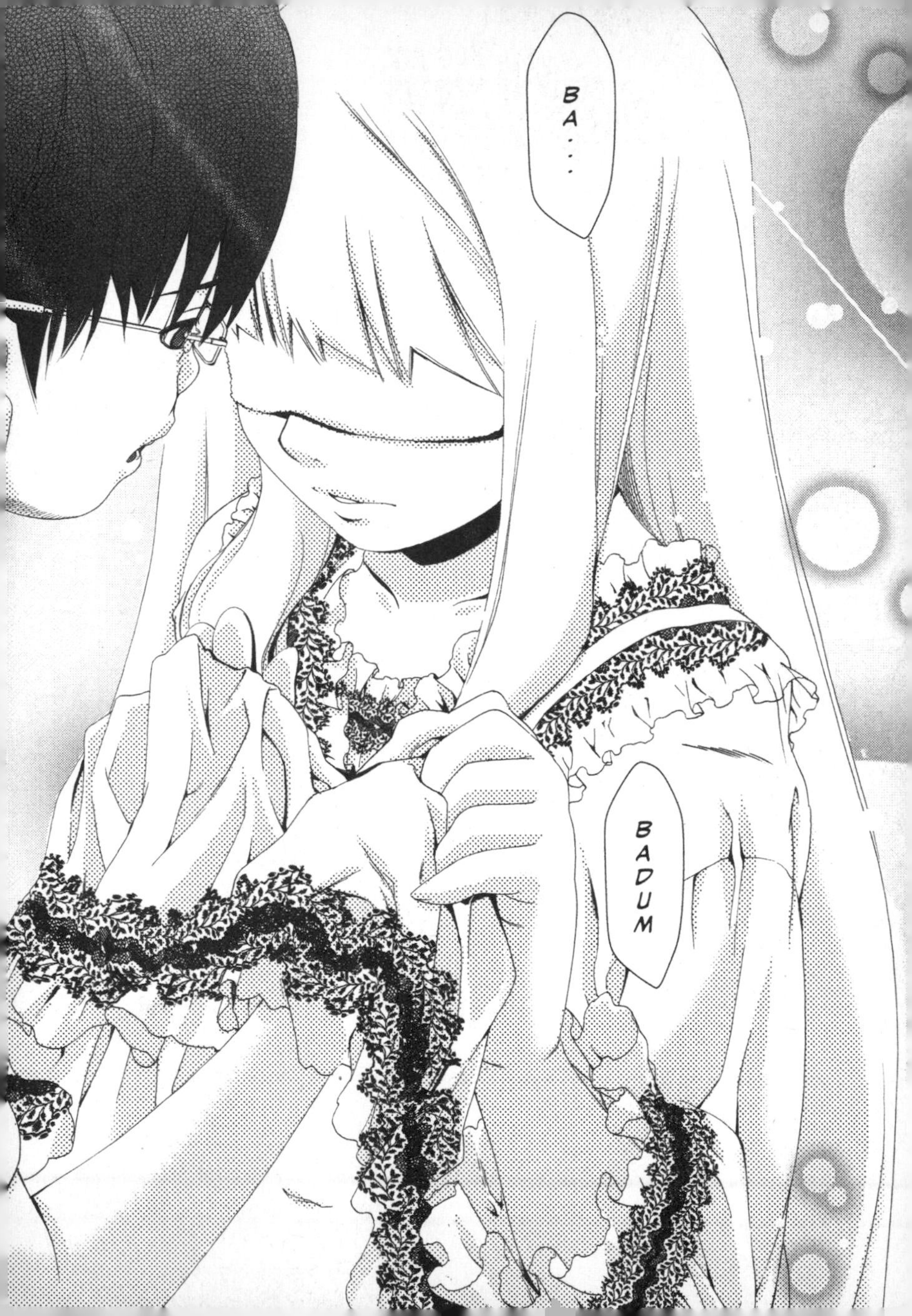
BA...
BADUM

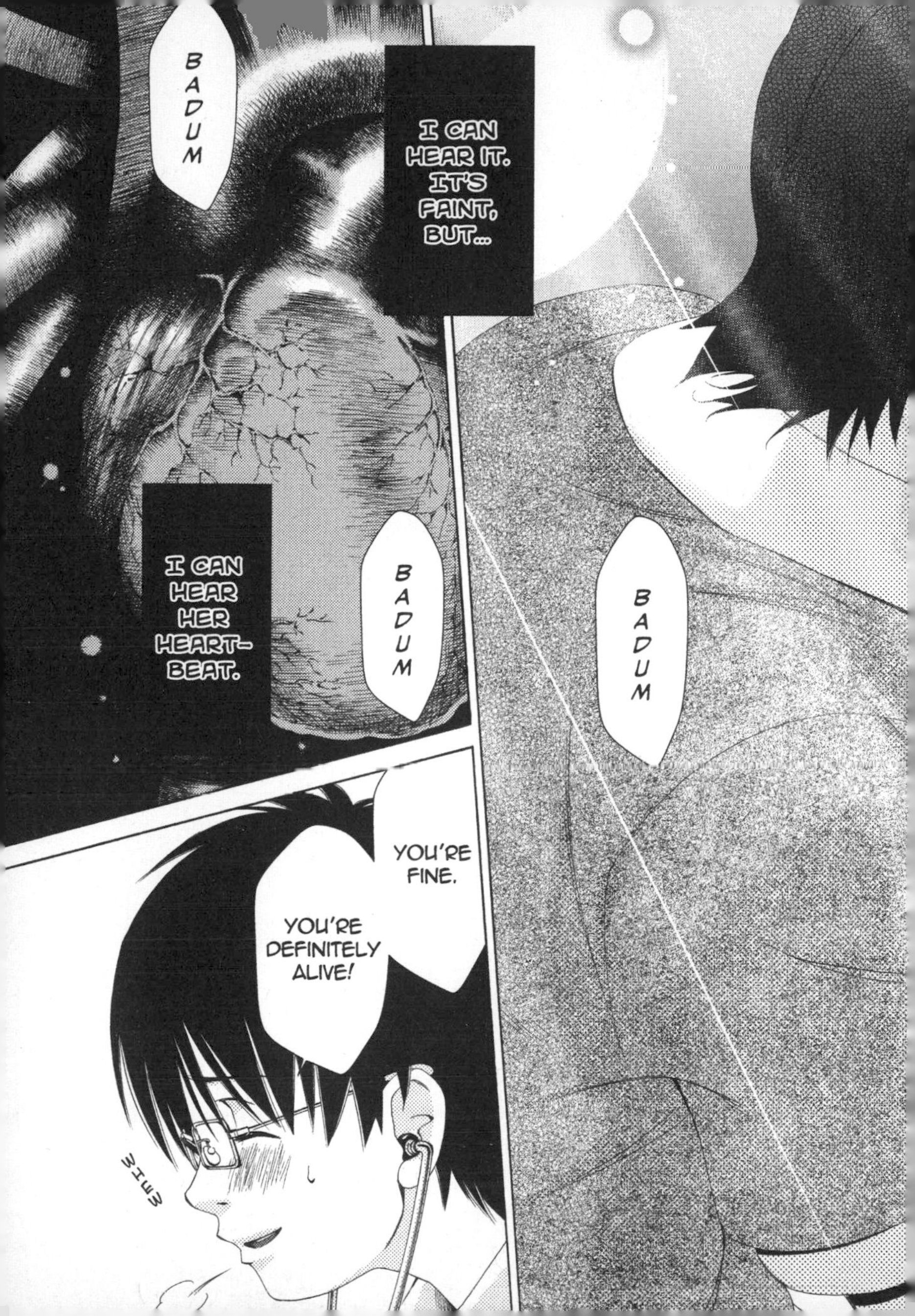
BADUM
I CAN HEAR IT. IT'S FAINT, BUT...
BADUM
BADUM
I CAN HEAR HER HEARTBEAT.
YOU'RE FINE.
YOU'RE DEFINITELY ALIVE!

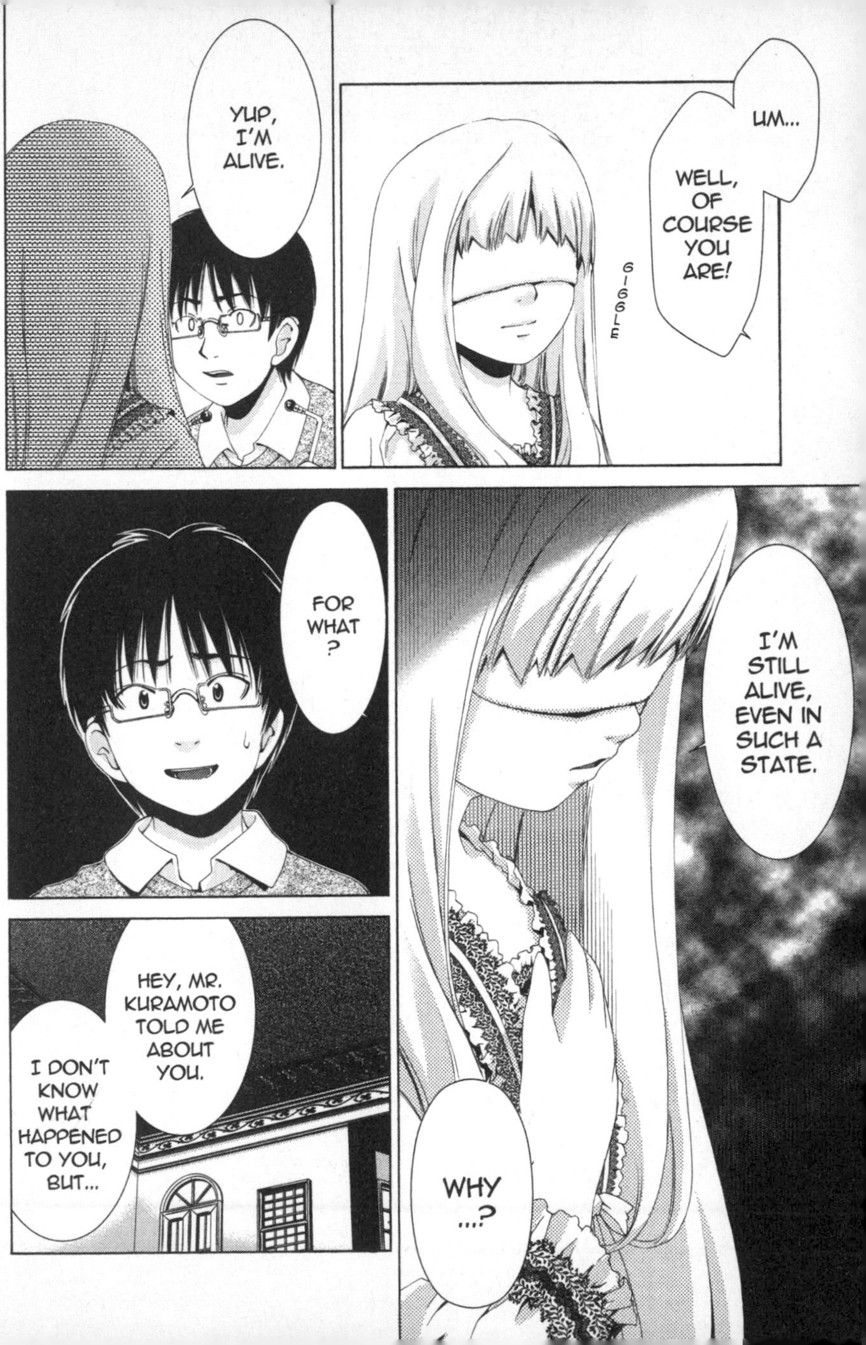
UM...
WELL, OF COURSE YOU ARE!
GIGGLE
YUP, I'M ALIVE.
I'M STILL ALIVE, EVEN IN SUCH A STATE.
WHY ...?
FOR WHAT?
HEY, MR. KURAMOTO TOLD ME ABOUT YOU.
I DON'T KNOW WHAT HAPPENED TO YOU, BUT...

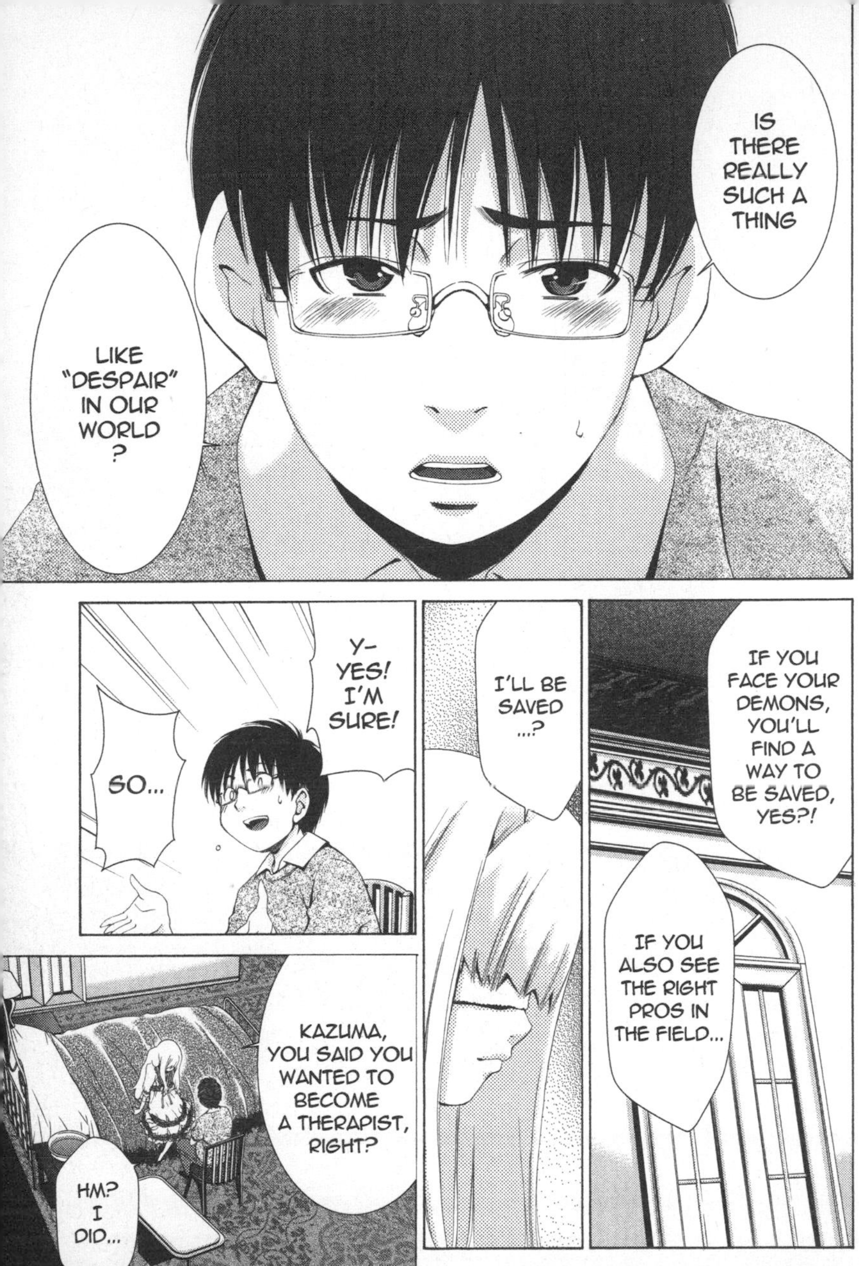
IS THERE REALLY SUCH A THING
LIKE "DESPAIR" IN OUR WORLD ?
IF YOU FACE YOUR DEMONS, YOU'LL FIND A WAY TO BE SAVED, YES?!
IF YOU ALSO SEE THE RIGHT PROS IN THE FIELD...
I'LL BE SAVED ...?
Y- YES! I'M SURE!
SO...
KAZUMA, YOU SAID YOU WANTED TO BECOME A THERAPIST, RIGHT?
HM? I DID...

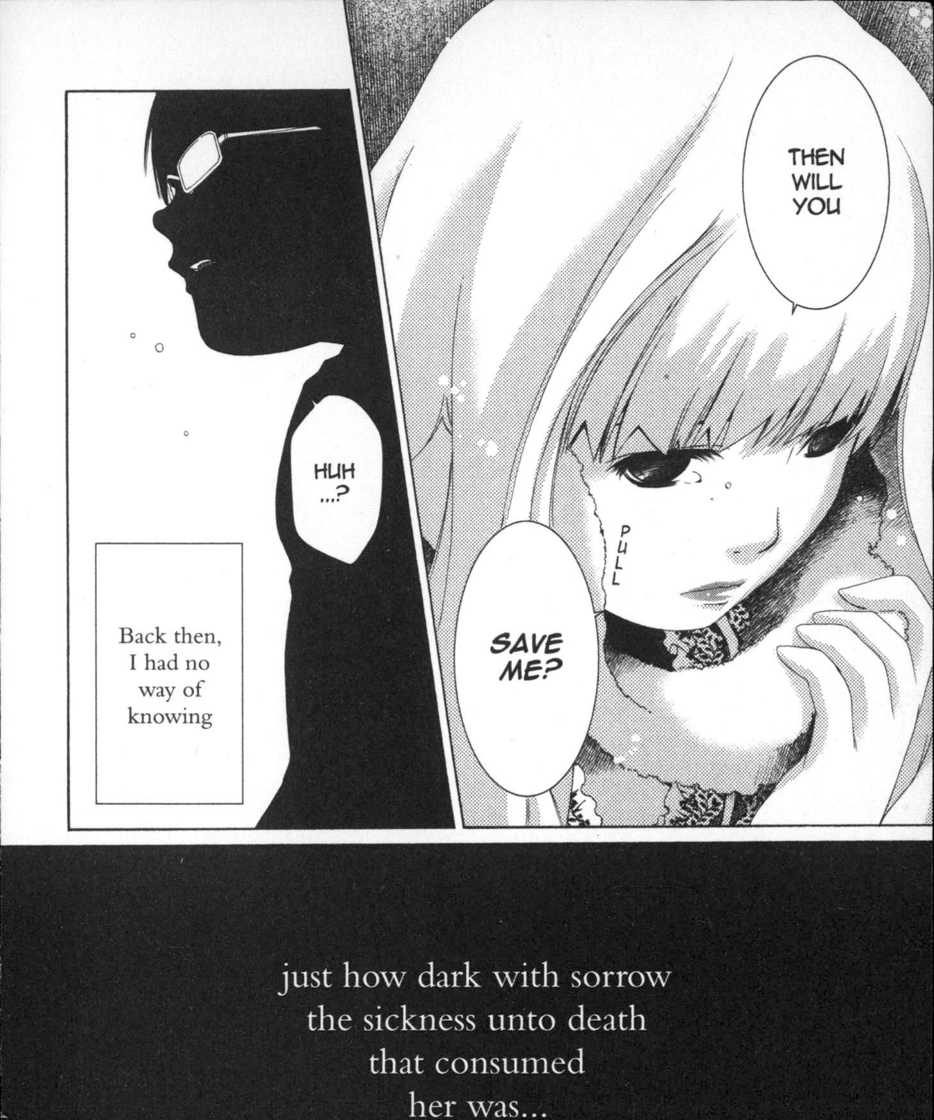
THEN WILL YOU
PULL
SAVE ME?
HUH ...?
Back then, I had no way of knowing

just how dark with sorrow
the sickness unto death
that consumed
her was...

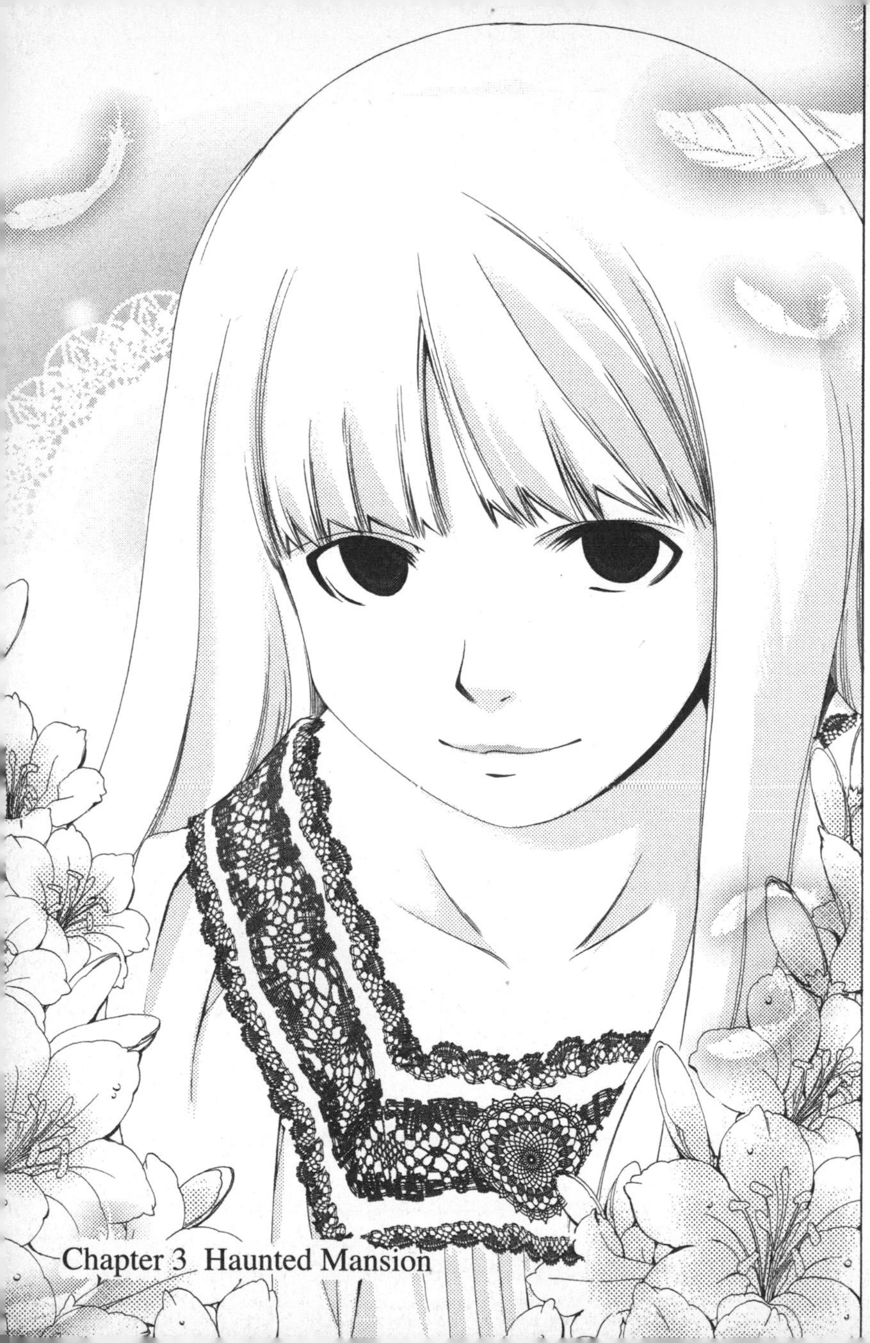
Chapter 3 Haunted Mansion

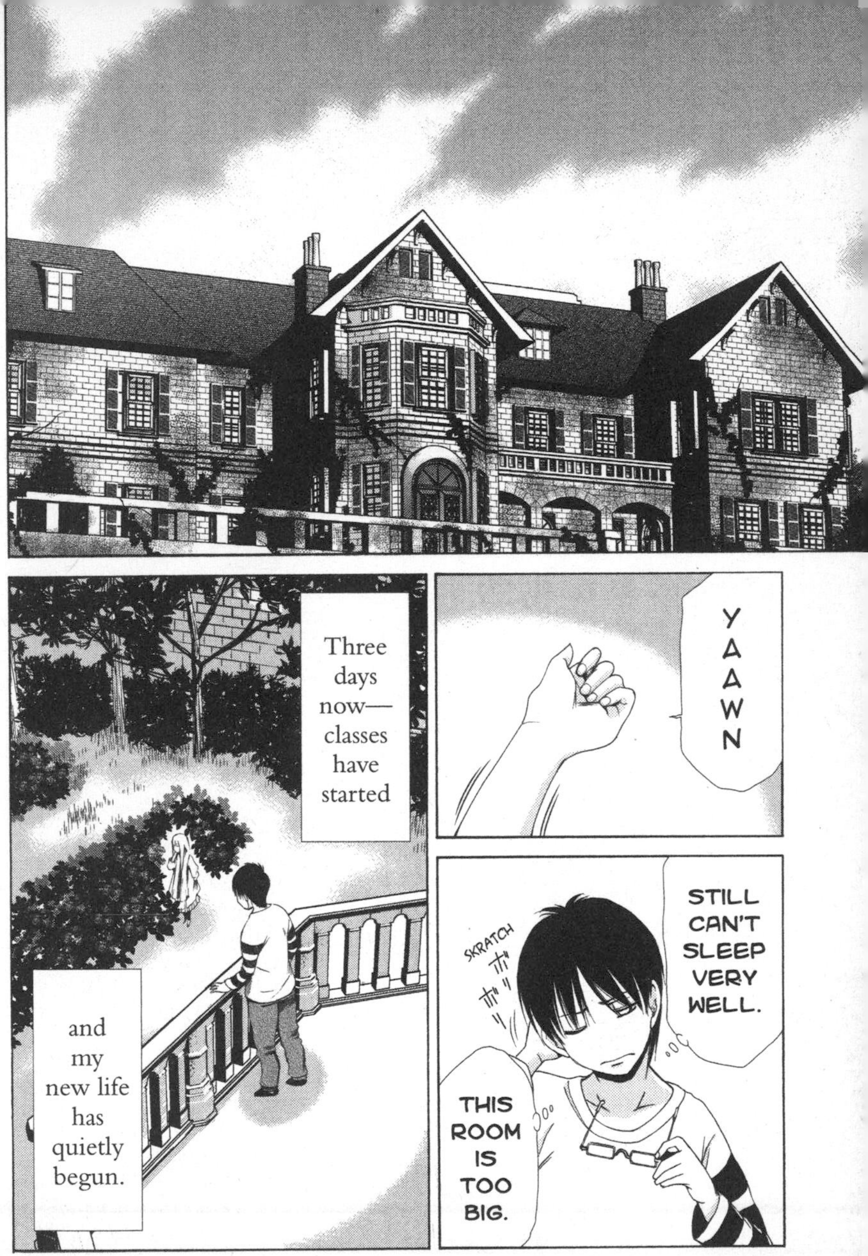
YAAWN
STILL CAN'T SLEEP VERY WELL.
SKRATCH
THIS ROOM IS TOO BIG.
Three days now—classes have started
and my new life has quietly begun.

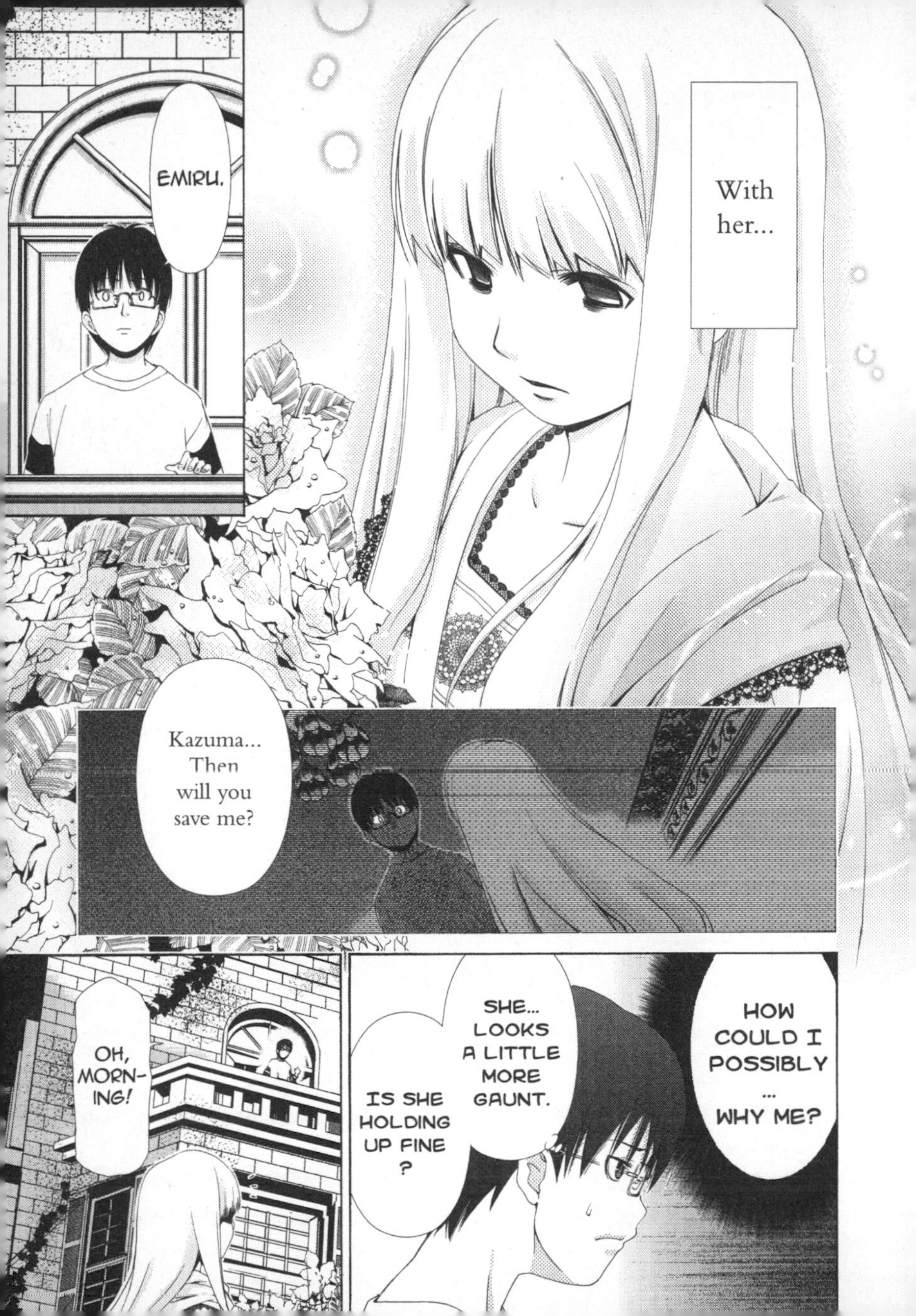
With her...
EMIRU.
Kazuma... Then will you save me?
HOW COULD I POSSIBLY ... WHY ME?
SHE... LOOKS A LITTLE MORE GAUNT.
IS SHE HOLDING UP FINE ?
OH, MORNING!

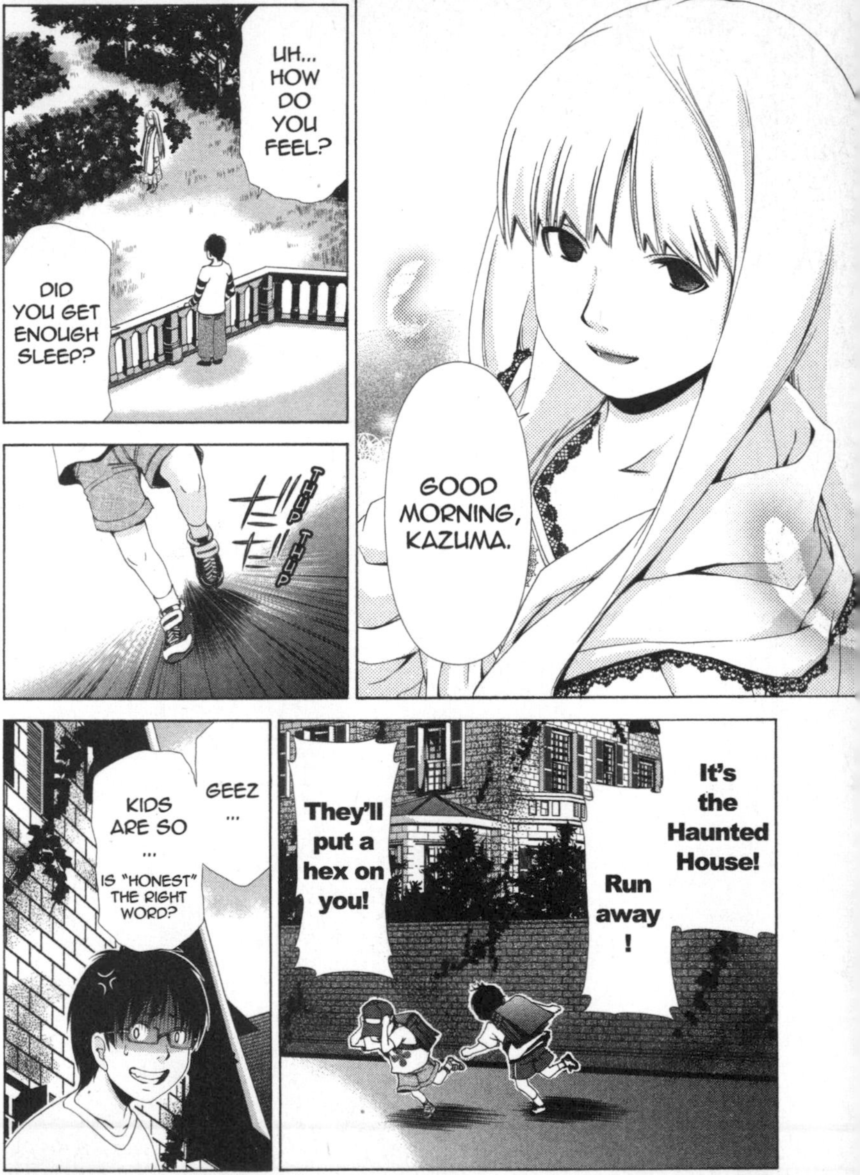
GOOD MORNING, KAZUMA.
UH... HOW DO YOU FEEL?
DID YOU GET ENOUGH SLEEP?
THUMP THUMP
It's the Haunted House!
Run away!
They'll put a hex on you!
GEEZ ...
KIDS ARE SO ...
IS "HONEST" THE RIGHT WORD?

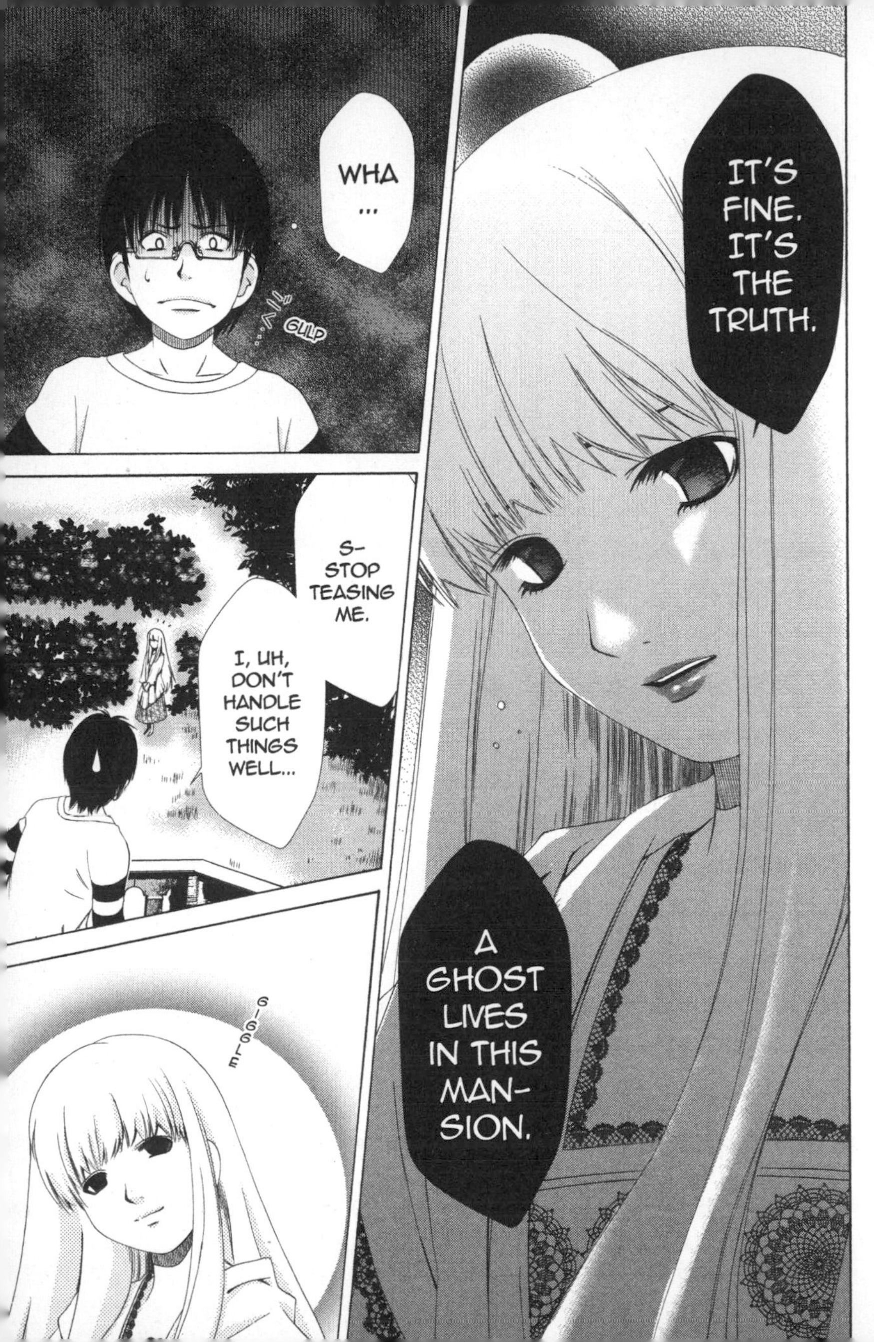
IT'S FINE. IT'S THE TRUTH.
A GHOST LIVES IN THIS MAN-SION.
WHA ...
GULP
S-STOP TEASING ME.
I, UH, DON'T HANDLE SUCH THINGS WELL...
GIGGLE

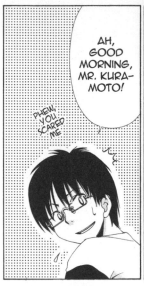

BOOM
GOOD MORNING-ING.
JOLT
AH, GOOD MORNING, MR. KURA-MOTO!
PHEW, YOU SCARED ME
BY THE WAY, I'LL BE ABSENT FROM THE MANSION FOR THE NEXT TWO DAYS.
PLEASE LOOK AFTER MISS EMIRU WHILE I'M GONE.
HUH ...?
I'M GETTING A THOROUGH MEDICAL CHECKUP AS PER MISS EMIRU'S ADVICE.
I AM OF AGE, YOU SEE.
ALL RIGHT, GOT IT.
SO, WHAT, I'LL BE ALL ALONE WITH HER?

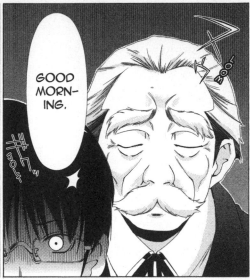

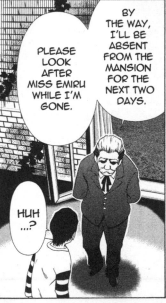

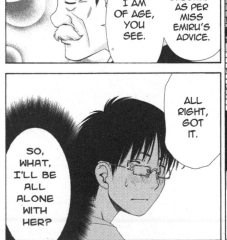

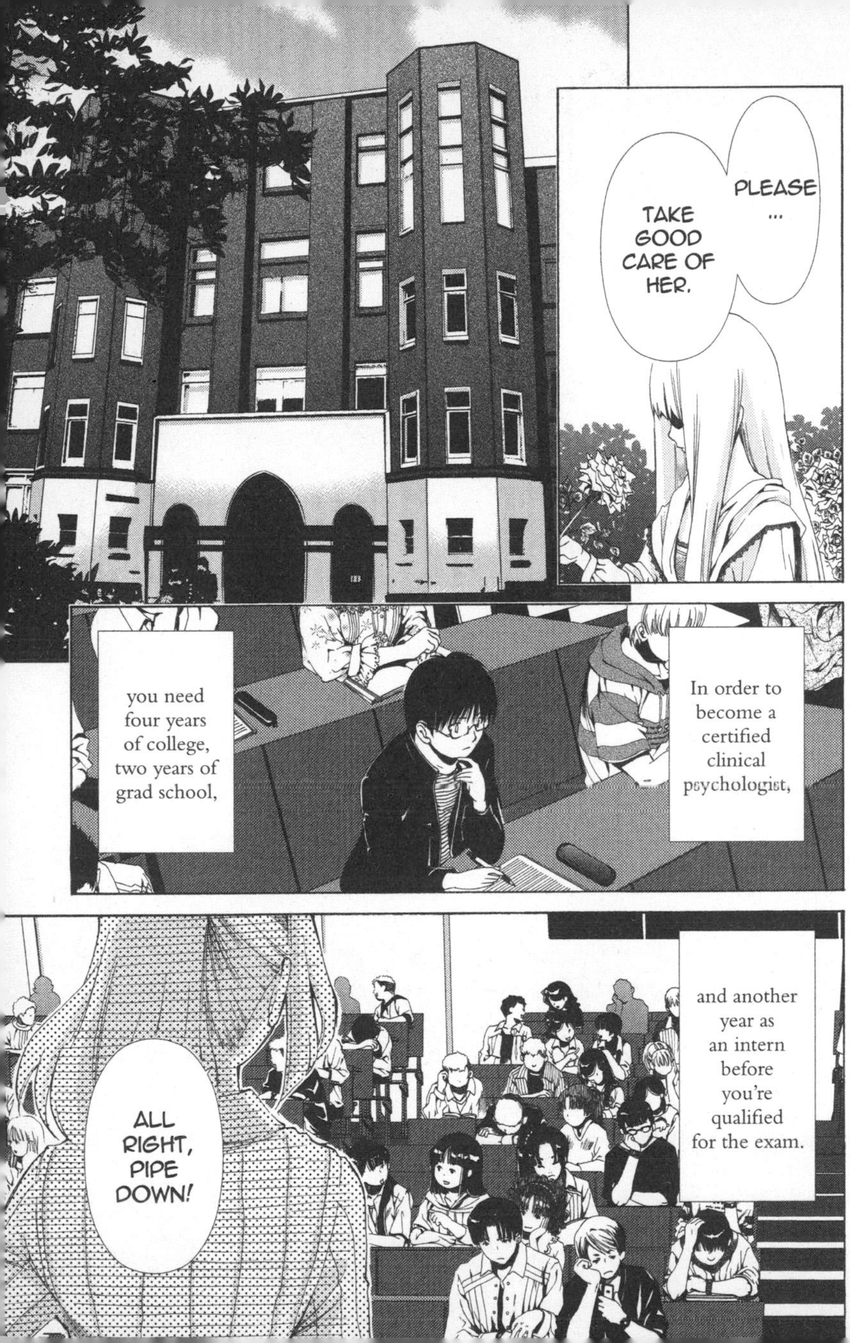
PLEASE ...
TAKE GOOD CARE OF HER.
In order to become a certified clinical psychologist,
you need four years of college, two years of grad school,
and another year as an intern before you're qualified for the exam.
ALL RIGHT, PIPE DOWN!

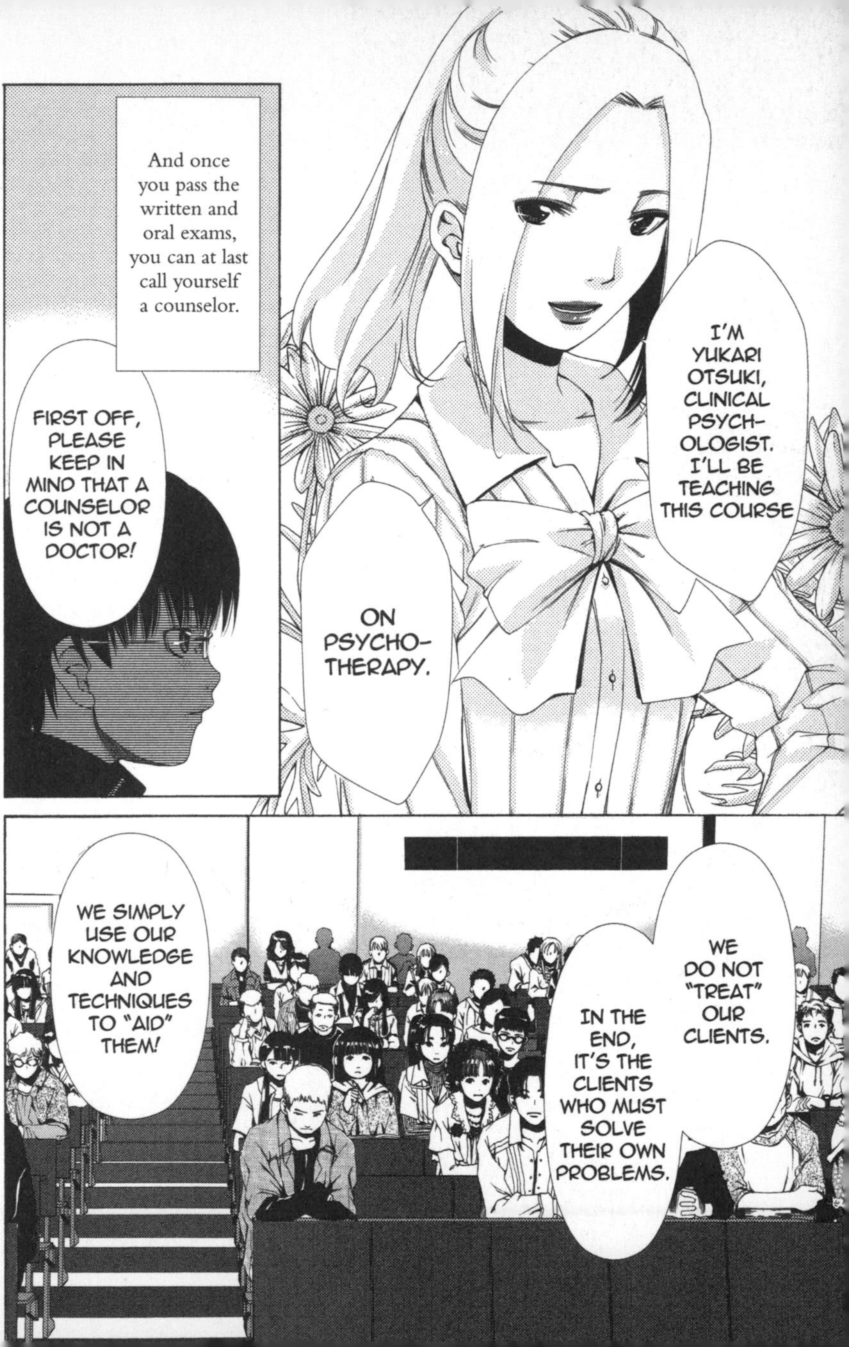
I'M YUKARI OTSUKI, CLINICAL PSYCH-OLOGIST. I'LL BE TEACHING THIS COURSE
ON PSYCHO-THERAPY.
And once you pass the written and oral exams, you can at last call yourself a counselor.
FIRST OFF, PLEASE KEEP IN MIND THAT A COUNSELOR IS NOT A DOCTOR!
WE DO NOT "TREAT" OUR CLIENTS.
IN THE END, IT'S THE CLIENTS WHO MUST SOLVE THEIR OWN PROBLEMS.
WE SIMPLY USE OUR KNOWLEDGE AND TECHNIQUES TO "AID" THEM!

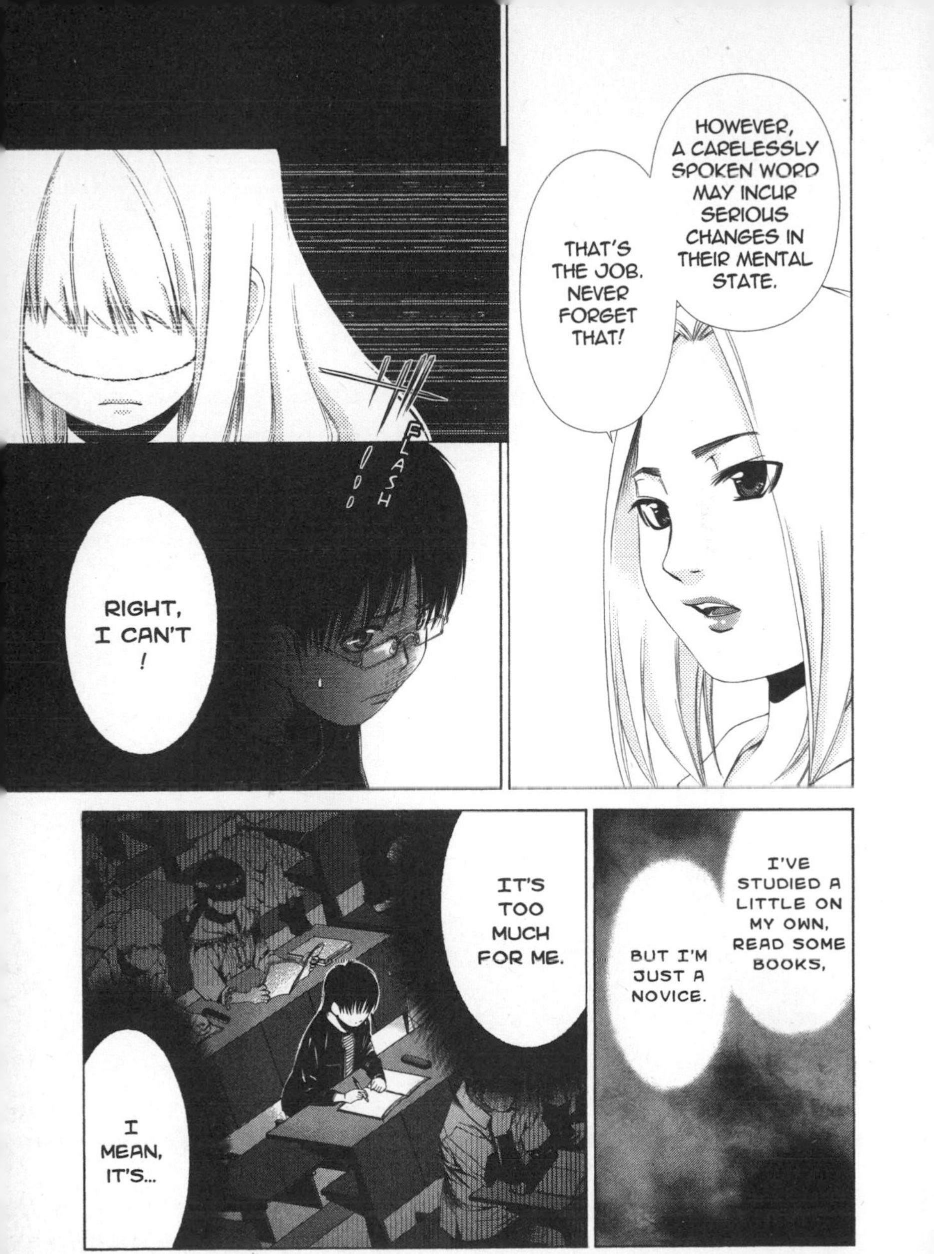
HOWEVER, A CARELESSLY SPOKEN WORD MAY INCUR SERIOUS CHANGES IN THEIR MENTAL STATE.
THAT'S THE JOB. NEVER FORGET THAT!
FLASH
RIGHT, I CAN'T!
I'VE STUDIED A LITTLE ON MY OWN, READ SOME BOOKS,
BUT I'M JUST A NOVICE.
IT'S TOO MUCH FOR ME.
I MEAN, IT'S...

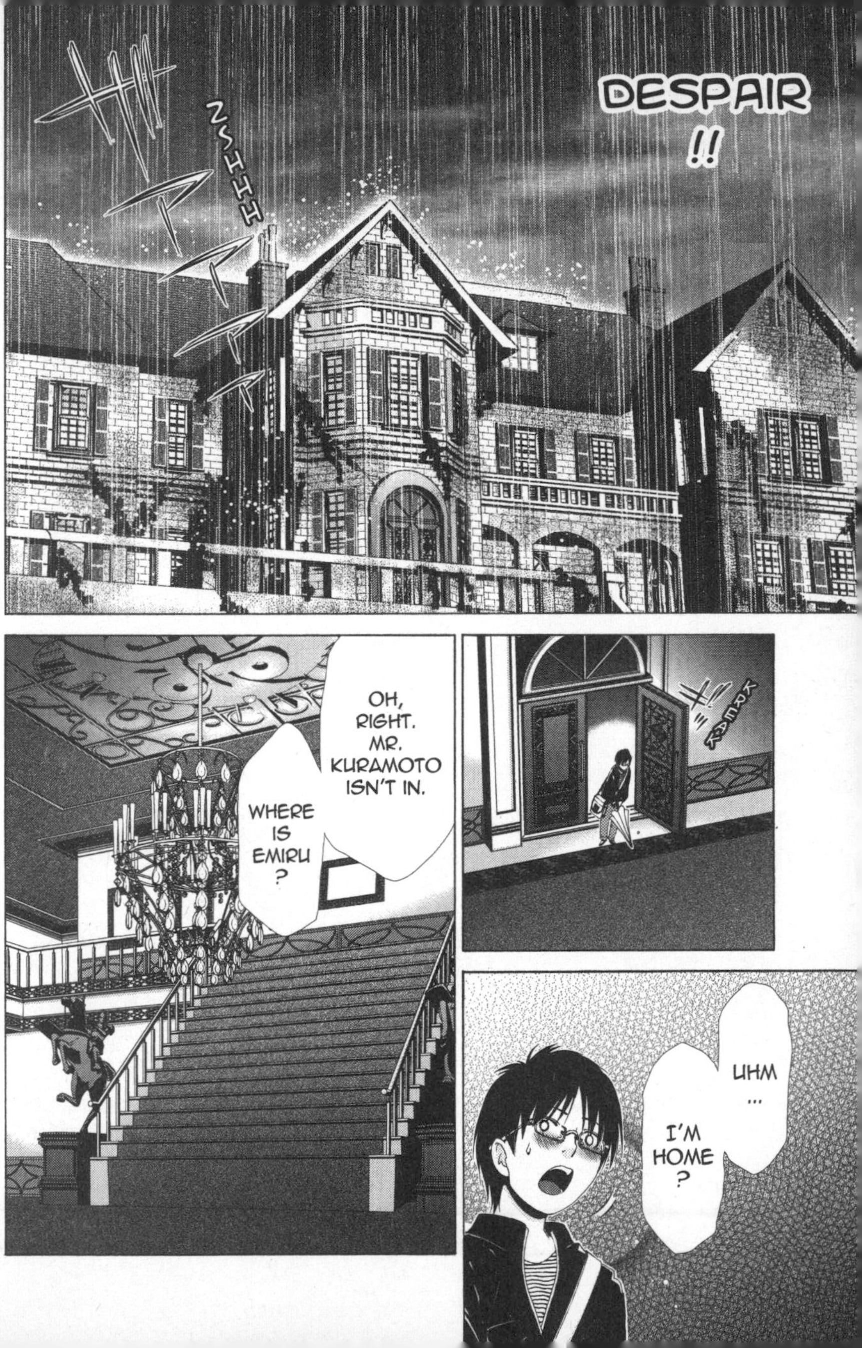
DESPAIR !!
UHM ...
I'M HOME ?
OH, RIGHT. MR. KURAMOTO ISN'T IN.
WHERE IS EMIRU ?

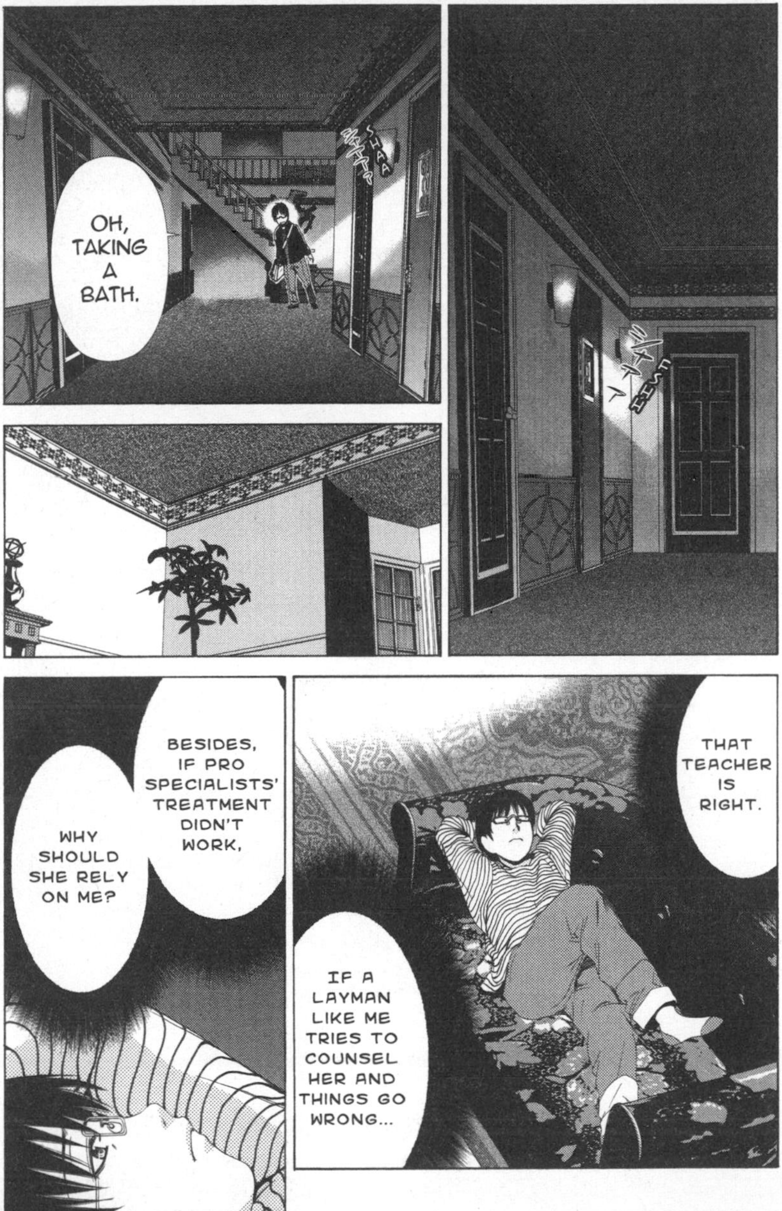
SHAA
OH, TAKING A BATH.
THAT TEACHER IS RIGHT.
IF A LAYMAN LIKE ME TRIES TO COUNSEL HER AND THINGS GO WRONG...
BESIDES, IF PRO SPECIALISTS' TREATMENT DIDN'T WORK,
WHY SHOULD SHE RELY ON ME?

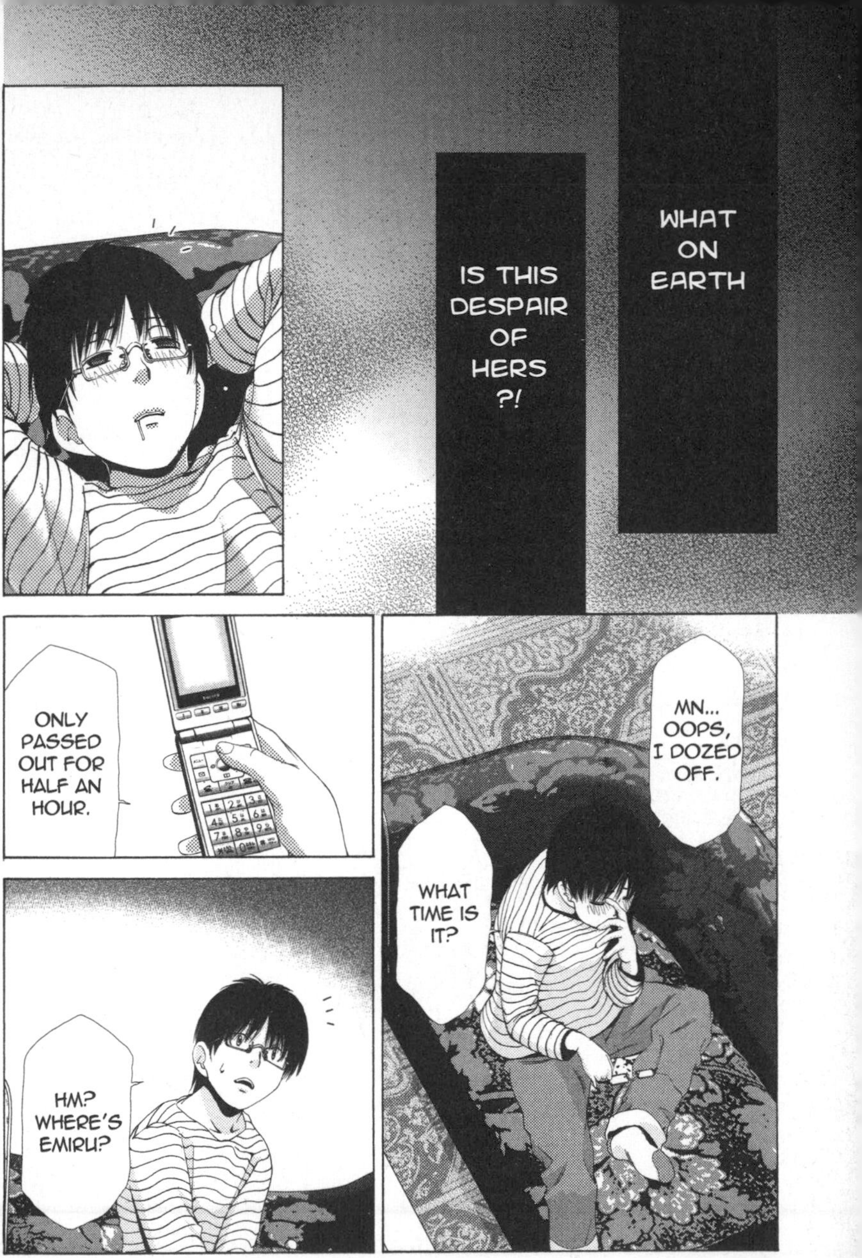
WHAT ON EARTH
IS THIS DESPAIR OF HERS ?!
MN... OOPS, I DOZED OFF.
WHAT TIME IS IT?
ONLY PASSED OUT FOR HALF AN HOUR.
HM? WHERE'S EMIRU?

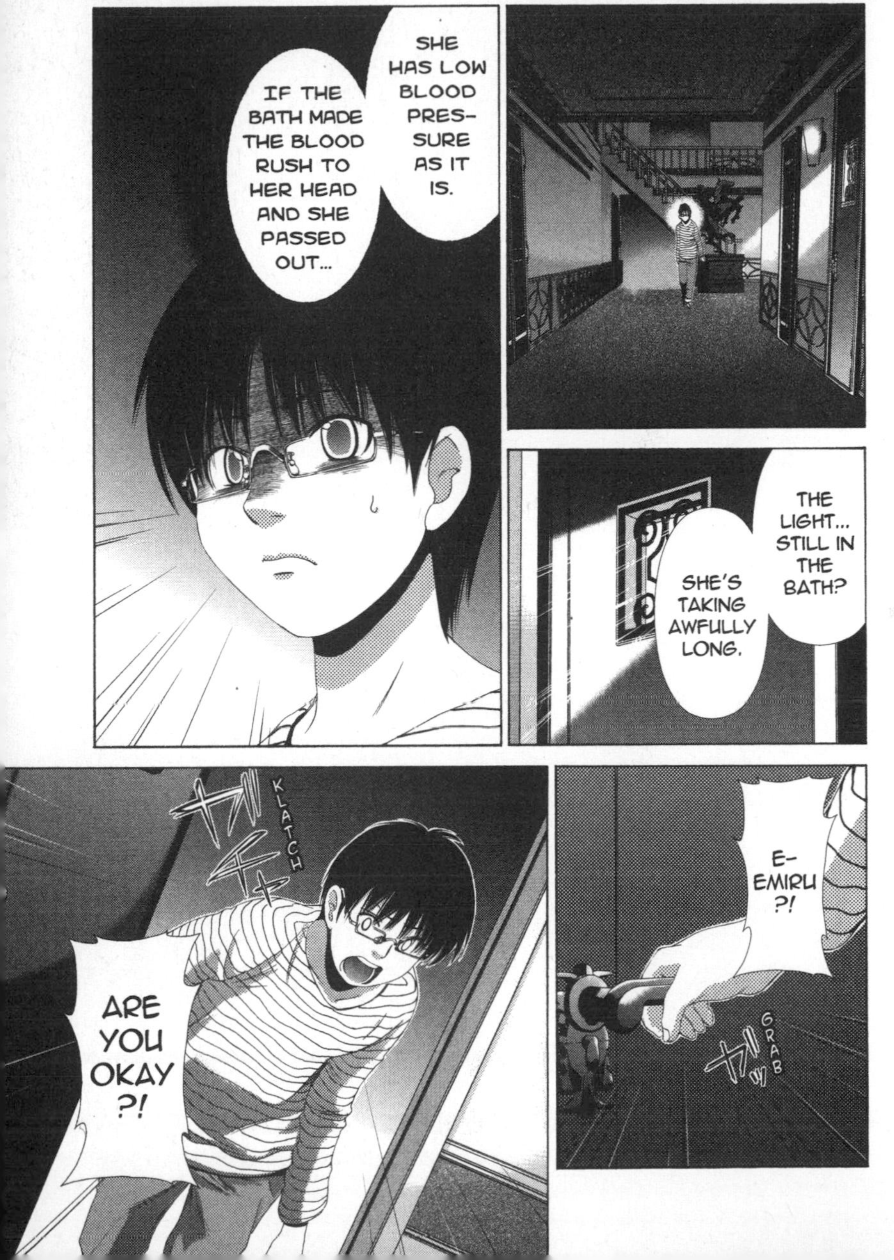
THE LIGHT... STILL IN THE BATH?
SHE'S TAKING AWFULLY LONG.
SHE HAS LOW BLOOD PRES-SURE AS IT IS.
IF THE BATH MADE THE BLOOD RUSH TO HER HEAD AND SHE PASSED OUT...
E-EMIRU?!
GRAB
KLATCH
ARE YOU OKAY?!

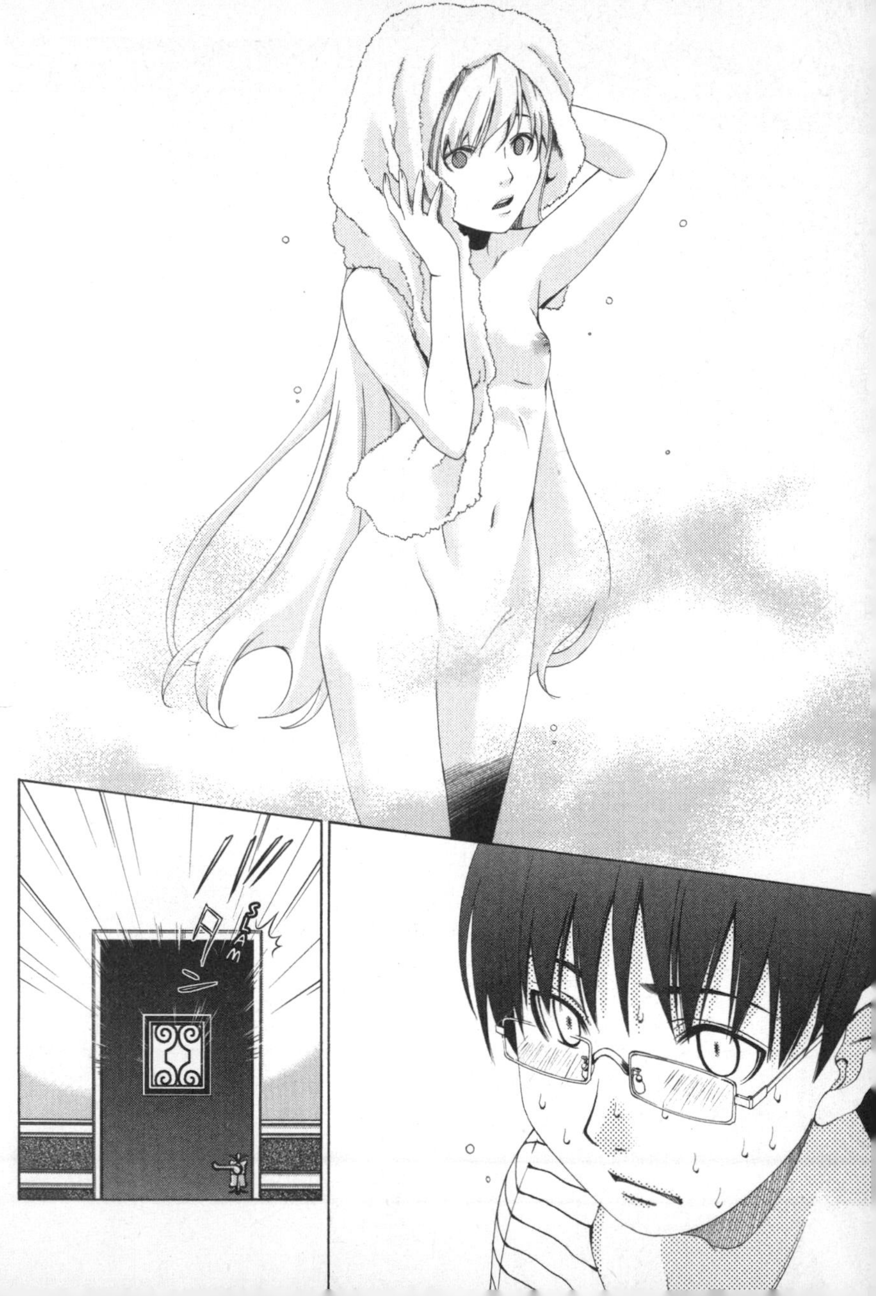
SLAM

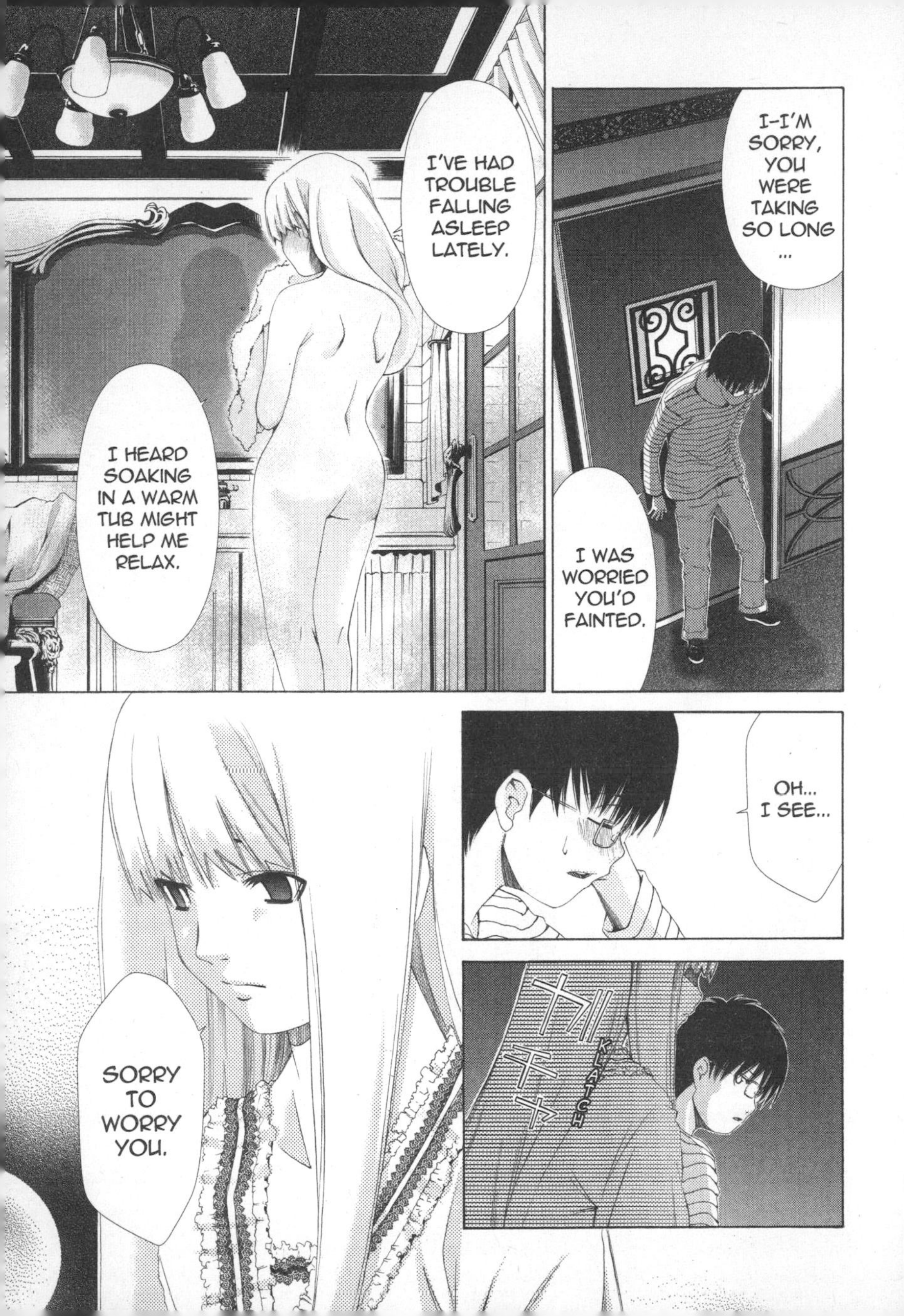
I-I'M SORRY, YOU WERE TAKING SO LONG ...
I WAS WORRIED YOU'D FAINTED.
I'VE HAD TROUBLE FALLING ASLEEP LATELY.
I HEARD SOAKING IN A WARM TUB MIGHT HELP ME RELAX.
OH... I SEE...
KLATCH
SORRY TO WORRY YOU.

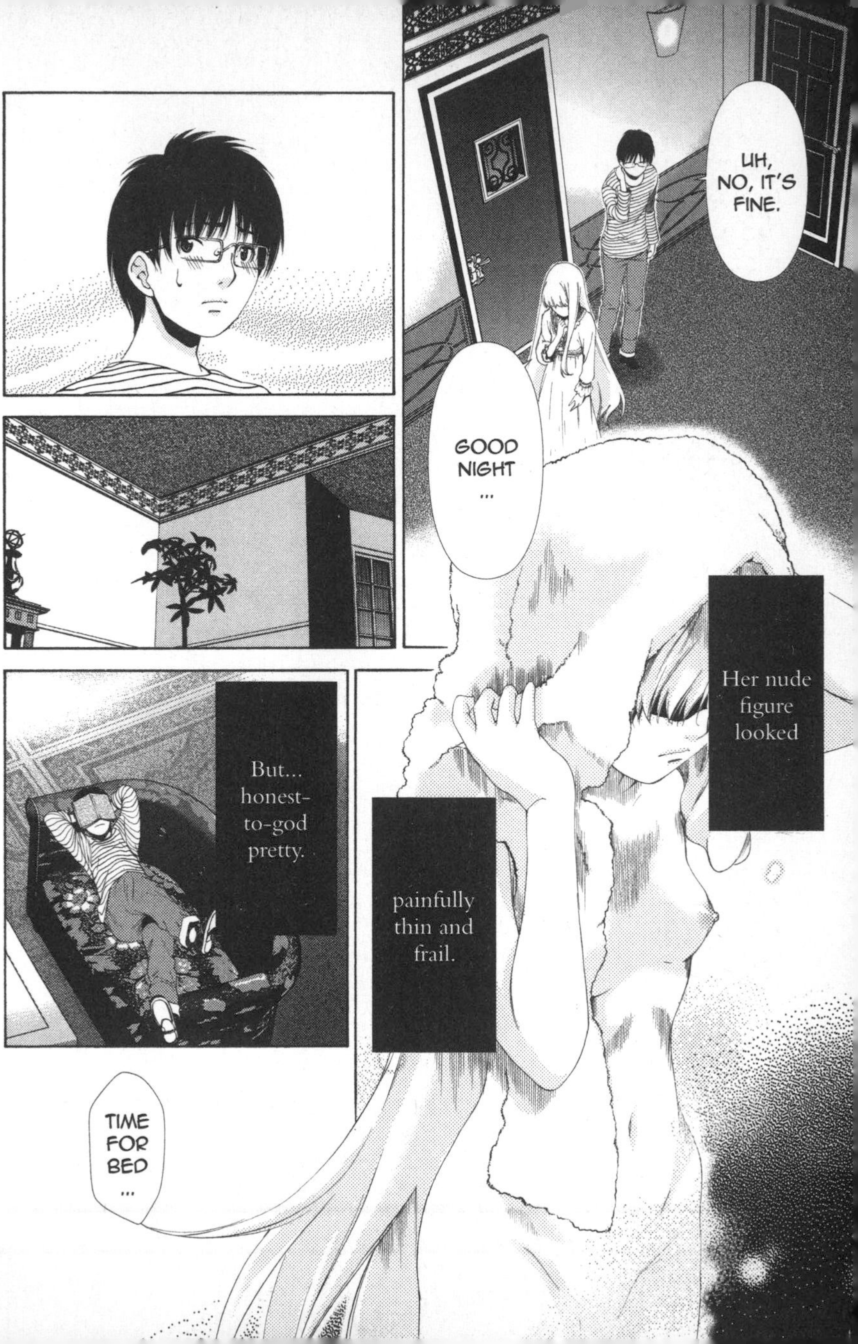
UH, NO, IT'S FINE.
GOOD NIGHT ...
Her nude figure looked
painfully thin and frail.
But... honest-to-god pretty.
TIME FOR BED ...

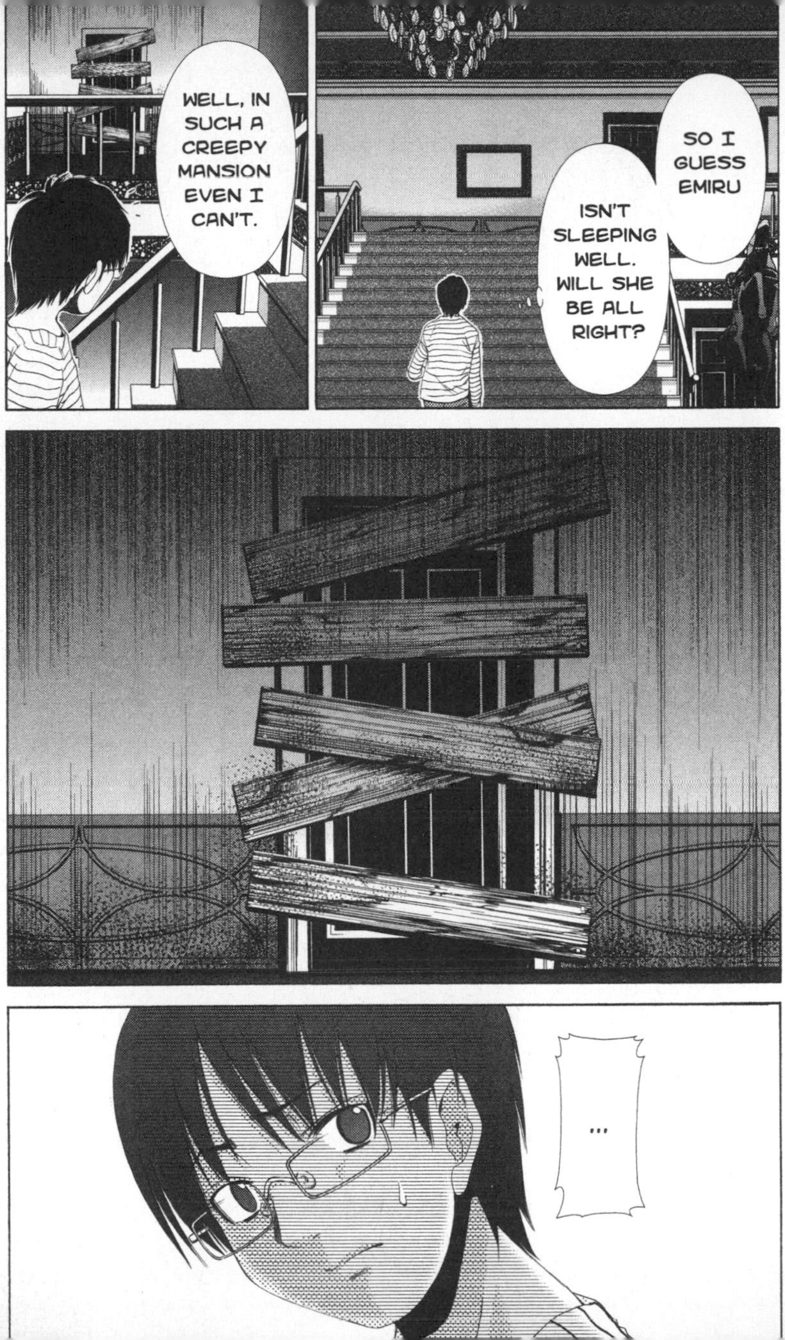
SO I GUESS EMIRU
ISN'T SLEEPING WELL. WILL SHE BE ALL RIGHT?
WELL, IN SUCH A CREEPY MANSION EVEN I CAN'T.
...

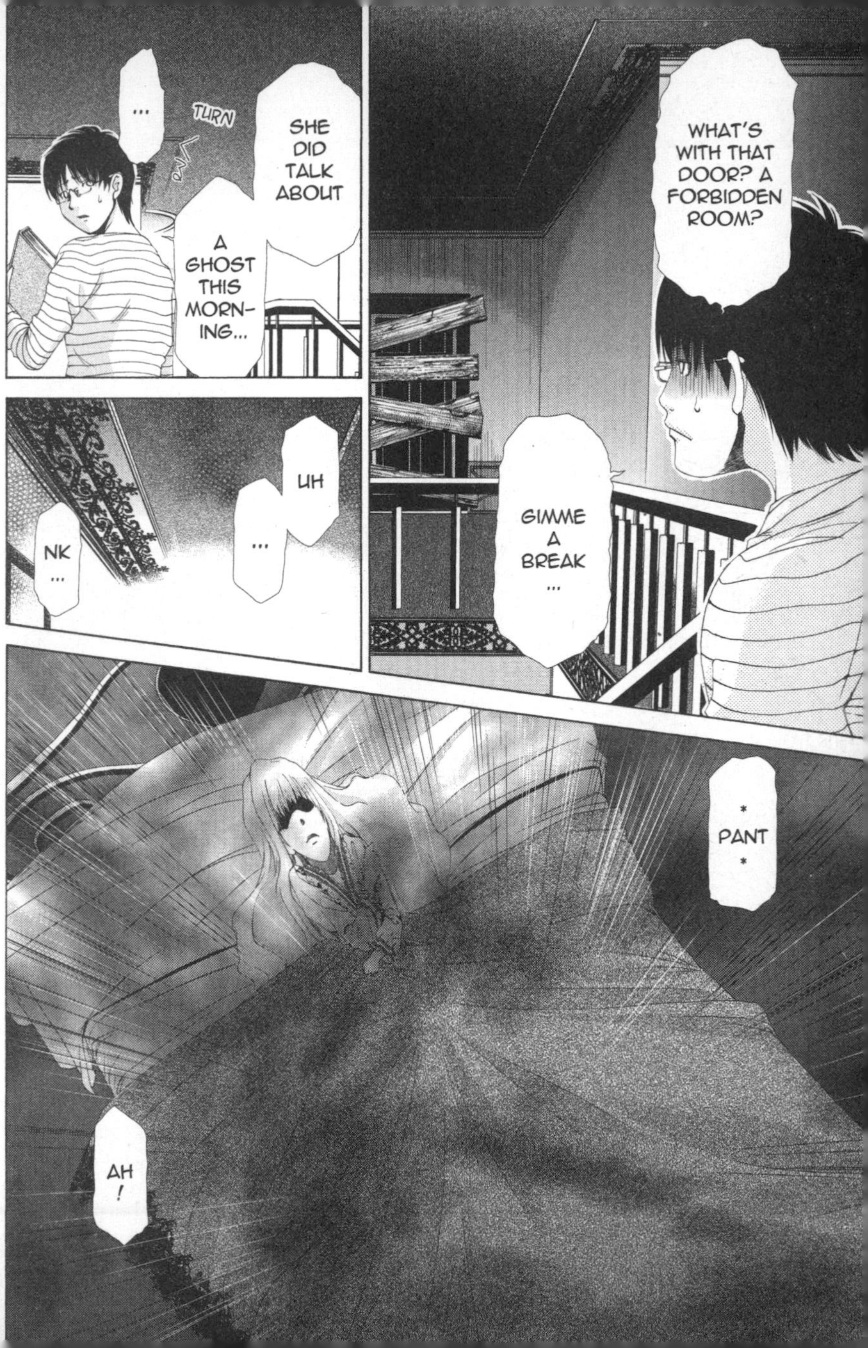
WHAT'S WITH THAT DOOR? A FORBIDDEN ROOM?
GIMME A BREAK ...
SHE DID TALK ABOUT
TURN
...
A GHOST THIS MORNING-ING...
UH
...
NK ...
* PANT *
AH !

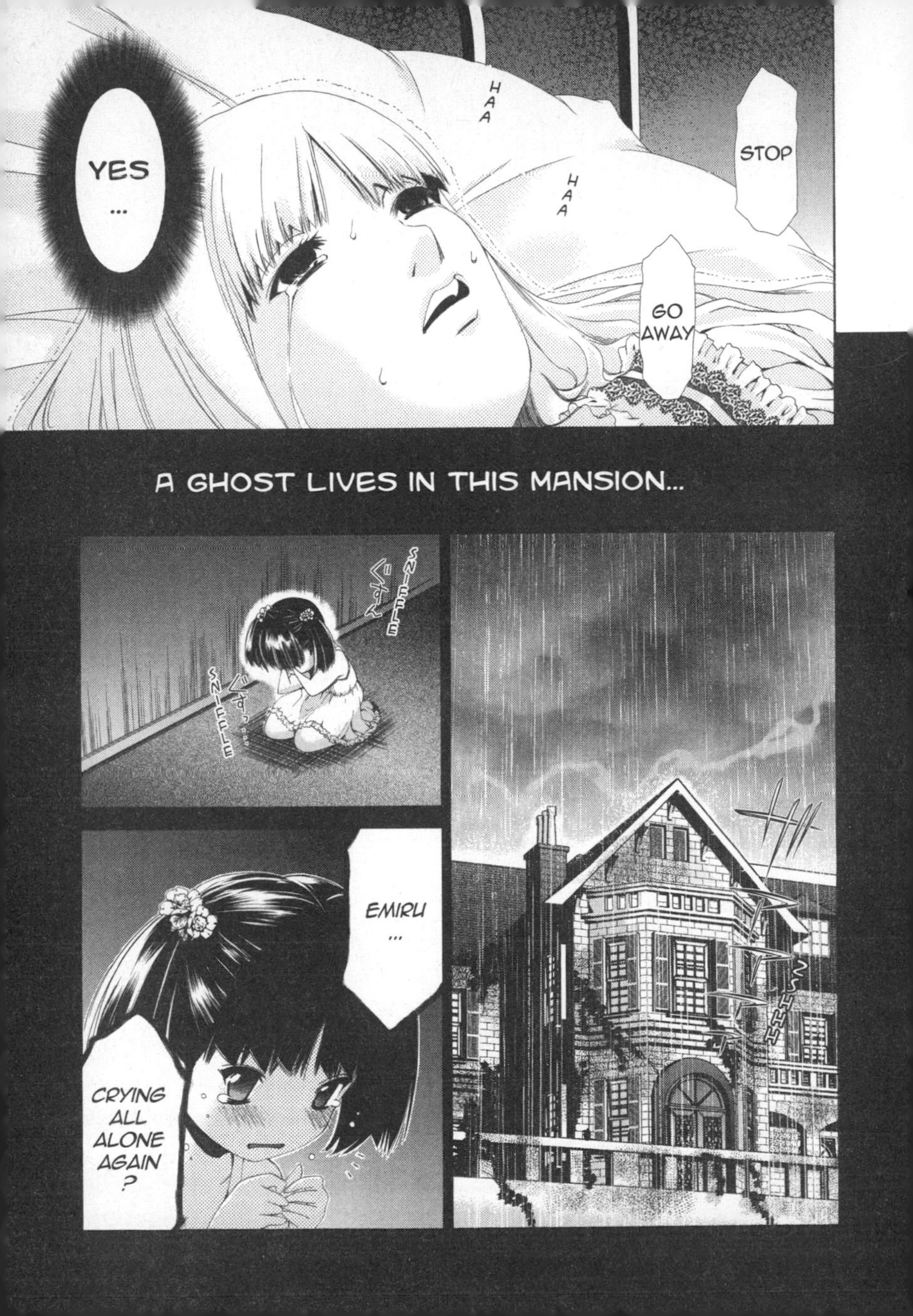
STOP
HAA
HAA
GO AWAY
YES ...
A GHOST LIVES IN THIS MANSION...
SHHHH
SNIFFLE
SNIFFLE
EMIRU ...
CRYING ALL ALONE AGAIN ?

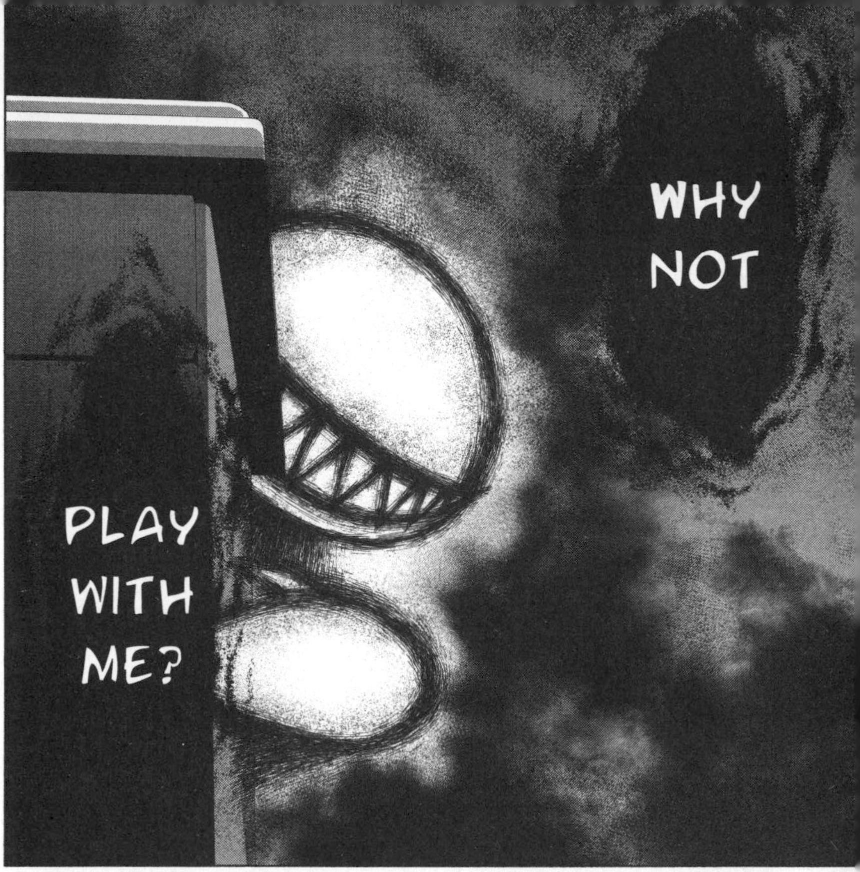
WHY NOT
PLAY WITH ME?
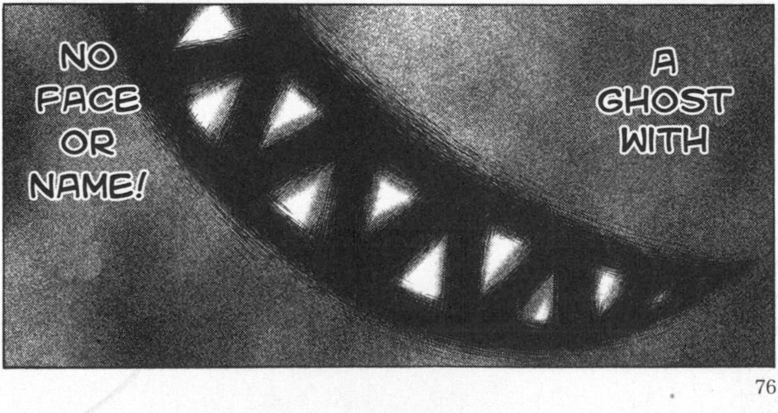
A GHOST WITH
NO FACE OR NAME!

Chapter 4 Sharing a Bed

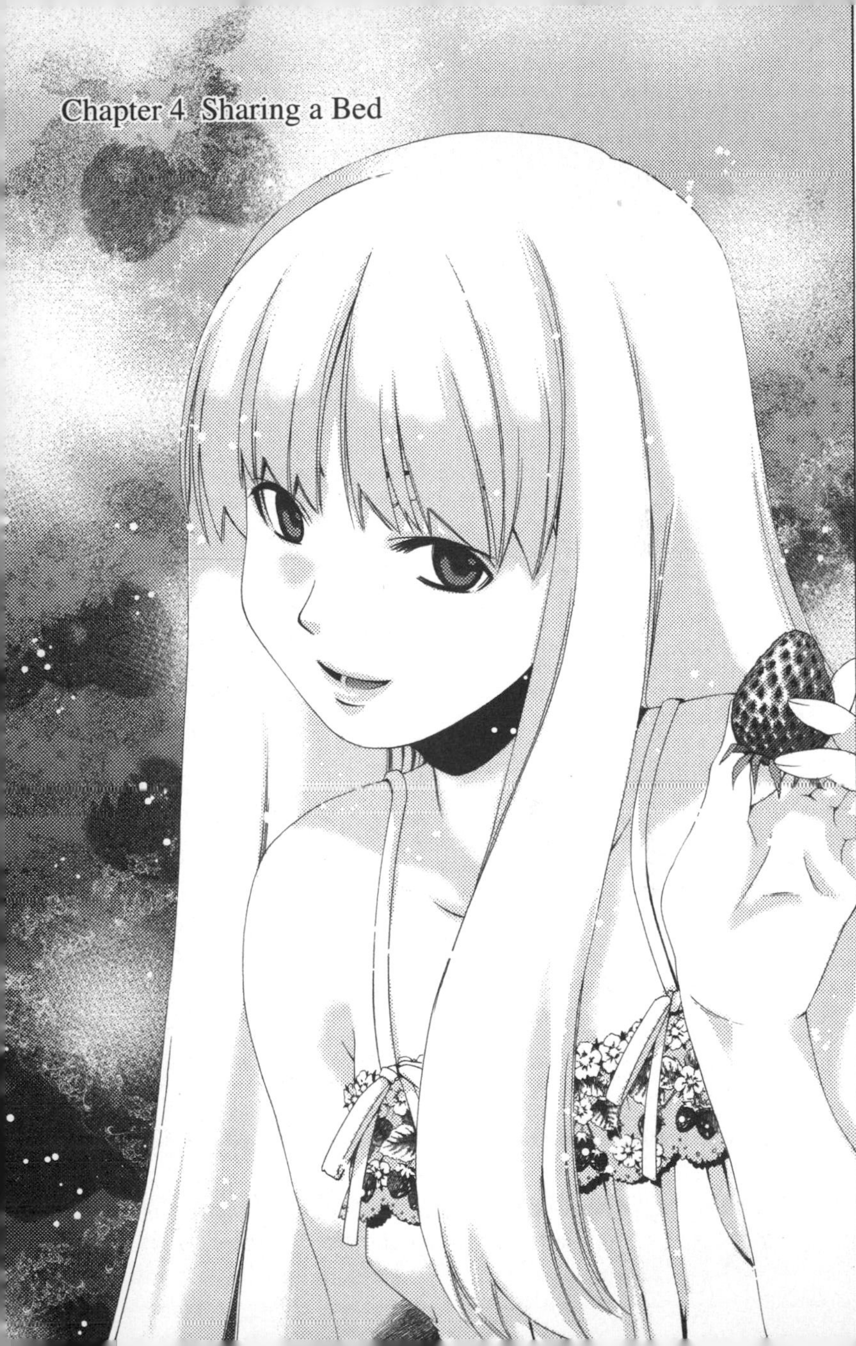

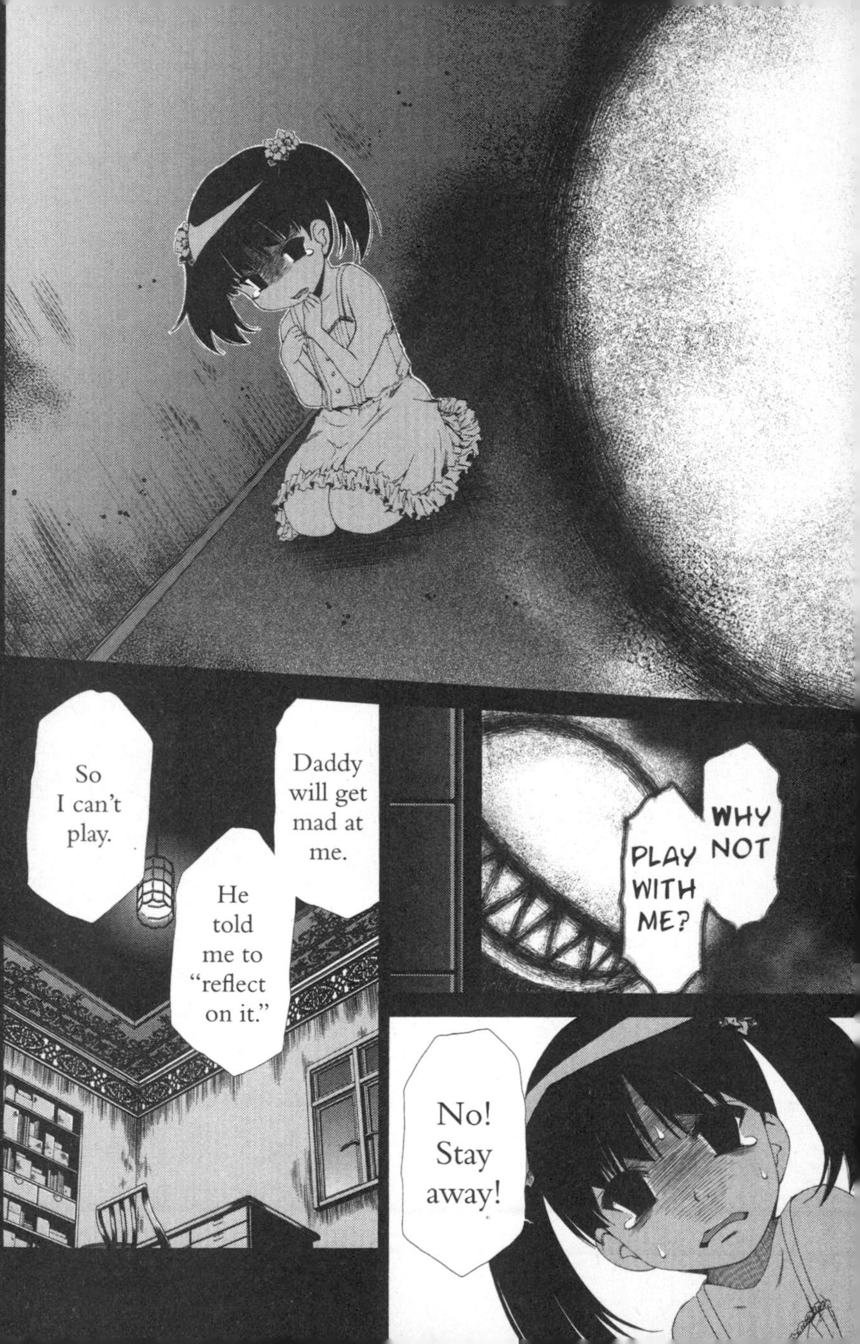
WHY NOT PLAY WITH ME?
Daddy will get mad at me.
He told me to "reflect on it."
So I can't play.
No! Stay away!

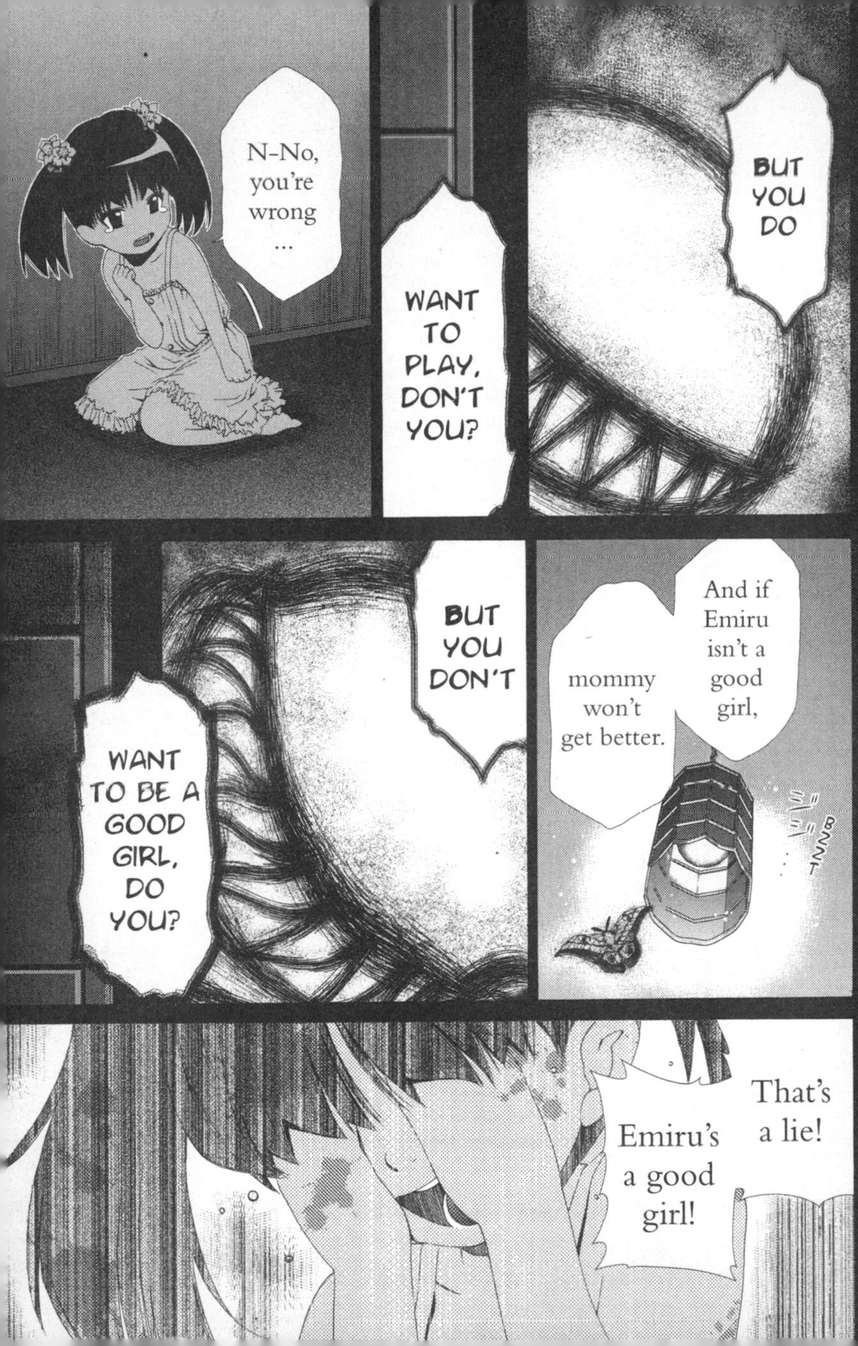
BUT YOU DO
WANT TO PLAY, DON'T YOU?
N-No, you're wrong ...
And if Emiru isn't a good girl,
mommy won't get better.
BZZT
BUT YOU DON'T
WANT TO BE A GOOD GIRL, DO YOU?
That's a lie!
Emiru's a good girl!

HIC

SOB

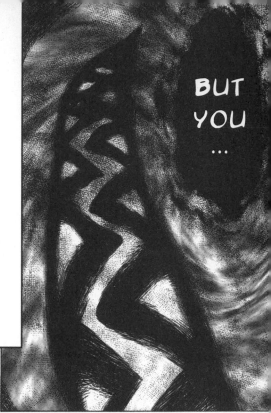

BUT YOU ...

FROM EMIRU'S ROOM ?

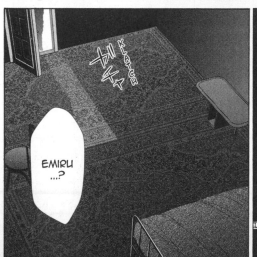

KLAKTCH

EMIRU ....?

KNOK KNOK

HEY, EMIRU ?

ARE YOU OKAY ?

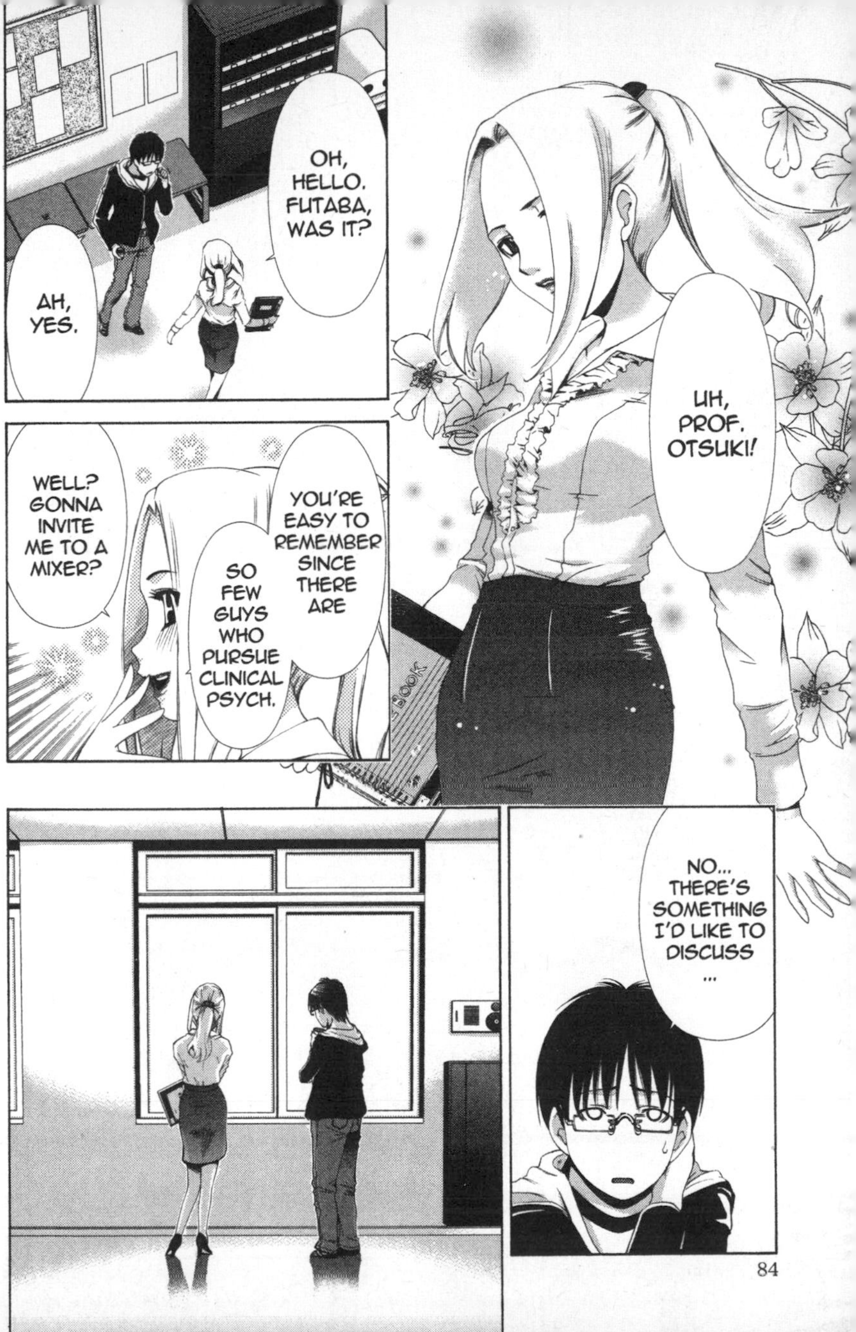
UH, PROF. OTSUKI!
OH, HELLO. FUTABA, WAS IT?
AH, YES.
YOU'RE EASY TO REMEMBER SINCE THERE ARE
SO FEW GUYS WHO PURSUE CLINICAL PSYCH.
WELL? GONNA INVITE ME TO A MIXER?
NO... THERE'S SOMETHING I'D LIKE TO DISCUSS ...

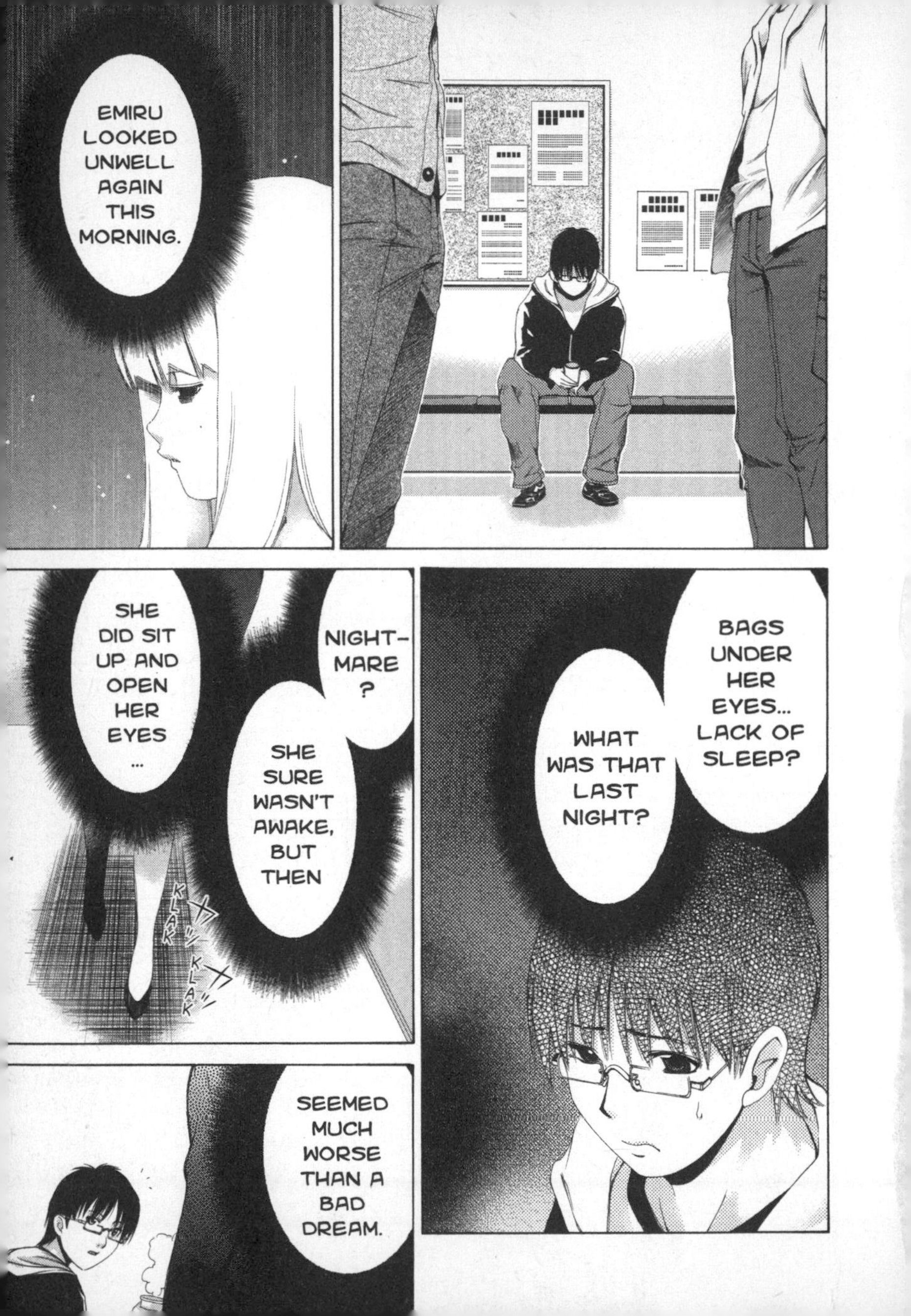
EMIRU LOOKED UNWELL AGAIN THIS MORNING.
BAGS UNDER HER EYES... LACK OF SLEEP?
WHAT WAS THAT LAST NIGHT?
SHE DID SIT UP AND OPEN HER EYES ...
SHE SURE WASN'T AWAKE, BUT THEN
NIGHT-MARE ?
KLAK
KLAK
SEEMED MUCH WORSE THAN A BAD DREAM.

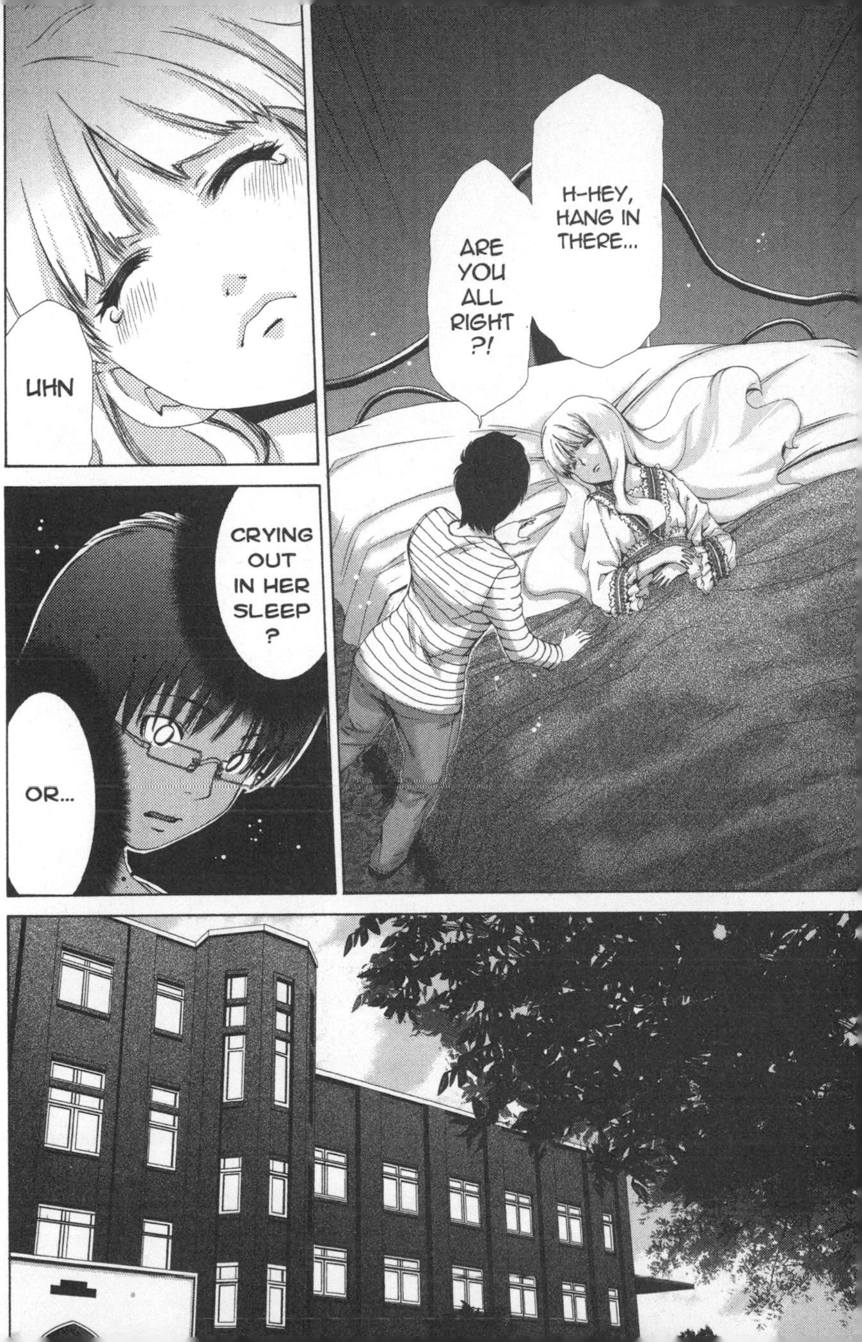
H-HEY, HANG IN THERE...
ARE YOU ALL RIGHT ?!
UHN
CRYING OUT IN HER SLEEP ?
OR...

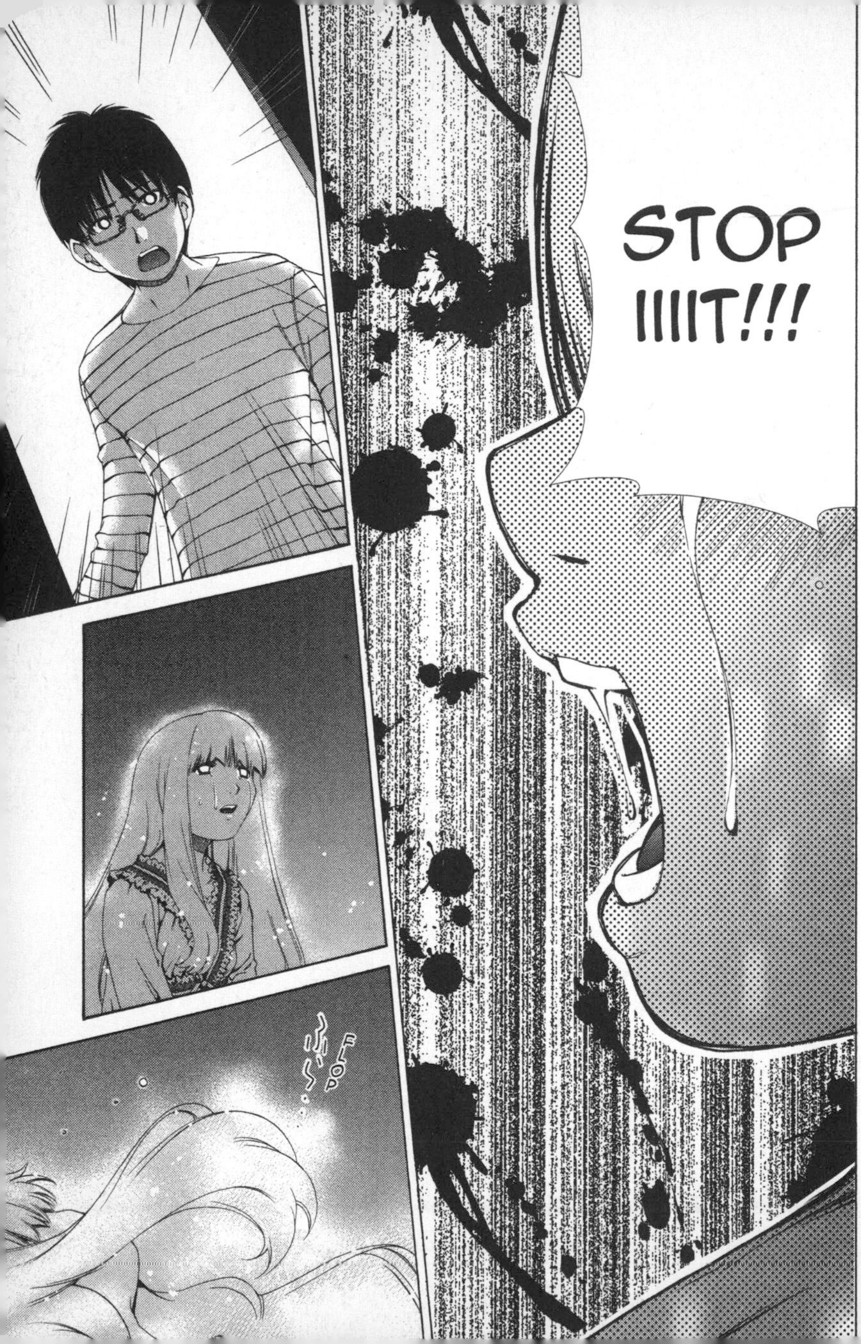
STOP IIIIT!!!
FLOP

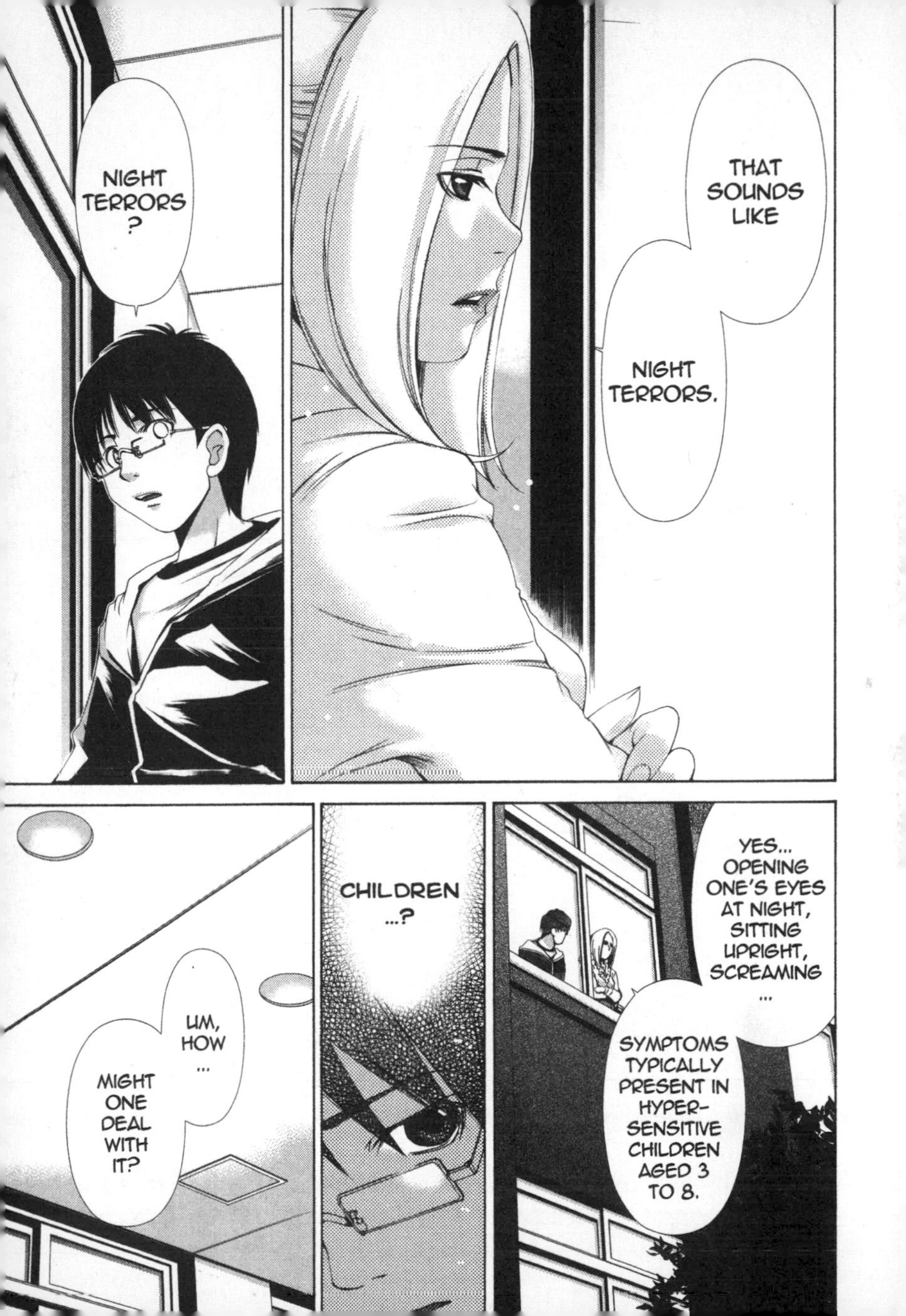
THAT SOUNDS LIKE
NIGHT TERRORS.
NIGHT TERRORS ?
YES... OPENING ONE'S EYES AT NIGHT, SITTING UPRIGHT, SCREAMING ...
SYMPTOMS TYPICALLY PRESENT IN HYPER-SENSITIVE CHILDREN AGED 3 TO 8.
CHILDREN ...?
UM, HOW ...
MIGHT ONE DEAL WITH IT?

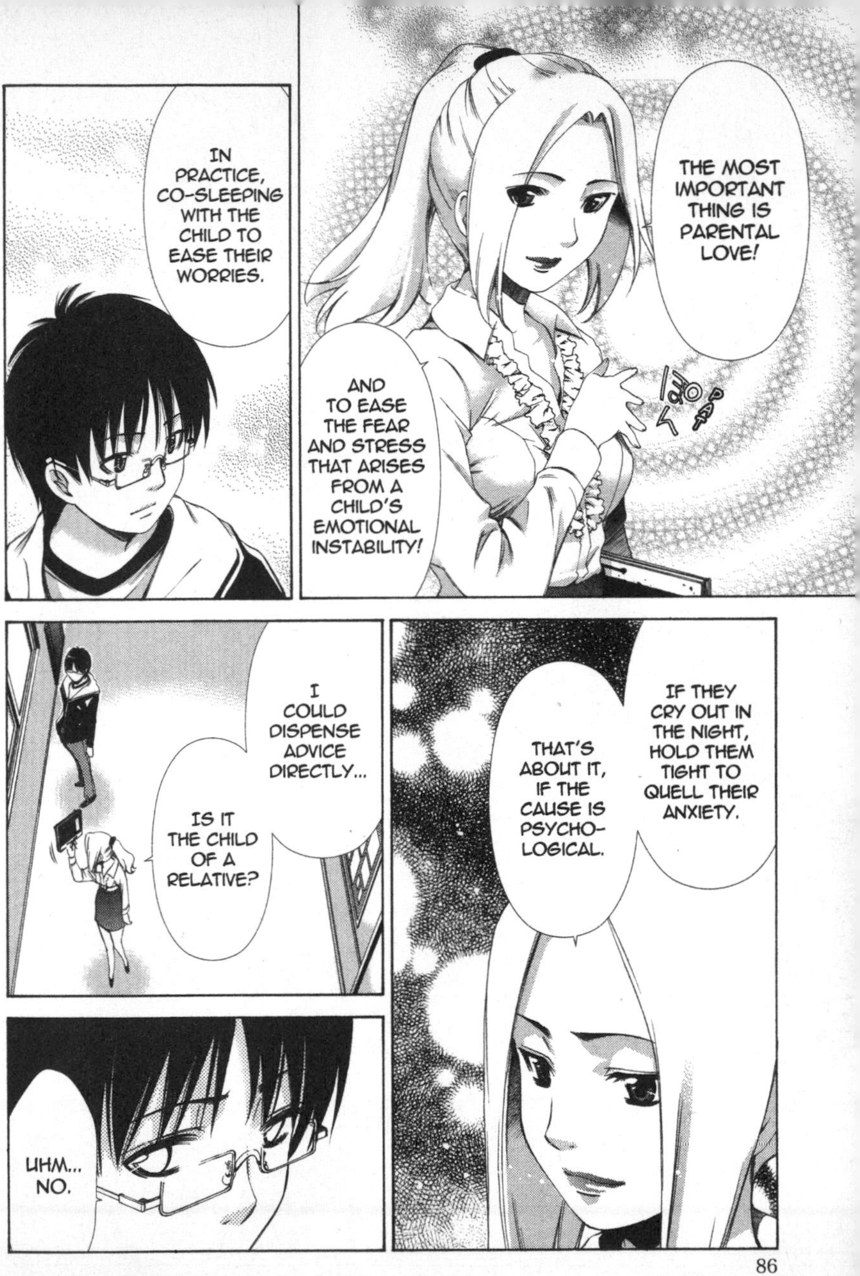
THE MOST IMPORTANT THING IS PARENTAL LOVE!
PAT
AND TO EASE THE FEAR AND STRESS THAT ARISES FROM A CHILD'S EMOTIONAL INSTABILITY!
IN PRACTICE, CO-SLEEPING WITH THE CHILD TO EASE THEIR WORRIES.
IF THEY CRY OUT IN THE NIGHT, HOLD THEM TIGHT TO QUELL THEIR ANXIETY.
THAT'S ABOUT IT, IF THE CAUSE IS PSYCHO-LOGICAL.
I COULD DISPENSE ADVICE DIRECTLY...
IS IT THE CHILD OF A RELATIVE?
UHM... NO.

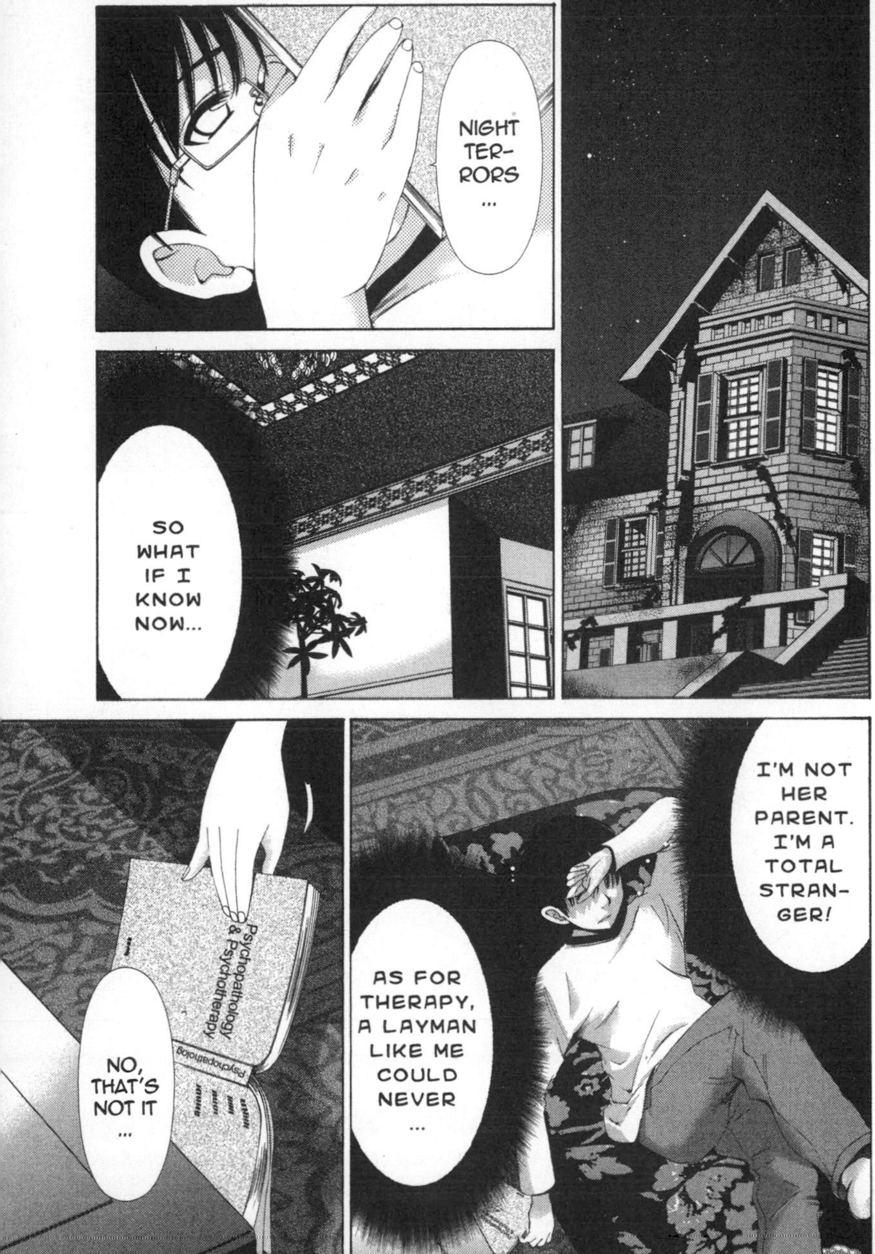
NIGHT TERRORS ...
SO WHAT IF I KNOW NOW...
I'M NOT HER PARENT. I'M A TOTAL STRANGER!
AS FOR THERAPY, A LAYMAN LIKE ME COULD NEVER ...
Psychopathology & Psychotherapy
Psychopatholog
NO, THAT'S NOT IT ...

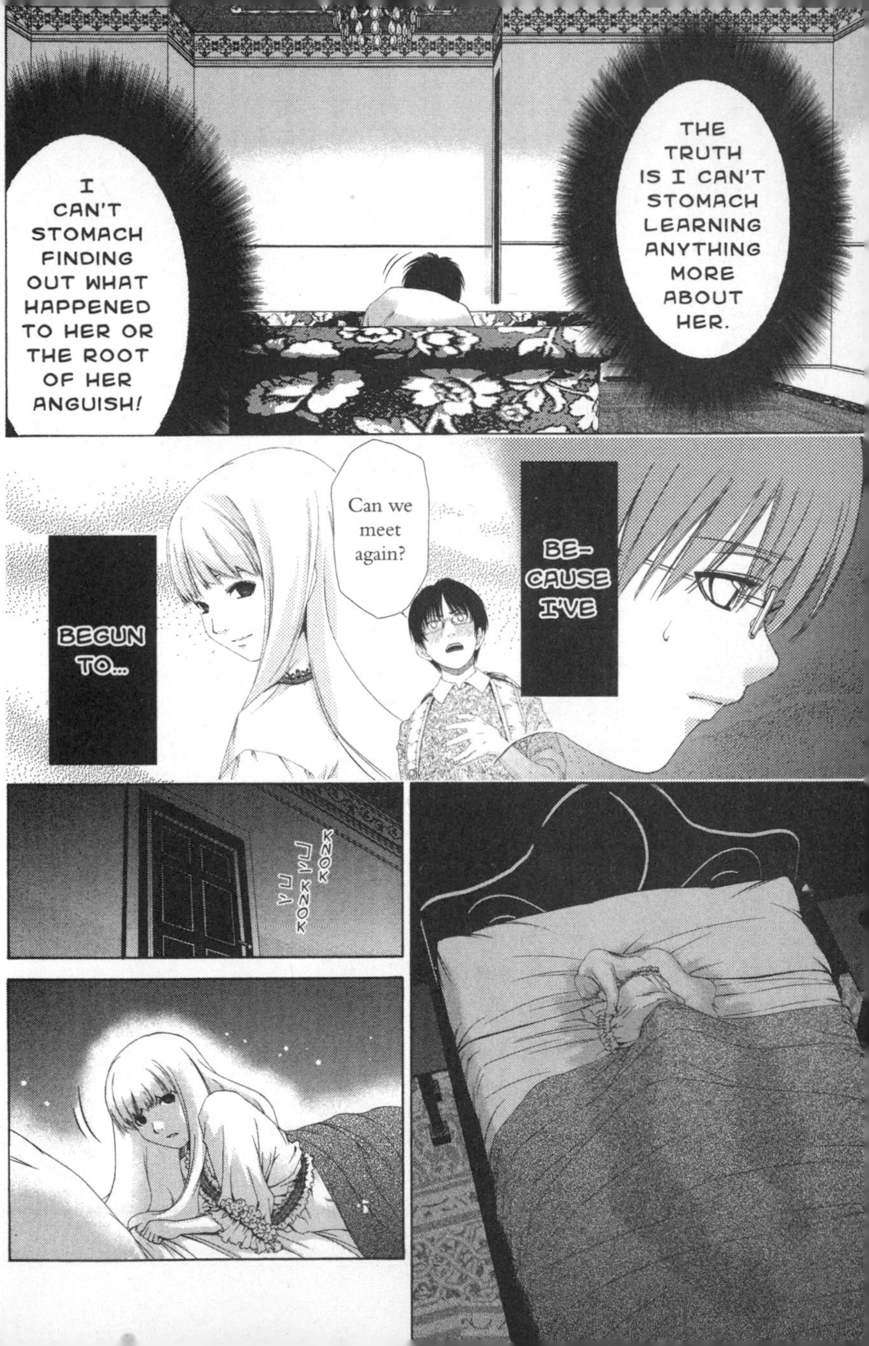
THE TRUTH IS I CAN'T STOMACH LEARNING ANYTHING MORE ABOUT HER.
I CAN'T STOMACH FINDING OUT WHAT HAPPENED TO HER OR THE ROOT OF HER ANGUISH!
BE-CAUSE I'VE
Can we meet again?
BEGUN TO...
KNOK
KNOK

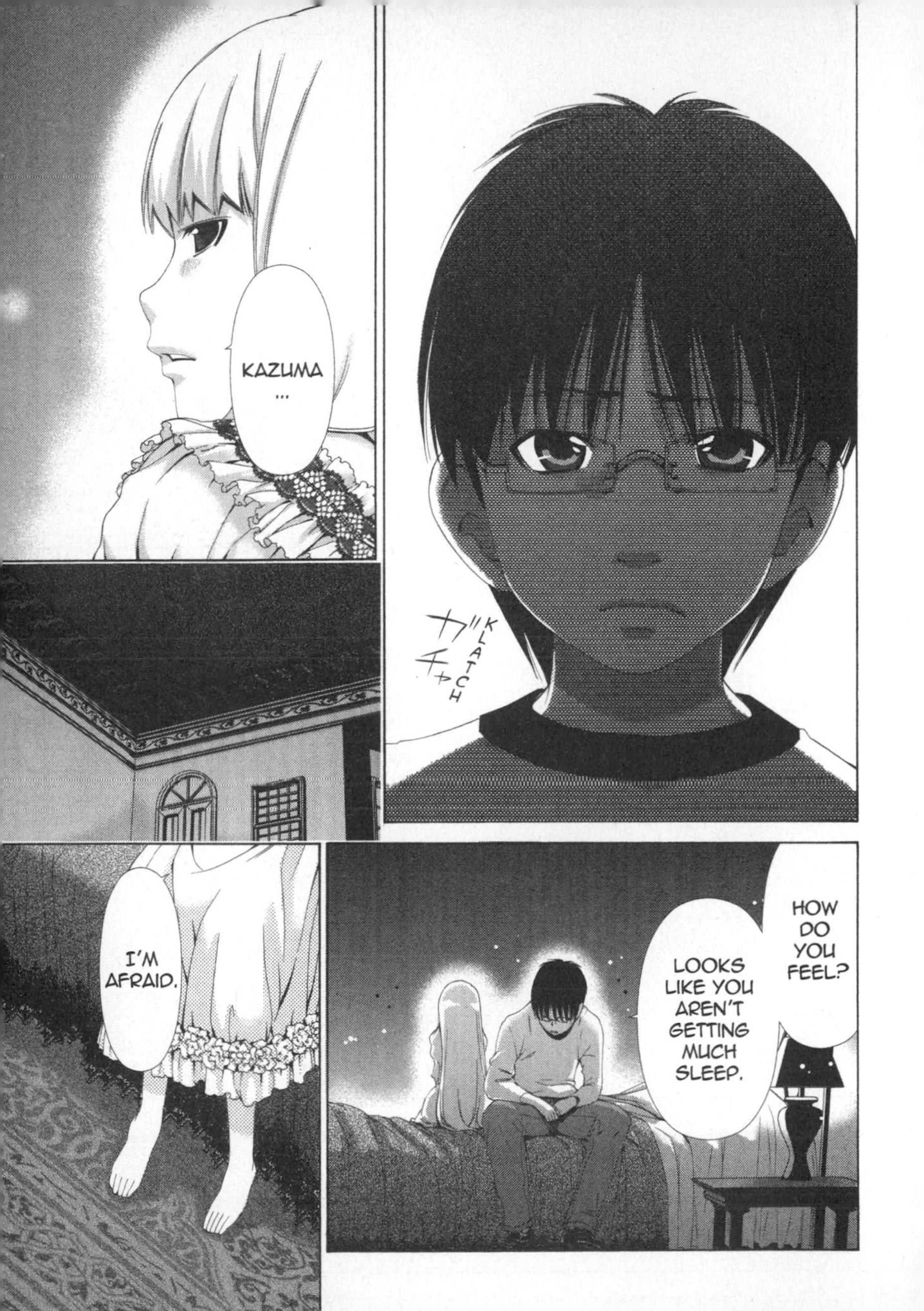
ガチャ
KLATCH
KAZUMA ...
HOW DO YOU FEEL?
LOOKS LIKE YOU AREN'T GETTING MUCH SLEEP.
I'M AFRAID.

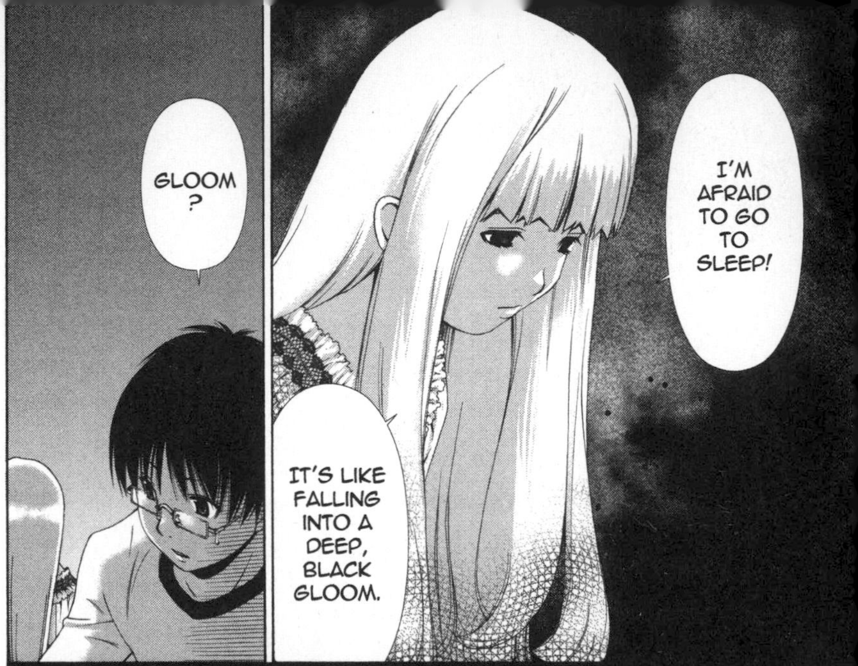
I'M AFRAID TO GO TO SLEEP!
IT'S LIKE FALLING INTO A DEEP, BLACK GLOOM.
GLOOM?

THE MOST IMPORTANT THING IS PARENTAL LOVE

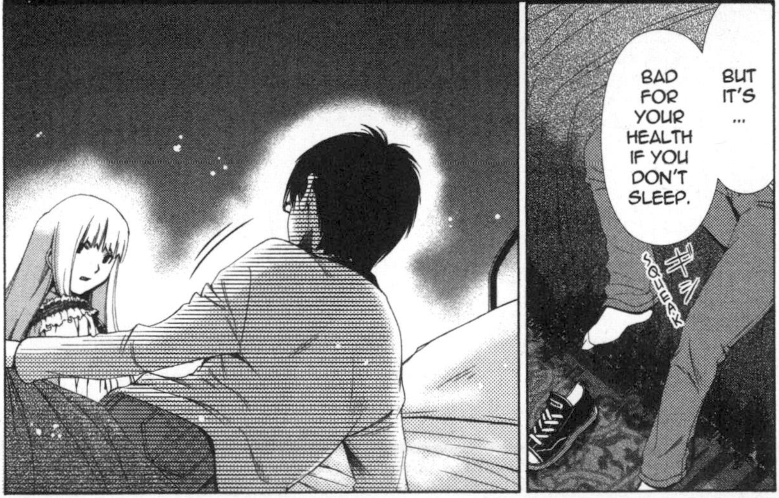
BUT IT'S ...
BAD FOR YOUR HEALTH IF YOU DON'T SLEEP.
SQUEAK

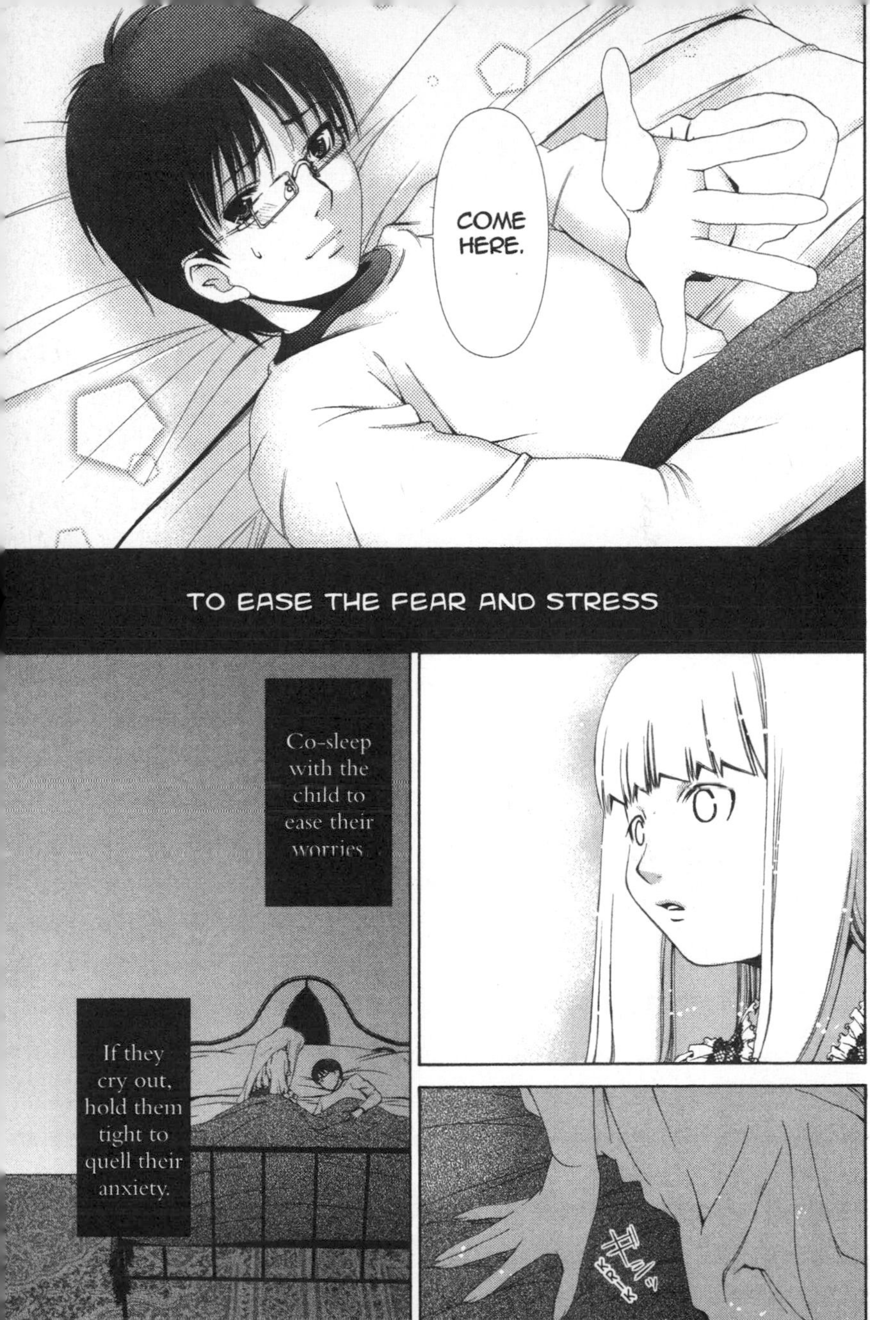
COME HERE.
TO EASE THE FEAR AND STRESS
Co-sleep with the child to ease their worries.
If they cry out, hold them tight to quell their anxiety.

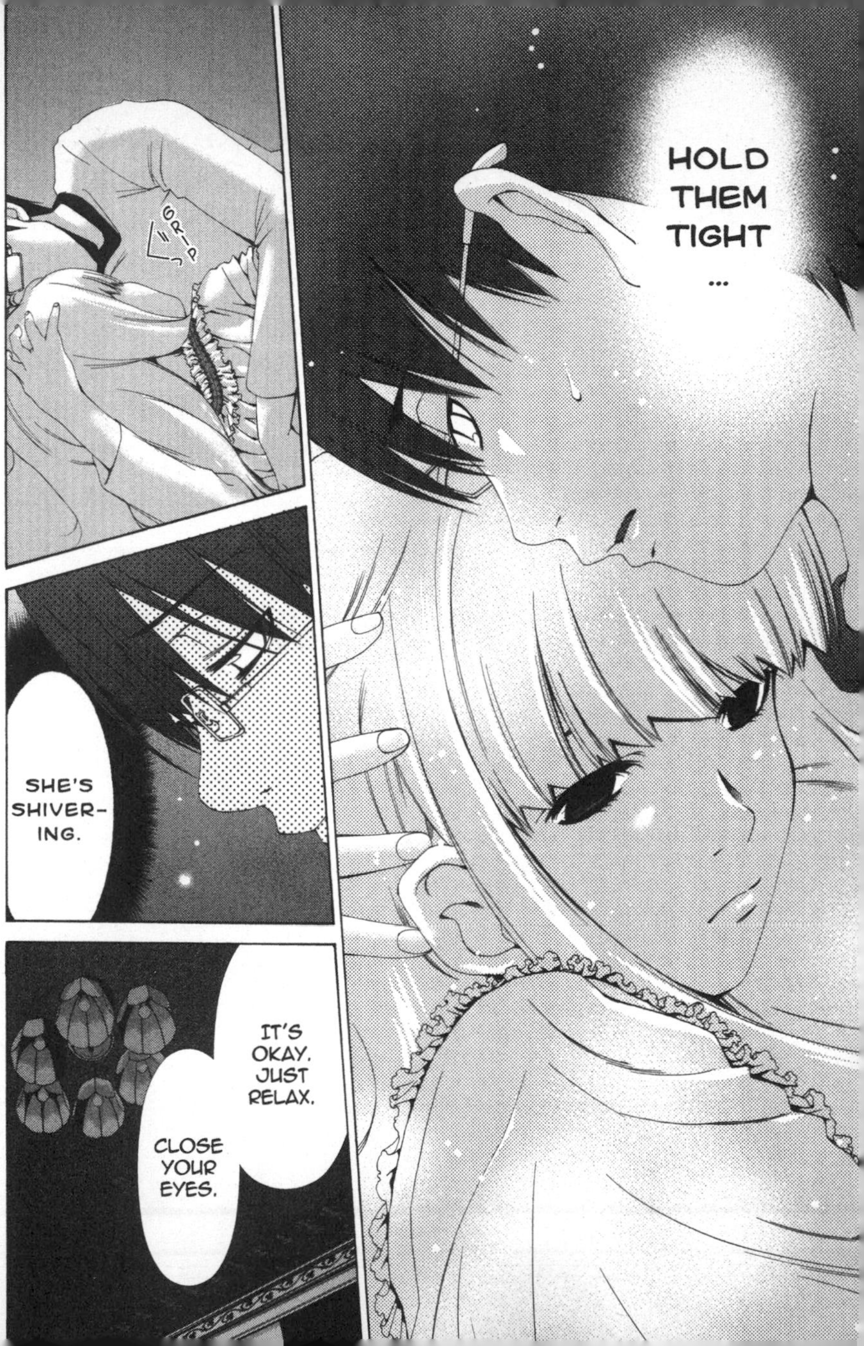
HOLD THEM TIGHT ...
GRIP
SHE'S SHIVERING.
IT'S OKAY. JUST RELAX.
CLOSE YOUR EYES.

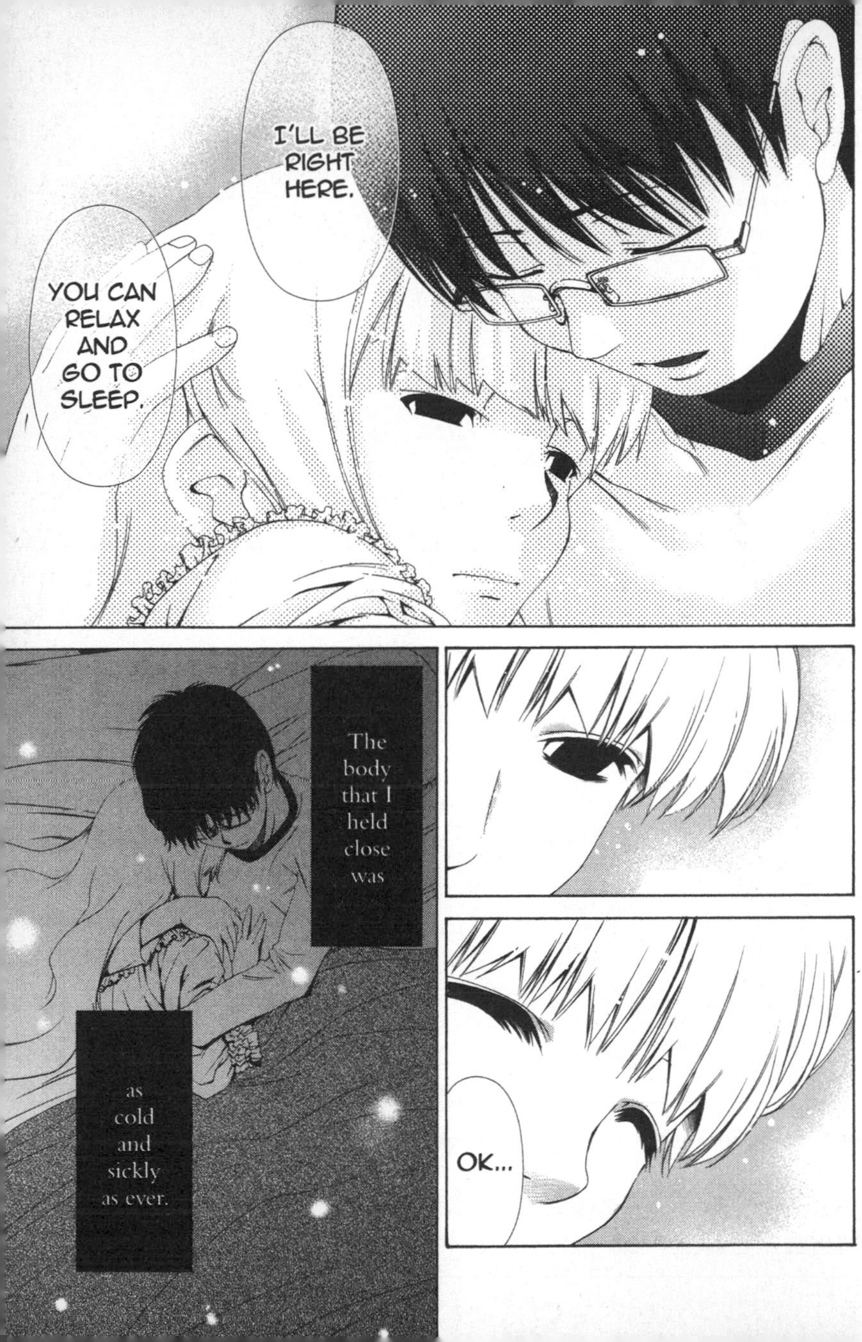
I'LL BE RIGHT HERE.
YOU CAN RELAX AND GO TO SLEEP.
OK...
The body that I held close was
as cold and sickly as ever.

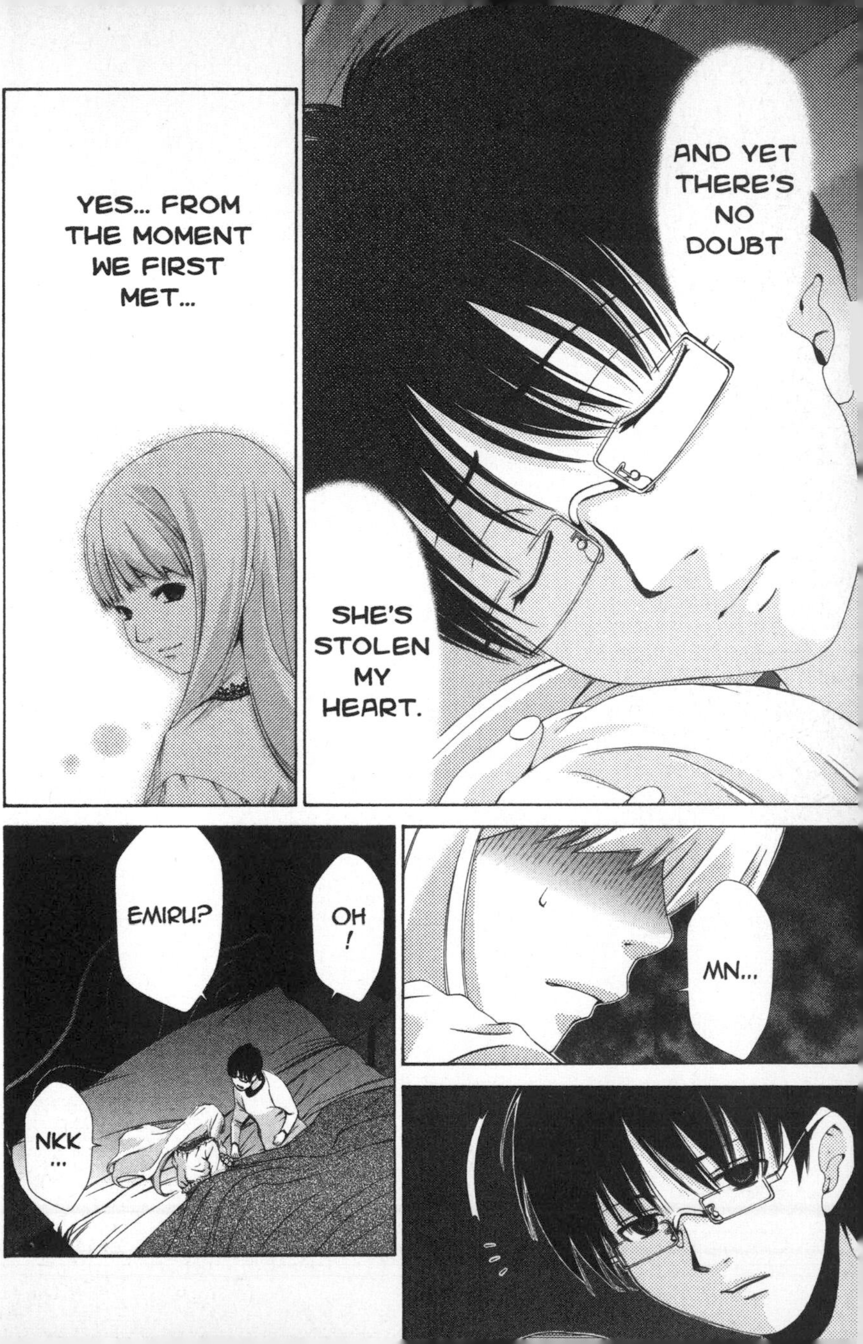
AND YET THERE'S NO DOUBT
SHE'S STOLEN MY HEART.
YES... FROM THE MOMENT WE FIRST MET...
MN...
OH !
EMIRU?
NKK ...

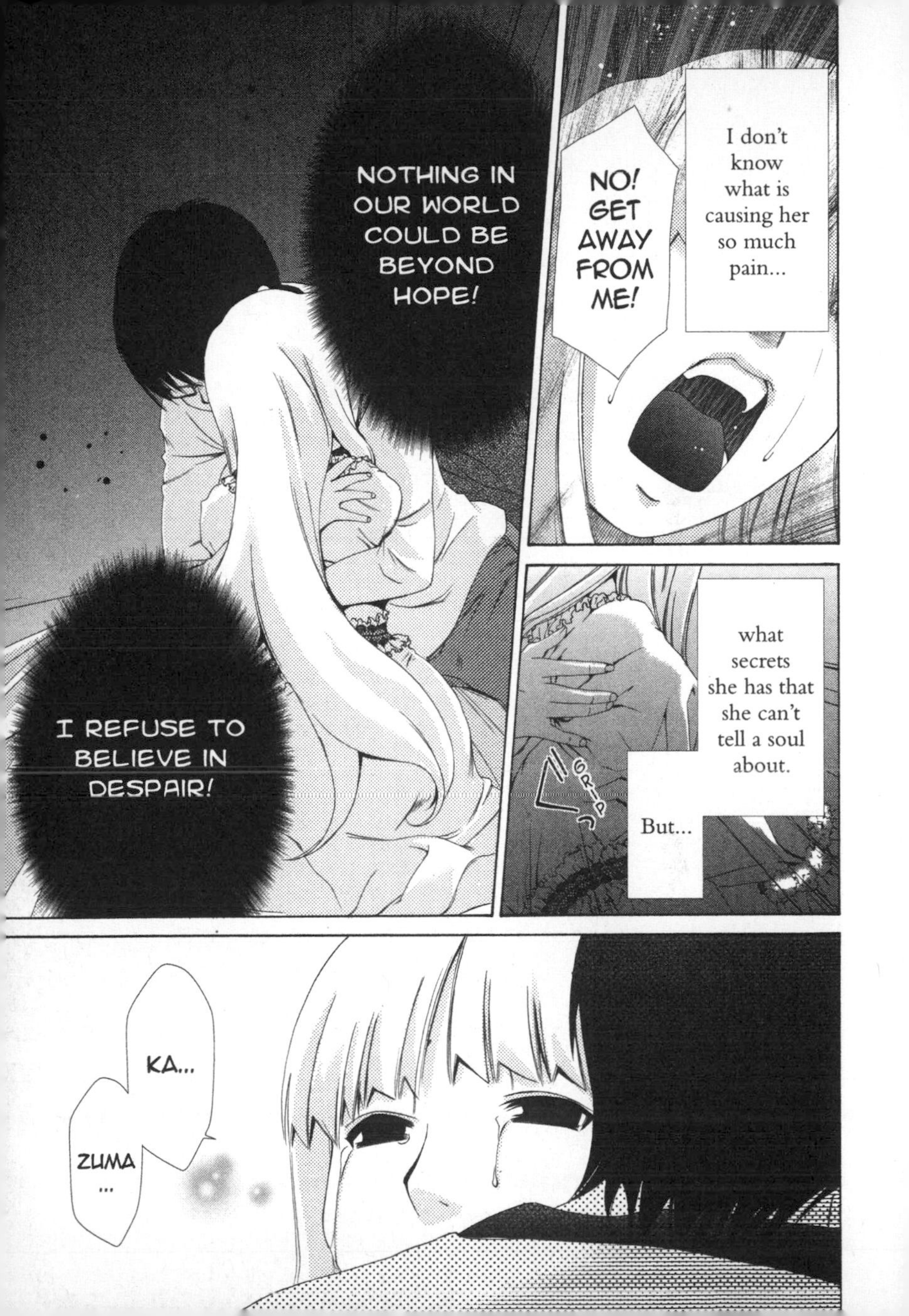
I don't know what is causing her so much pain...
NO! GET AWAY FROM ME!
what secrets she has that she can't tell a soul about.
GRIP
But...
NOTHING IN OUR WORLD COULD BE BEYOND HOPE!
I REFUSE TO BELIEVE IN DESPAIR!
KA...
ZUMA ...

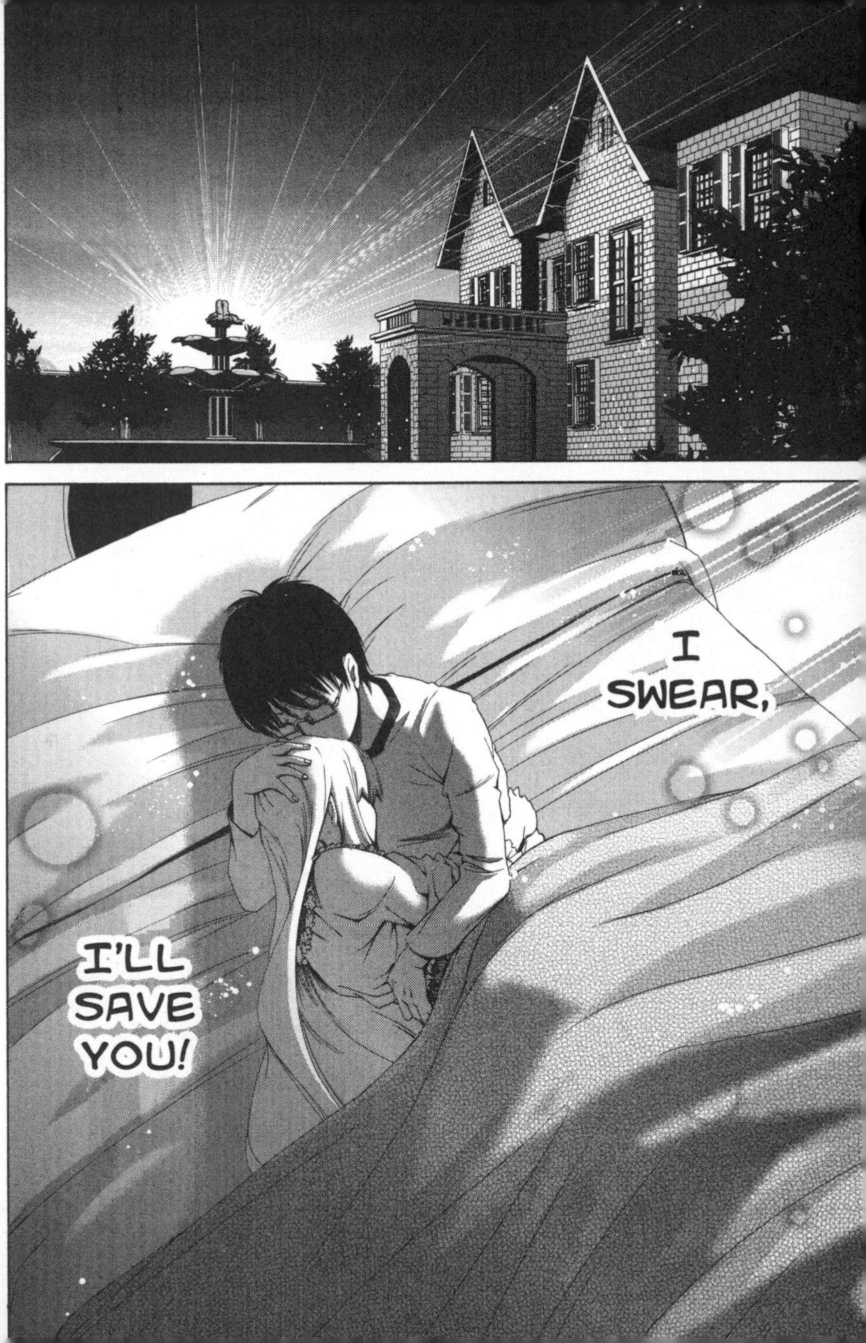
I SWEAR,
I'LL SAVE YOU!

Chapter 5 Psych Assessment

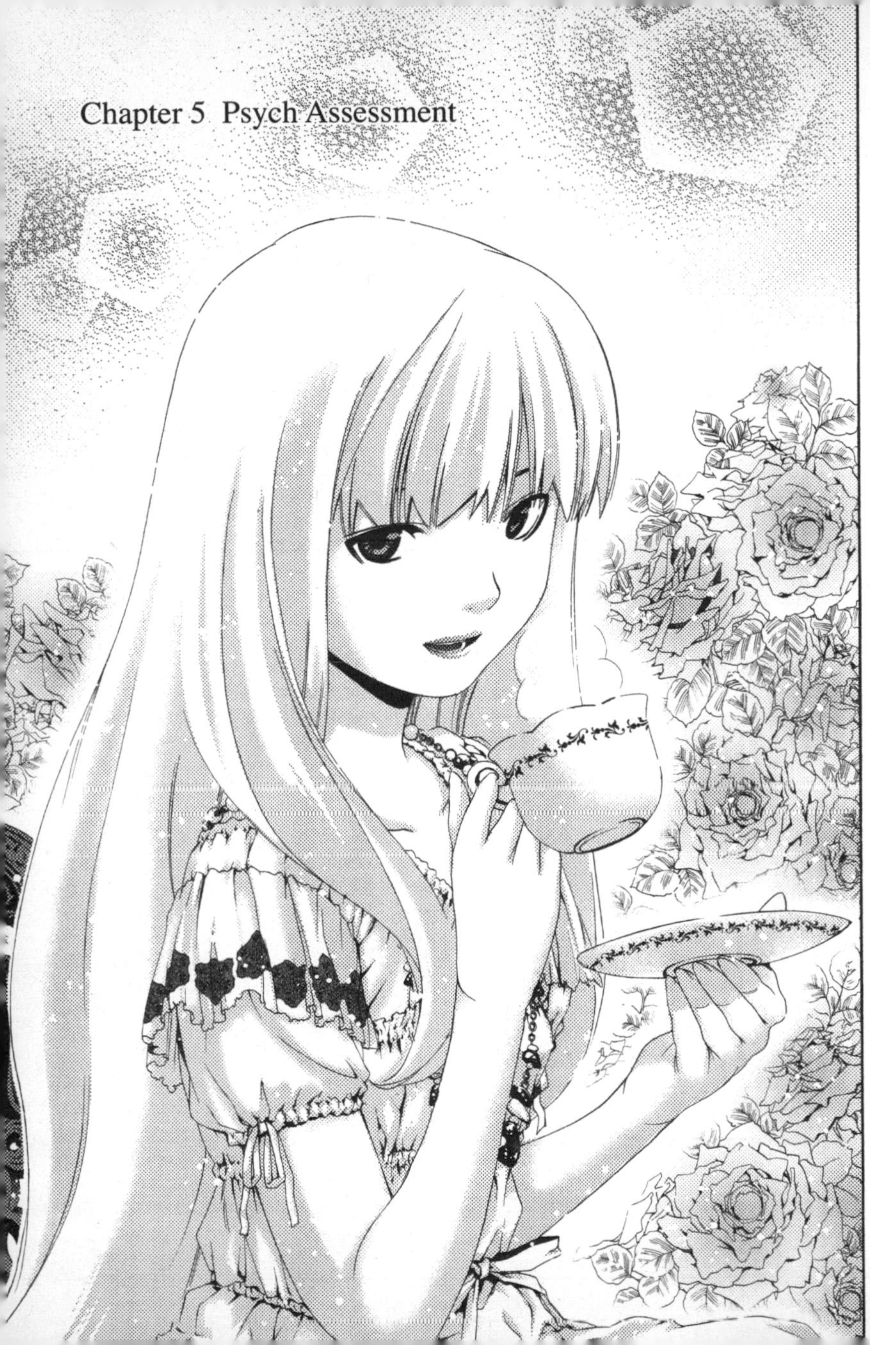

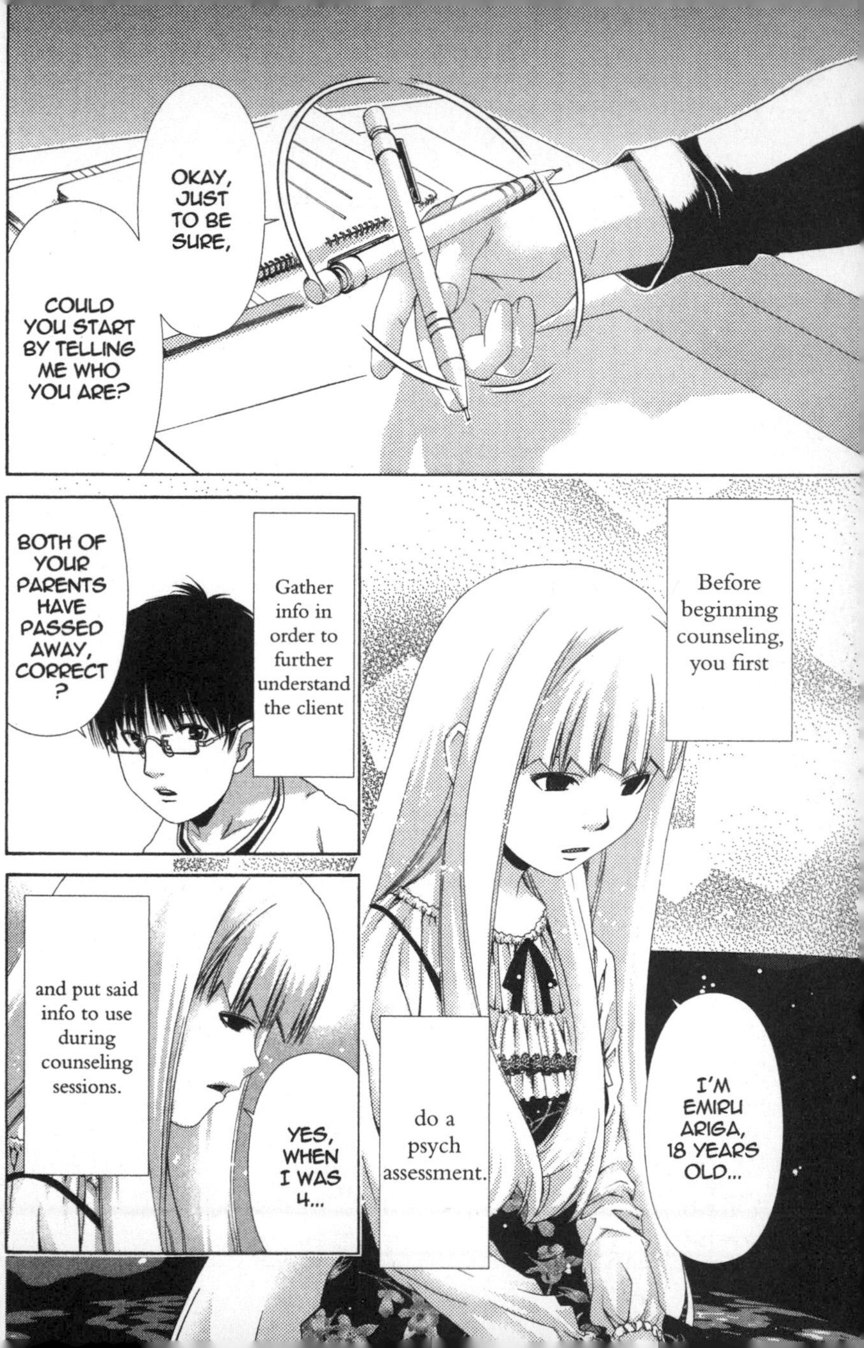
OKAY, JUST TO BE SURE,
COULD YOU START BY TELLING ME WHO YOU ARE?
Before beginning counseling, you first
I'M EMIRU ARIGA, 18 YEARS OLD...
do a psych assessment.
Gather info in order to further understand the client
BOTH OF YOUR PARENTS HAVE PASSED AWAY, CORRECT?
and put said info to use during counseling sessions.
YES, WHEN I WAS 4...

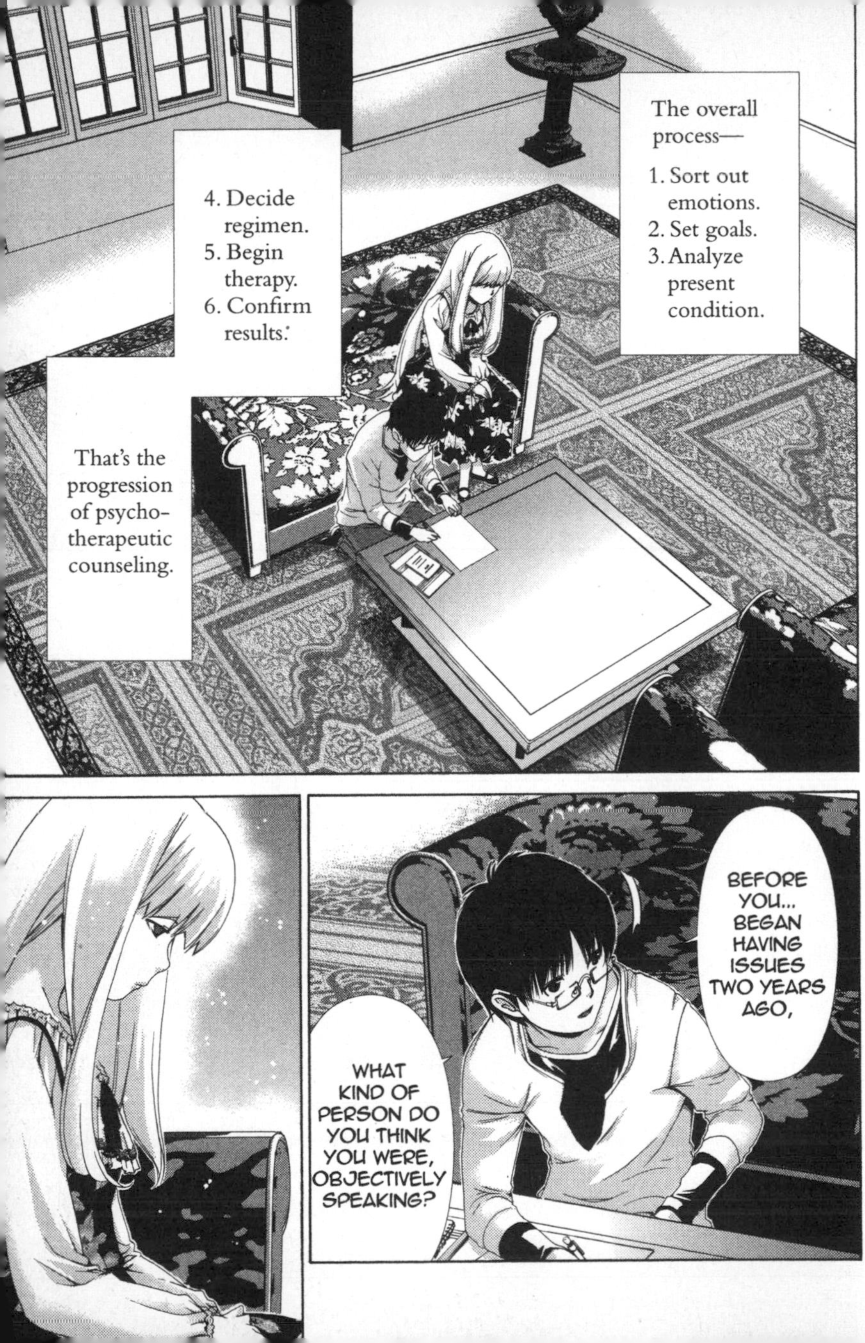
The overall process—
1. Sort out emotions.
2. Set goals.
3. Analyze present condition.
4. Decide regimen.
5. Begin therapy.
6. Confirm results.*
That's the progression of psycho-therapeutic counseling.
BEFORE YOU... BEGAN HAVING ISSUES TWO YEARS AGO,
WHAT KIND OF PERSON DO YOU THINK YOU WERE, OBJECTIVELY SPEAKING?

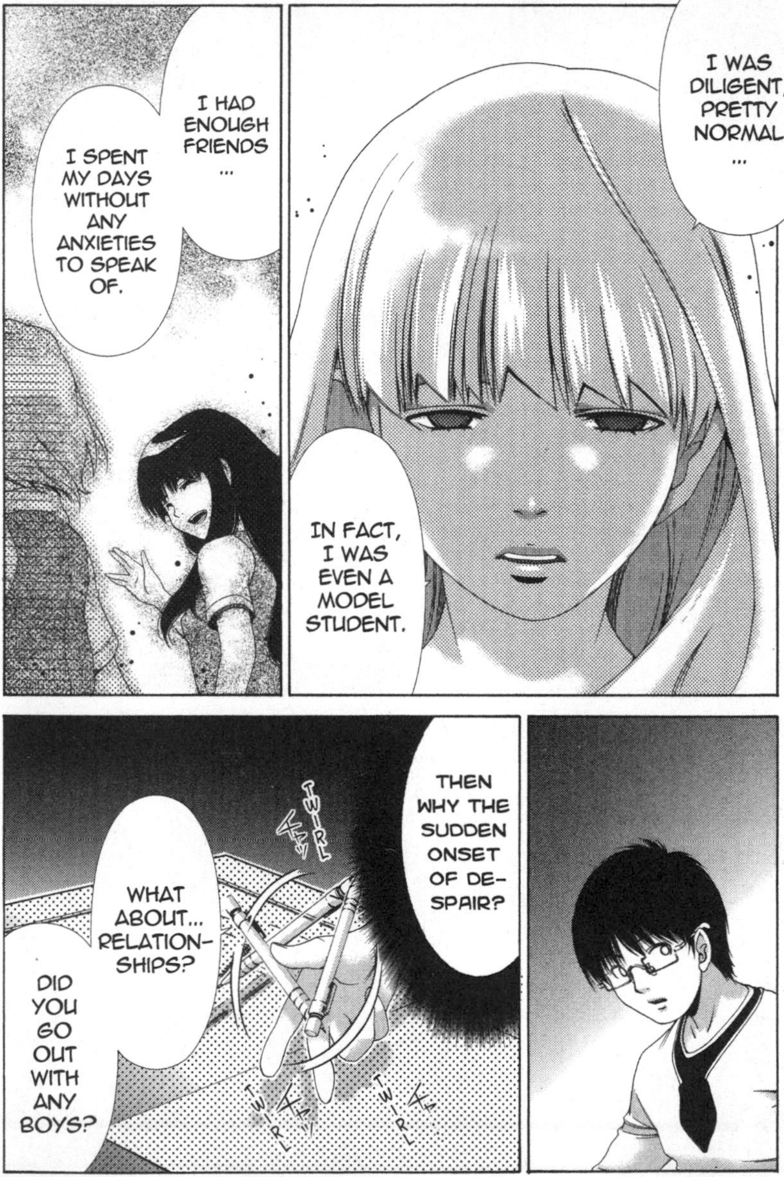
I WAS DILIGENT, PRETTY NORMAL ...
IN FACT, I WAS EVEN A MODEL STUDENT.
I HAD ENOUGH FRIENDS ...
I SPENT MY DAYS WITHOUT ANY ANXIETIES TO SPEAK OF.
THEN WHY THE SUDDEN ONSET OF DE-SPAIR?
TWIRL
WHAT ABOUT... RELATION-SHIPS?
DID YOU GO OUT WITH ANY BOYS?
TWIRL
TWIRL

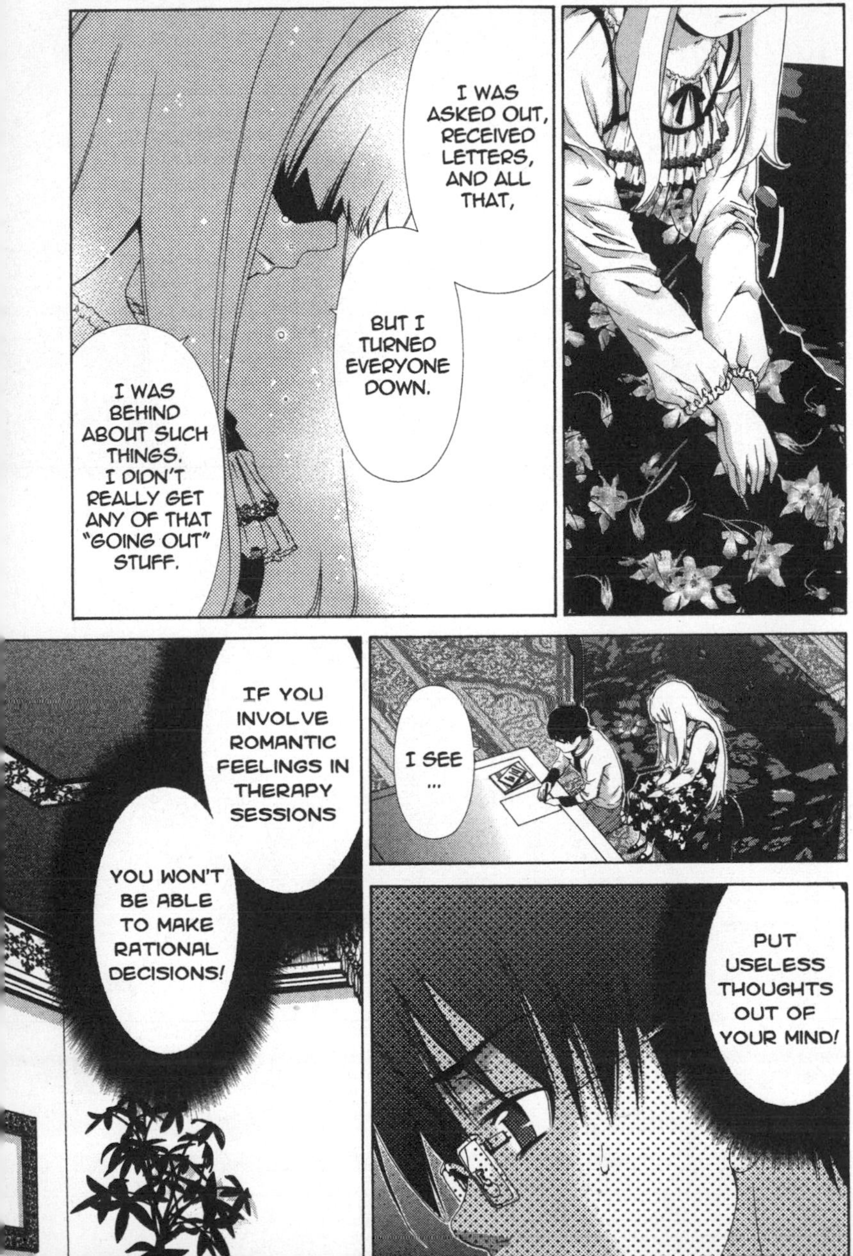
I WAS ASKED OUT, RECEIVED LETTERS, AND ALL THAT,
BUT I TURNED EVERYONE DOWN.
I WAS BEHIND ABOUT SUCH THINGS. I DIDN'T REALLY GET ANY OF THAT "GOING OUT" STUFF.
I SEE ...
PUT USELESS THOUGHTS OUT OF YOUR MIND!
IF YOU INVOLVE ROMANTIC FEELINGS IN THERAPY SESSIONS
YOU WON'T BE ABLE TO MAKE RATIONAL DECISIONS!

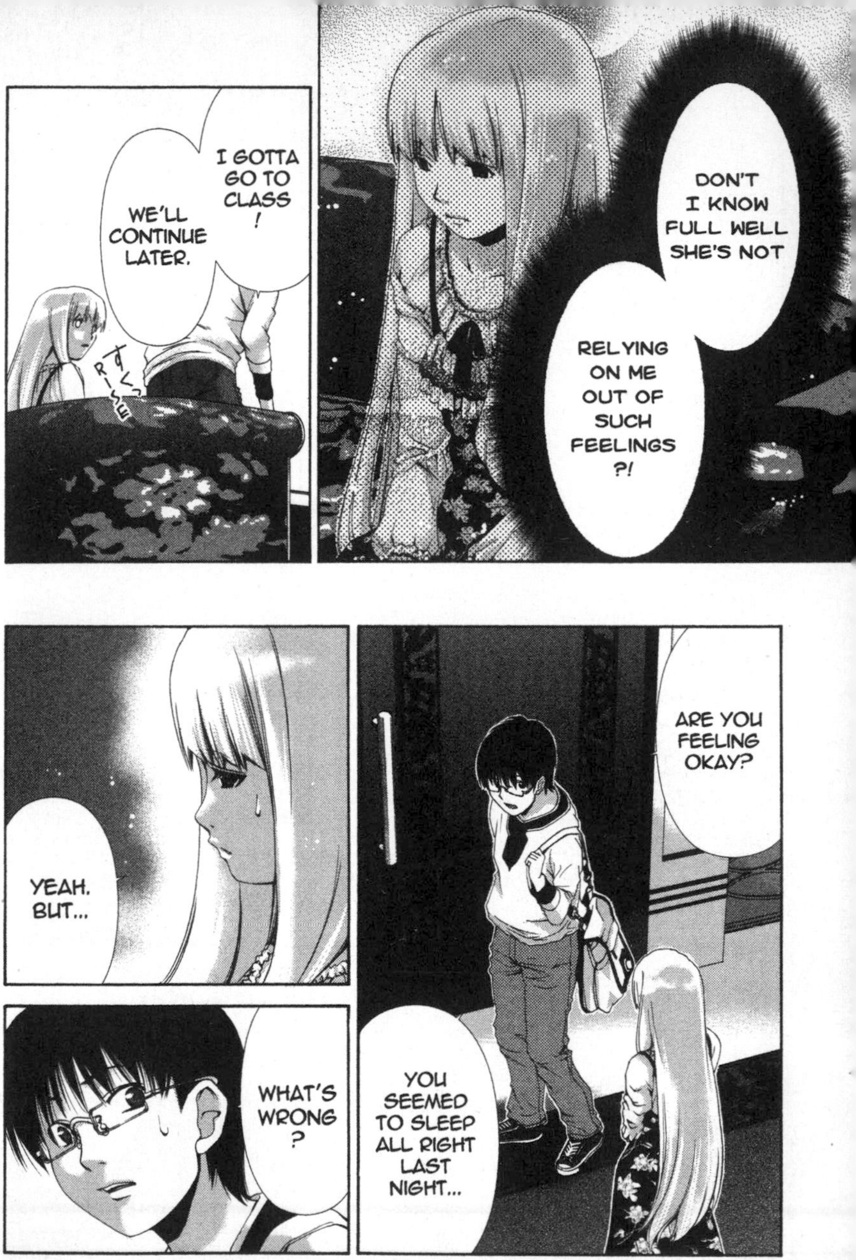
DON'T I KNOW FULL WELL SHE'S NOT
RELYING ON ME OUT OF SUCH FEELINGS ?!
I GOTTA GO TO CLASS !
WE'LL CONTINUE LATER.
すっ RISE
ARE YOU FEELING OKAY?
YOU SEEMED TO SLEEP ALL RIGHT LAST NIGHT...
YEAH. BUT...
WHAT'S WRONG ?

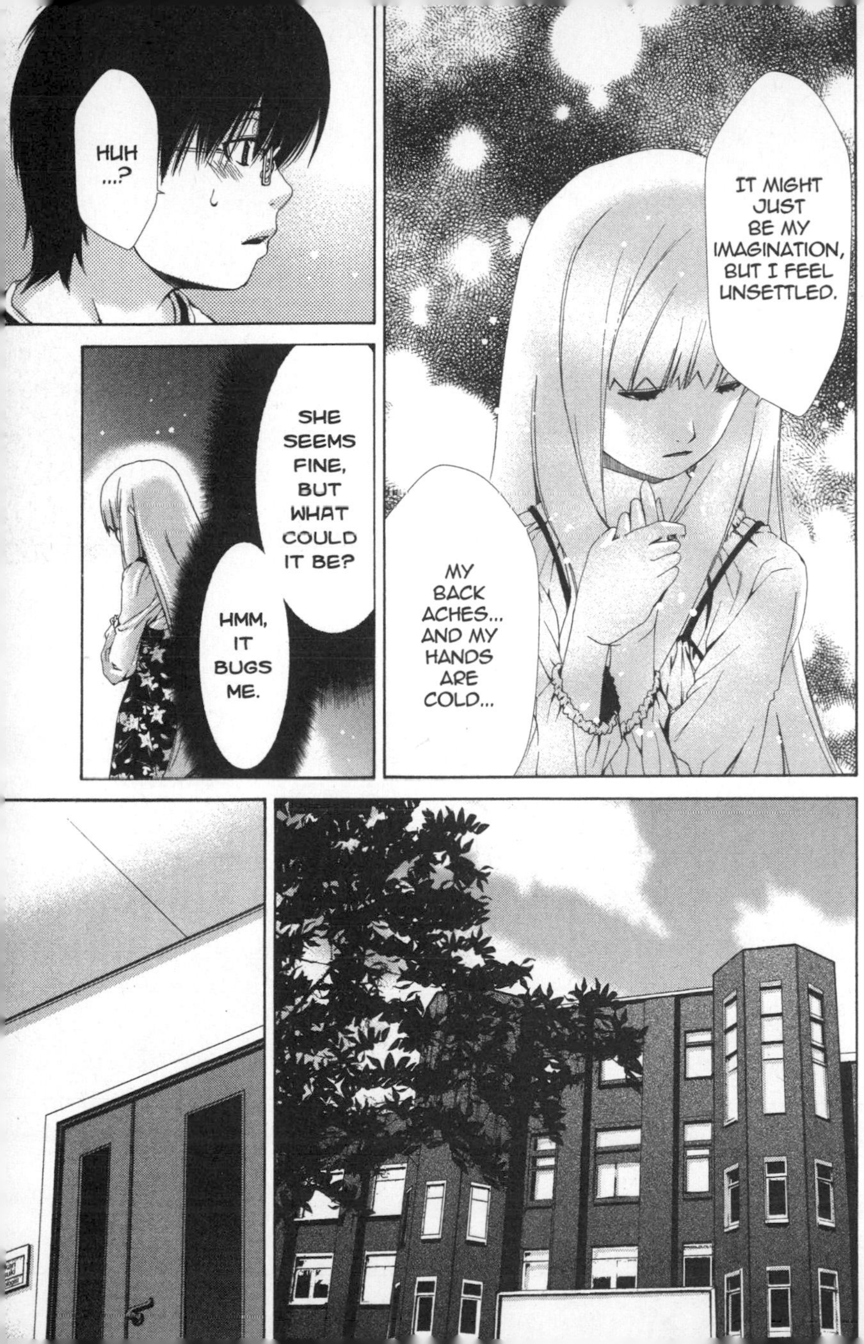
IT MIGHT JUST BE MY IMAGINATION, BUT I FEEL UNSETTLED.
MY BACK ACHES... AND MY HANDS ARE COLD...
HUH ...?
SHE SEEMS FINE, BUT WHAT COULD IT BE?
HMM, IT BUGS ME.

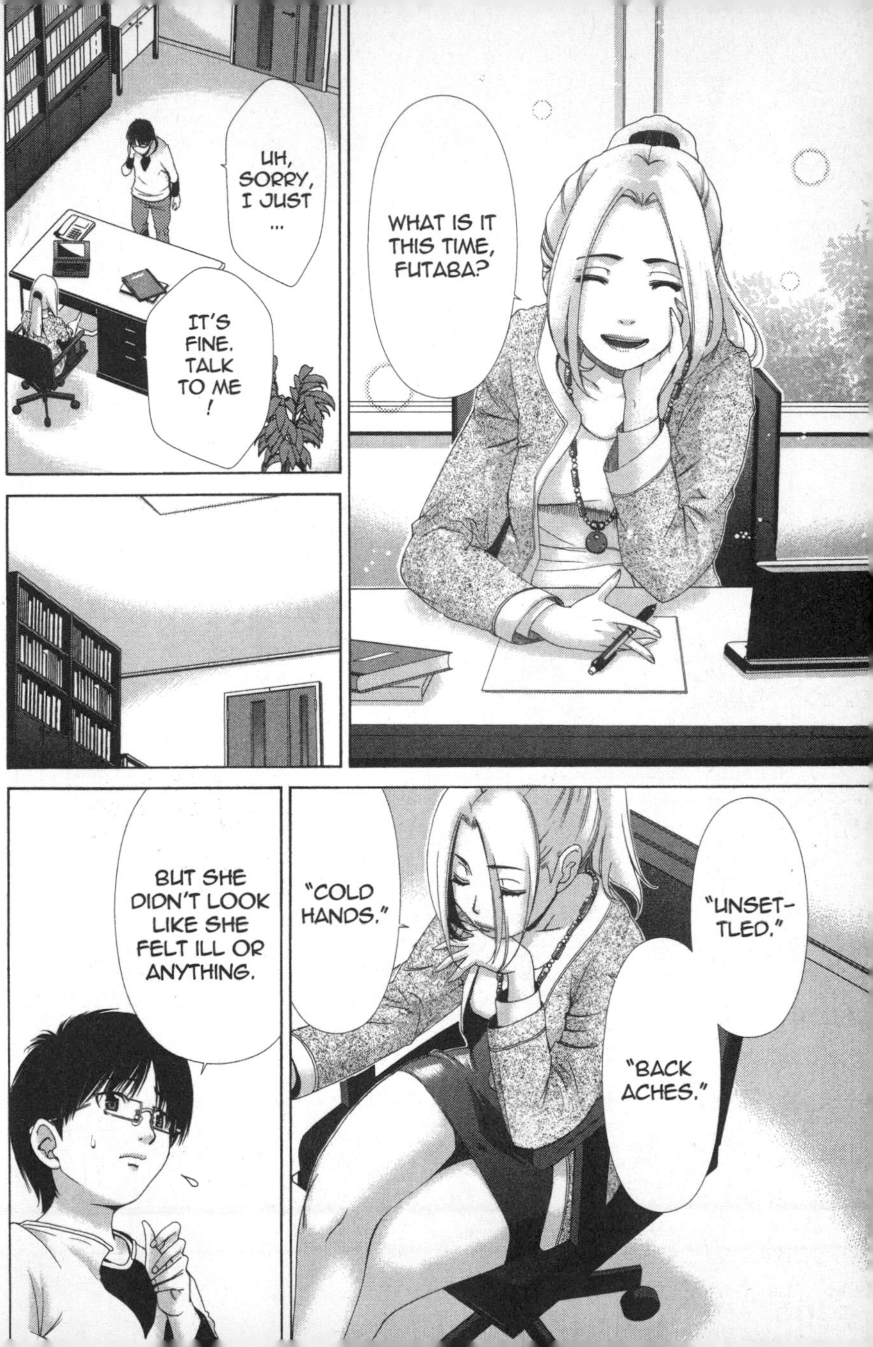
WHAT IS IT THIS TIME, FUTABA?
UH, SORRY, I JUST ...
IT'S FINE. TALK TO ME!
"UNSET-TLED."
"COLD HANDS."
"BACK ACHES."
BUT SHE DIDN'T LOOK LIKE SHE FELT ILL OR ANYTHING.

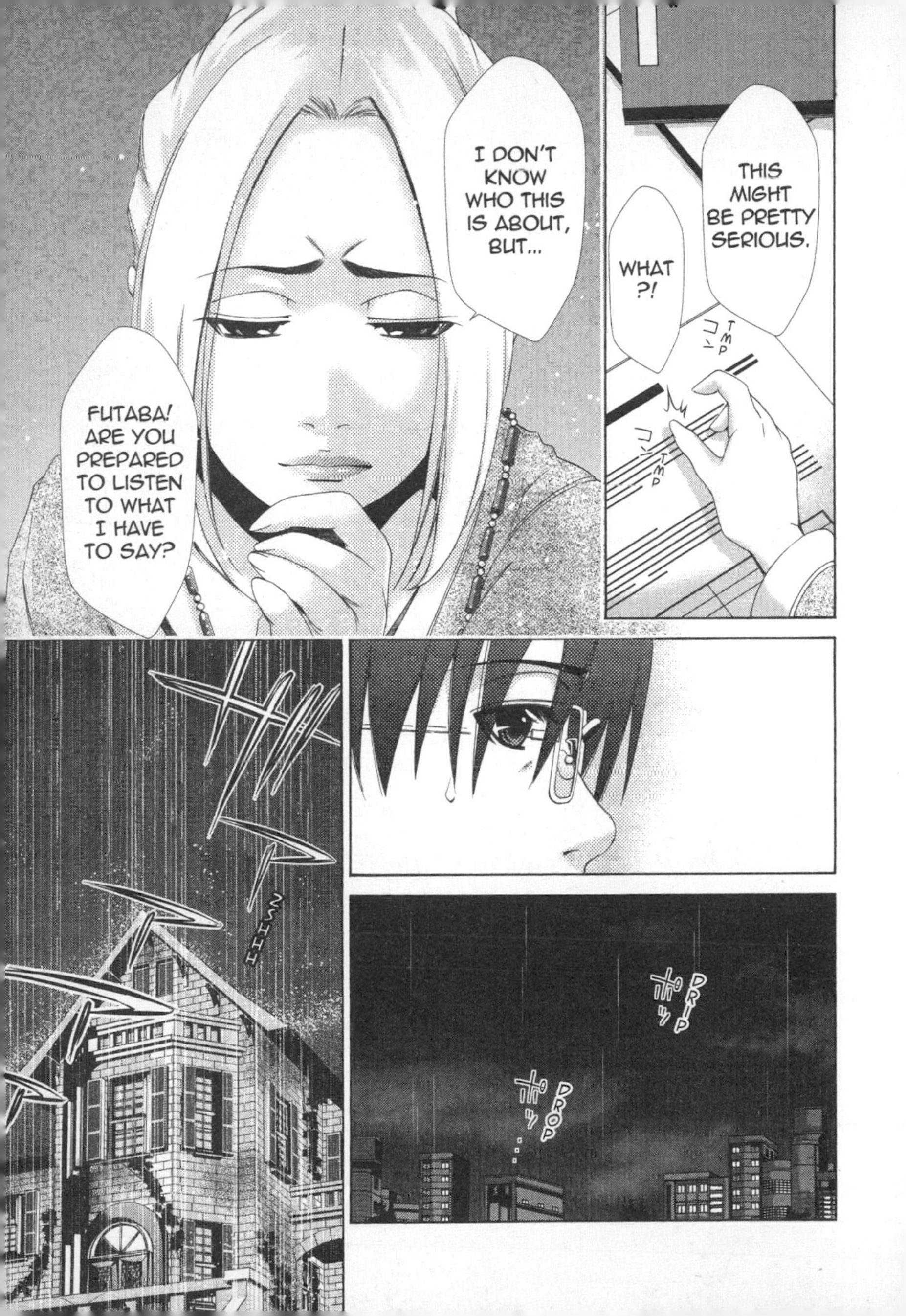
THIS MIGHT BE PRETTY SERIOUS.
WHAT ?!
TMP
TMP
I DON'T KNOW WHO THIS IS ABOUT, BUT...
FUTABA! ARE YOU PREPARED TO LISTEN TO WHAT I HAVE TO SAY?
DRIP
DROP
ZSHHH

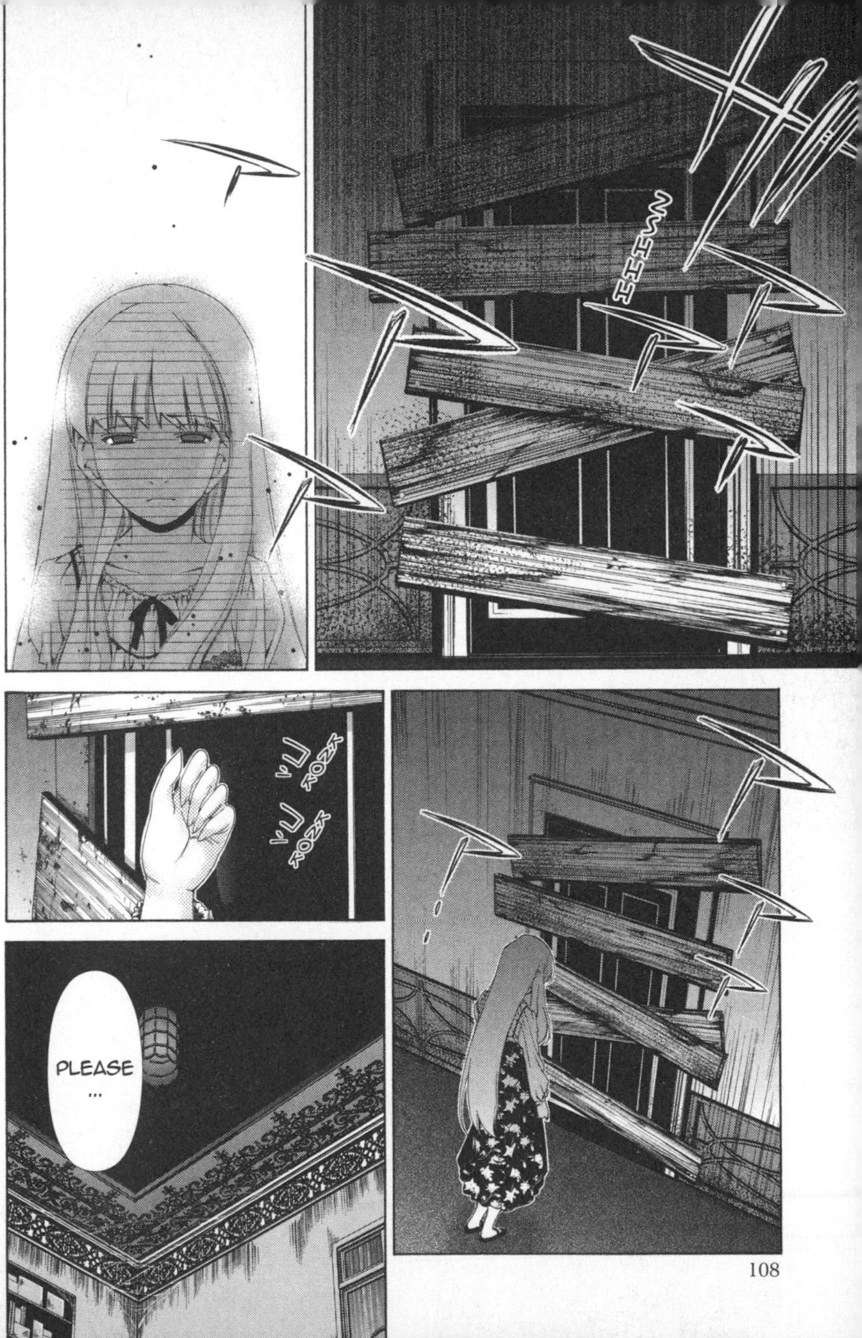
KONK
KONK
PLEASE ...

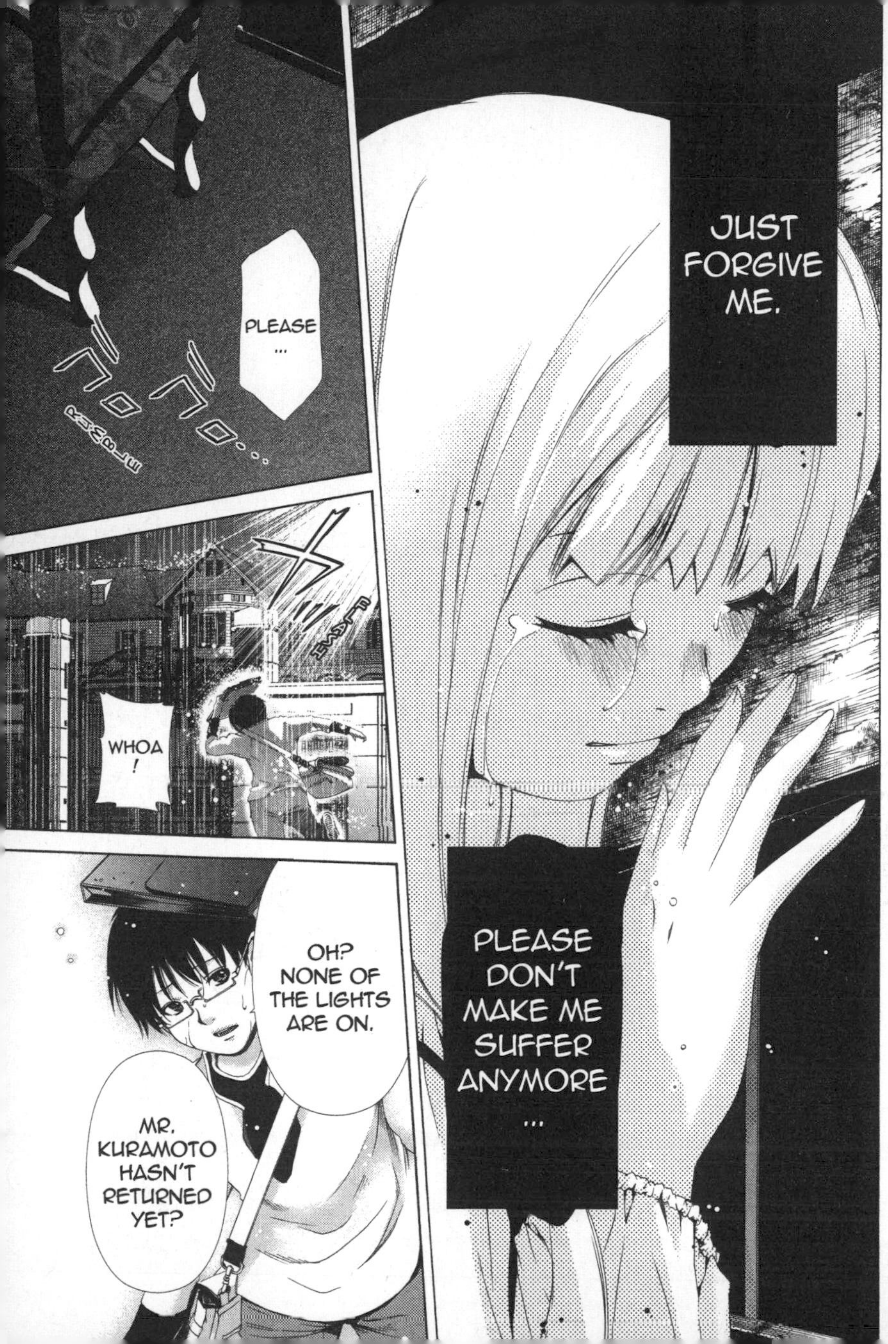
JUST FORGIVE ME.
PLEASE DON'T MAKE ME SUFFER ANYMORE ...
PLEASE ...
WHOA !
OH? NONE OF THE LIGHTS ARE ON.
MR. KURAMOTO HASN'T RETURNED YET?

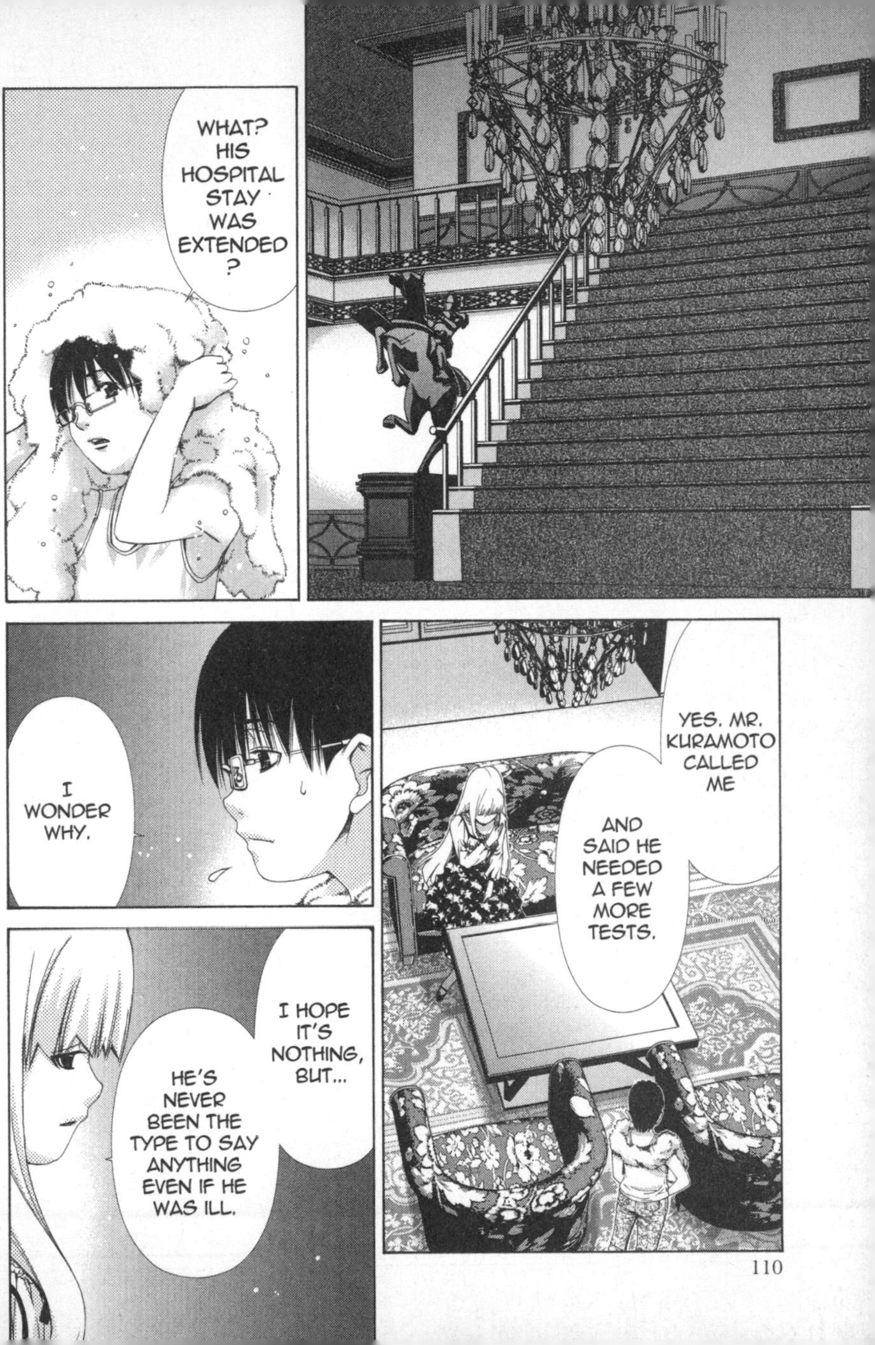
WHAT? HIS HOSPITAL STAY WAS EXTENDED?
YES. MR. KURAMOTO CALLED ME
AND SAID HE NEEDED A FEW MORE TESTS.
I WONDER WHY.
I HOPE IT'S NOTHING, BUT...
HE'S NEVER BEEN THE TYPE TO SAY ANYTHING EVEN IF HE WAS ILL.

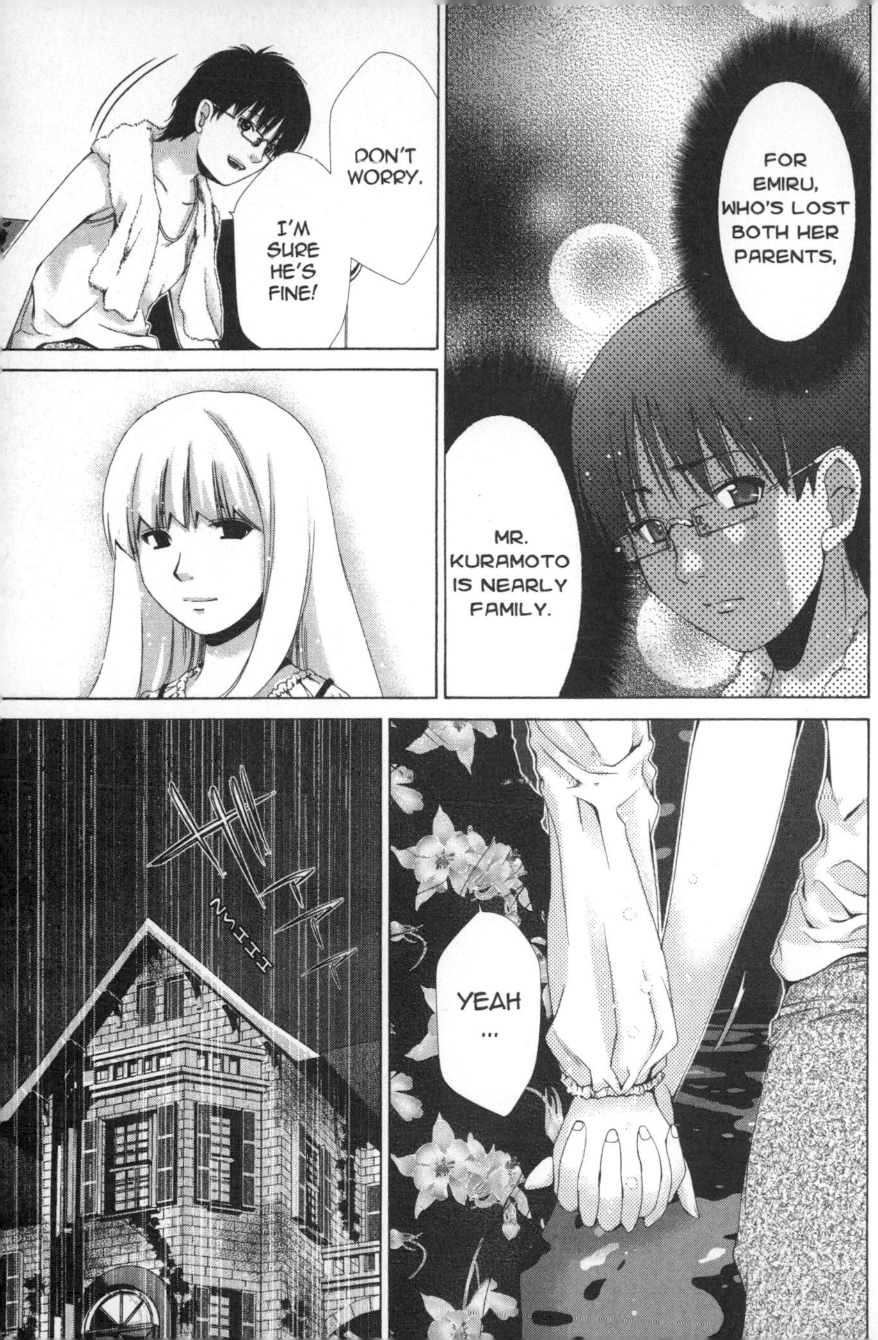
FOR EMIRU, WHO'S LOST BOTH HER PARENTS,
MR. KURAMOTO IS NEARLY FAMILY.
DON'T WORRY.
I'M SURE HE'S FINE!
YEAH ...

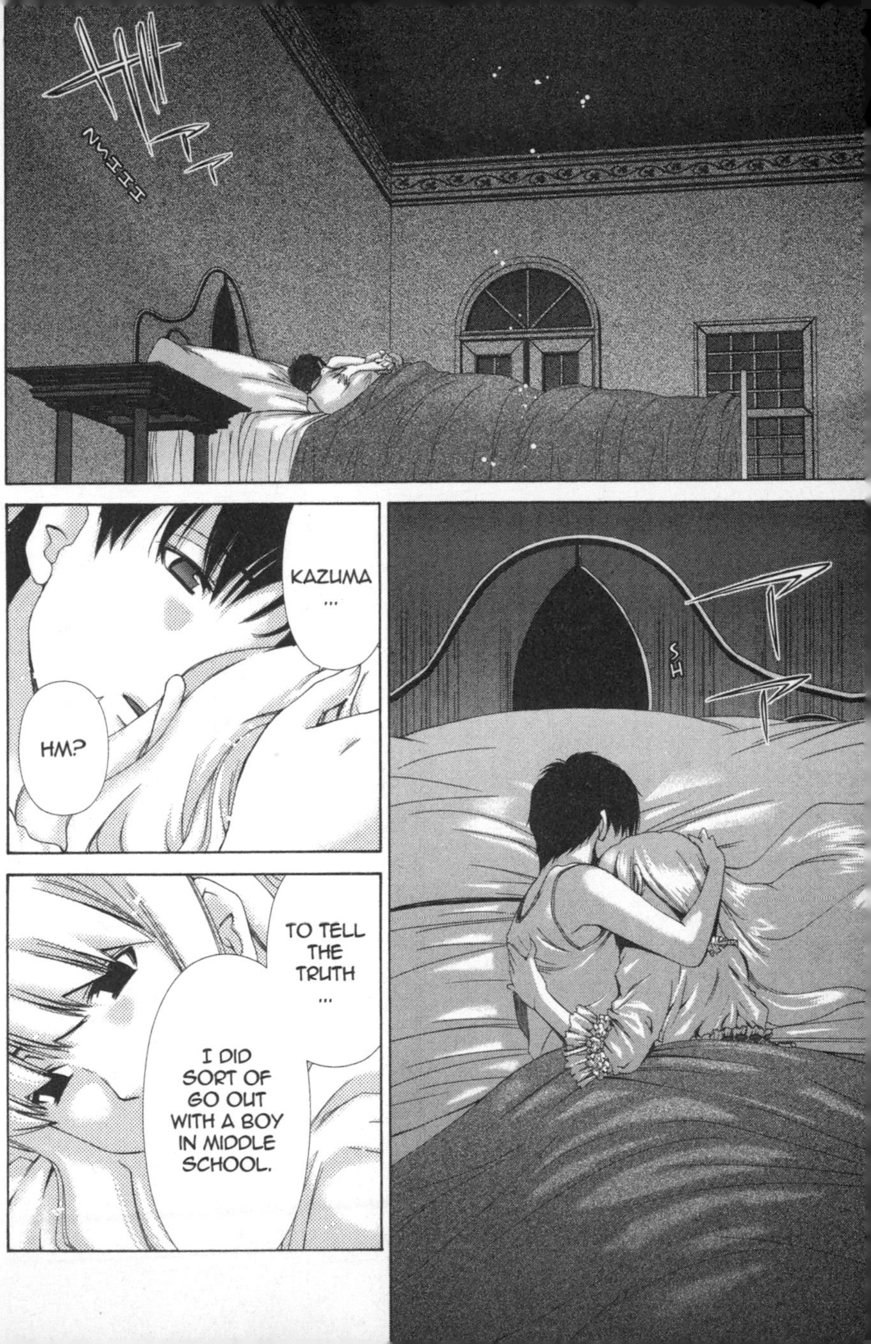
FIIIIN
SH
KAZUMA ...
HM?
TO TELL THE TRUTH ...
I DID SORT OF GO OUT WITH A BOY IN MIDDLE SCHOOL.

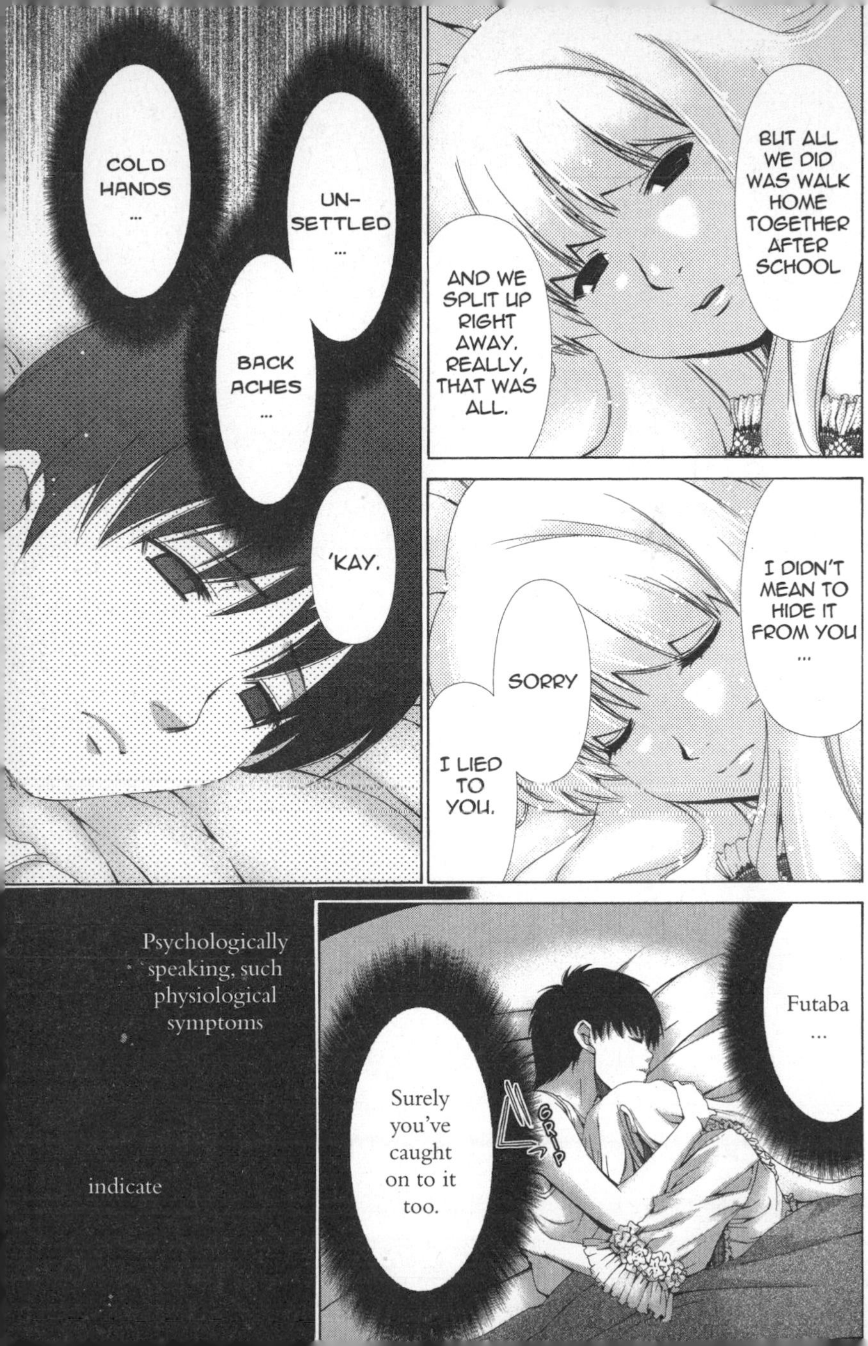
BUT ALL WE DID WAS WALK HOME TOGETHER AFTER SCHOOL
AND WE SPLIT UP RIGHT AWAY. REALLY, THAT WAS ALL.
I DIDN'T MEAN TO HIDE IT FROM YOU ...
SORRY
I LIED TO YOU.
UN-SETTLED ...
COLD HANDS ...
BACK ACHES ...
'KAY.
Futaba ...
GRIP
Surely you've caught on to it too.
Psychologically speaking, such physiological symptoms
indicate

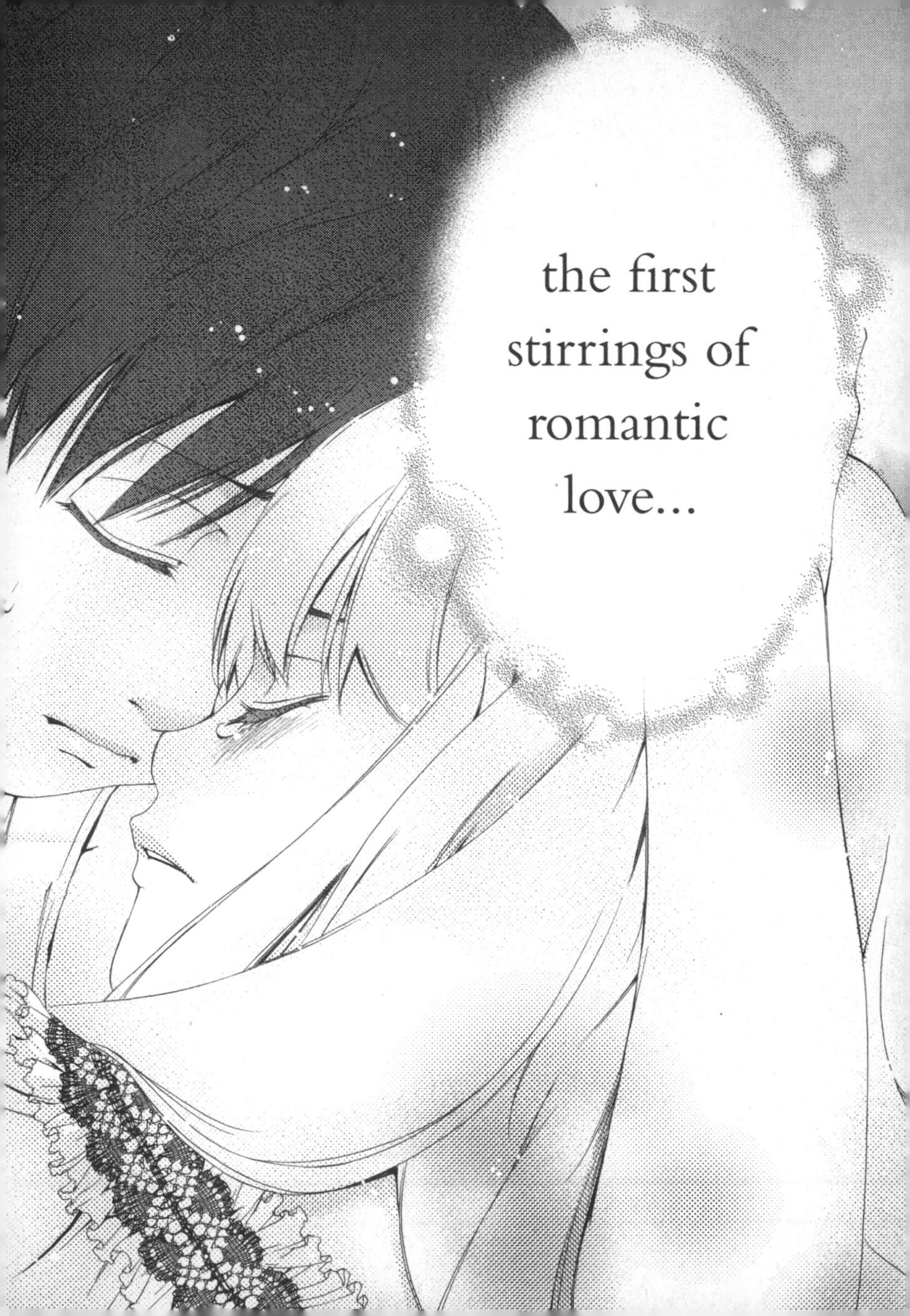
the first stirrings of romantic love...

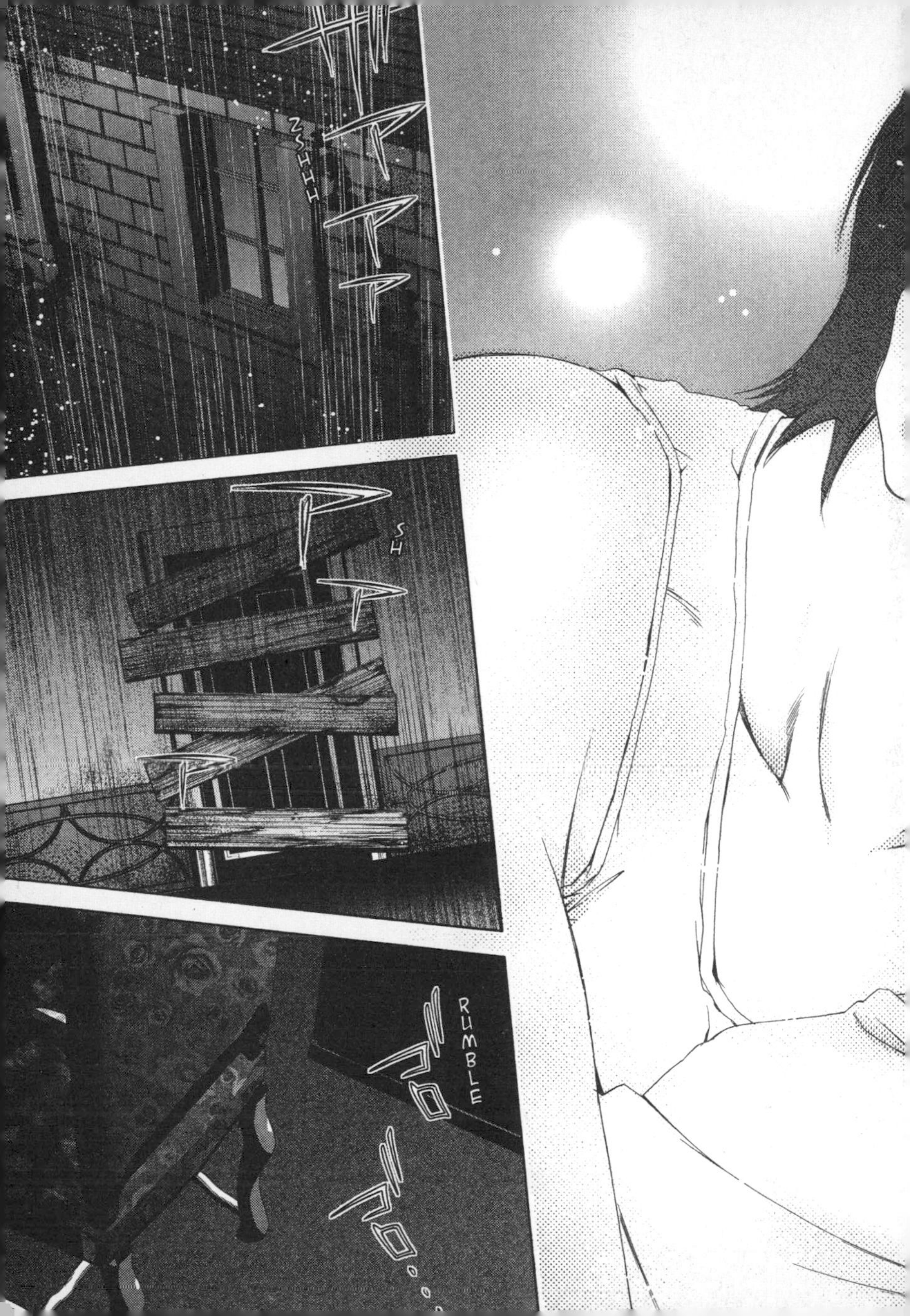
ザァァァァ
ZSHHH
アァァ
SH
ゴロ
RUMBLE
ゴロ…

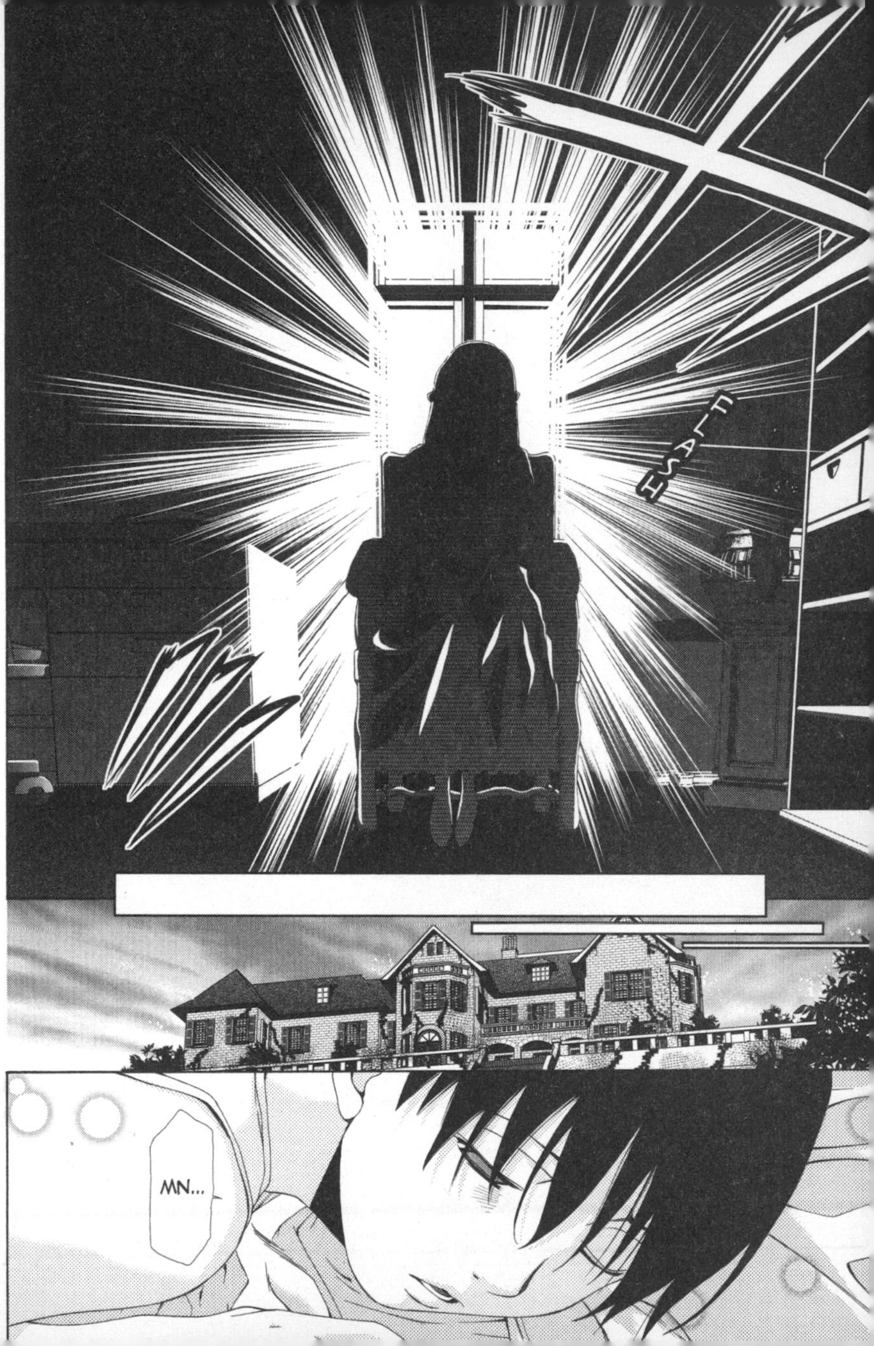
FLASH
MN...

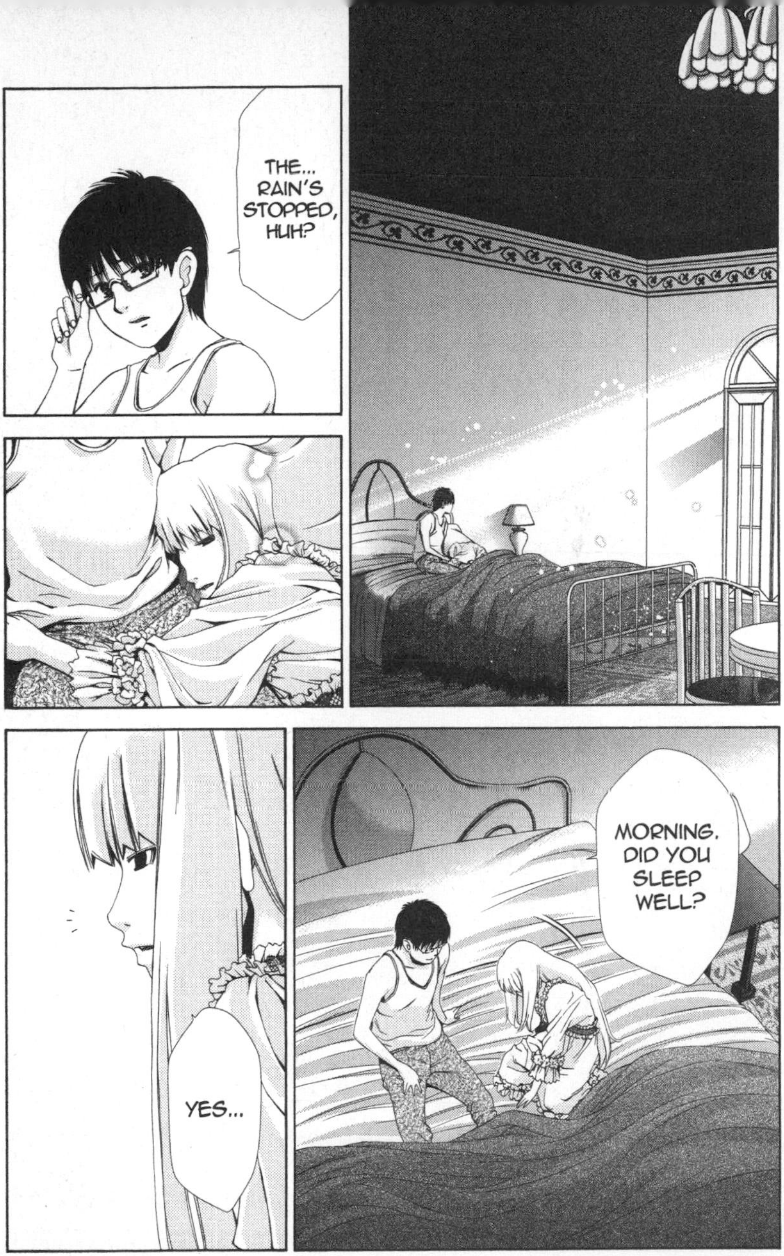
THE... RAIN'S STOPPED, HUH?
MORNING. DID YOU SLEEP WELL?
YES...

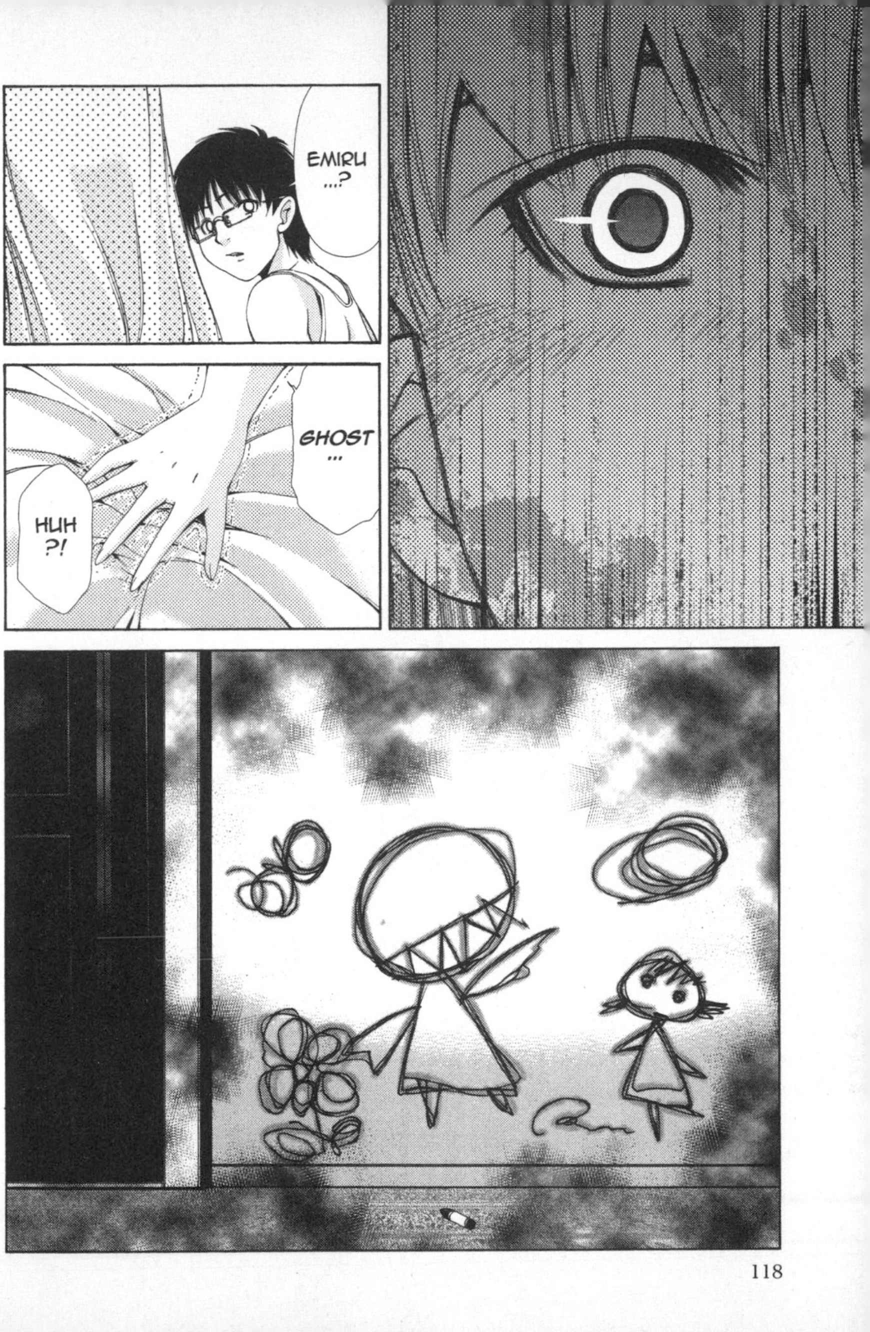
EMIRU ...?
GHOST ...
HUH ?!

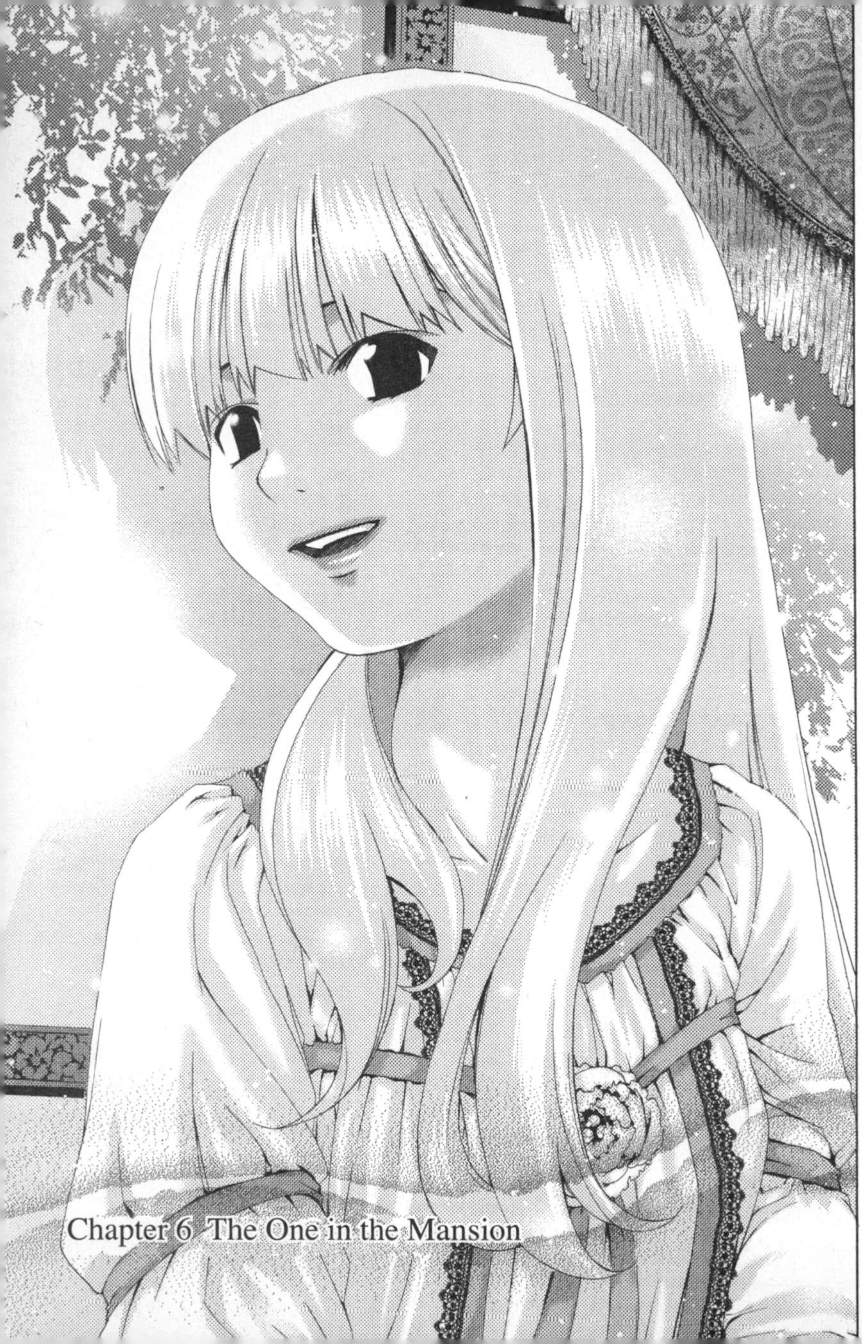
Chapter 6 The One in the Mansion

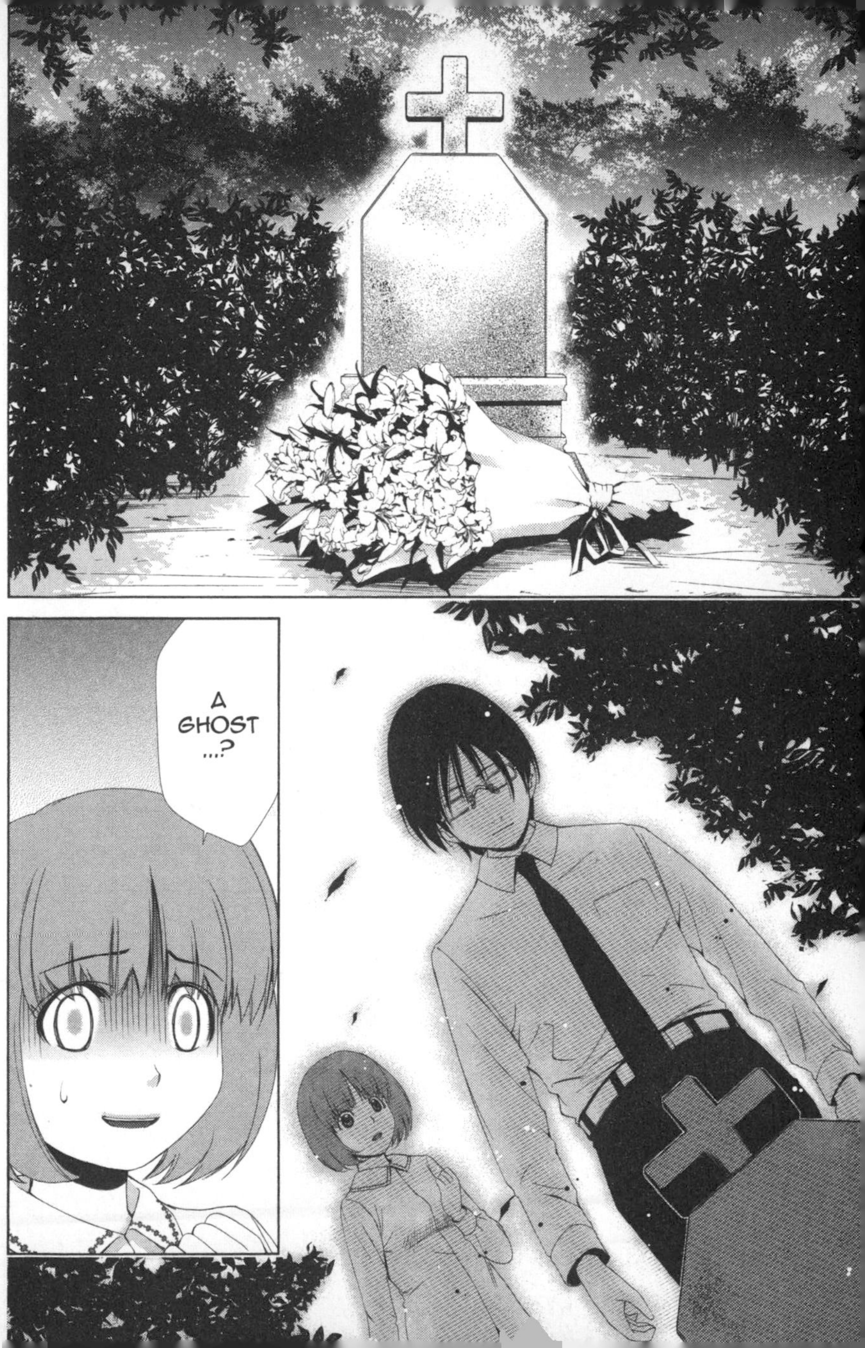
A GHOST ...?

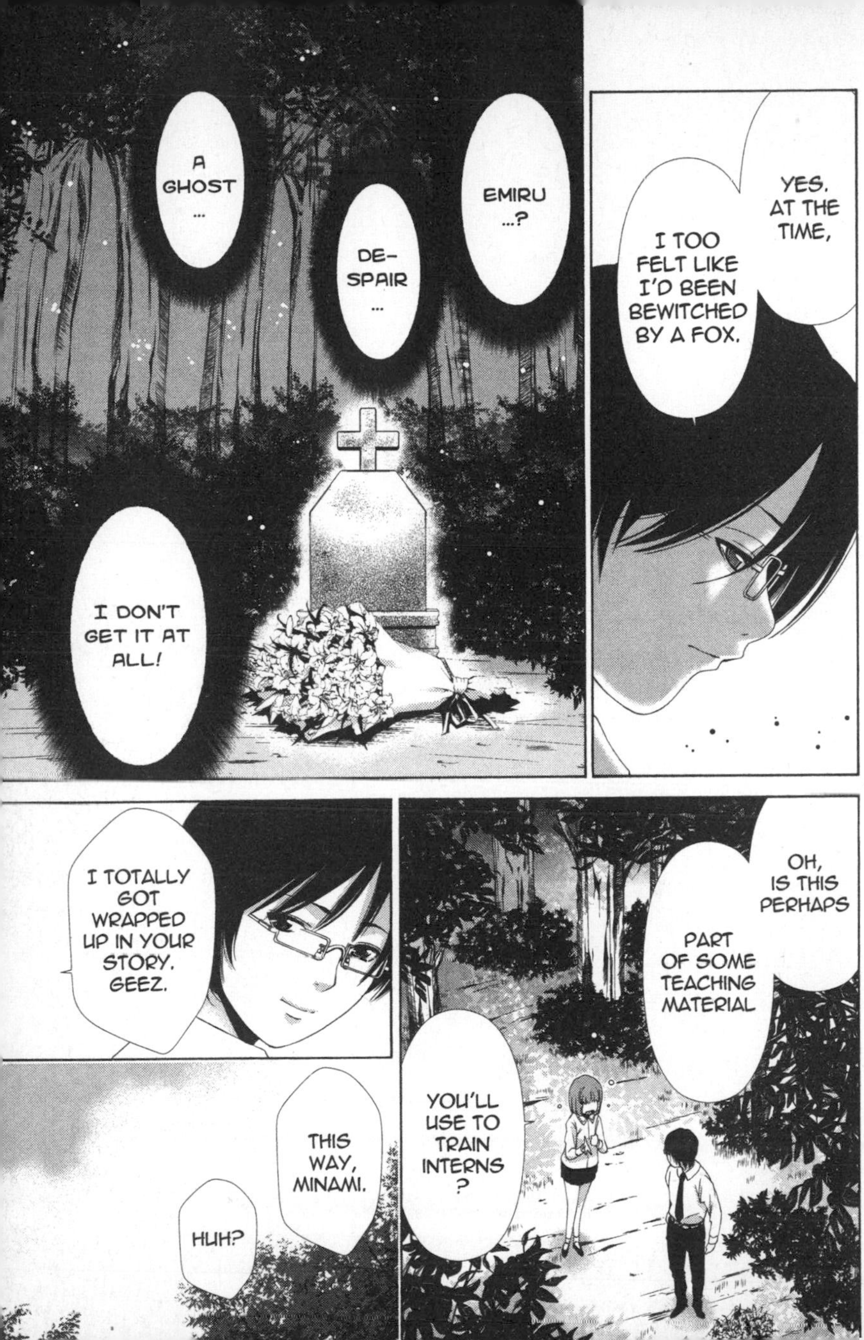
YES. AT THE TIME,
I TOO FELT LIKE I'D BEEN BEWITCHED BY A FOX.
EMIRU ...?
DE-SPAIR ...
A GHOST ...
I DON'T GET IT AT ALL!
OH, IS THIS PERHAPS
PART OF SOME TEACHING MATERIAL
YOU'LL USE TO TRAIN INTERNS ?
I TOTALLY GOT WRAPPED UP IN YOUR STORY. GEEZ.
THIS WAY, MINAMI.
HUH?

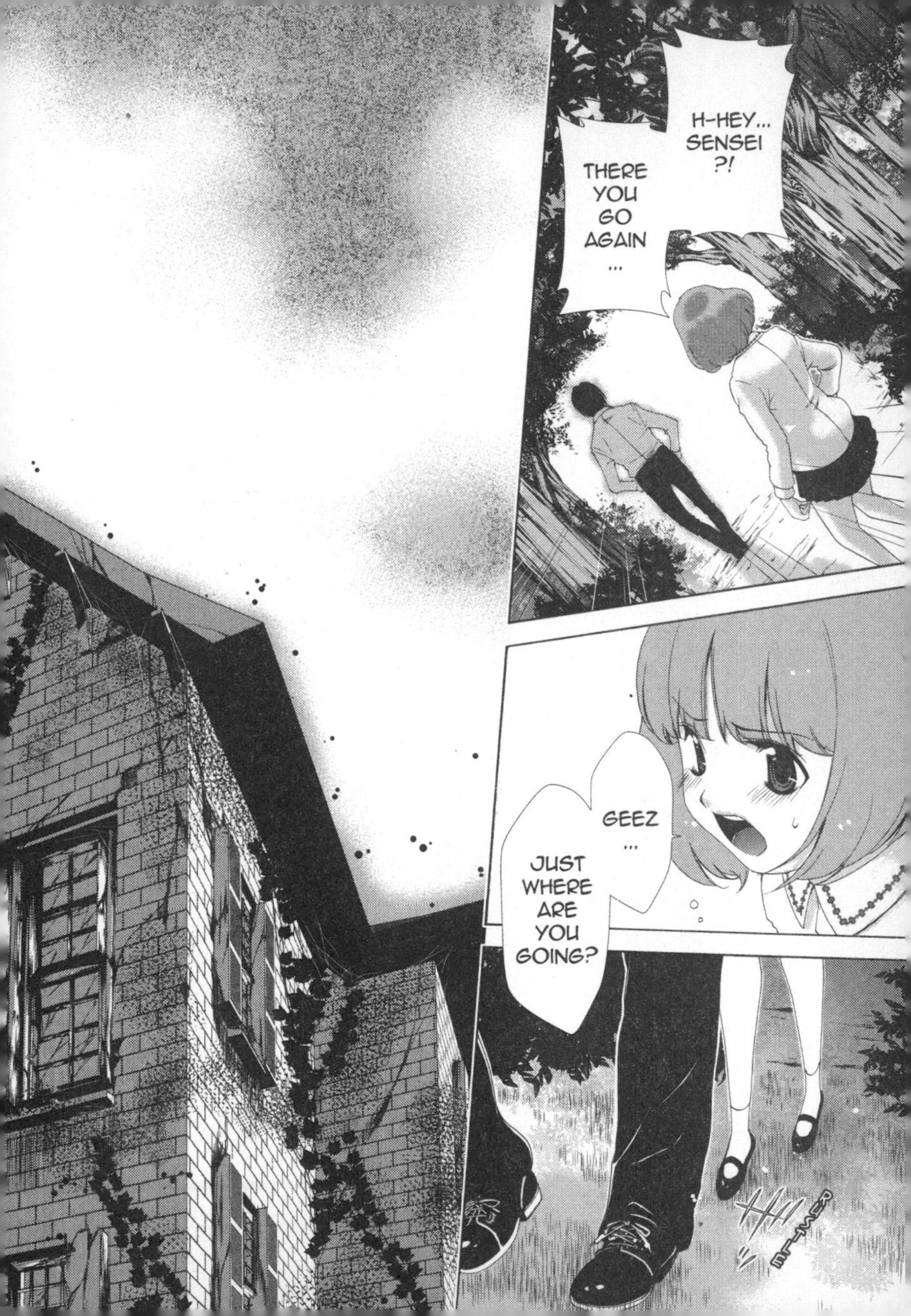
H-HEY... SENSEI ?!
THERE YOU GO AGAIN ...
GEEZ ...
JUST WHERE ARE YOU GOING?

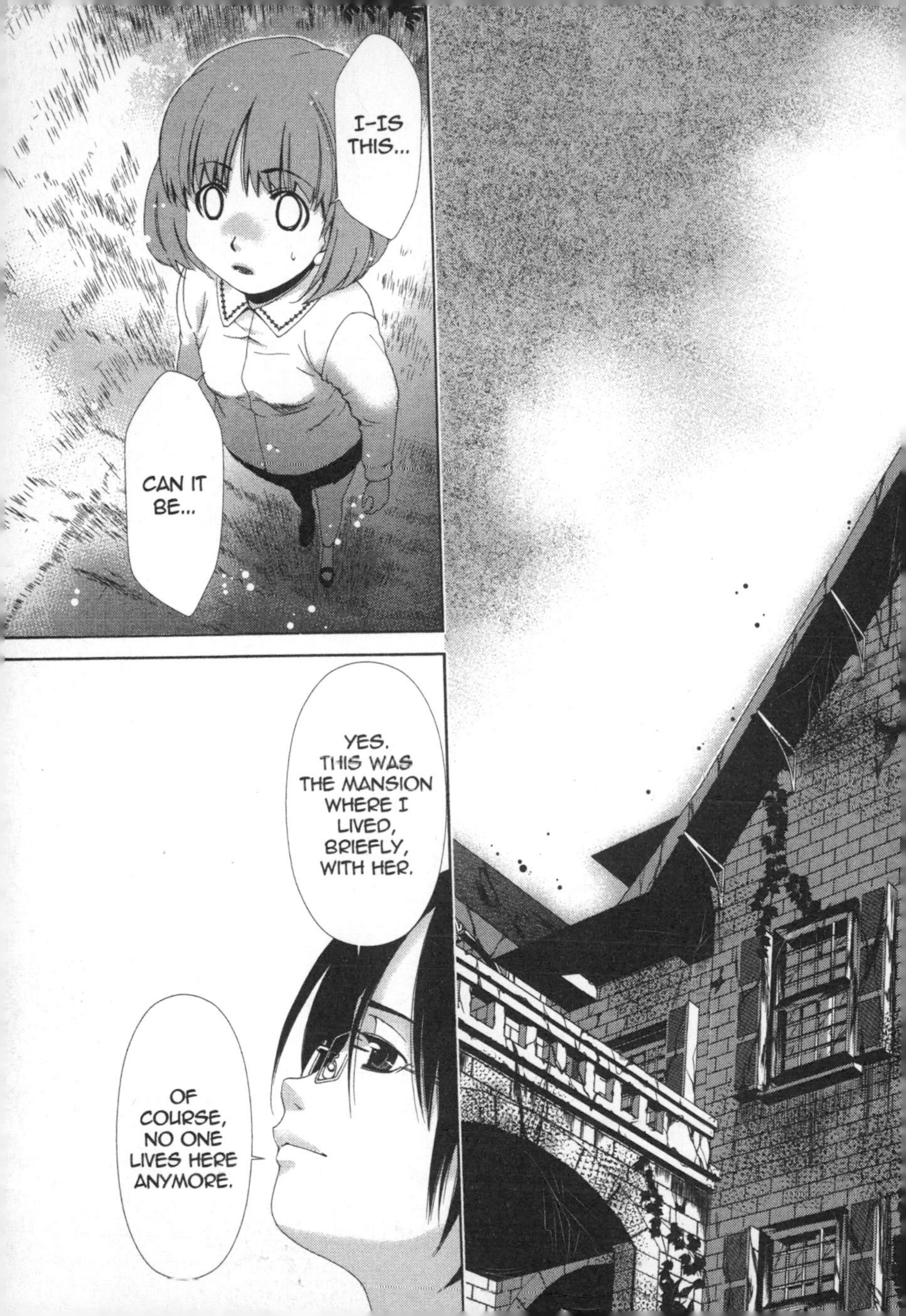
I-IS THIS...
CAN IT BE...
YES. THIS WAS THE MANSION WHERE I LIVED, BRIEFLY, WITH HER.
OF COURSE, NO ONE LIVES HERE ANYMORE.

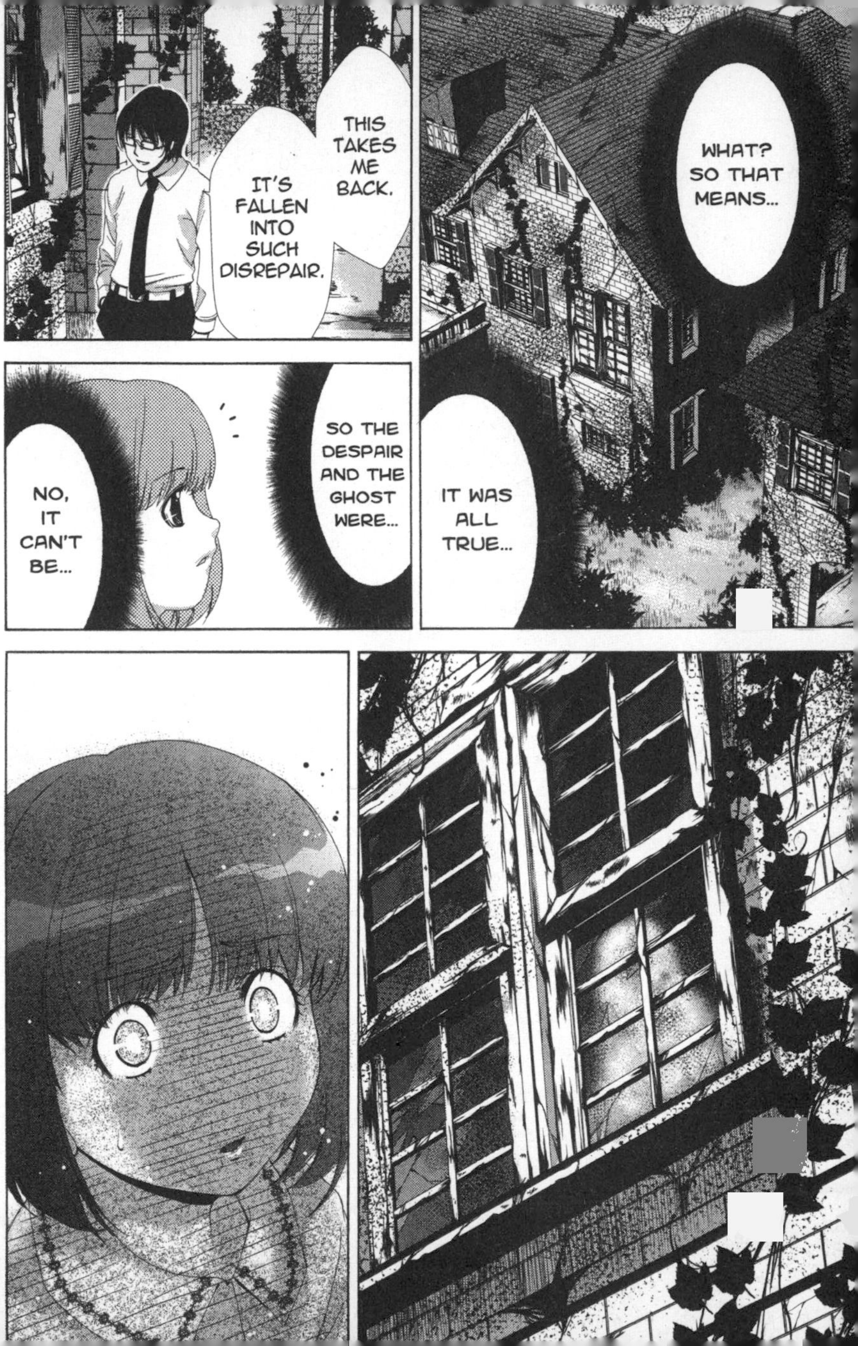
WHAT? SO THAT MEANS...
IT WAS ALL TRUE...
THIS TAKES ME BACK.
IT'S FALLEN INTO SUCH DISREPAIR.
SO THE DESPAIR AND THE GHOST WERE...
NO, IT CAN'T BE...

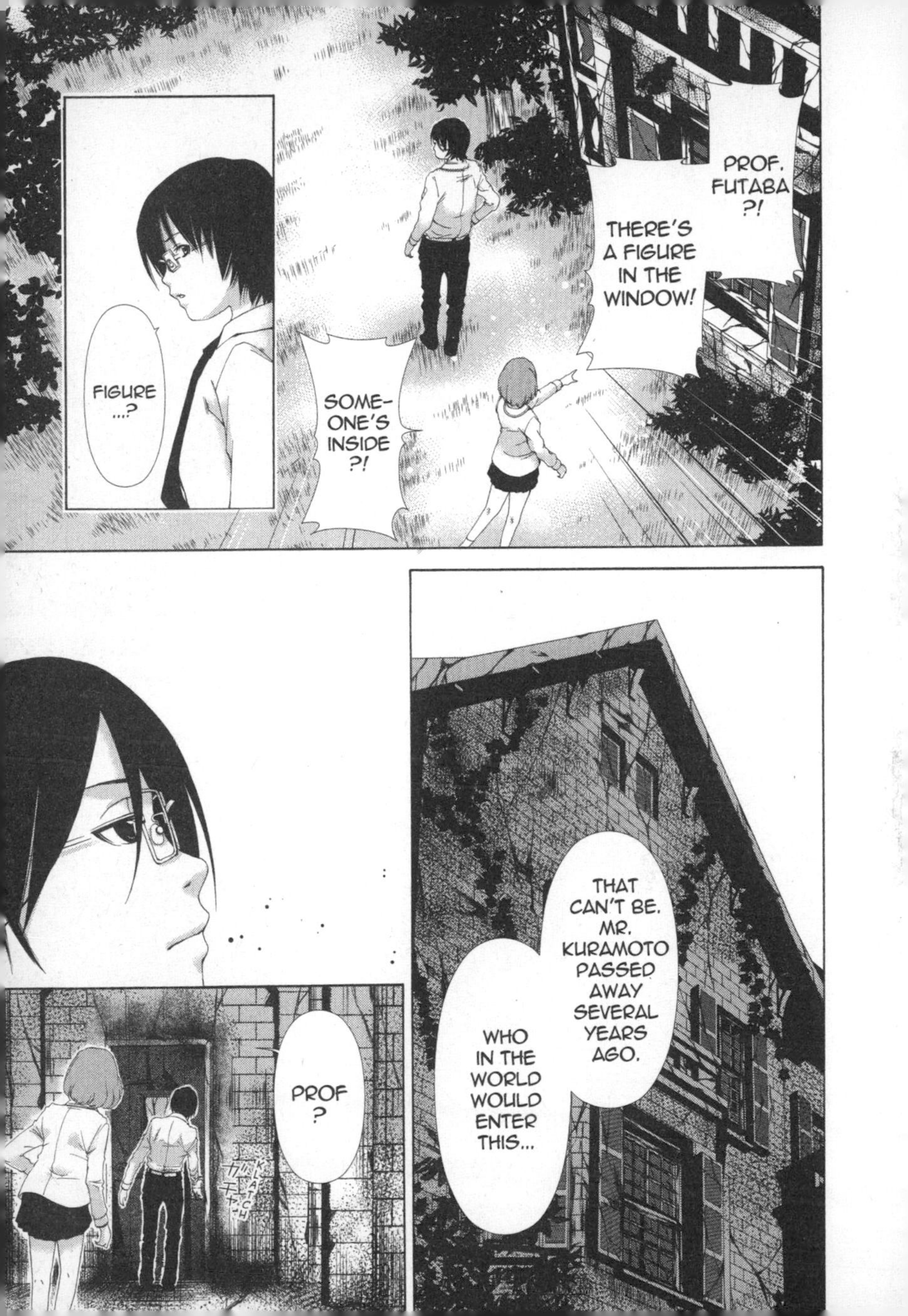
PROF. FUTABA ?!
THERE'S A FIGURE IN THE WINDOW!
SOME-ONE'S INSIDE ?!
FIGURE ...?
THAT CAN'T BE. MR. KURAMOTO PASSED AWAY SEVERAL YEARS AGO.
WHO IN THE WORLD WOULD ENTER THIS...
PROF ?
KLATCH

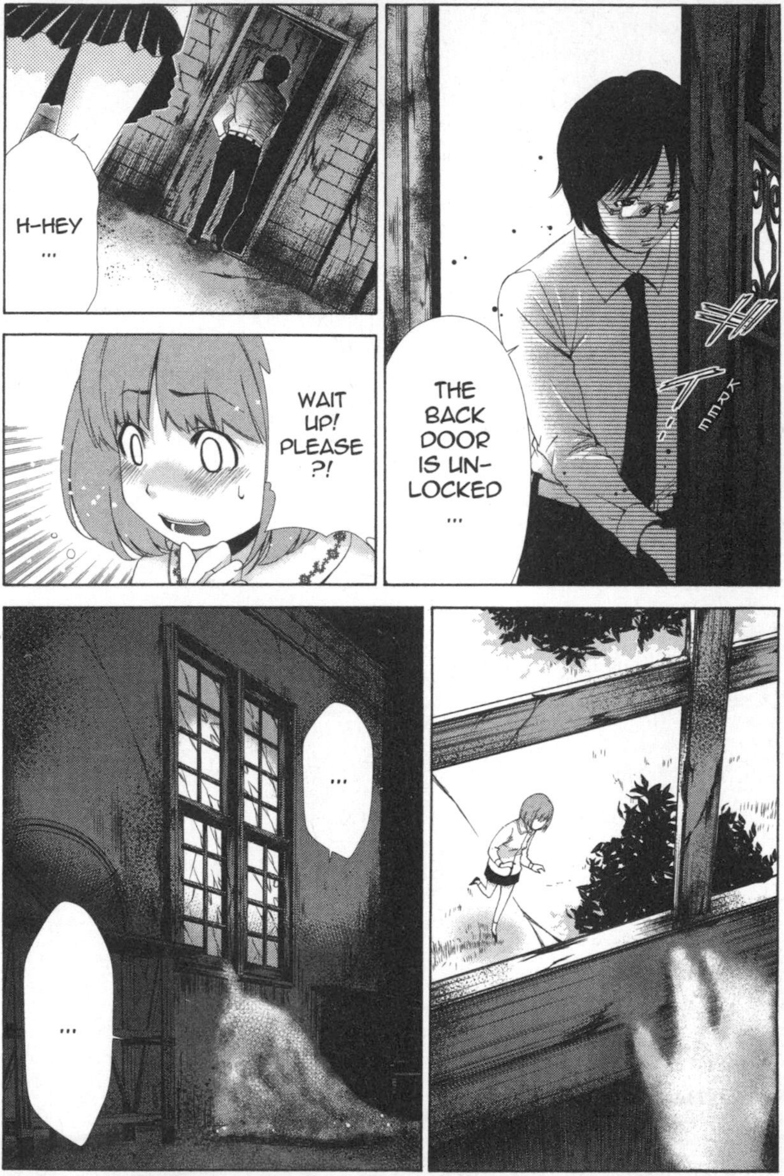
THE BACK DOOR IS UN-LOCKED ...
KREE
H-HEY ...
WAIT UP! PLEASE ?!
...
...

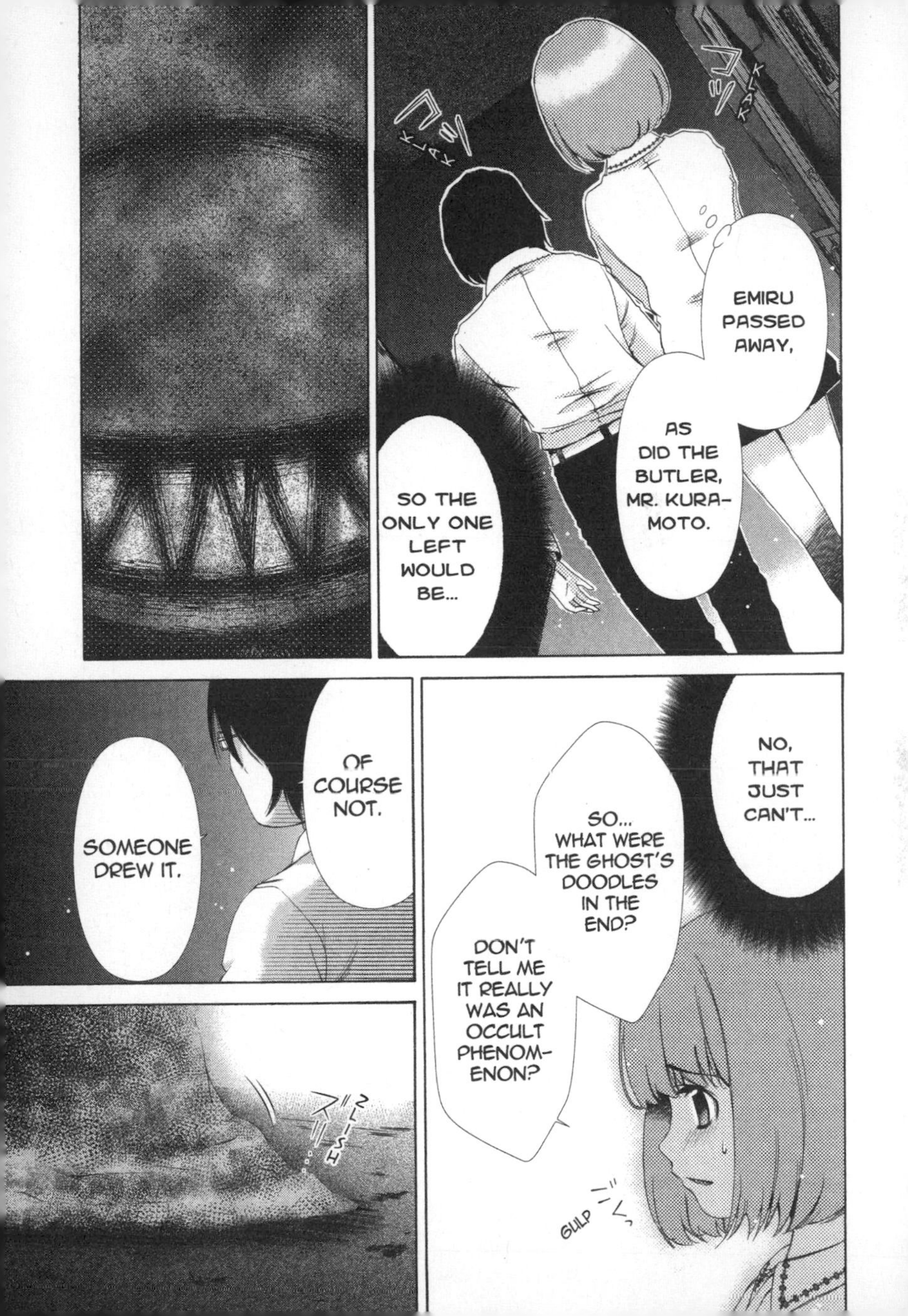
KLAK
KLAK
EMIRU PASSED AWAY,
AS DID THE BUTLER, MR. KURA-MOTO.
SO THE ONLY ONE LEFT WOULD BE...
NO, THAT JUST CAN'T...
SO... WHAT WERE THE GHOST'S DOODLES IN THE END?
DON'T TELL ME IT REALLY WAS AN OCCULT PHENOM-ENON?
GULP
OF COURSE NOT.
SOMEONE DREW IT.
SLISH

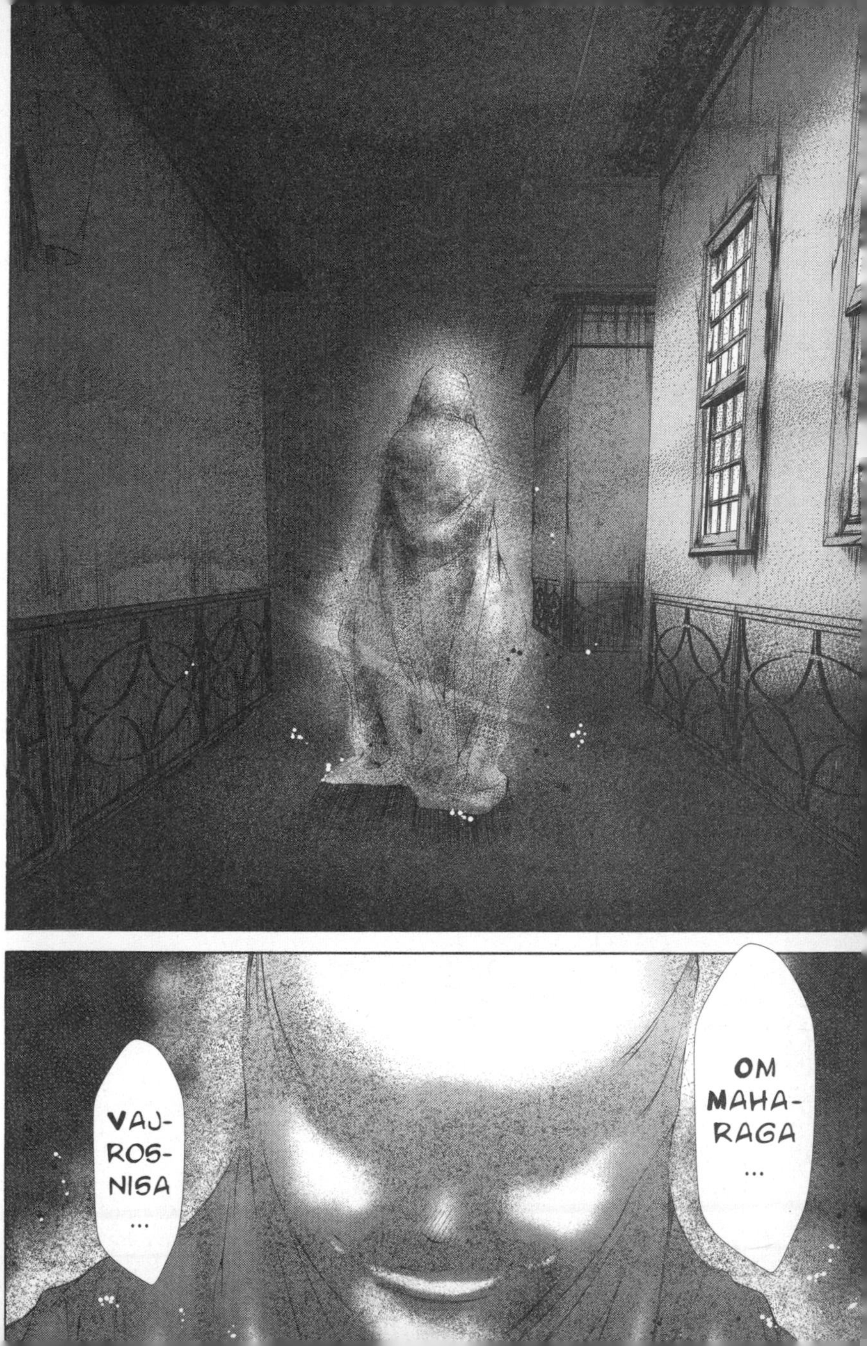
OM MAHA-RAGA ...
VAJ-ROS-NISA ...

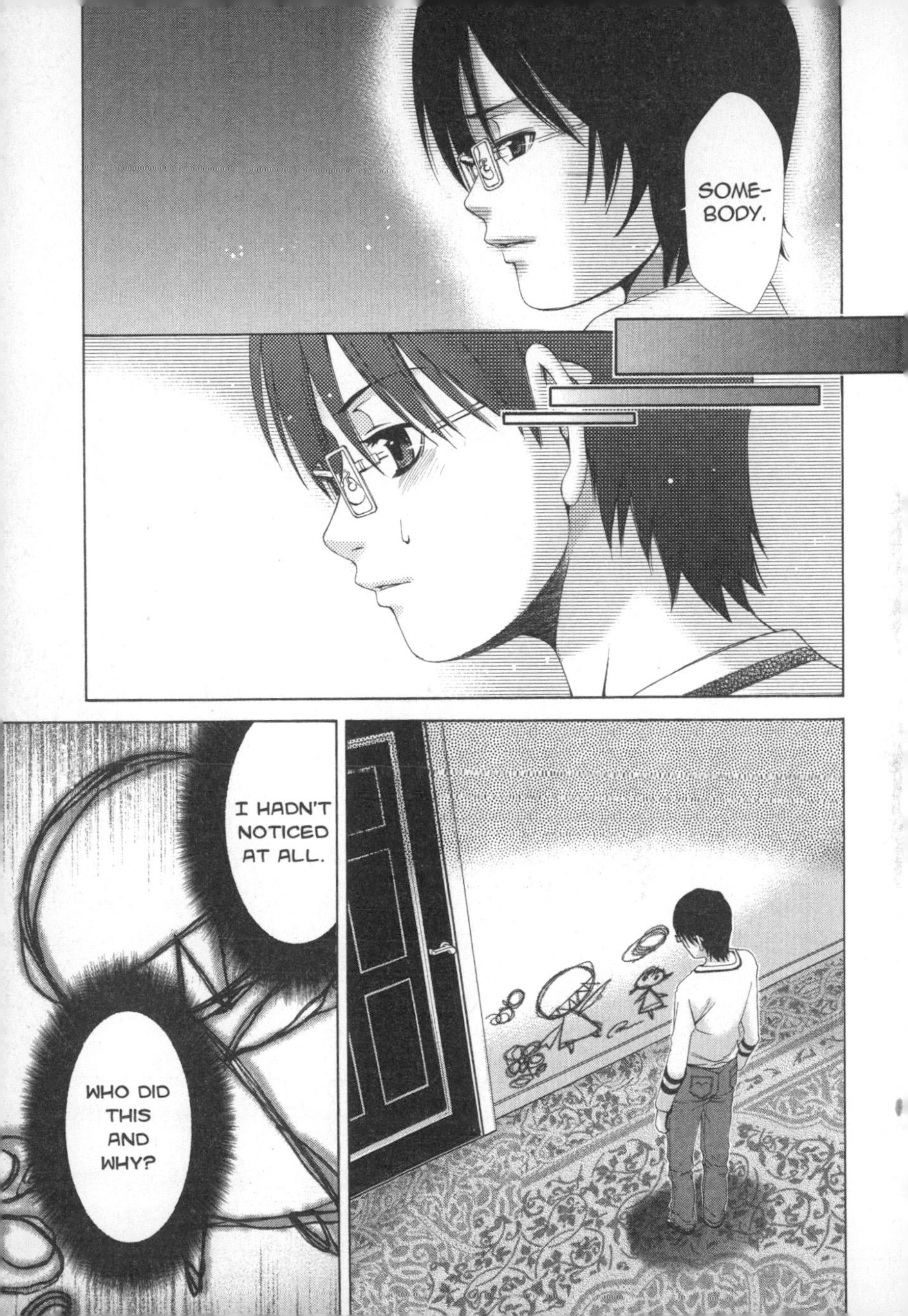
SOME-BODY.
I HADN'T NOTICED AT ALL.
WHO DID THIS AND WHY?

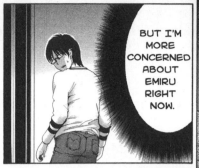

BUT I'M MORE CONCERNED ABOUT EMIRU RIGHT NOW.
SHE SEEMS TO HAVE SUFFERED QUITE A SHOCK.
KAZUMA ... PLEASE BRING
THE YOUNG MISTRESS SOME WATER.
MR. KURA-MOTO,
SORRY THIS HAPPENED ON MY WATCH.

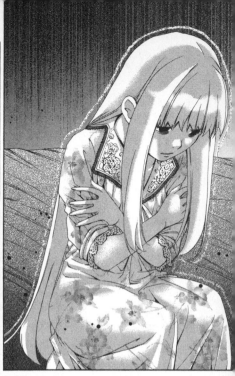

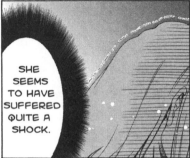

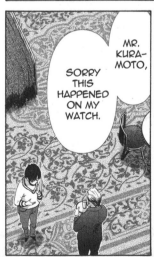

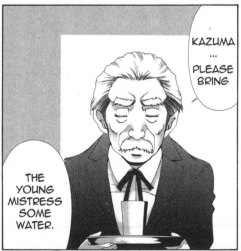

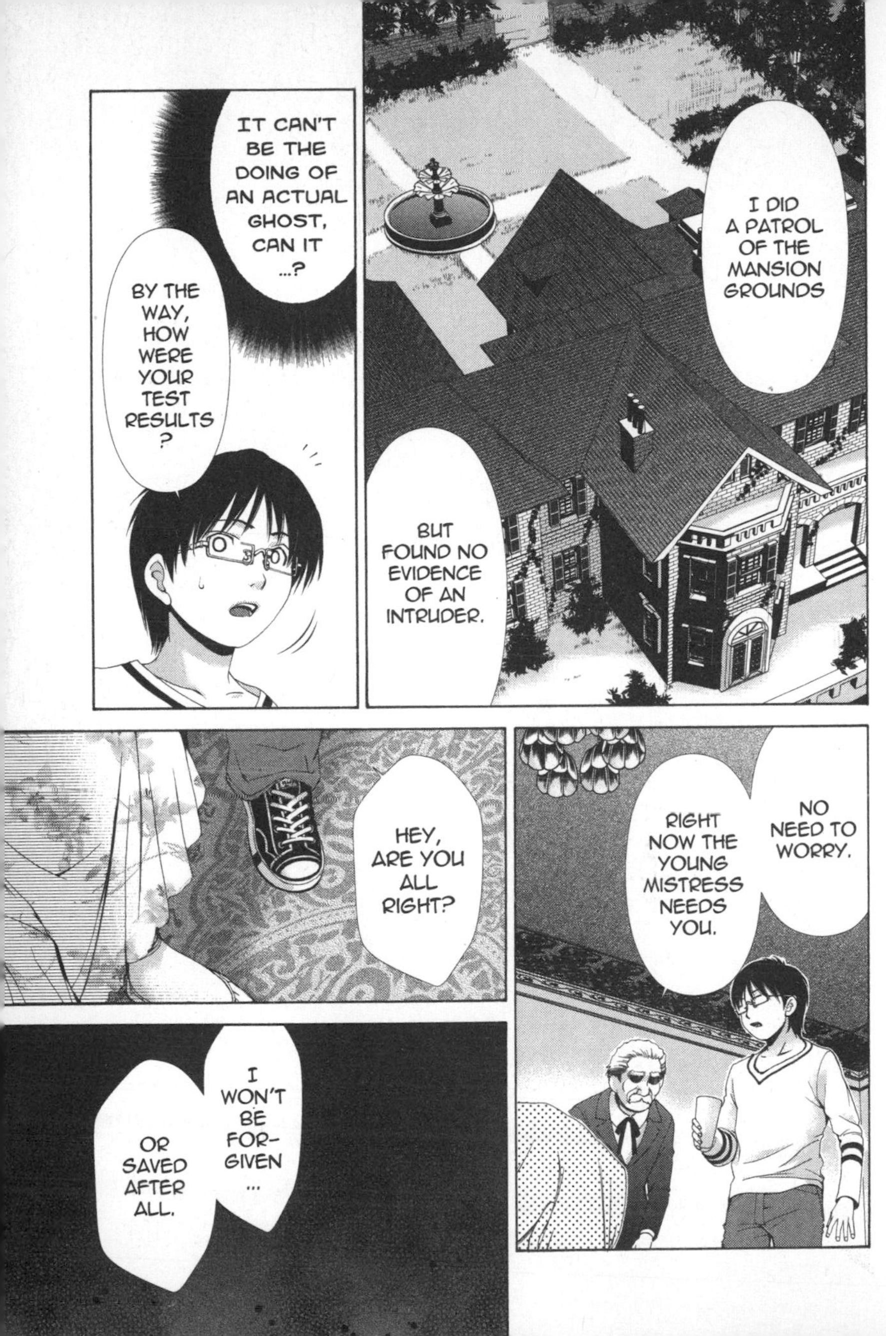
I DID A PATROL OF THE MANSION GROUNDS
BUT FOUND NO EVIDENCE OF AN INTRUDER.
IT CAN'T BE THE DOING OF AN ACTUAL GHOST, CAN IT ...?
BY THE WAY, HOW WERE YOUR TEST RESULTS?
NO NEED TO WORRY.
RIGHT NOW THE YOUNG MISTRESS NEEDS YOU.
HEY, ARE YOU ALL RIGHT?
I WON'T BE FOR-GIVEN ...
OR SAVED AFTER ALL.

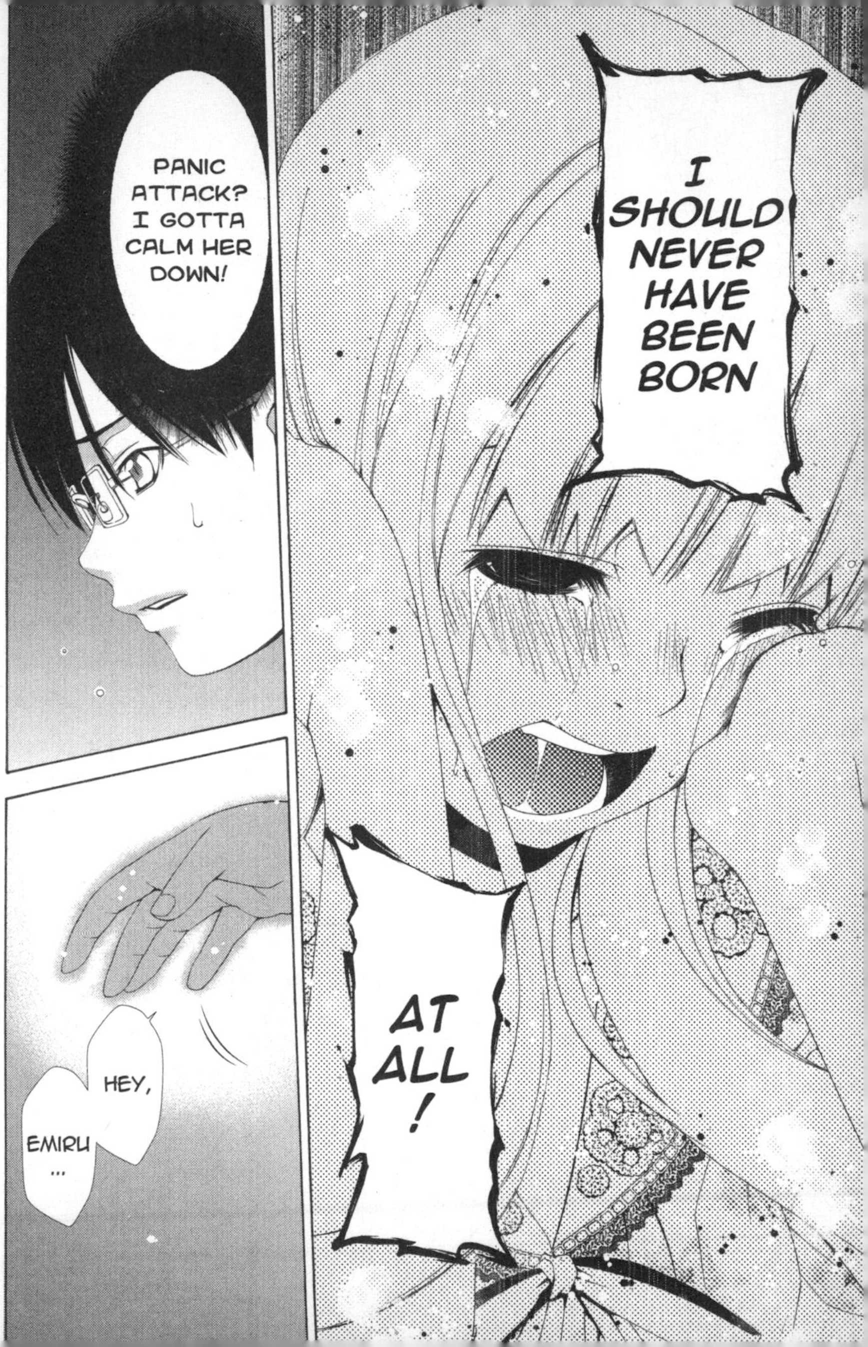
I SHOULD NEVER HAVE BEEN BORN
AT ALL!
PANIC ATTACK? I GOTTA CALM HER DOWN!
HEY,
EMIRU...

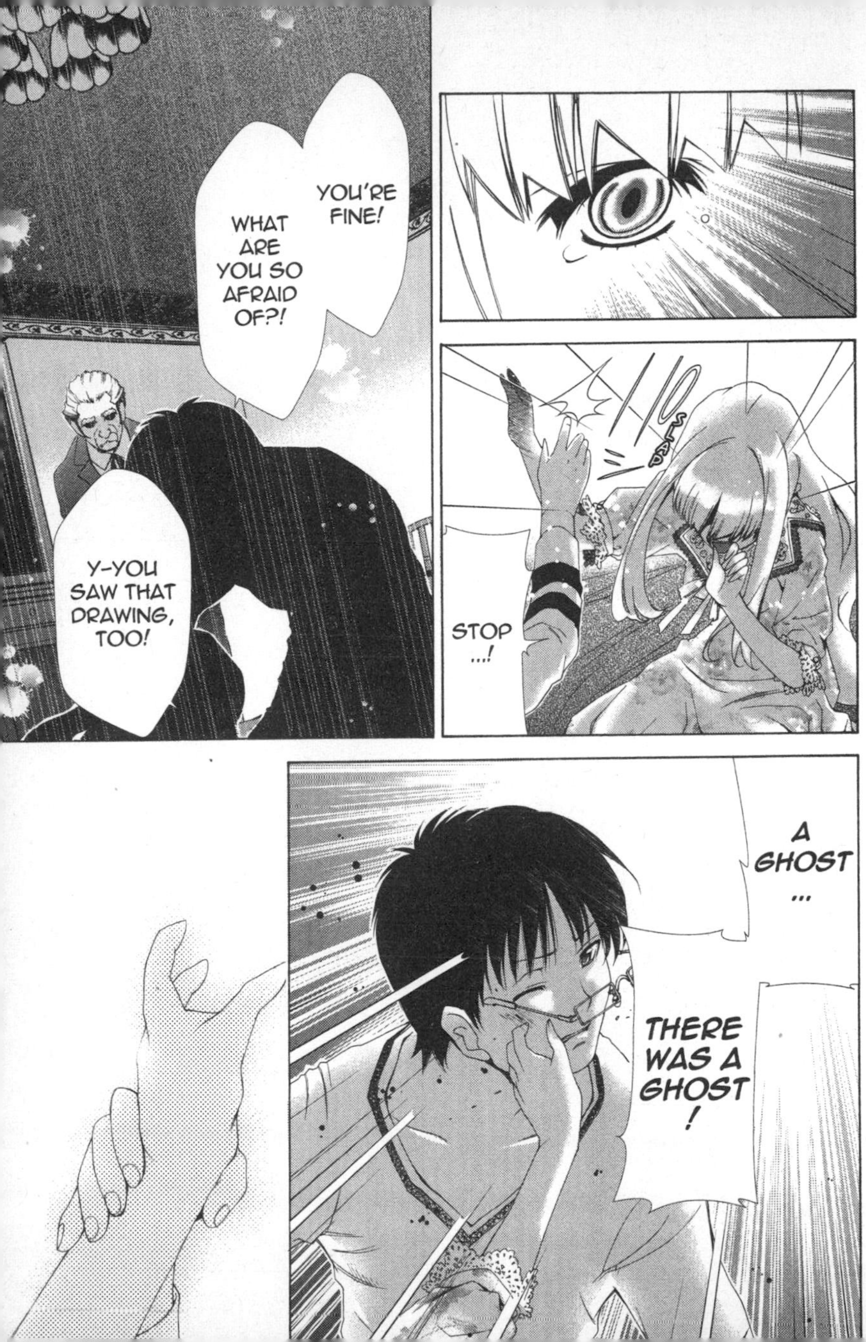
SLAP
STOP ...!
YOU'RE FINE!
WHAT ARE YOU SO AFRAID OF?!
Y-YOU SAW THAT DRAWING, TOO!
A GHOST ...
THERE WAS A GHOST!

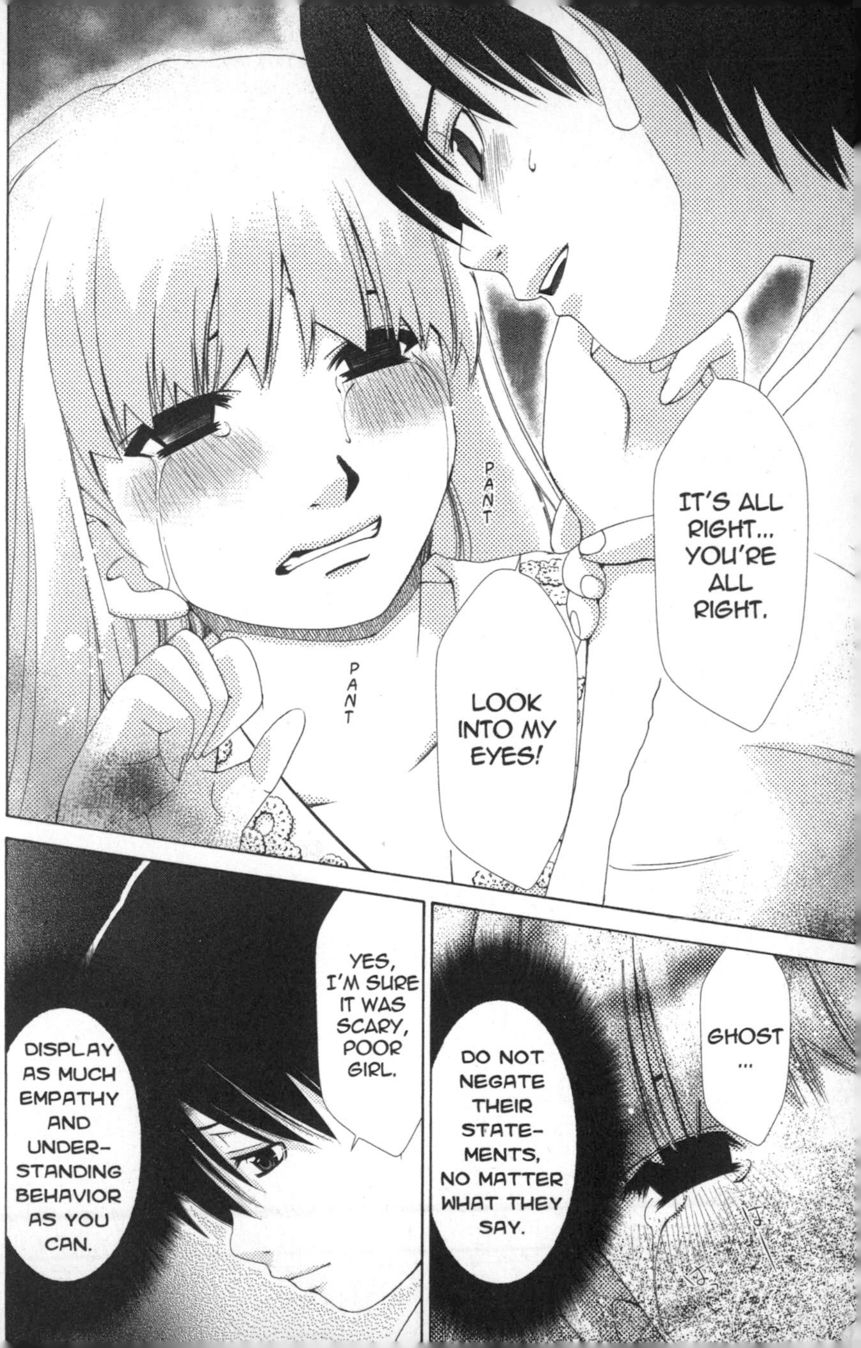
IT'S ALL RIGHT... YOU'RE ALL RIGHT.
PANT
LOOK INTO MY EYES!
PANT
GHOST ...
DO NOT NEGATE THEIR STATE-MENTS, NO MATTER WHAT THEY SAY.
YES, I'M SURE IT WAS SCARY, POOR GIRL.
DISPLAY AS MUCH EMPATHY AND UNDER-STANDING BEHAVIOR AS YOU CAN.

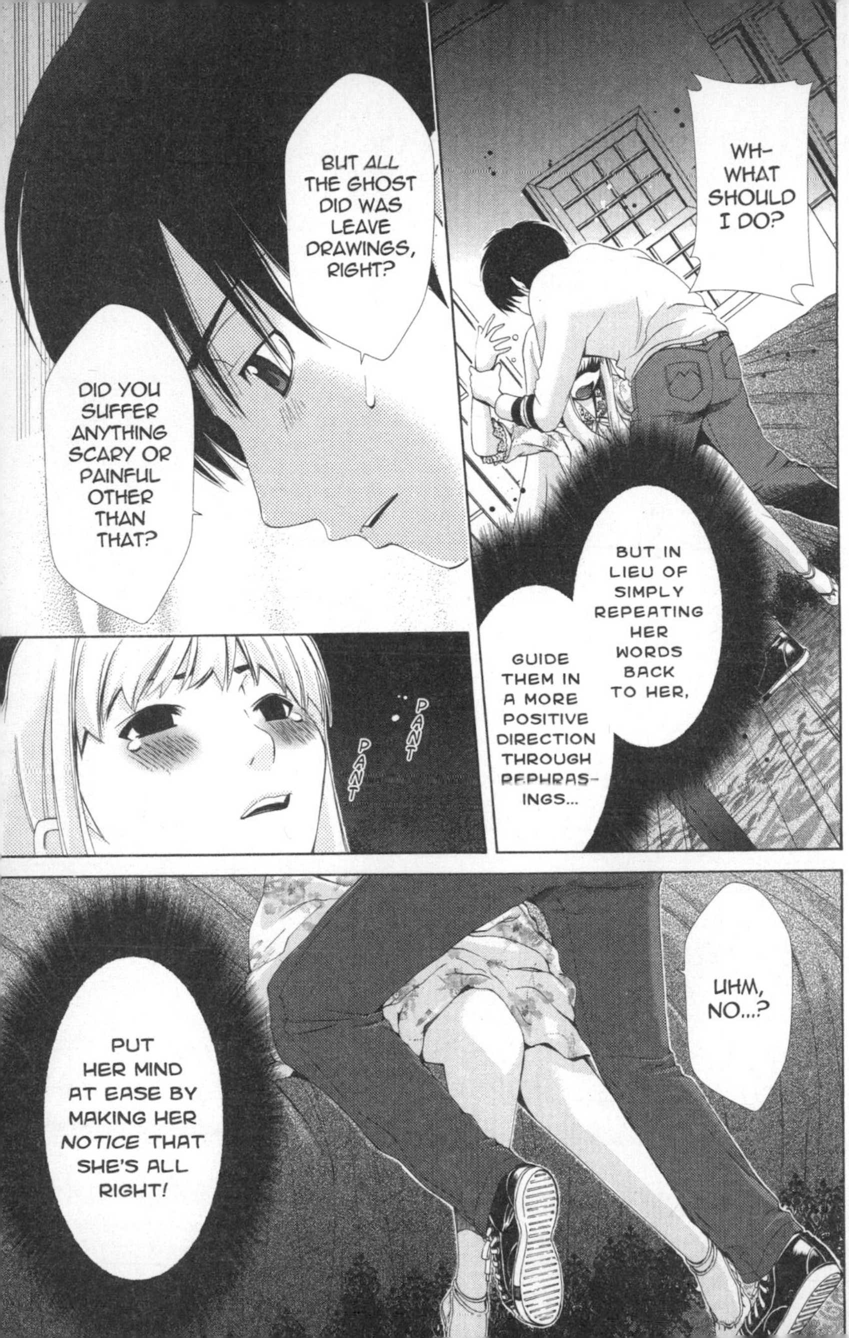
WH- WHAT SHOULD I DO?
BUT IN LIEU OF SIMPLY REPEATING HER WORDS BACK TO HER,
GUIDE THEM IN A MORE POSITIVE DIRECTION THROUGH REPHRAS- INGS...
BUT ALL THE GHOST DID WAS LEAVE DRAWINGS, RIGHT?
DID YOU SUFFER ANYTHING SCARY OR PAINFUL OTHER THAN THAT?
PANT
PANT
UHM, NO...?
PUT HER MIND AT EASE BY MAKING HER NOTICE THAT SHE'S ALL RIGHT!

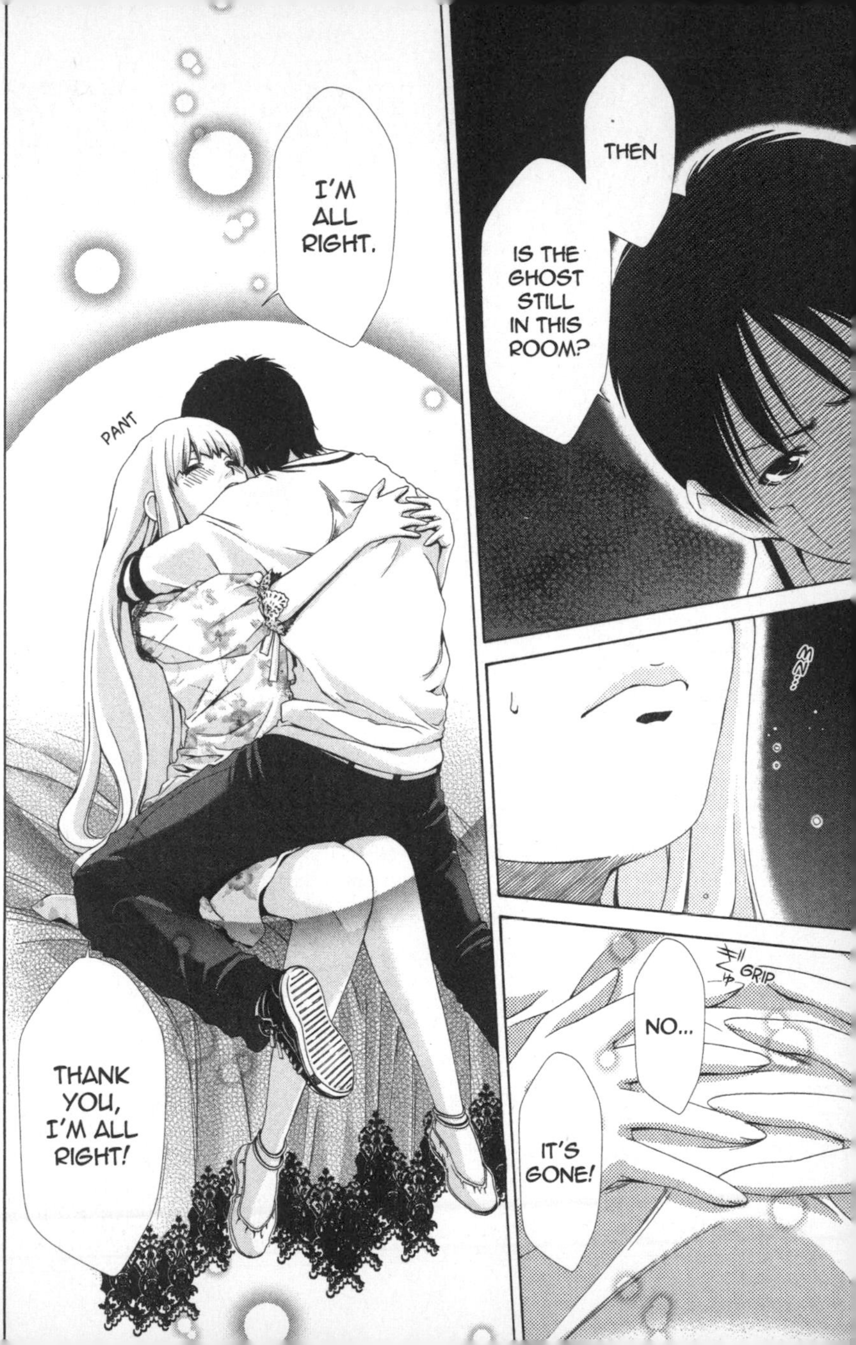
THEN
IS THE GHOST STILL IN THIS ROOM?
MN...
GRIP
NO...
IT'S GONE!
I'M ALL RIGHT.
PANT
THANK YOU, I'M ALL RIGHT!

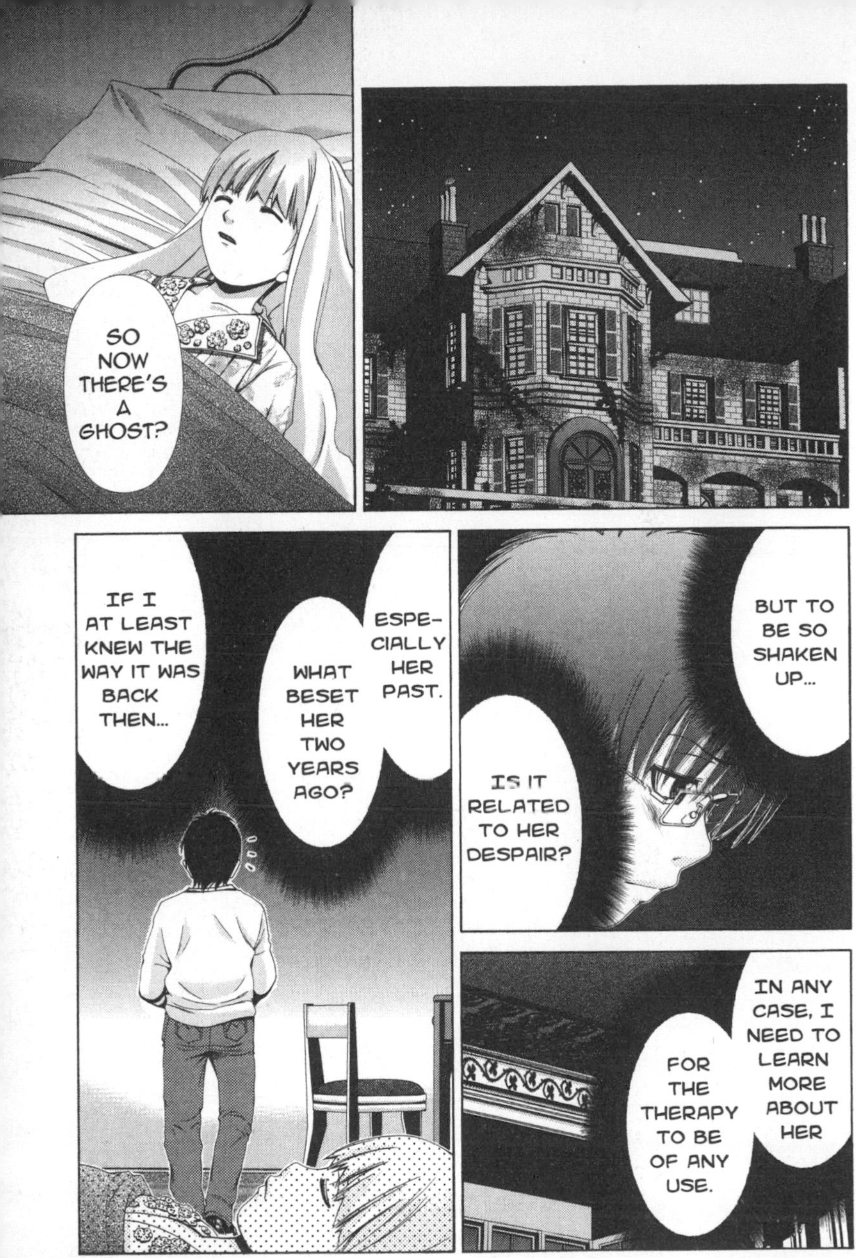
SO NOW THERE'S A GHOST?
BUT TO BE SO SHAKEN UP...
IS IT RELATED TO HER DESPAIR?
IN ANY CASE, I NEED TO LEARN MORE ABOUT HER
FOR THE THERAPY TO BE OF ANY USE.
ESPE-CIALLY HER PAST.
WHAT BESET HER TWO YEARS AGO?
IF I AT LEAST KNEW THE WAY IT WAS BACK THEN...

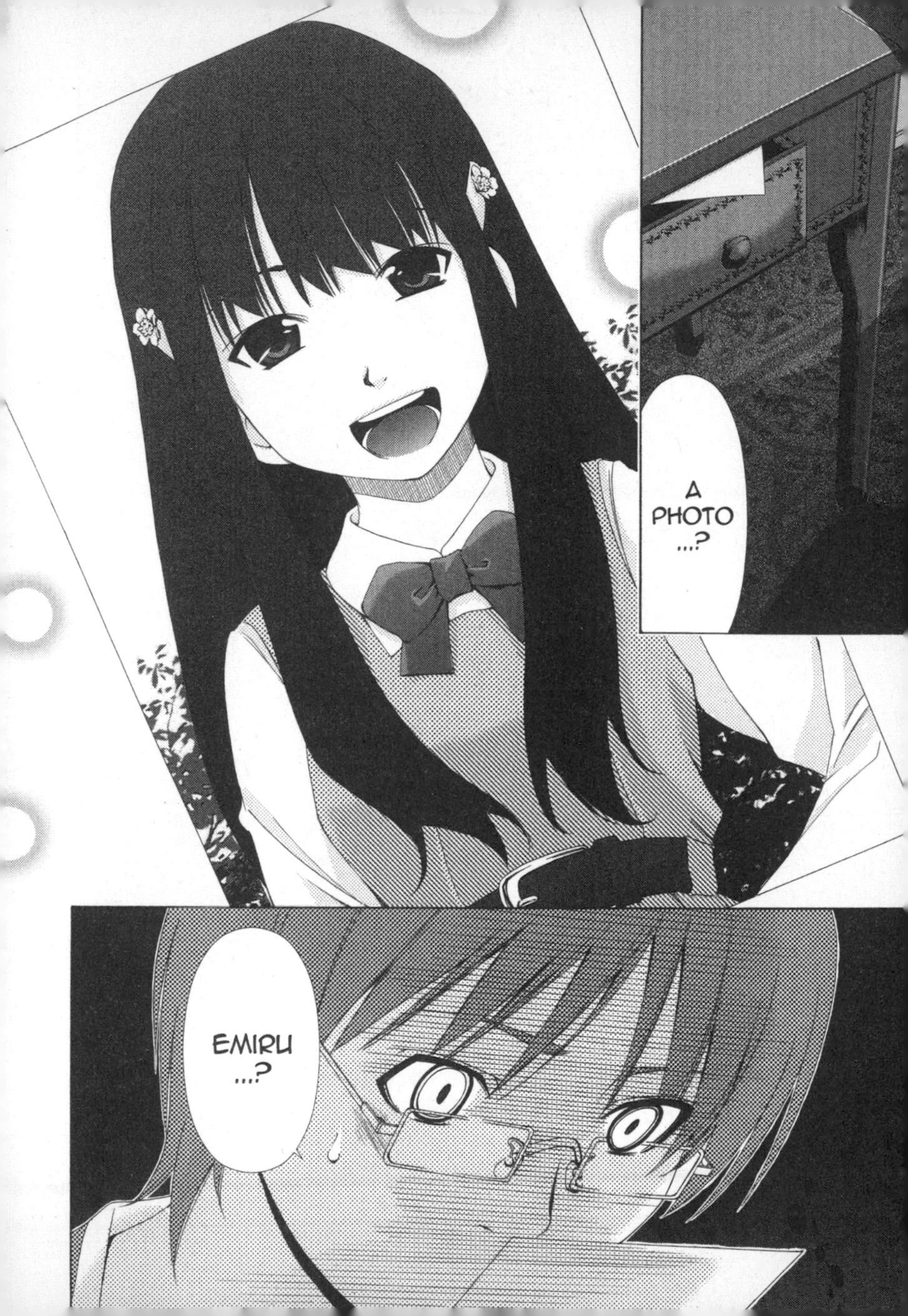
A PHOTO ...?
EMIRU ...?

Chapter 7
High School Years

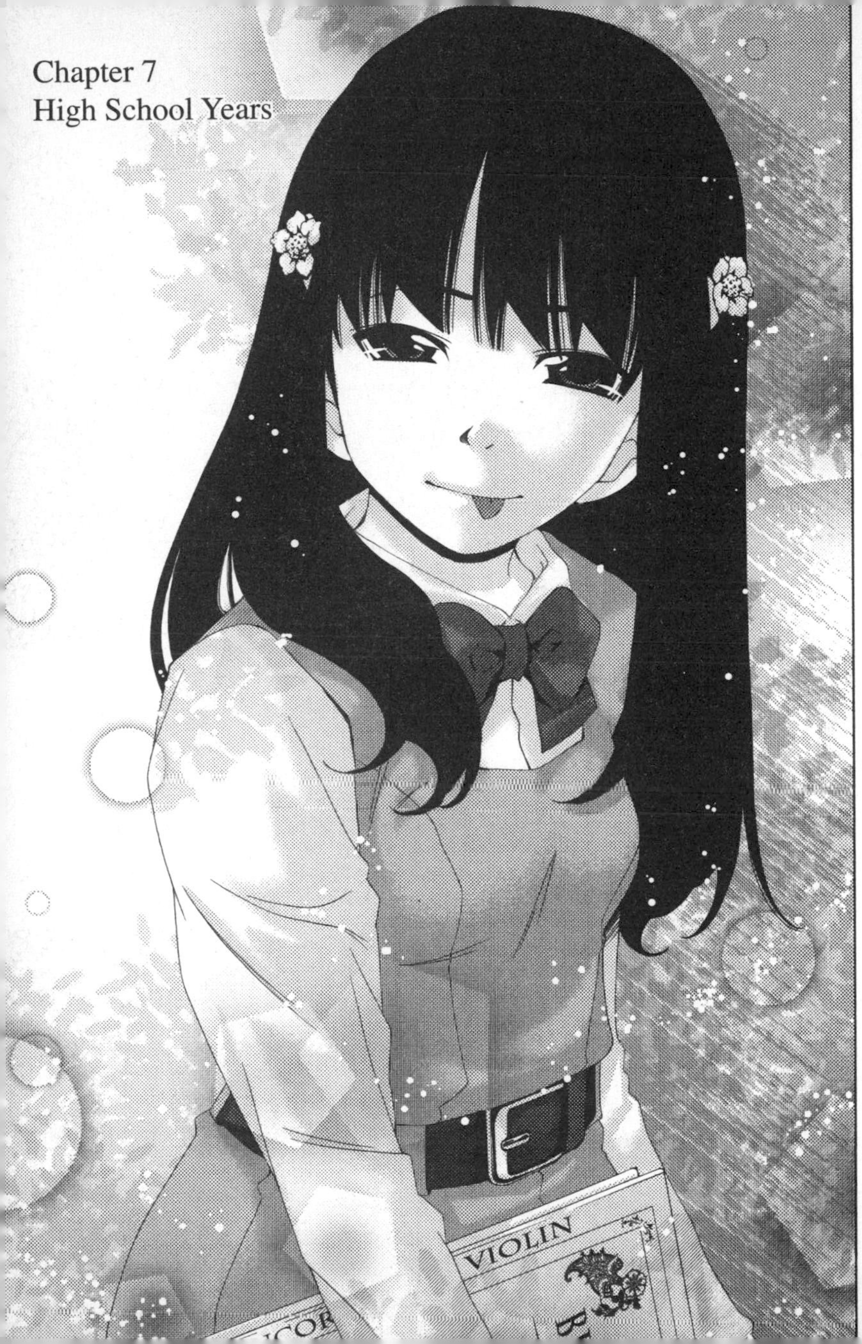
VIOLIN

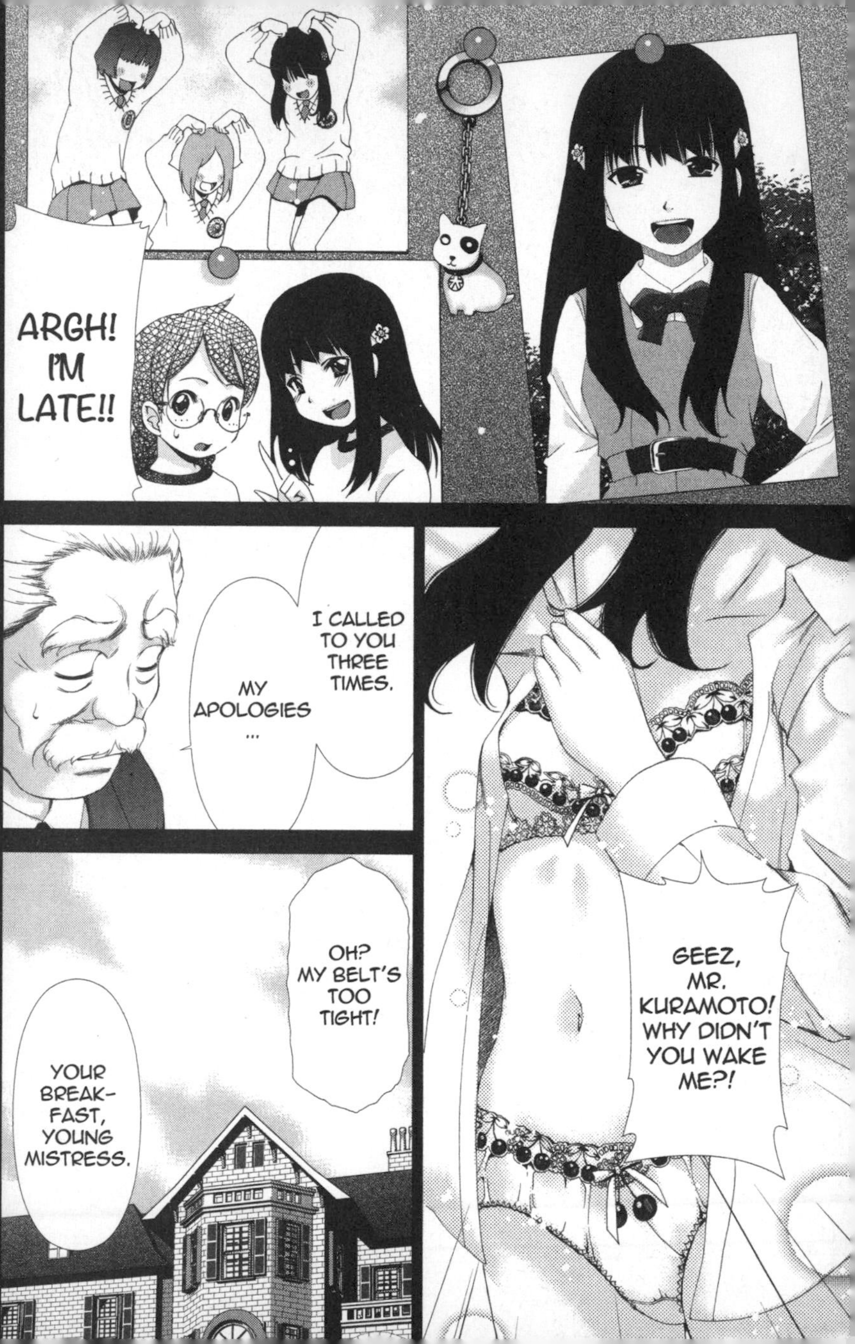
ARGH! I'M LATE!!
GEEZ, MR. KURAMOTO! WHY DIDN'T YOU WAKE ME?!
I CALLED TO YOU THREE TIMES.
MY APOLOGIES ...
OH? MY BELT'S TOO TIGHT!
YOUR BREAK-FAST, YOUNG MISTRESS.

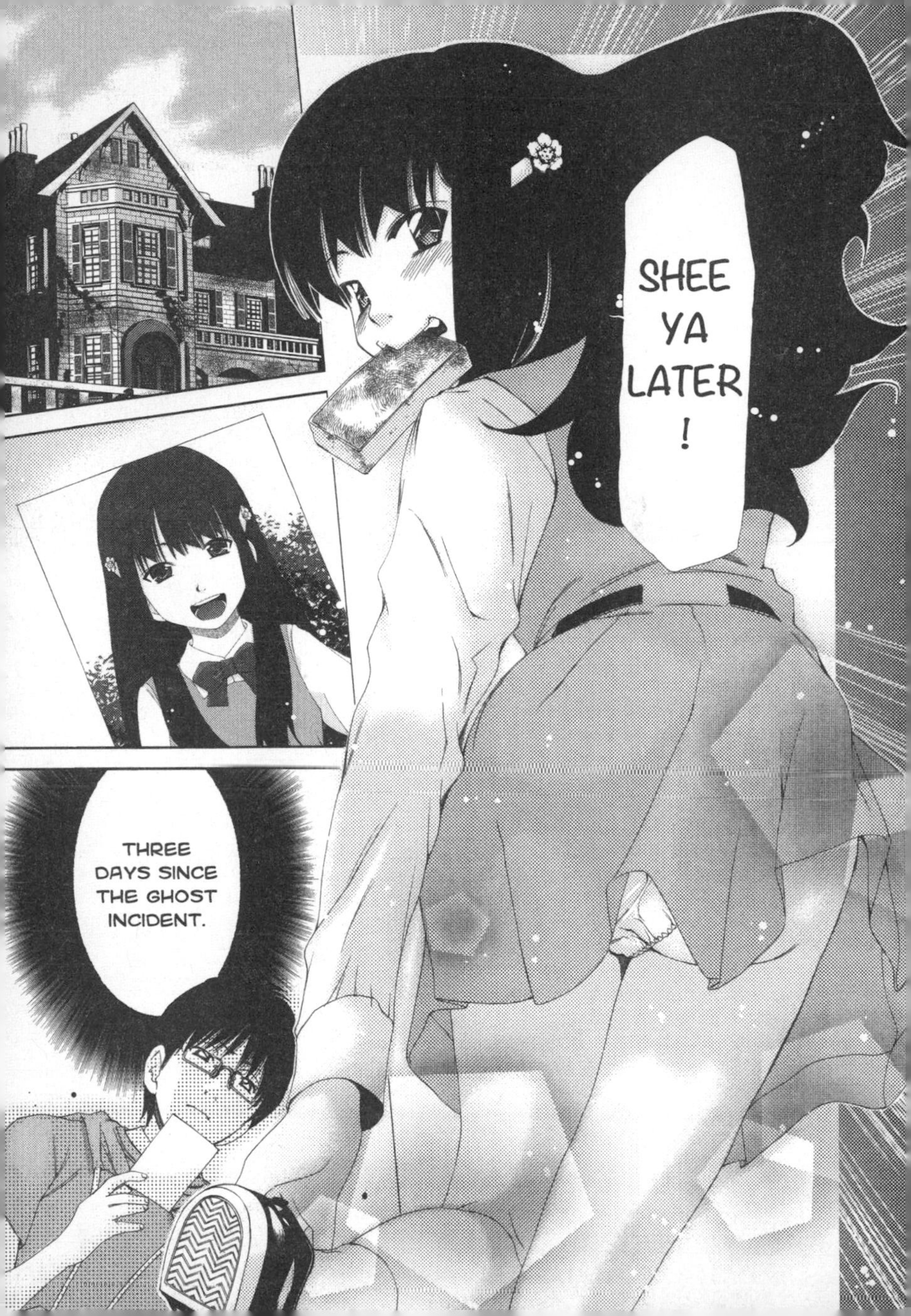
SHEE YA LATER !
THREE DAYS SINCE THE GHOST INCIDENT.

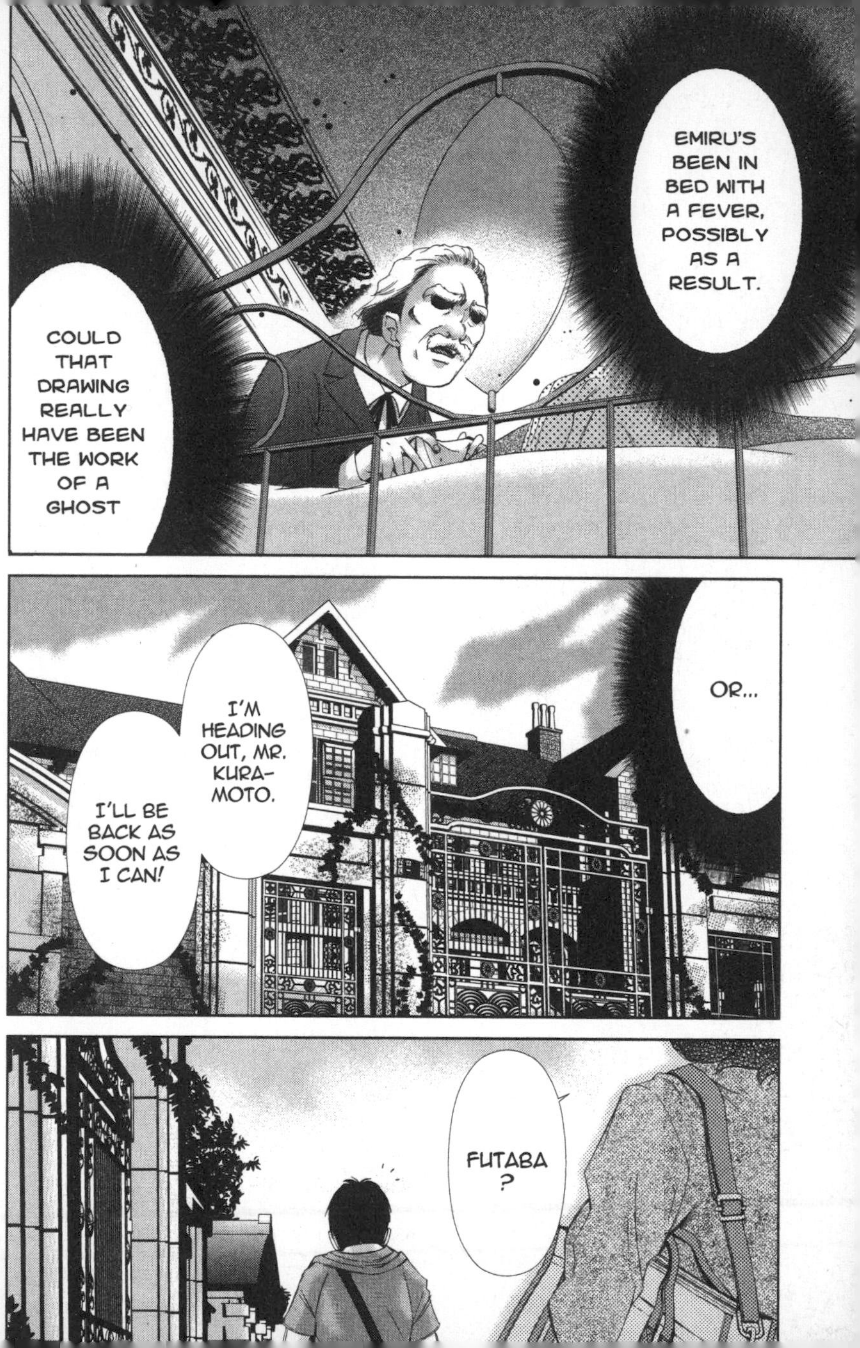
EMIRU'S BEEN IN BED WITH A FEVER, POSSIBLY AS A RESULT.
COULD THAT DRAWING REALLY HAVE BEEN THE WORK OF A GHOST
OR...
I'M HEADING OUT, MR. KURA-MOTO.
I'LL BE BACK AS SOON AS I CAN!
FUTABA ?

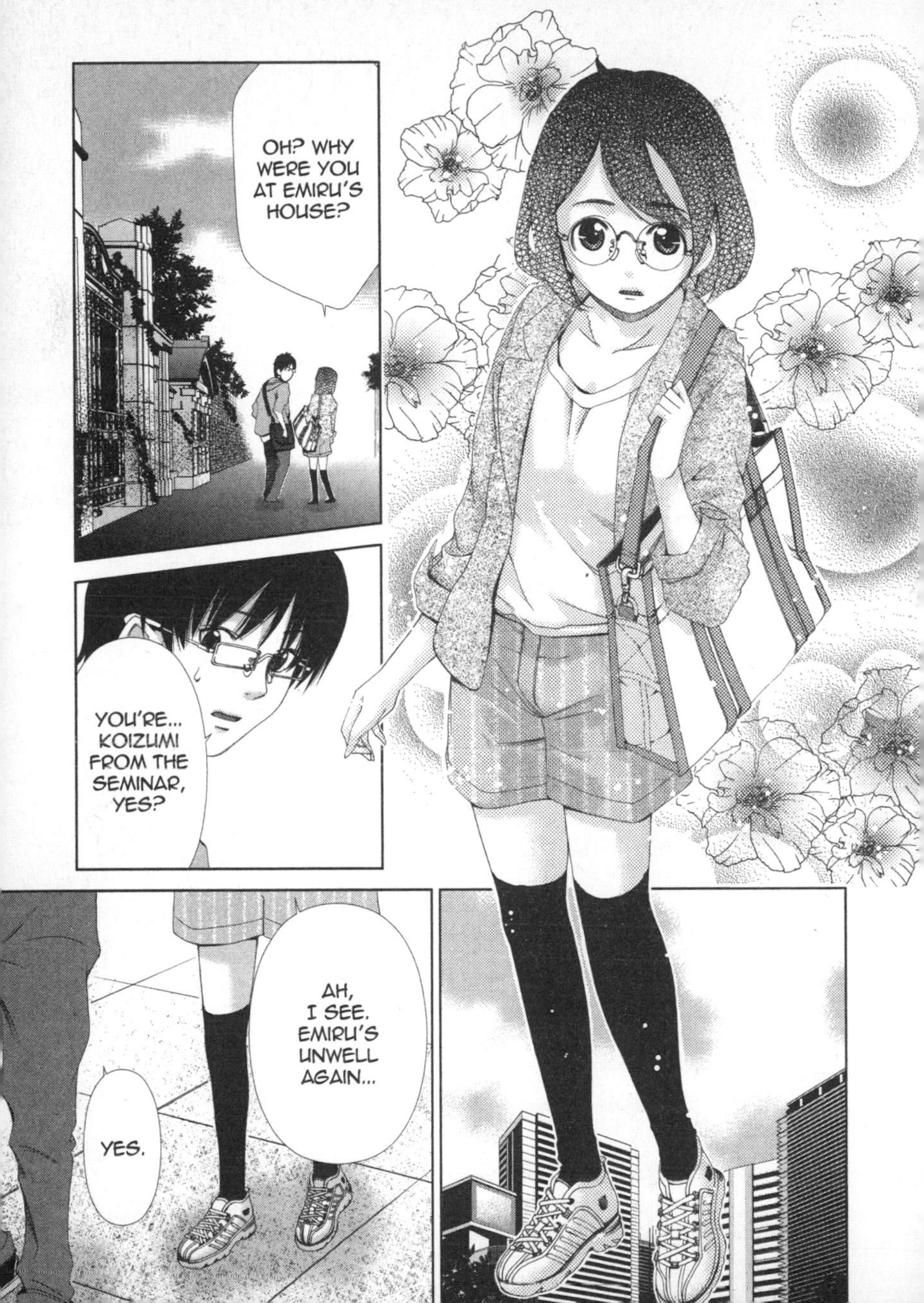
OH? WHY WERE YOU AT EMIRU'S HOUSE?
YOU'RE... KOIZUMI FROM THE SEMINAR, YES?
AH, I SEE. EMIRU'S UNWELL AGAIN...
YES.

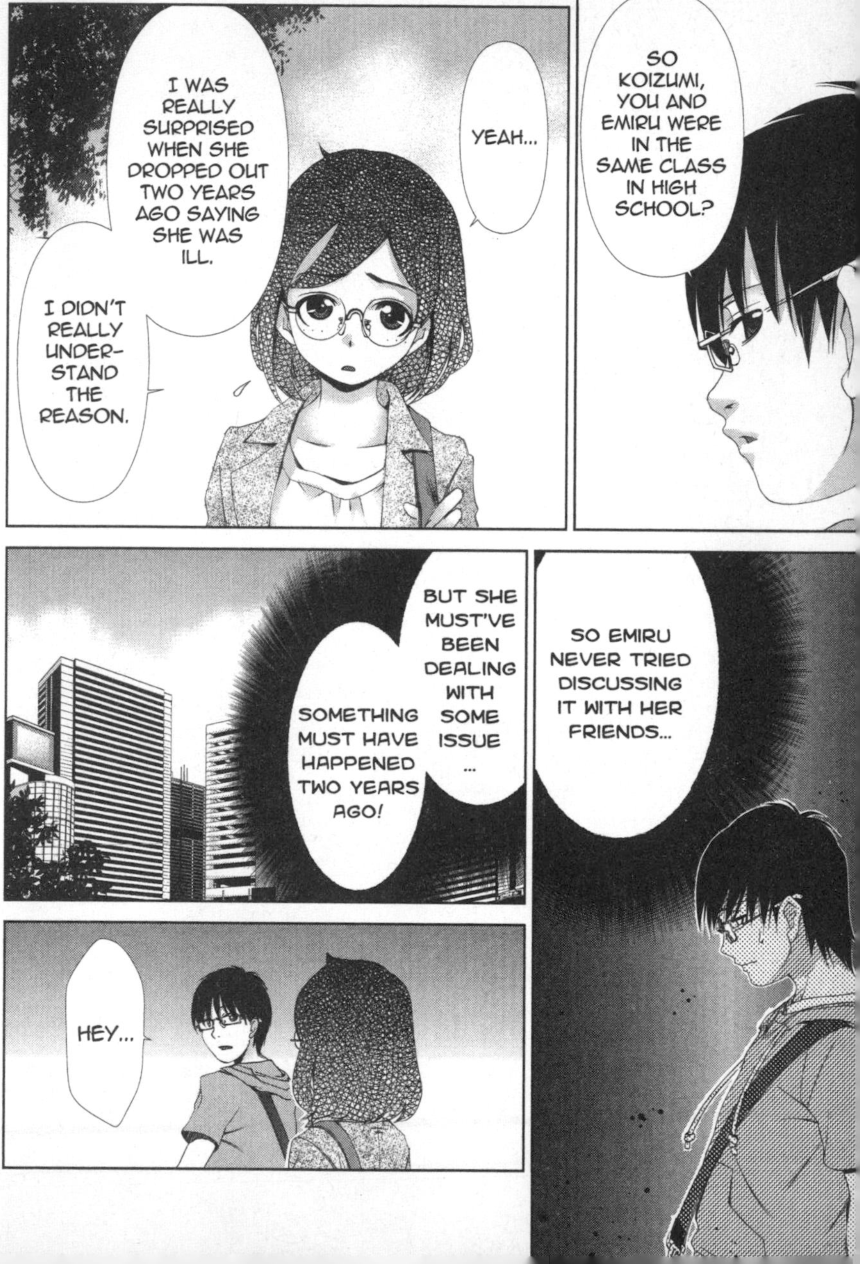
SO KOIZUMI, YOU AND EMIRU WERE IN THE SAME CLASS IN HIGH SCHOOL?
YEAH...
I WAS REALLY SURPRISED WHEN SHE DROPPED OUT TWO YEARS AGO SAYING SHE WAS ILL.
I DIDN'T REALLY UNDER-STAND THE REASON.
SO EMIRU NEVER TRIED DISCUSSING IT WITH HER FRIENDS...
BUT SHE MUST'VE BEEN DEALING WITH SOME ISSUE...
SOMETHING MUST HAVE HAPPENED TWO YEARS AGO!
HEY...

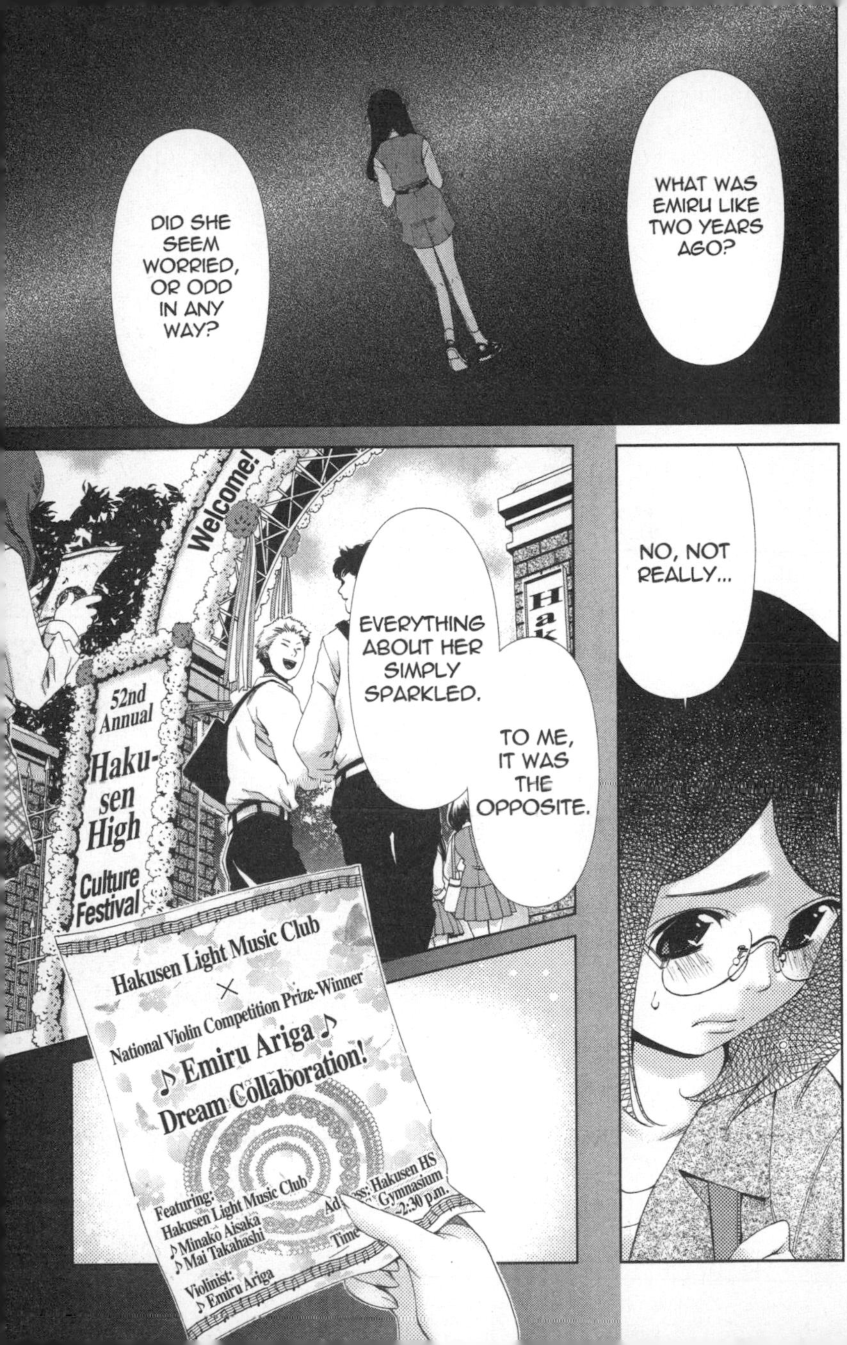
WHAT WAS EMIRU LIKE TWO YEARS AGO?
DID SHE SEEM WORRIED, OR ODD IN ANY WAY?
NO, NOT REALLY...
EVERYTHING ABOUT HER SIMPLY SPARKLED.
TO ME, IT WAS THE OPPOSITE.
Welcome!
52nd Annual Haku-sen High Culture Festival
Hakusen Light Music Club
×
National Violin Competition Prize-Winner
♪ Emiru Ariga ♪
Dream Collaboration!
Featuring:
Hakusen Light Music Club
♪ Minako Aisaka
♪ Mai Takahashi
Violinist:
♪ Emiru Ariga
Hakusen HS
Gymnasium
2:30 p.m.

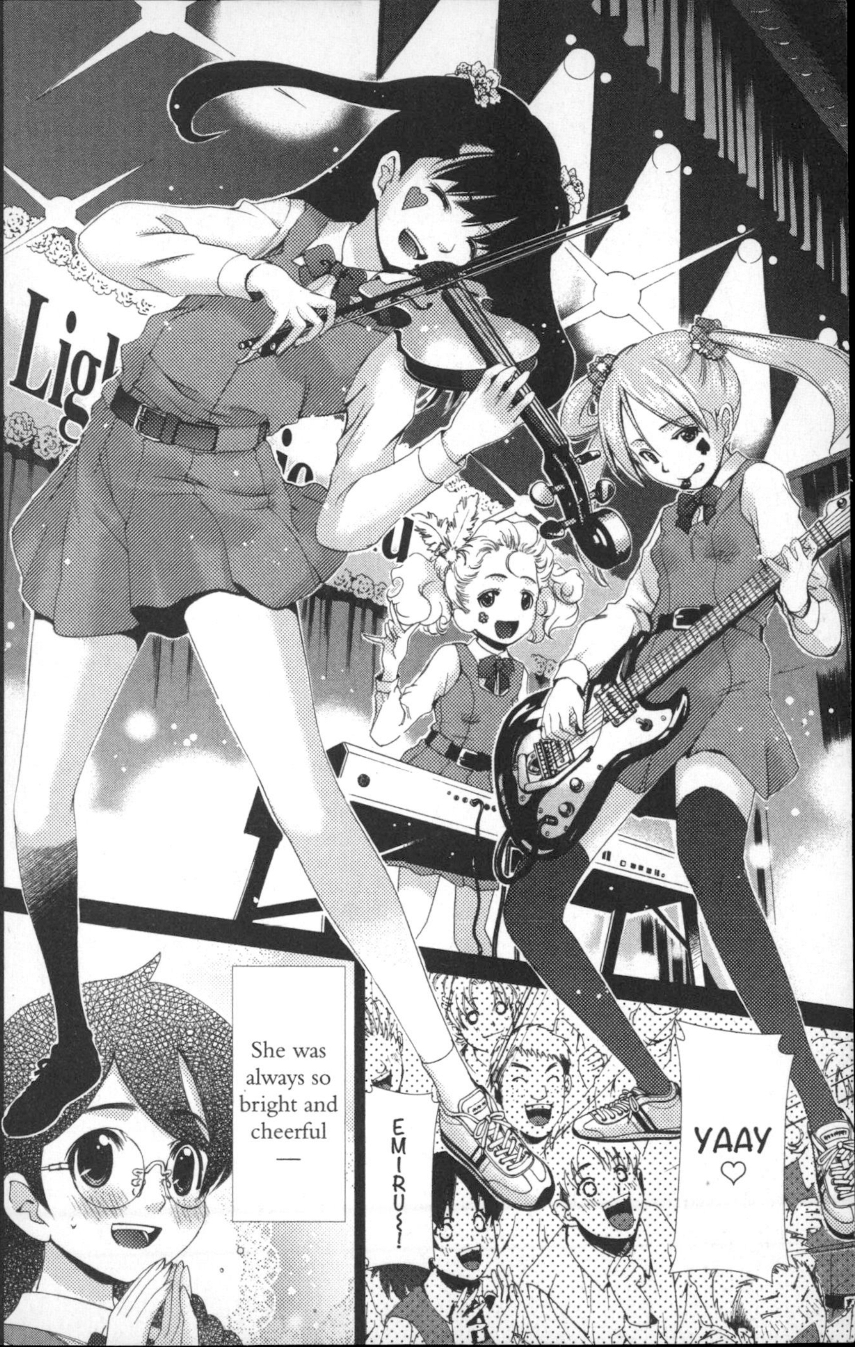
YAAY ♡
EMIRU~!
She was always so bright and cheerful —

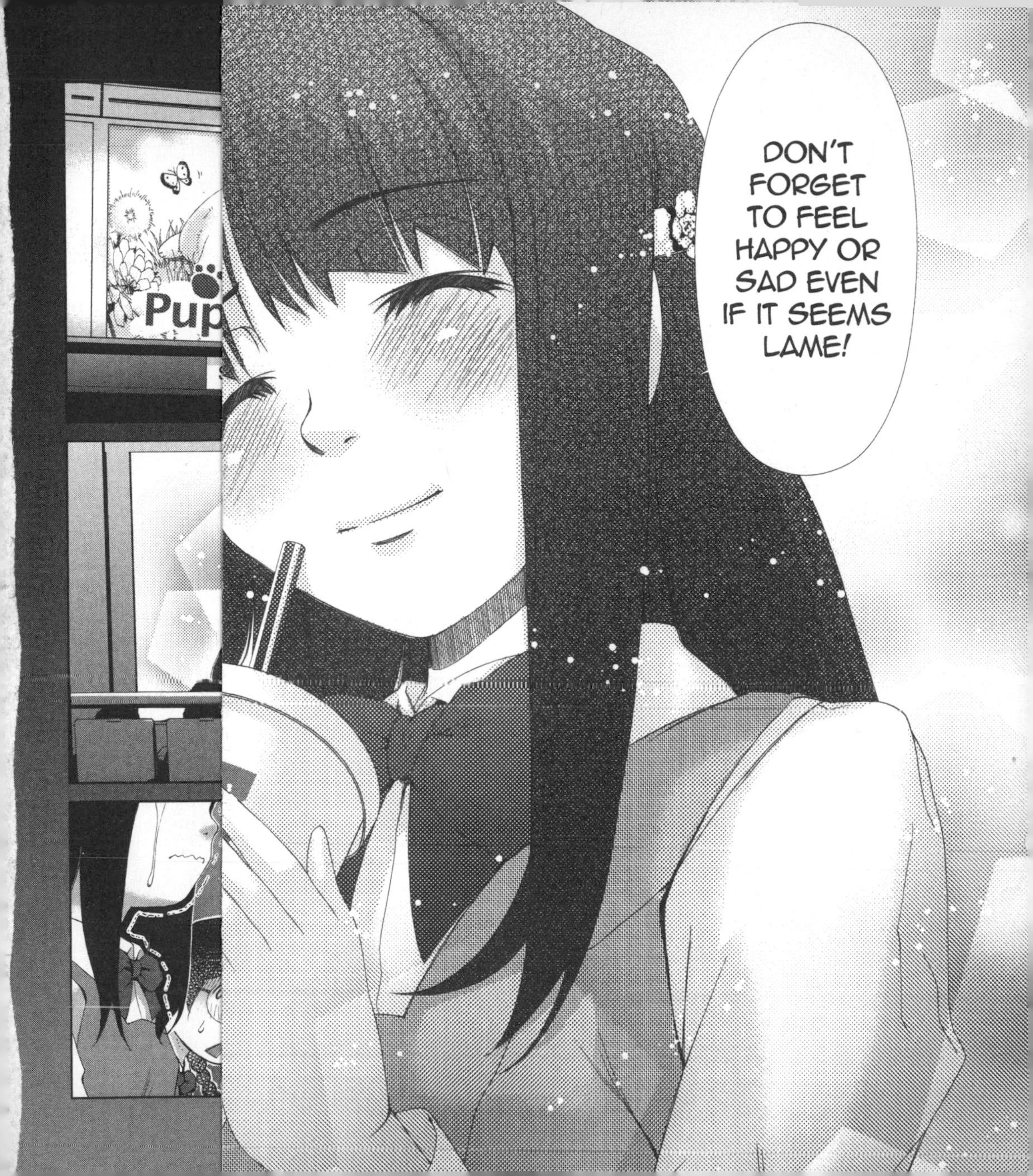
DON'T FORGET TO FEEL HAPPY OR SAD EVEN IF IT SEEMS LAME!

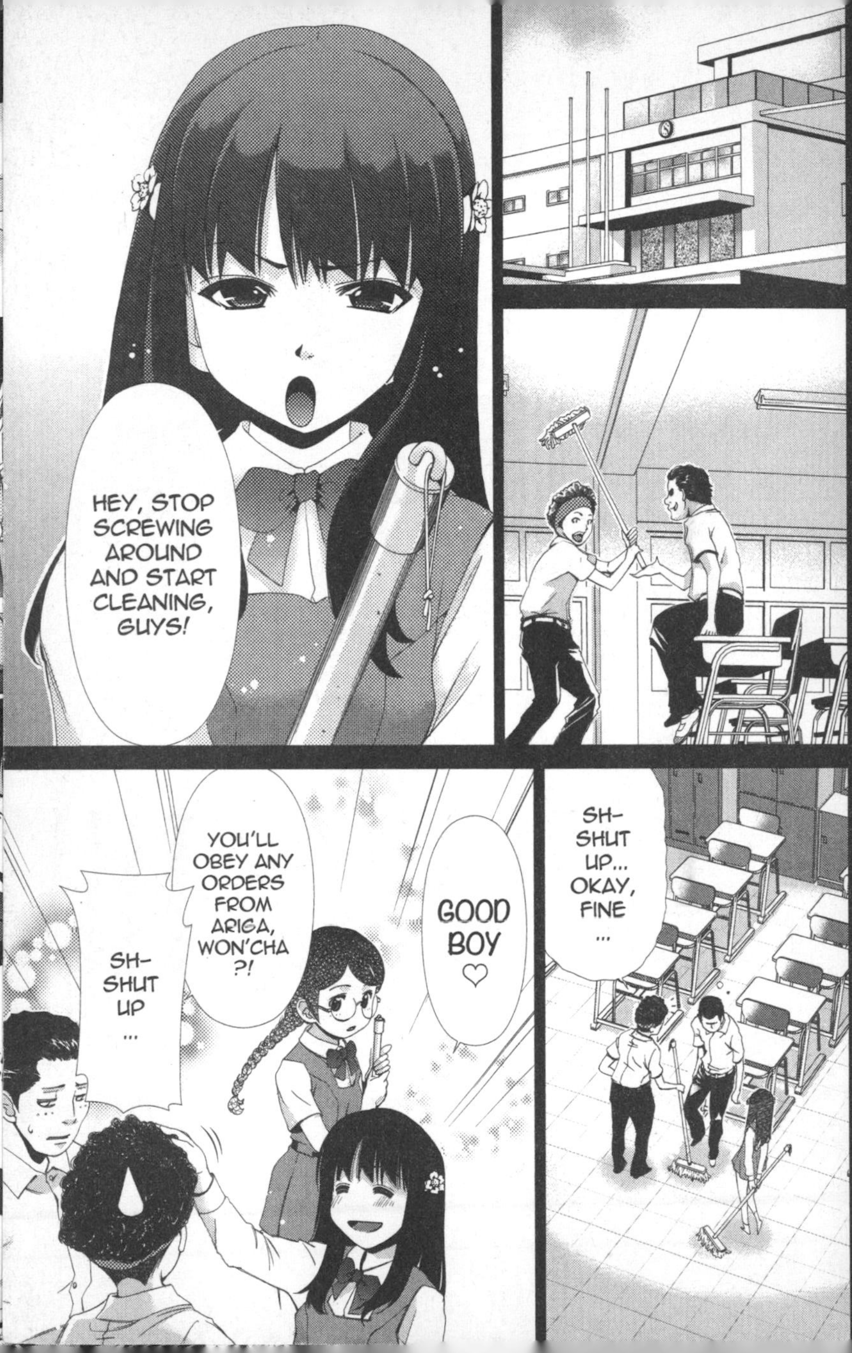
HEY, STOP SCREWING AROUND AND START CLEANING, GUYS!
SH-SHUT UP... OKAY, FINE ...
GOOD BOY ♥
YOU'LL OBEY ANY ORDERS FROM ARIGA, WON'CHA ?!
SH-SHUT UP ...

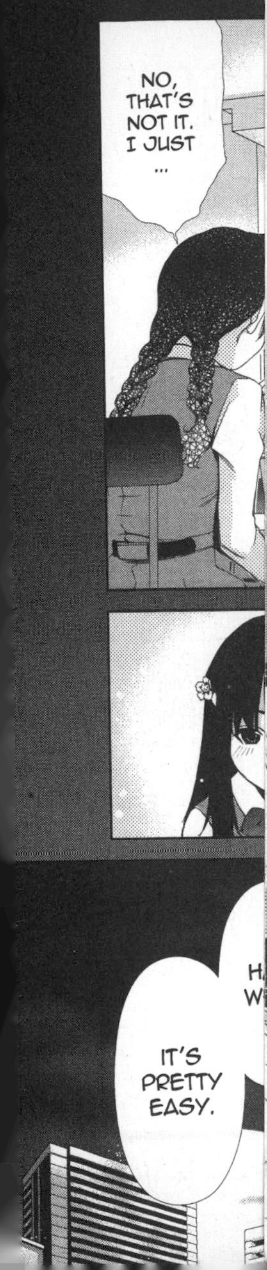
NO, THAT'S NOT IT. I JUST ...
IT'S PRETTY EASY.

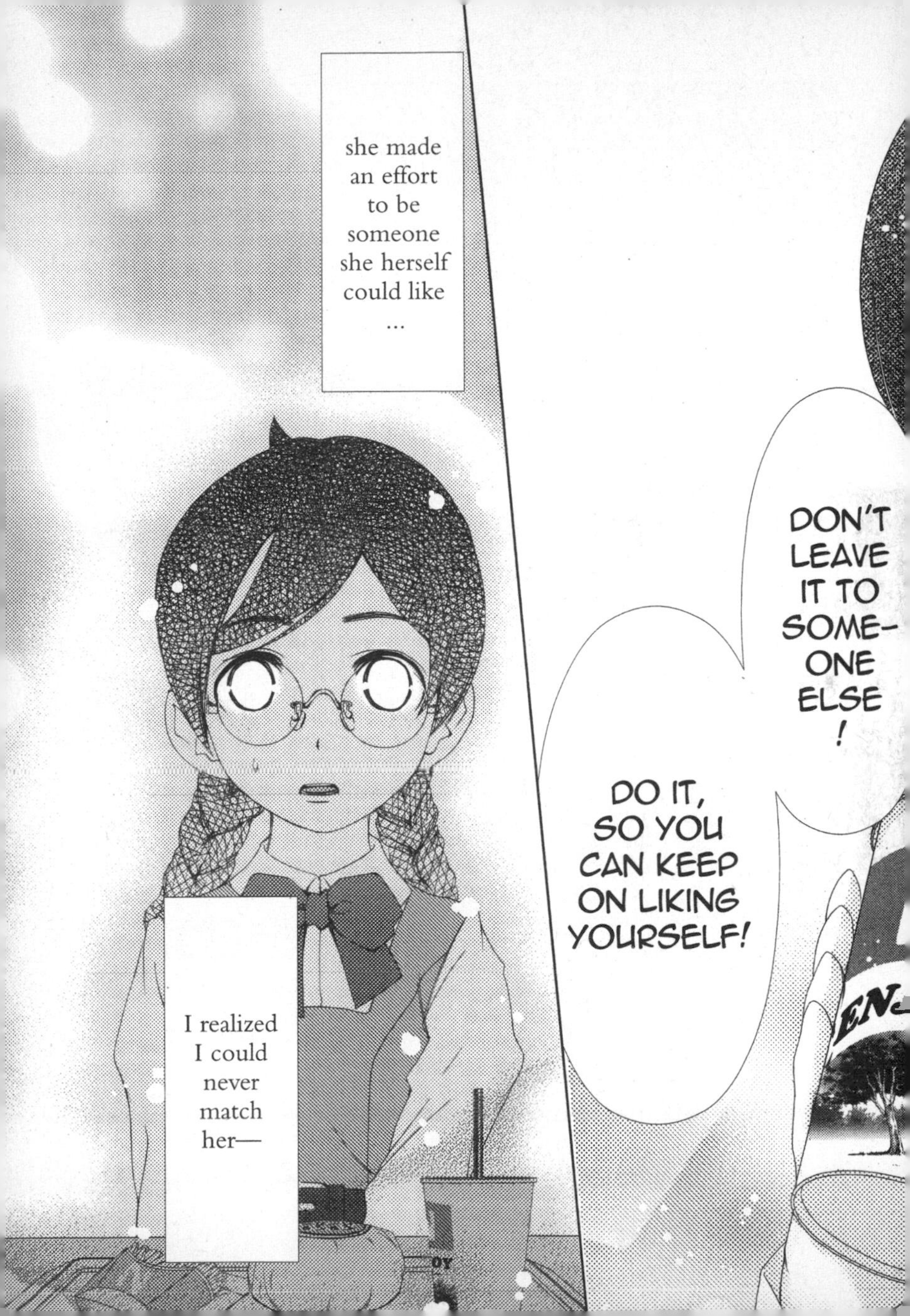
DON'T LEAVE IT TO SOME-ONE ELSE!
DO IT, SO YOU CAN KEEP ON LIKING YOURSELF!
she made an effort to be someone she herself could like ...
I realized I could never match her—

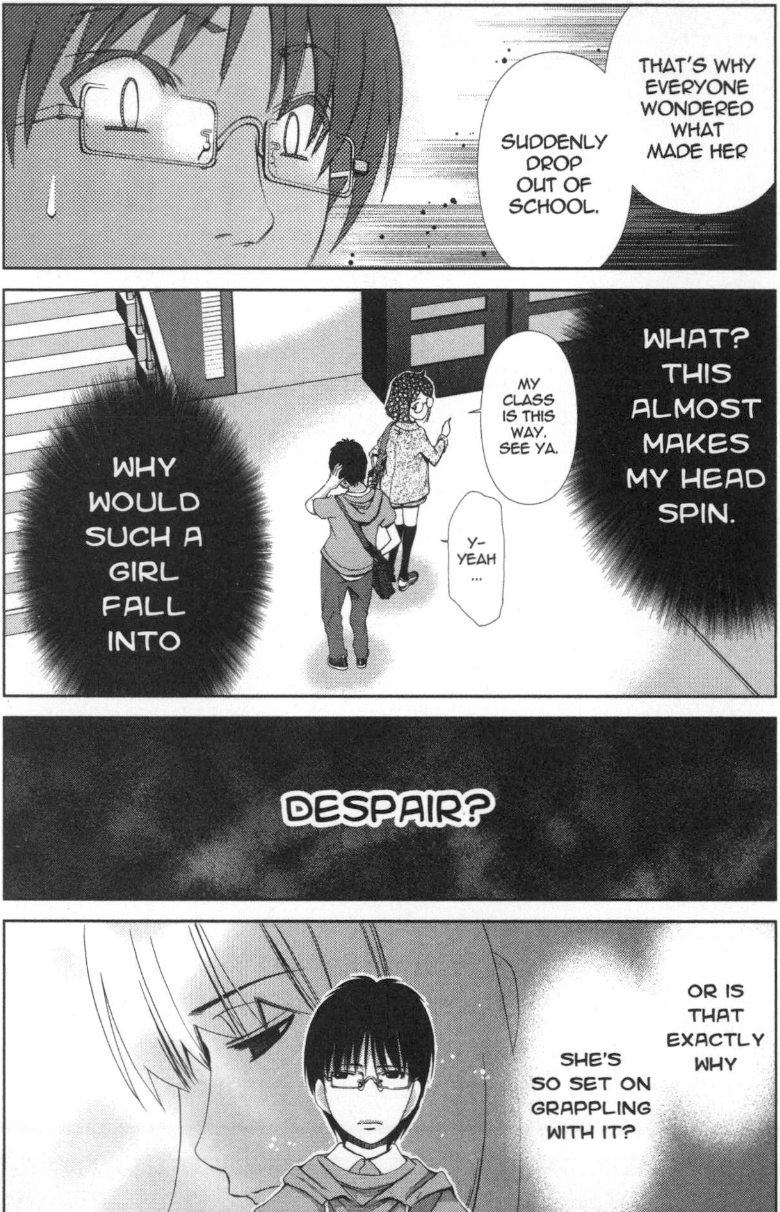
THAT'S WHY EVERYONE WONDERED WHAT MADE HER
SUDDENLY DROP OUT OF SCHOOL.
WHAT? THIS ALMOST MAKES MY HEAD SPIN.
MY CLASS IS THIS WAY. SEE YA.
Y-YEAH ...
WHY WOULD SUCH A GIRL FALL INTO
DESPAIR?
OR IS THAT EXACTLY WHY
SHE'S SO SET ON GRAPPLING WITH IT?

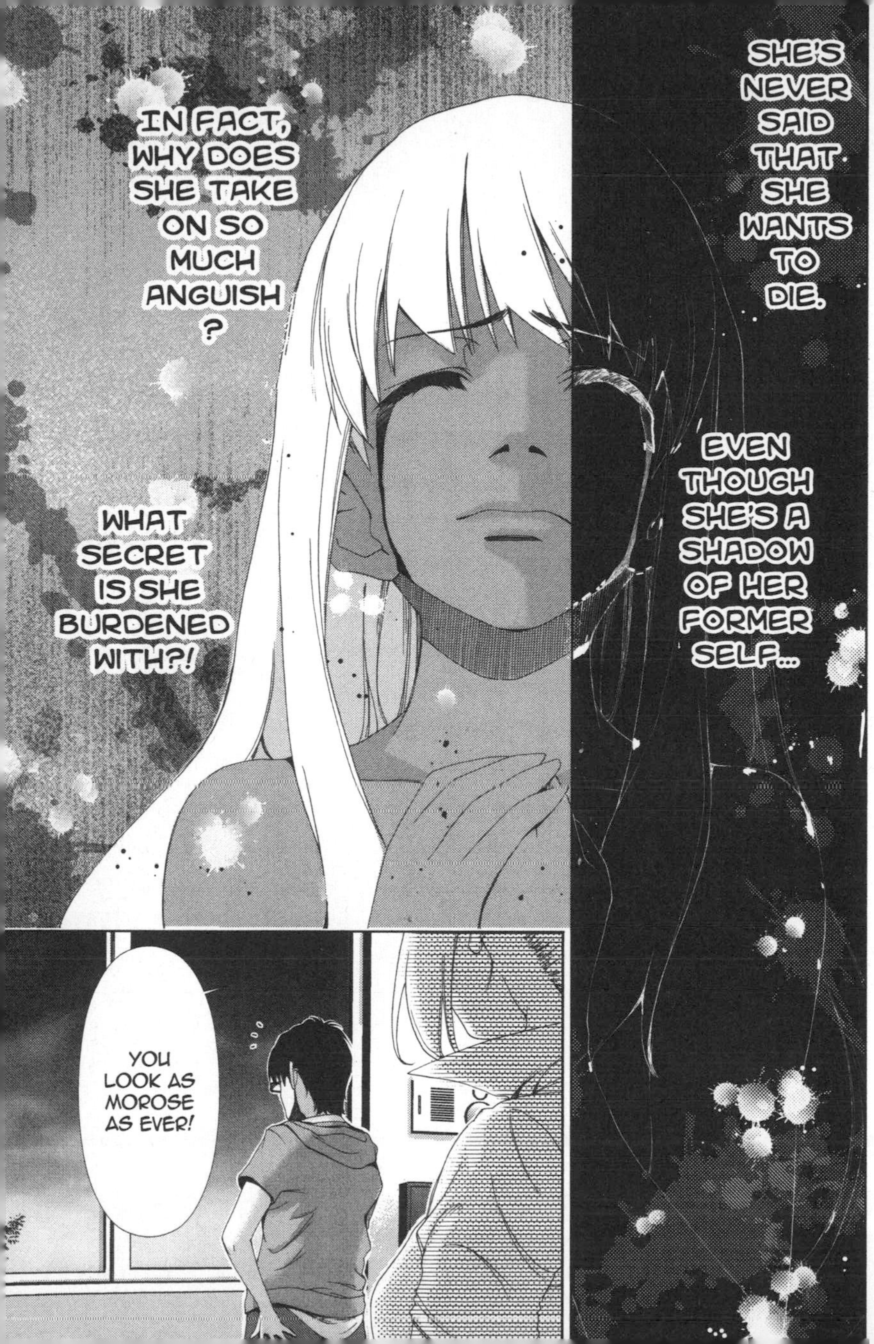
SHE'S NEVER SAID THAT SHE WANTS TO DIE.
EVEN THOUGH SHE'S A SHADOW OF HER FORMER SELF...
IN FACT, WHY DOES SHE TAKE ON SO MUCH ANGUISH?
WHAT SECRET IS SHE BURDENED WITH?!
YOU LOOK AS MOROSE AS EVER!

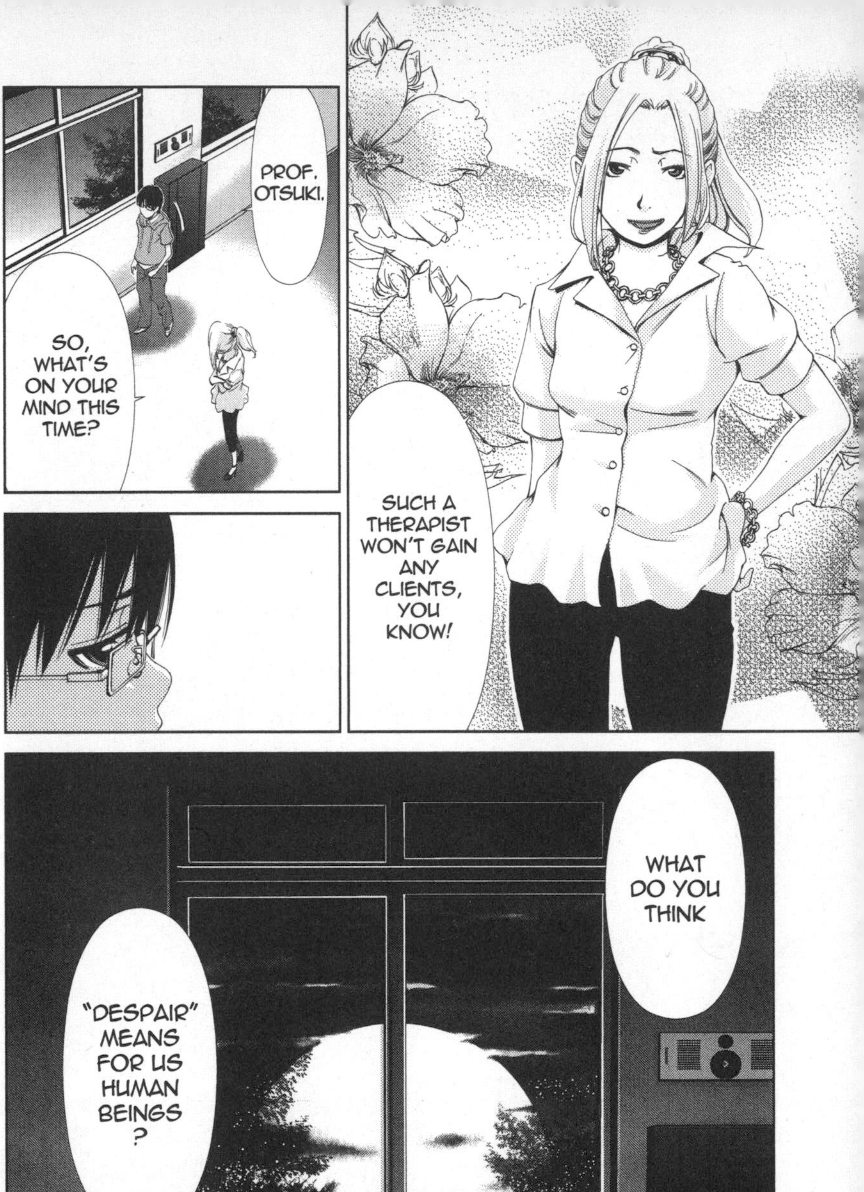
SUCH A THERAPIST WON'T GAIN ANY CLIENTS, YOU KNOW!
PROF. OTSUKI.
SO, WHAT'S ON YOUR MIND THIS TIME?
WHAT DO YOU THINK
"DESPAIR" MEANS FOR US HUMAN BEINGS ?

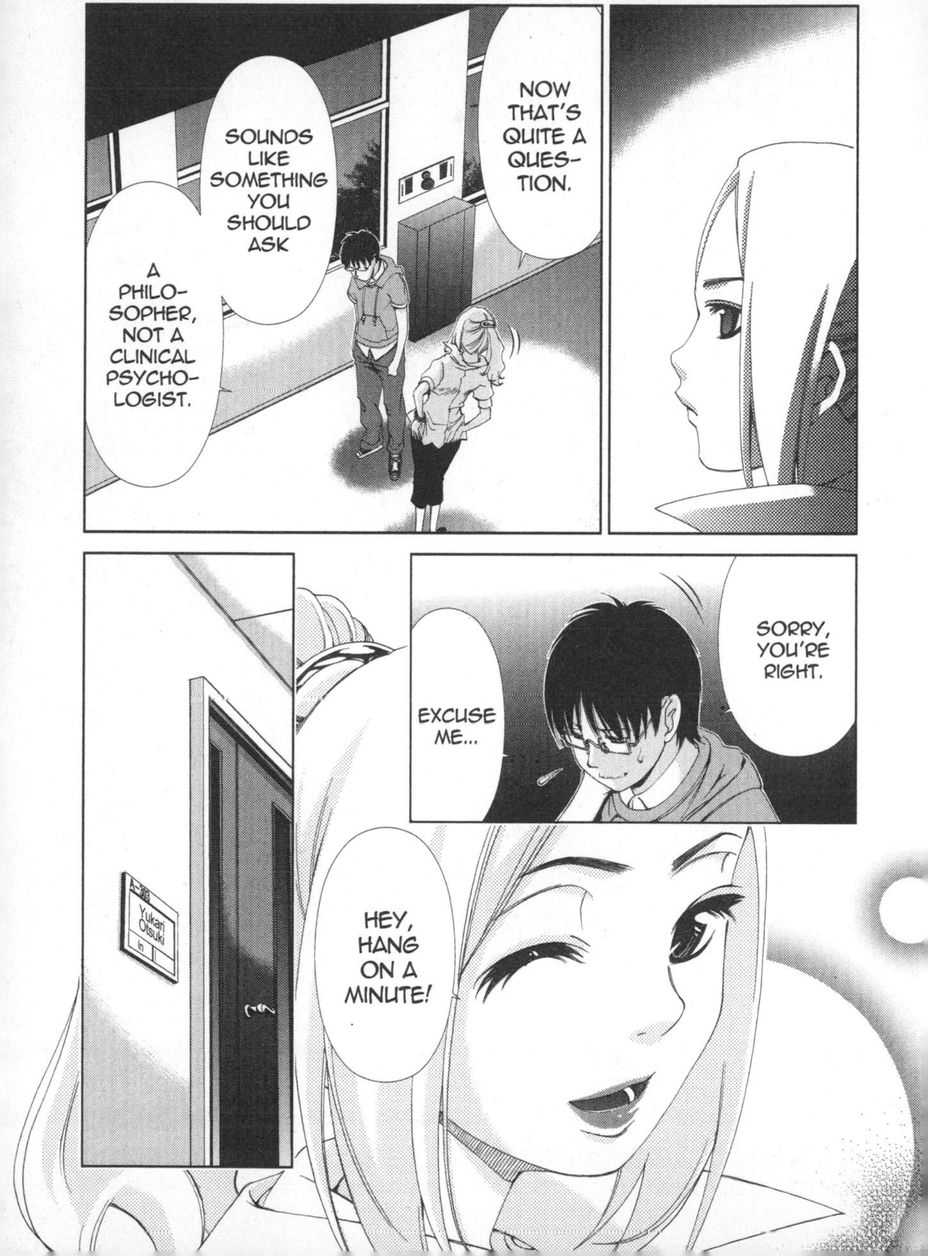
NOW THAT'S QUITE A QUES-TION.
SOUNDS LIKE SOMETHING YOU SHOULD ASK
A PHILO-SOPHER, NOT A CLINICAL PSYCHO-LOGIST.
SORRY, YOU'RE RIGHT.
EXCUSE ME...
HEY, HANG ON A MINUTE!
Yukari Otsuki
In

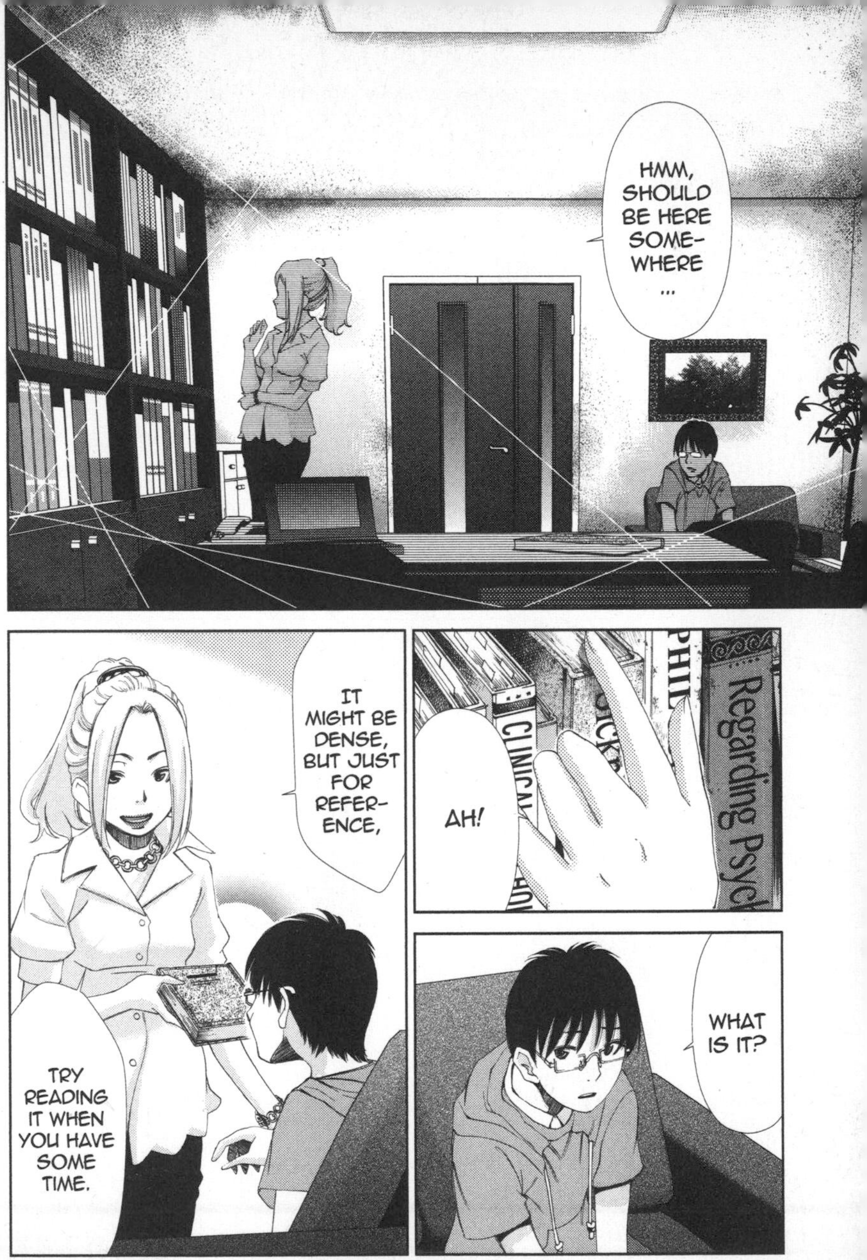
HMM, SHOULD BE HERE SOME-WHERE ...
Regarding Psych
AH!
WHAT IS IT?
IT MIGHT BE DENSE, BUT JUST FOR REFER-ENCE,
TRY READING IT WHEN YOU HAVE SOME TIME.

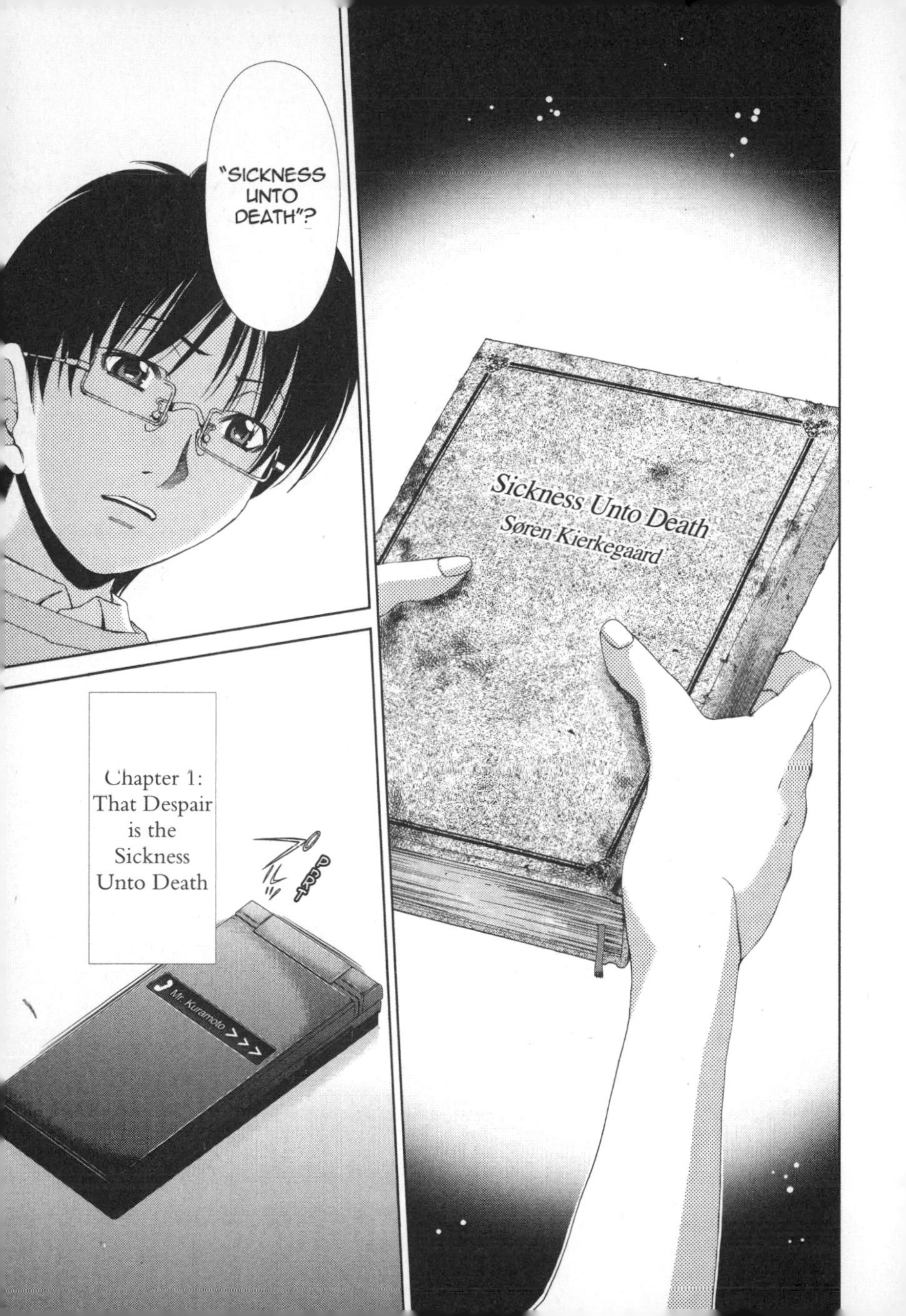
Sickness Unto Death
Søren Kierkegaard
"SICKNESS UNTO DEATH"?
Chapter 1: That Despair is the Sickness Unto Death
B-BRT
Mr. Kuramoto >>>

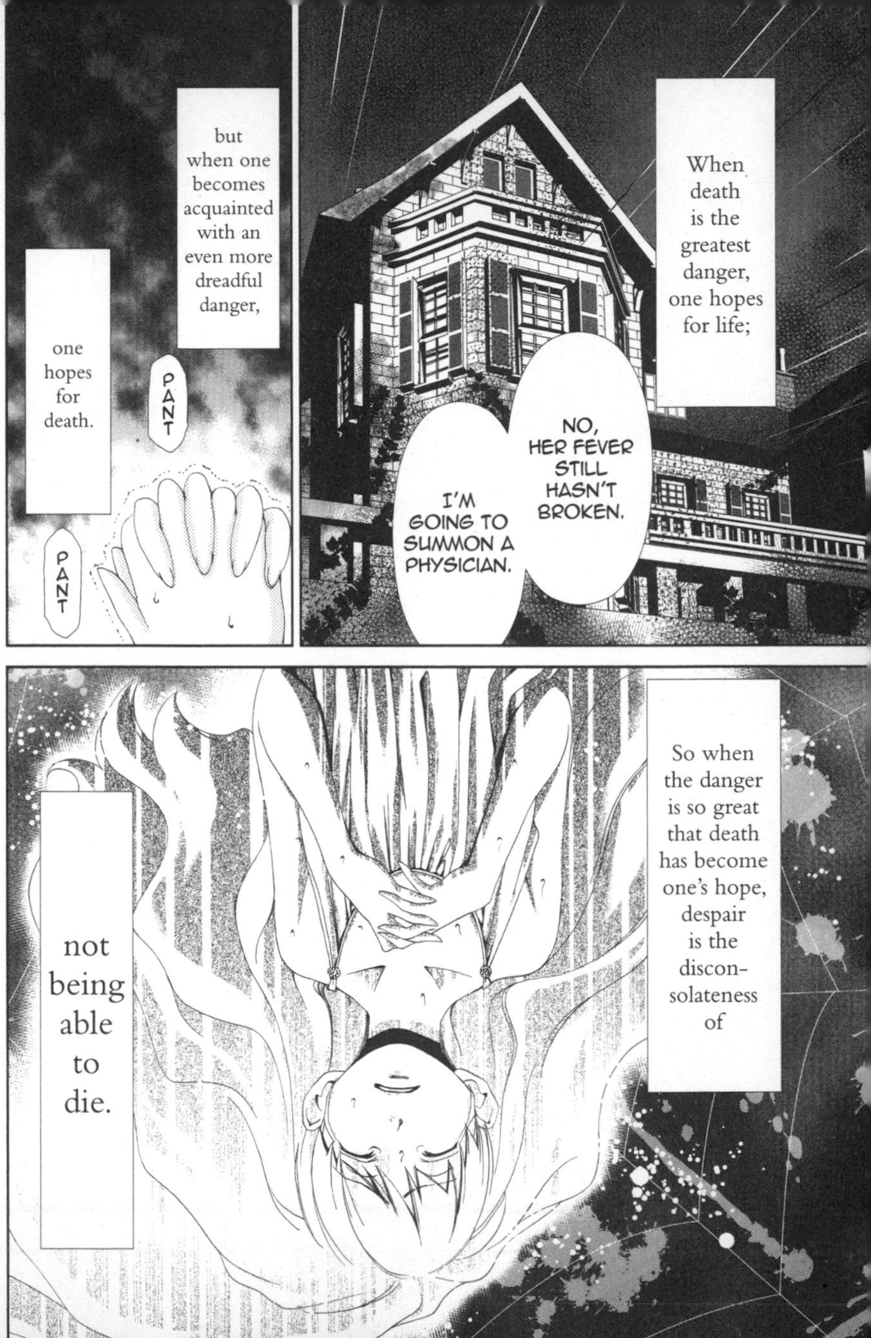
When death is the greatest danger, one hopes for life;
NO, HER FEVER STILL HASN'T BROKEN.
I'M GOING TO SUMMON A PHYSICIAN.
but when one becomes acquainted with an even more dreadful danger,
one hopes for death.
PANT
PANT
So when the danger is so great that death has become one's hope, despair is the discon-solateness of
not being able to die.

Chapter 8 Forbidden Line

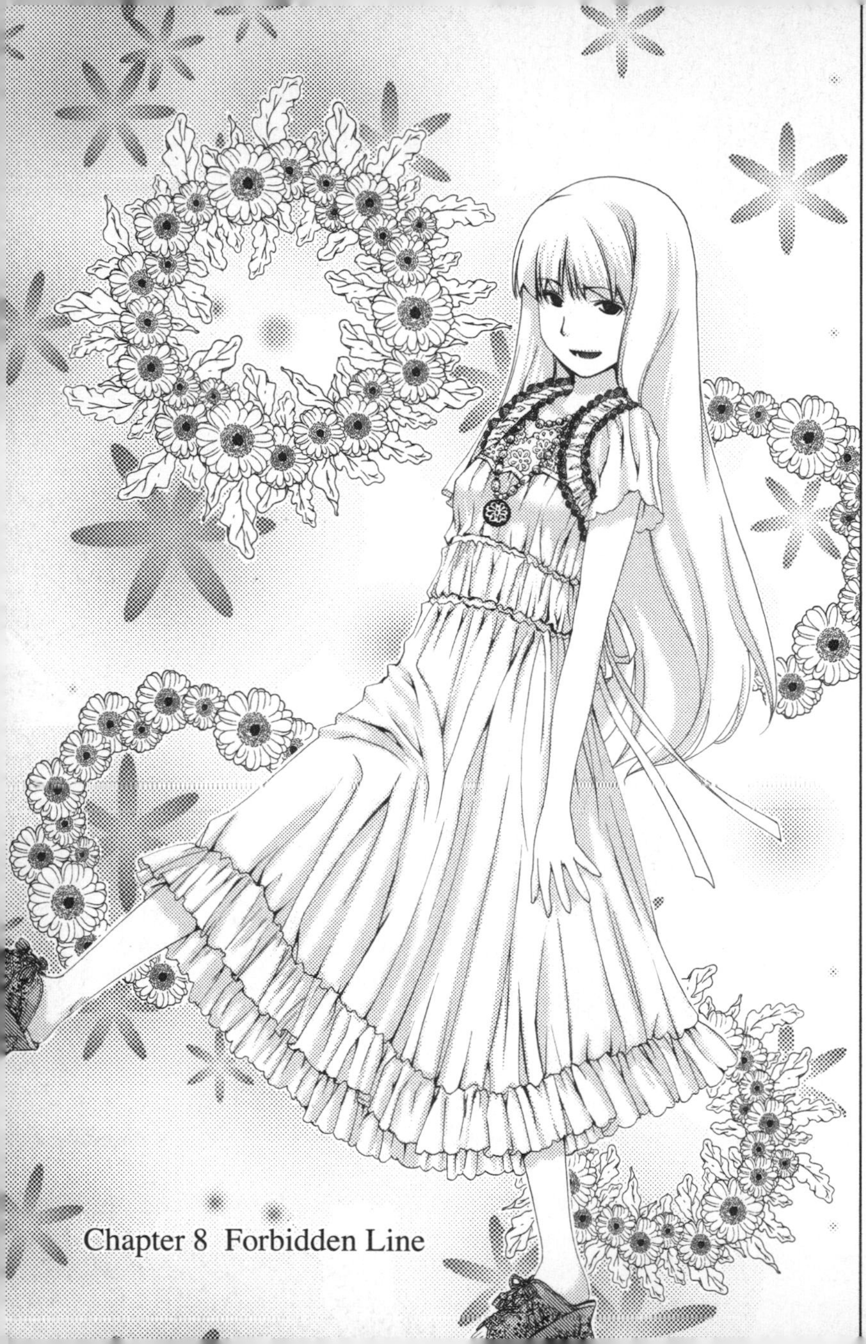

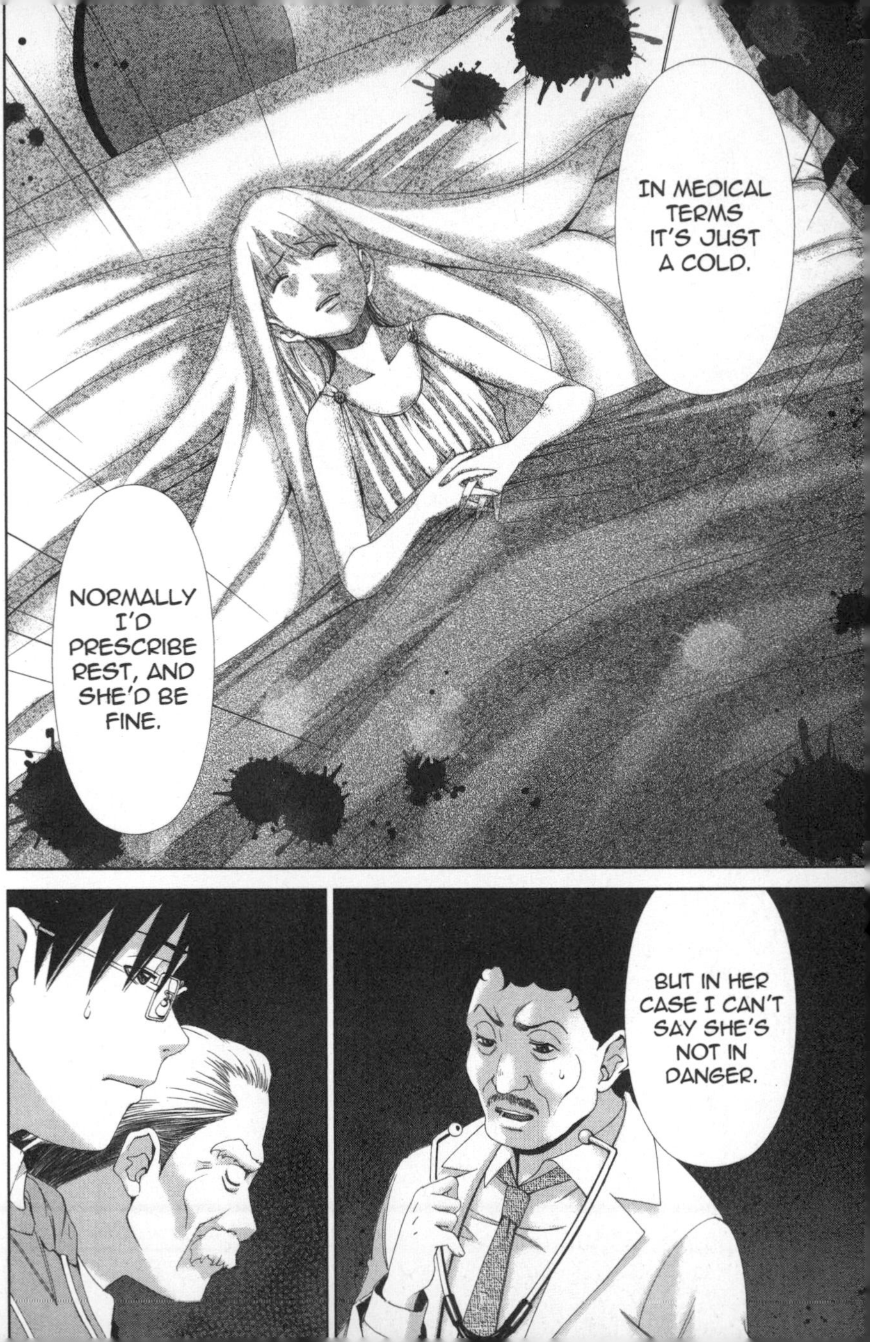
IN MEDICAL TERMS IT'S JUST A COLD.
NORMALLY I'D PRESCRIBE REST, AND SHE'D BE FINE.
BUT IN HER CASE I CAN'T SAY SHE'S NOT IN DANGER.

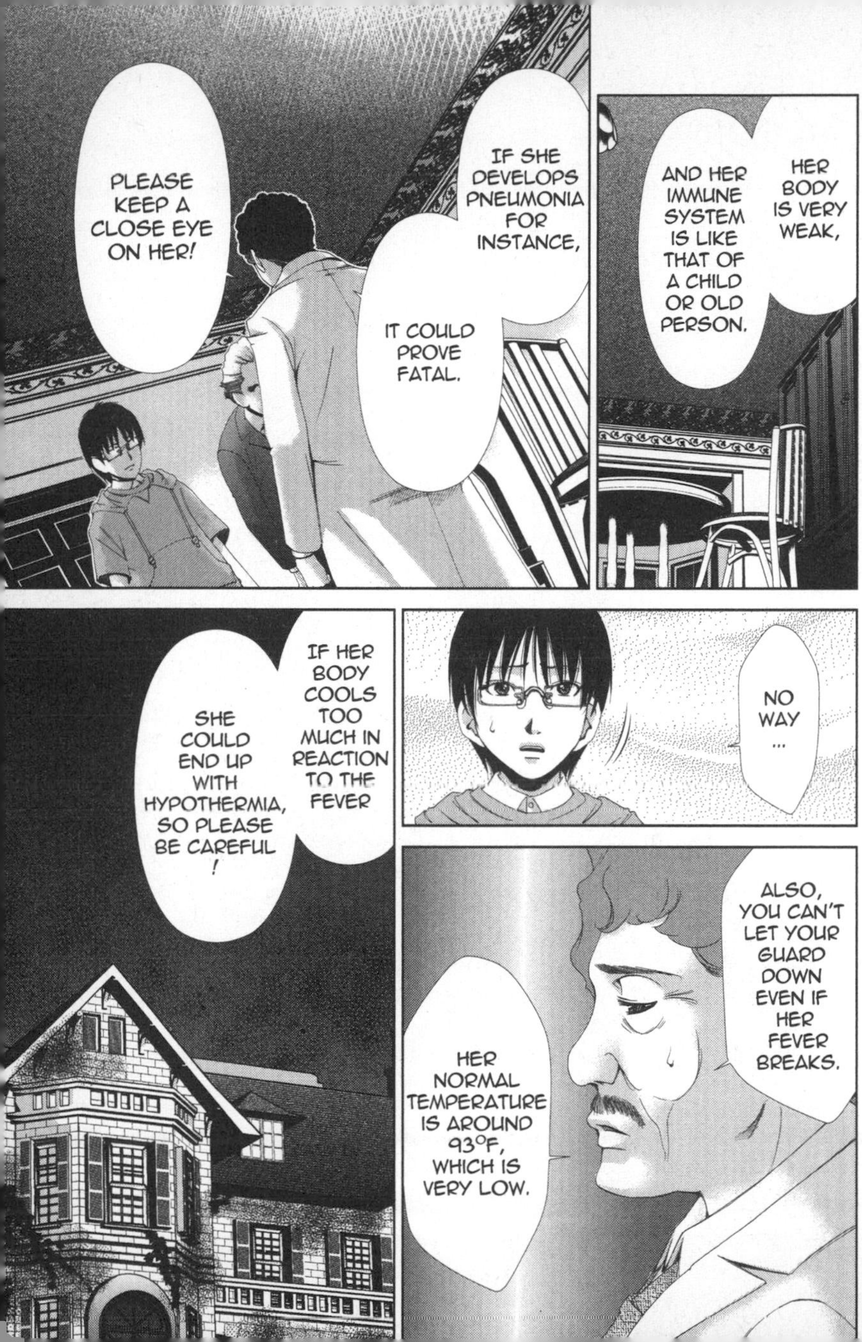
HER BODY IS VERY WEAK,
AND HER IMMUNE SYSTEM IS LIKE THAT OF A CHILD OR OLD PERSON.
IF SHE DEVELOPS PNEUMONIA FOR INSTANCE,
IT COULD PROVE FATAL.
PLEASE KEEP A CLOSE EYE ON HER!
NO WAY ...
ALSO, YOU CAN'T LET YOUR GUARD DOWN EVEN IF HER FEVER BREAKS.
HER NORMAL TEMPERATURE IS AROUND 93°F, WHICH IS VERY LOW.
IF HER BODY COOLS TOO MUCH IN REACTION TO THE FEVER
SHE COULD END UP WITH HYPOTHERMIA, SO PLEASE BE CAREFUL!

SHE HAS TO SUFFER THIS BADLY EVEN FROM A SIMPLE COLD.

here I am, utterly drawn to her.

It might be indecent of me to be thinking this,

Yet ...

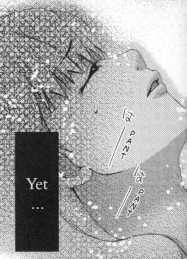

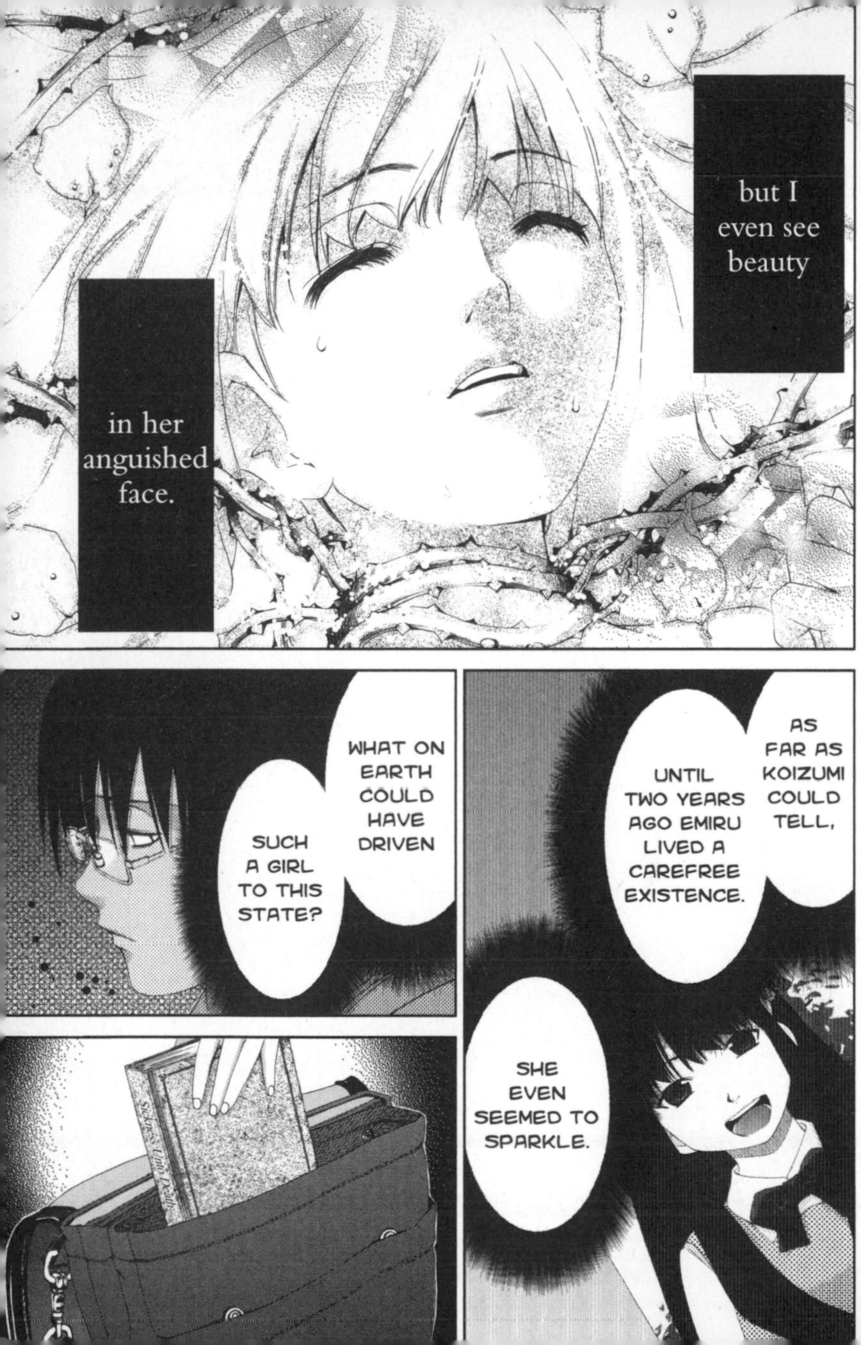
but I even see beauty
in her anguished face.
AS FAR AS KOIZUMI COULD TELL,
UNTIL TWO YEARS AGO EMIRU LIVED A CAREFREE EXISTENCE.
SHE EVEN SEEMED TO SPARKLE.
WHAT ON EARTH COULD HAVE DRIVEN
SUCH A GIRL TO THIS STATE?
Sickness Unto Death

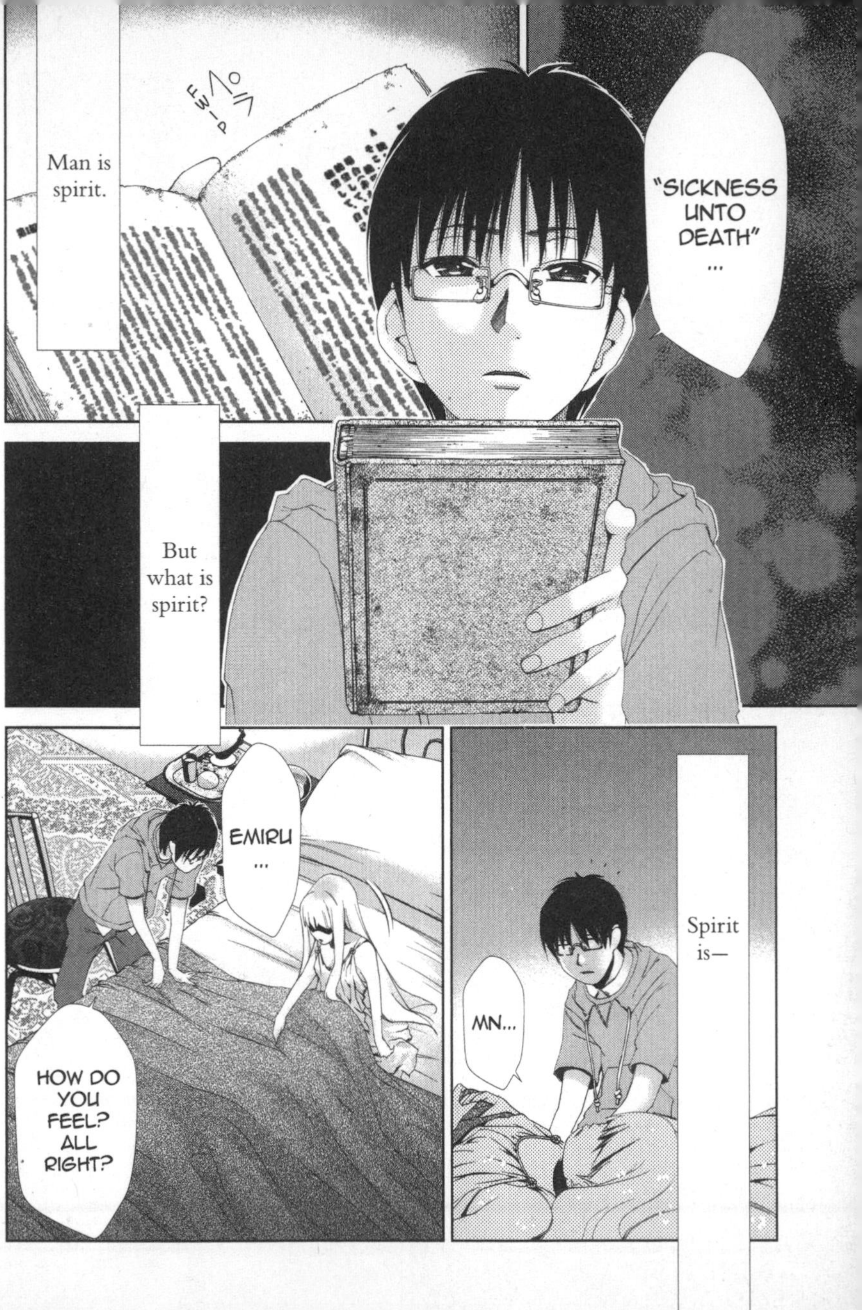
"SICKNESS UNTO DEATH" ...
FWIP
Man is spirit.
But what is spirit?
Spirit is—
MN...
EMIRU ...
HOW DO YOU FEEL? ALL RIGHT?

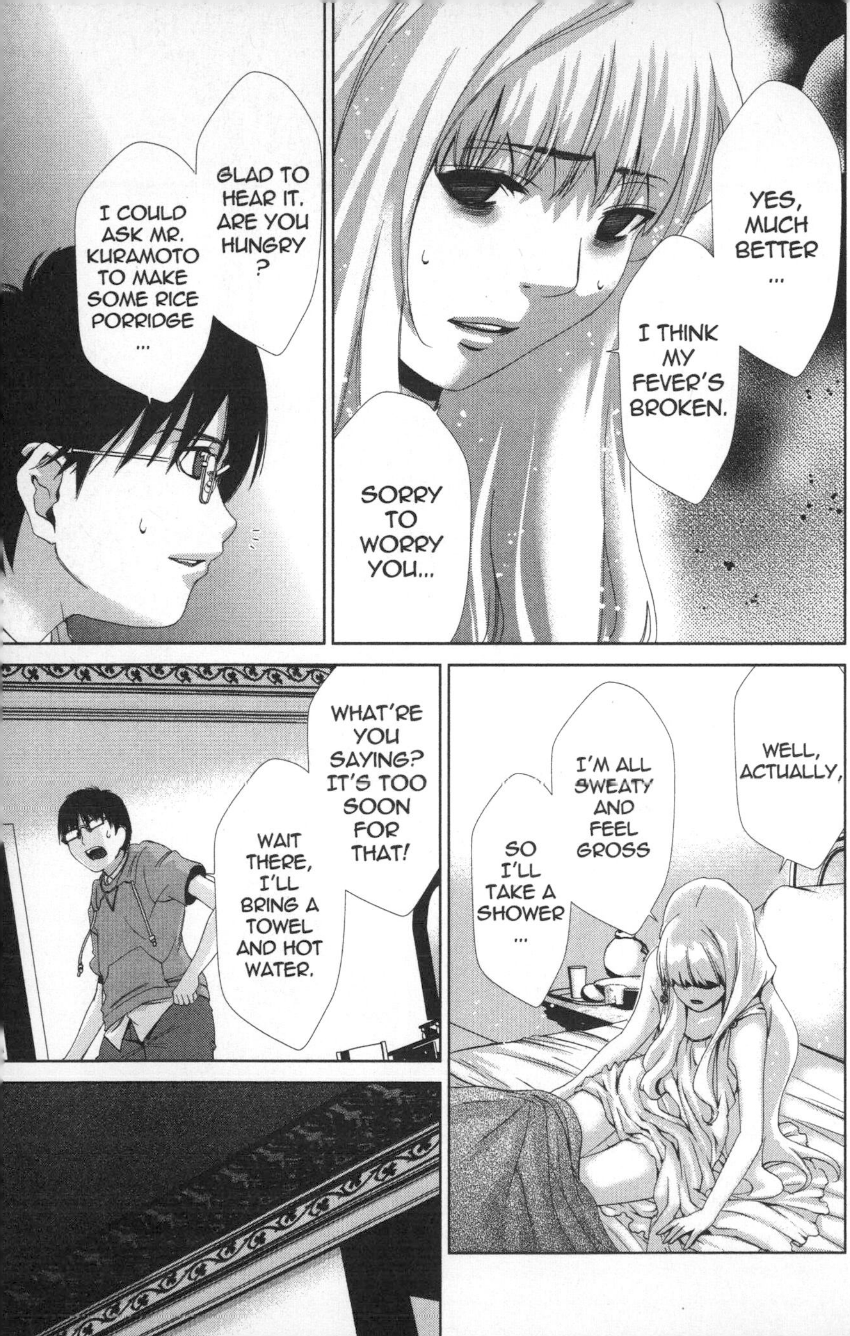
YES, MUCH BETTER ...
I THINK MY FEVER'S BROKEN.
SORRY TO WORRY YOU...
GLAD TO HEAR IT. ARE YOU HUNGRY ?
I COULD ASK MR. KURAMOTO TO MAKE SOME RICE PORRIDGE ...
WELL, ACTUALLY,
I'M ALL SWEATY AND FEEL GROSS
SO I'LL TAKE A SHOWER ...
WHAT'RE YOU SAYING? IT'S TOO SOON FOR THAT!
WAIT THERE, I'LL BRING A TOWEL AND HOT WATER.

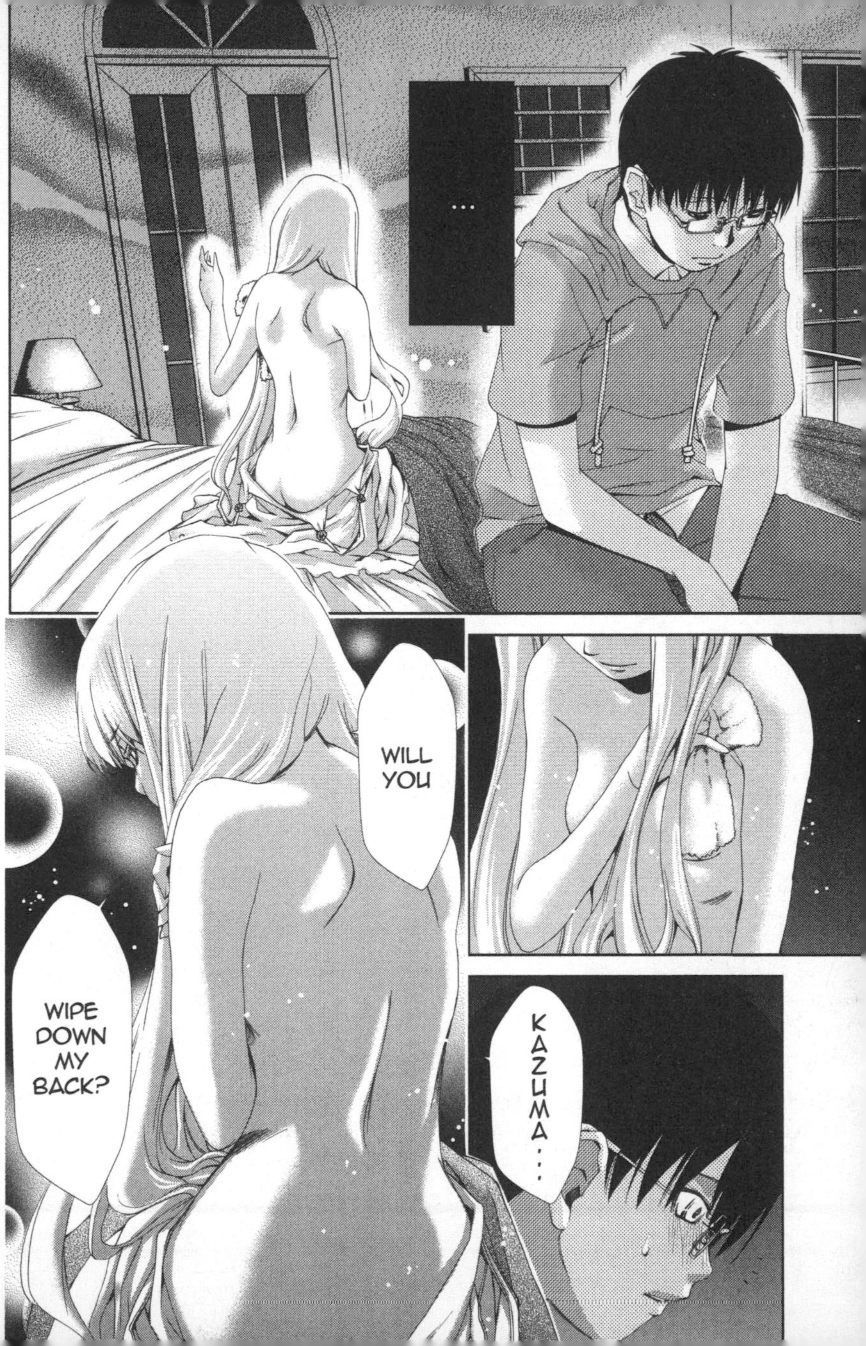
...
KAZUMA...
WILL YOU
WIPE DOWN MY BACK?

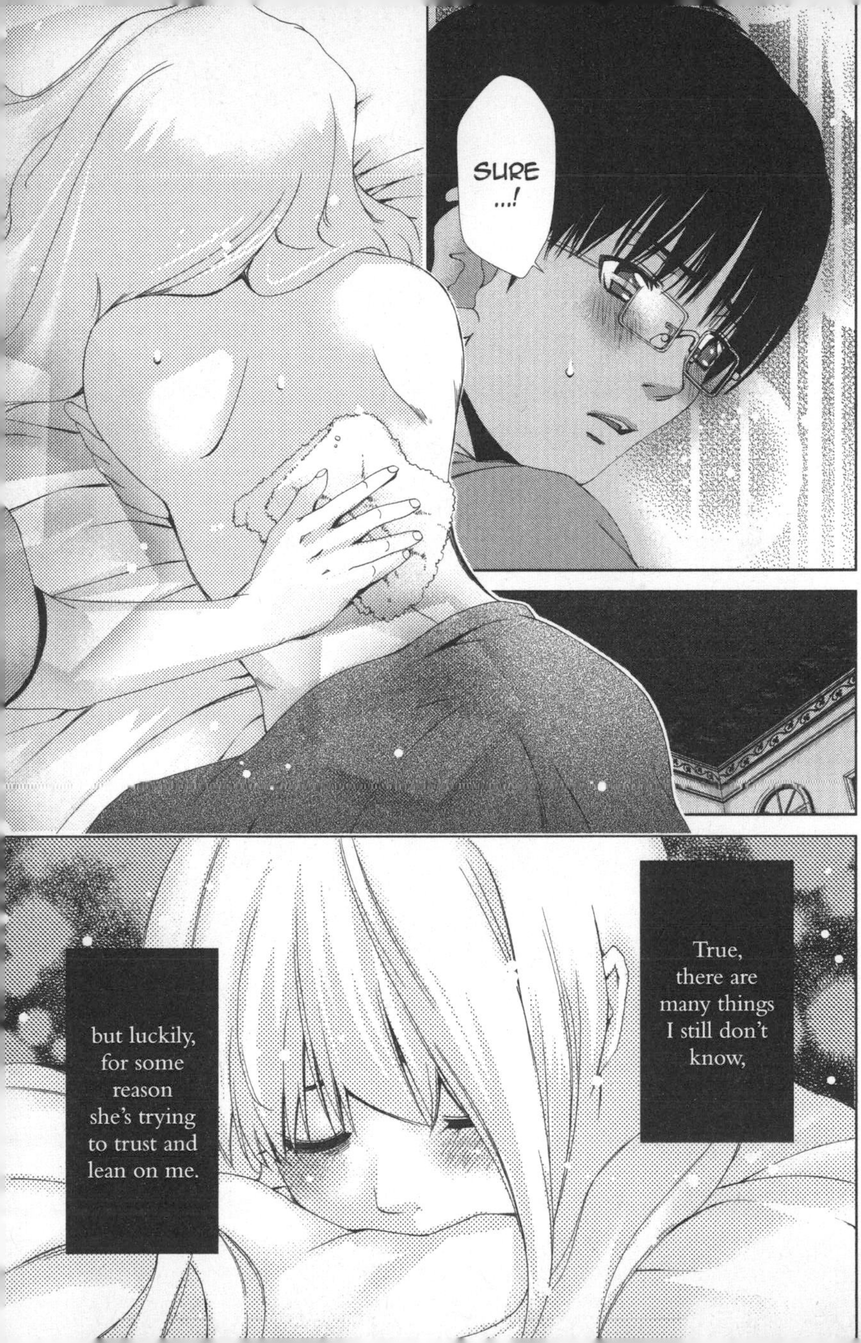
SURE ...!
True, there are many things I still don't know,
but luckily, for some reason she's trying to trust and lean on me.

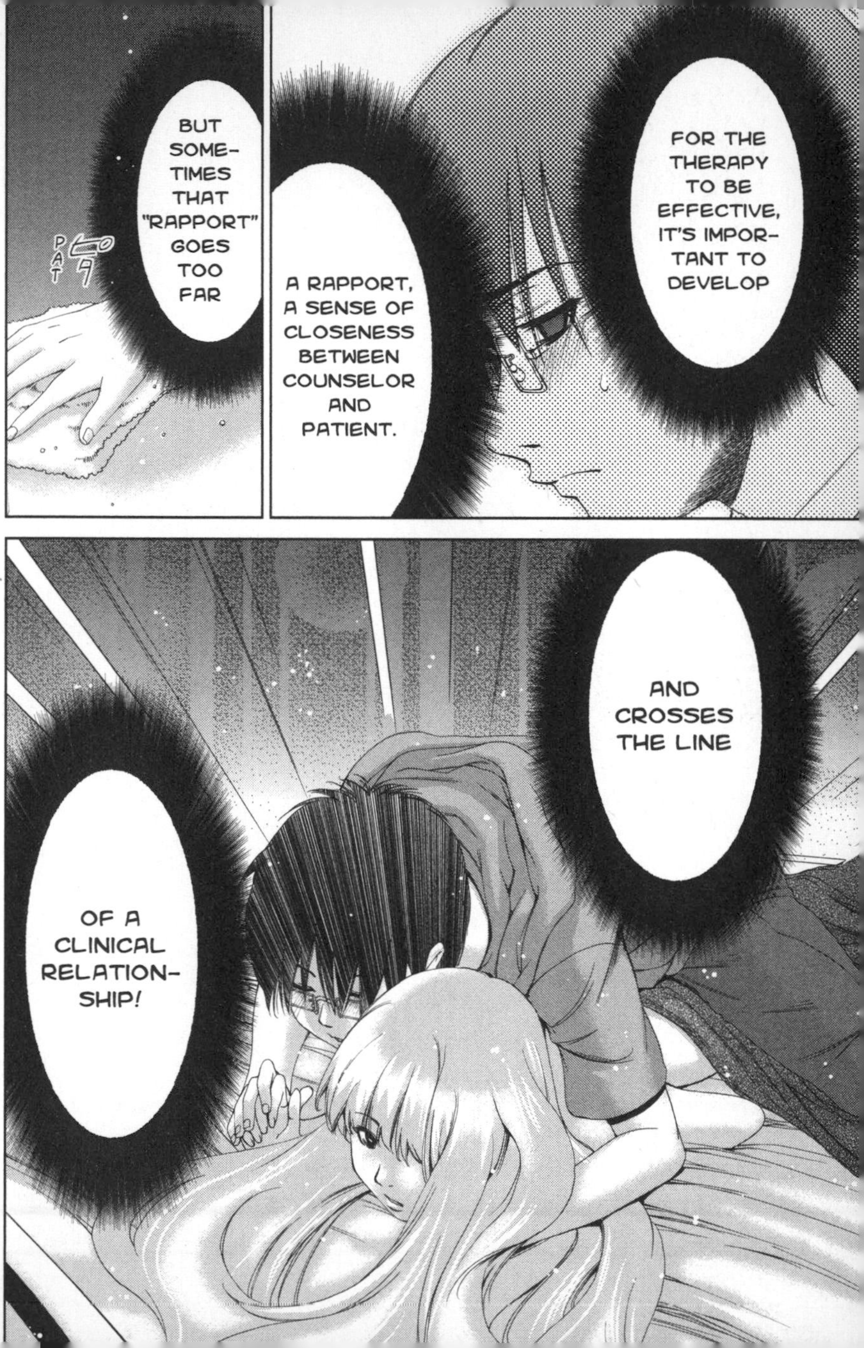
FOR THE THERAPY TO BE EFFECTIVE, IT'S IMPORTANT TO DEVELOP
A RAPPORT, A SENSE OF CLOSENESS BETWEEN COUNSELOR AND PATIENT.
PAT
BUT SOMETIMES THAT "RAPPORT" GOES TOO FAR
AND CROSSES THE LINE
OF A CLINICAL RELATIONSHIP!

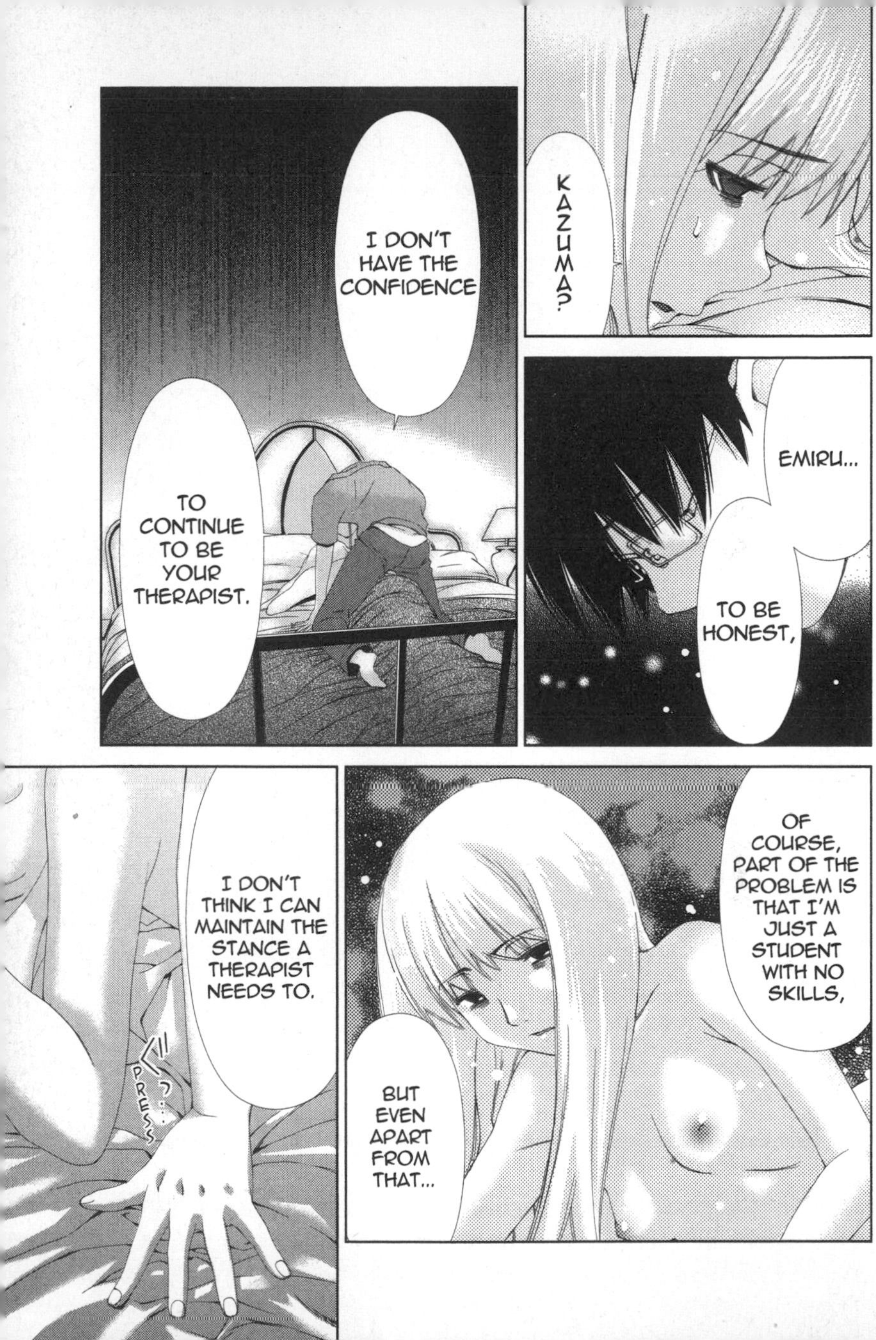
KAZUMA?
EMIRU...
TO BE HONEST,
I DON'T HAVE THE CONFIDENCE
TO CONTINUE TO BE YOUR THERAPIST.
OF COURSE, PART OF THE PROBLEM IS THAT I'M JUST A STUDENT WITH NO SKILLS,
BUT EVEN APART FROM THAT...
I DON'T THINK I CAN MAINTAIN THE STANCE A THERAPIST NEEDS TO.
PRESS

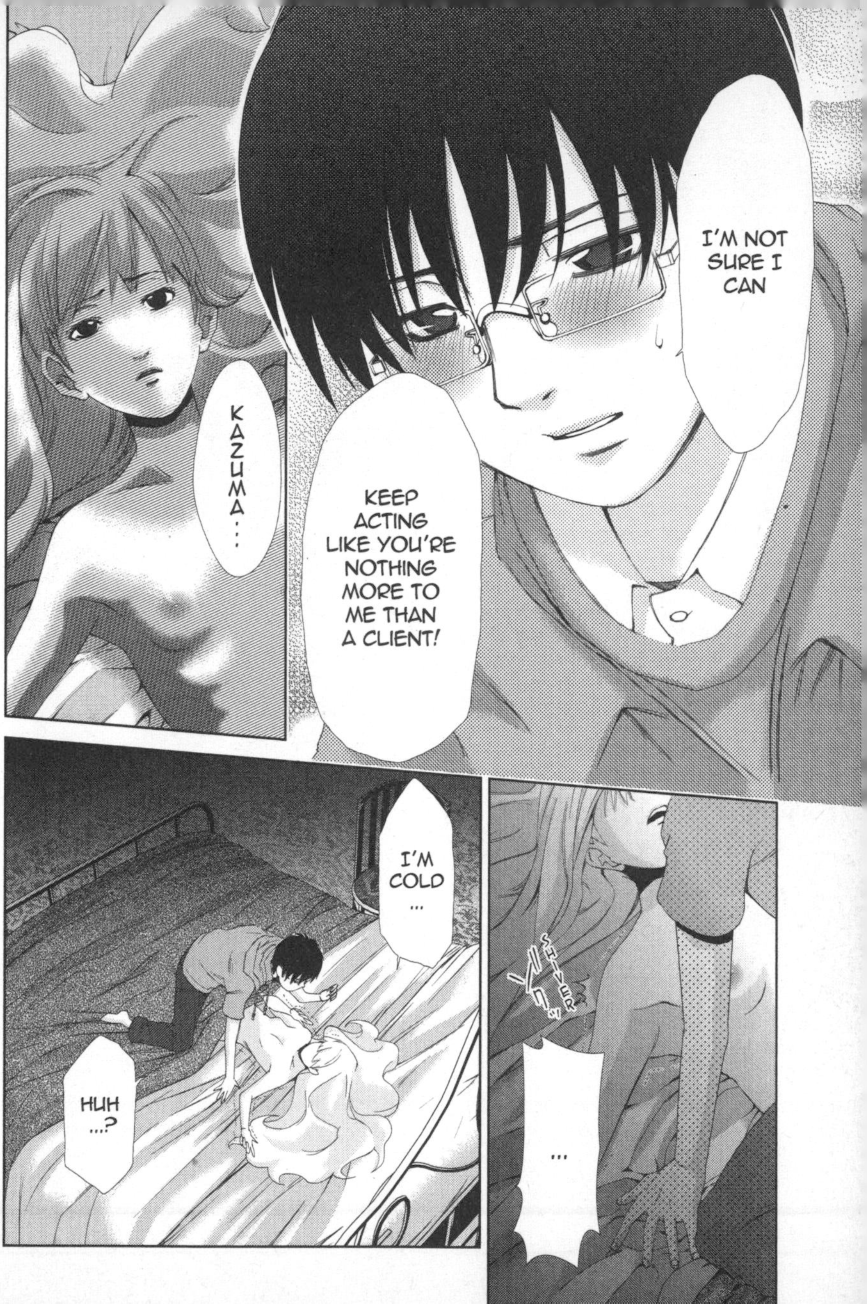
I'M NOT SURE I CAN
KEEP ACTING LIKE YOU'RE NOTHING MORE TO ME THAN A CLIENT!
KAZUMA...
SHIVER
...
I'M COLD ...
HUH ...?

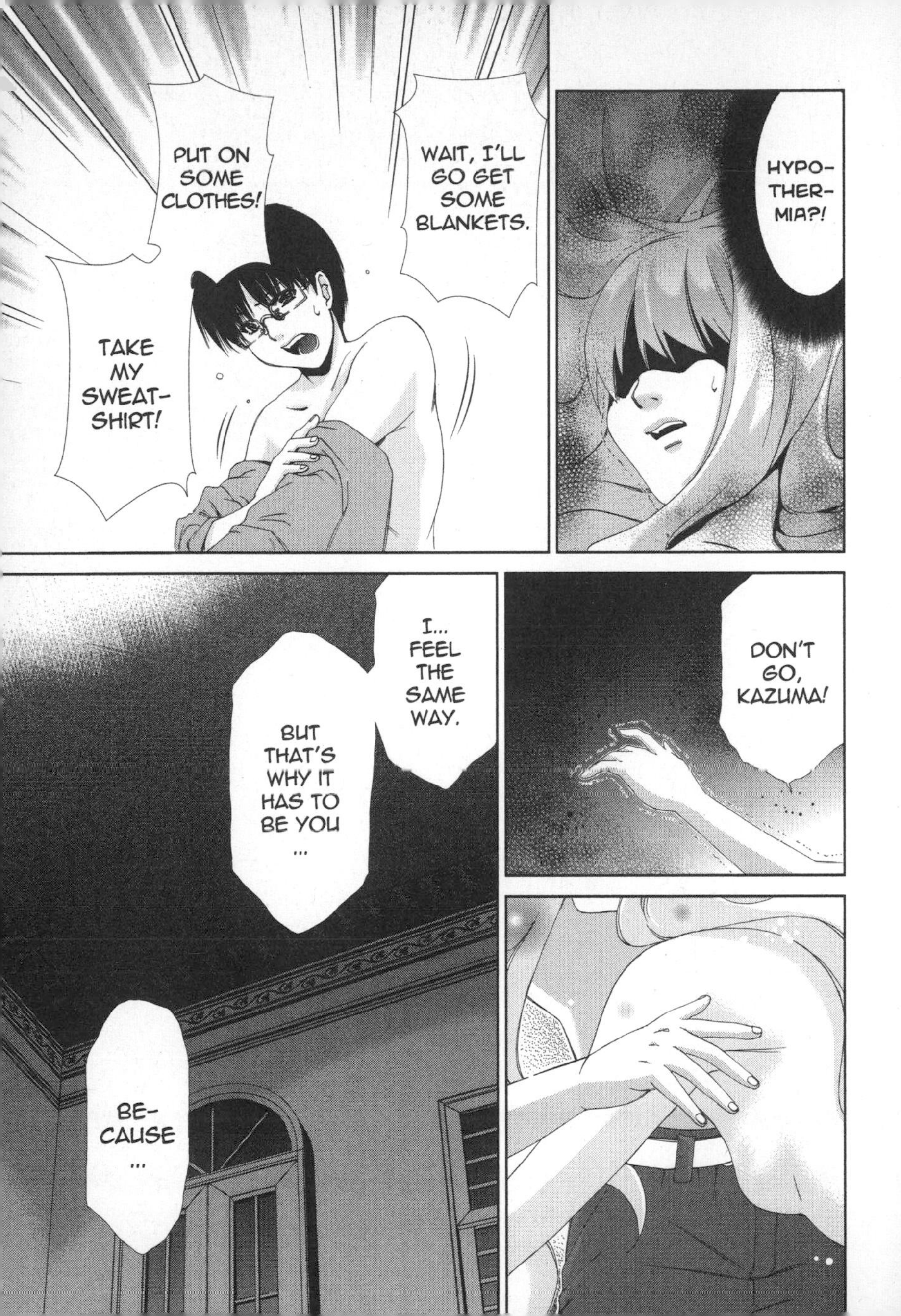
HYPO-
THER-
MIA?!
WAIT, I'LL GO GET SOME BLANKETS.
PUT ON SOME CLOTHES!
TAKE MY SWEAT-SHIRT!
DON'T GO, KAZUMA!
I... FEEL THE SAME WAY.
BUT THAT'S WHY IT HAS TO BE YOU ...
BE-CAUSE ...

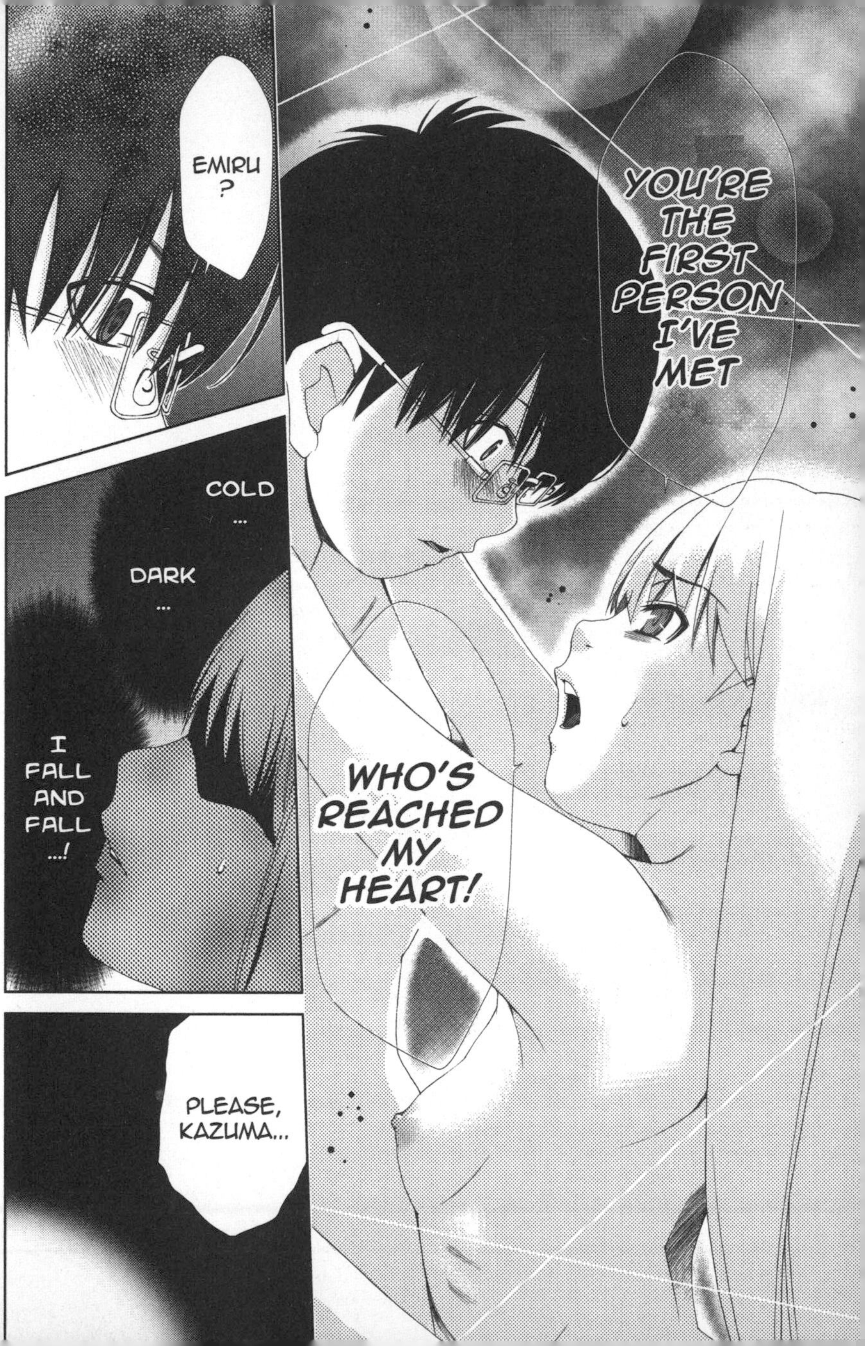
YOU'RE THE FIRST PERSON I'VE MET
WHO'S REACHED MY HEART!
EMIRU?
COLD...
DARK...
I FALL AND FALL...!
PLEASE, KAZUMA...

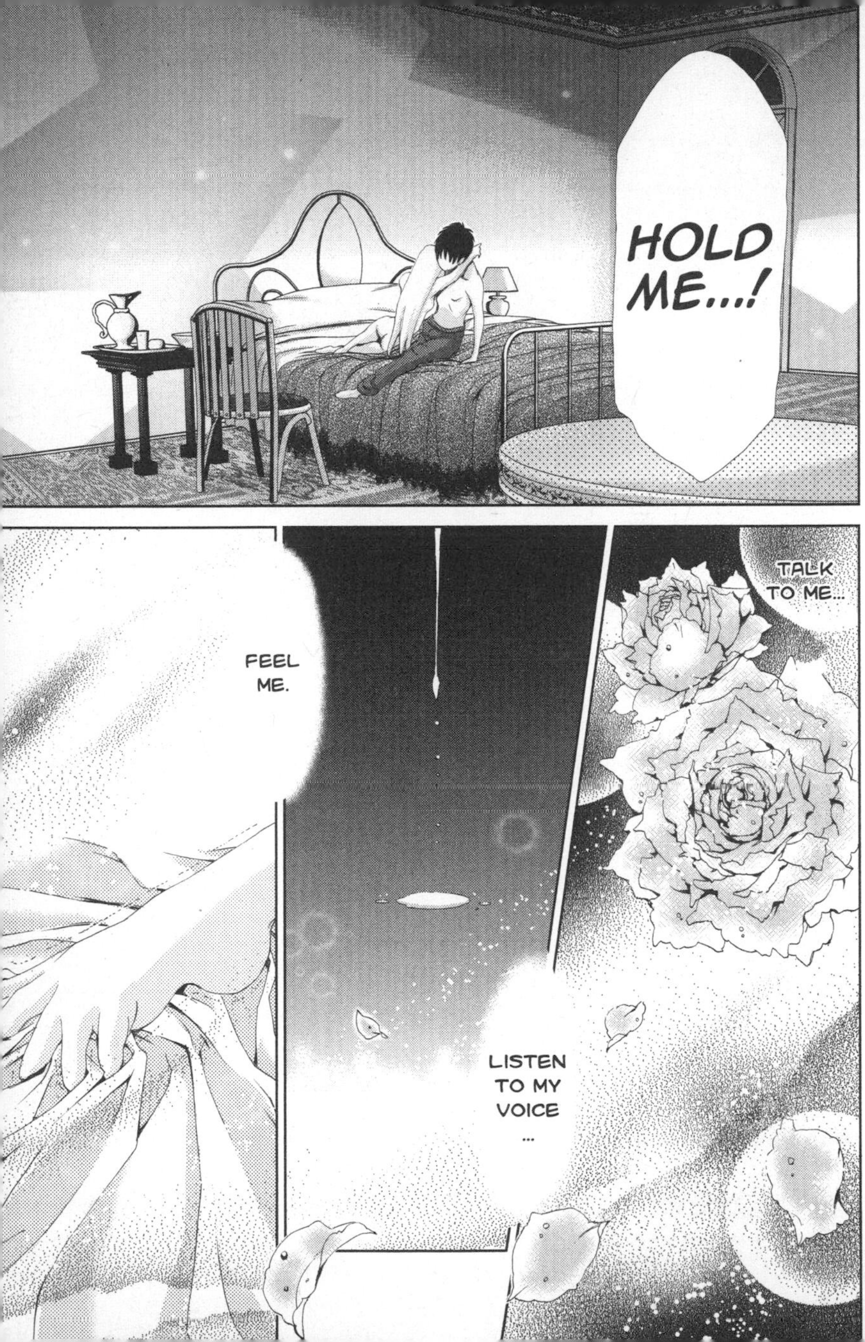
HOLD ME...!
TALK TO ME...
LISTEN TO MY VOICE ...
FEEL ME.

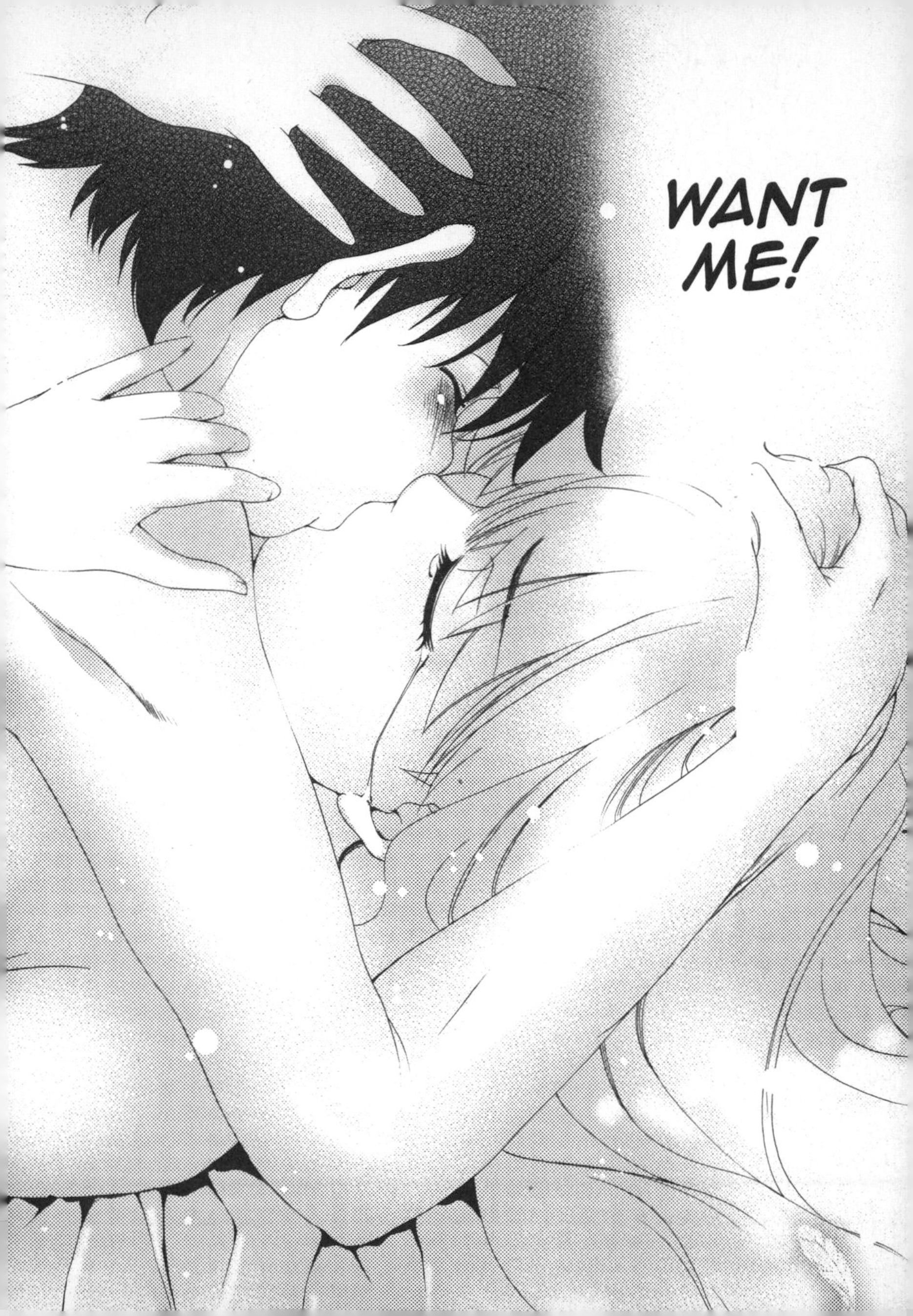
WANT ME!

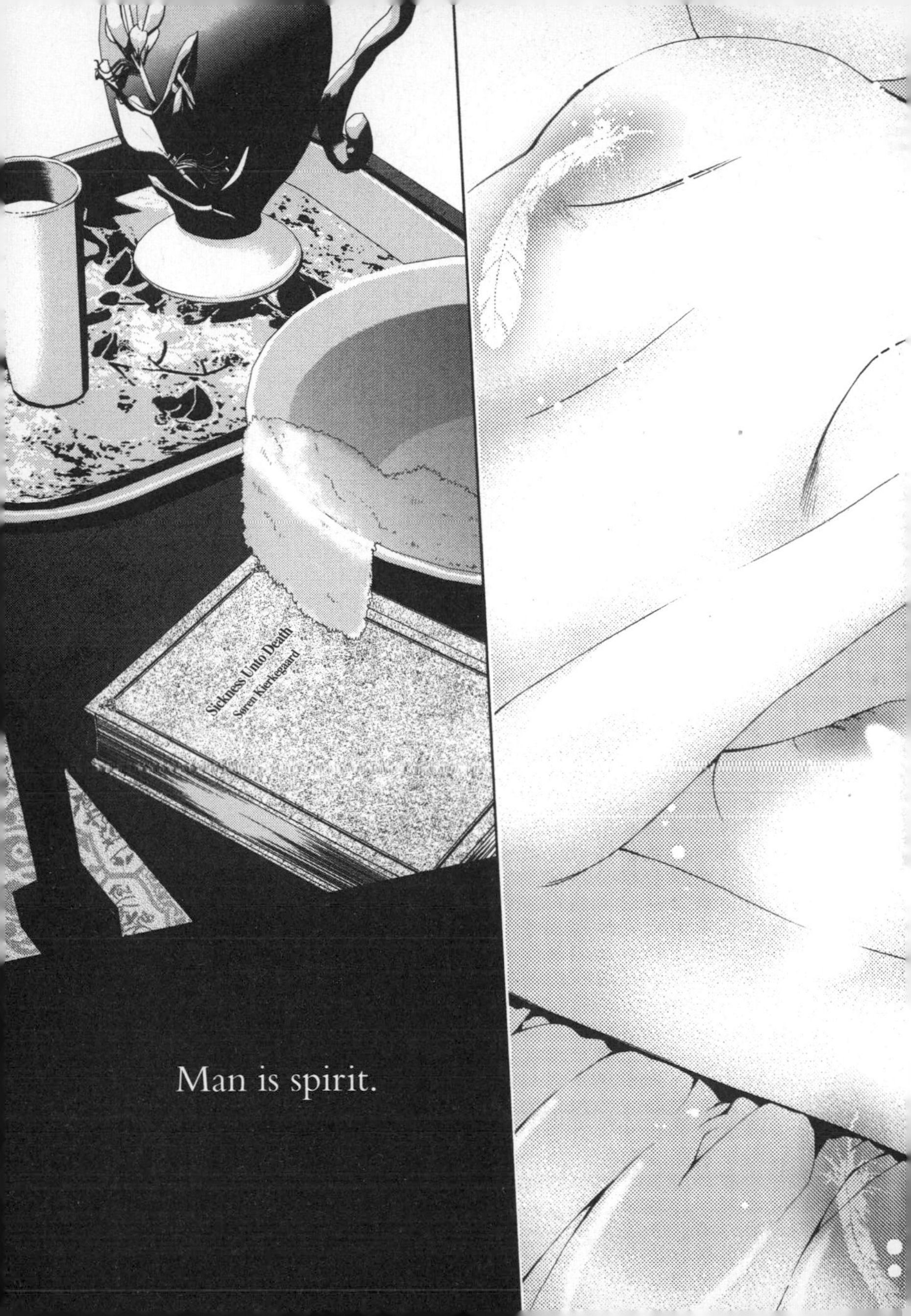
Sickness Unto Death
Soren Kierkegaard
Man is spirit.

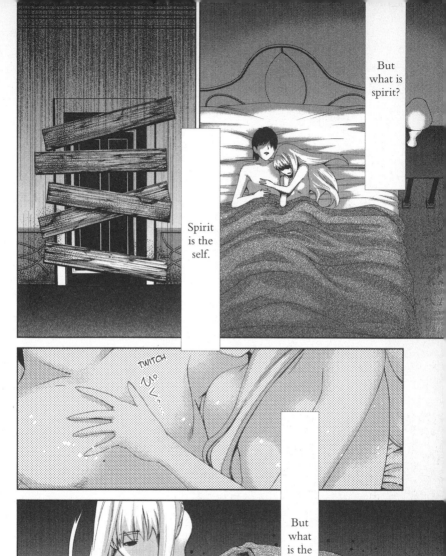

But what is spirit?

Spirit is the self.

TWITCH

But what is the self?

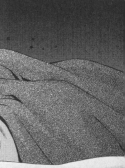

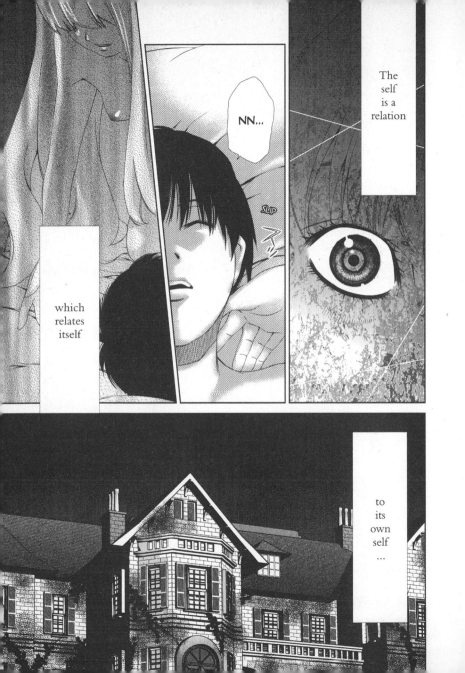

The
self
is a
relation

NN...

SLIP

which
relates
itself

to
its
own
self
...

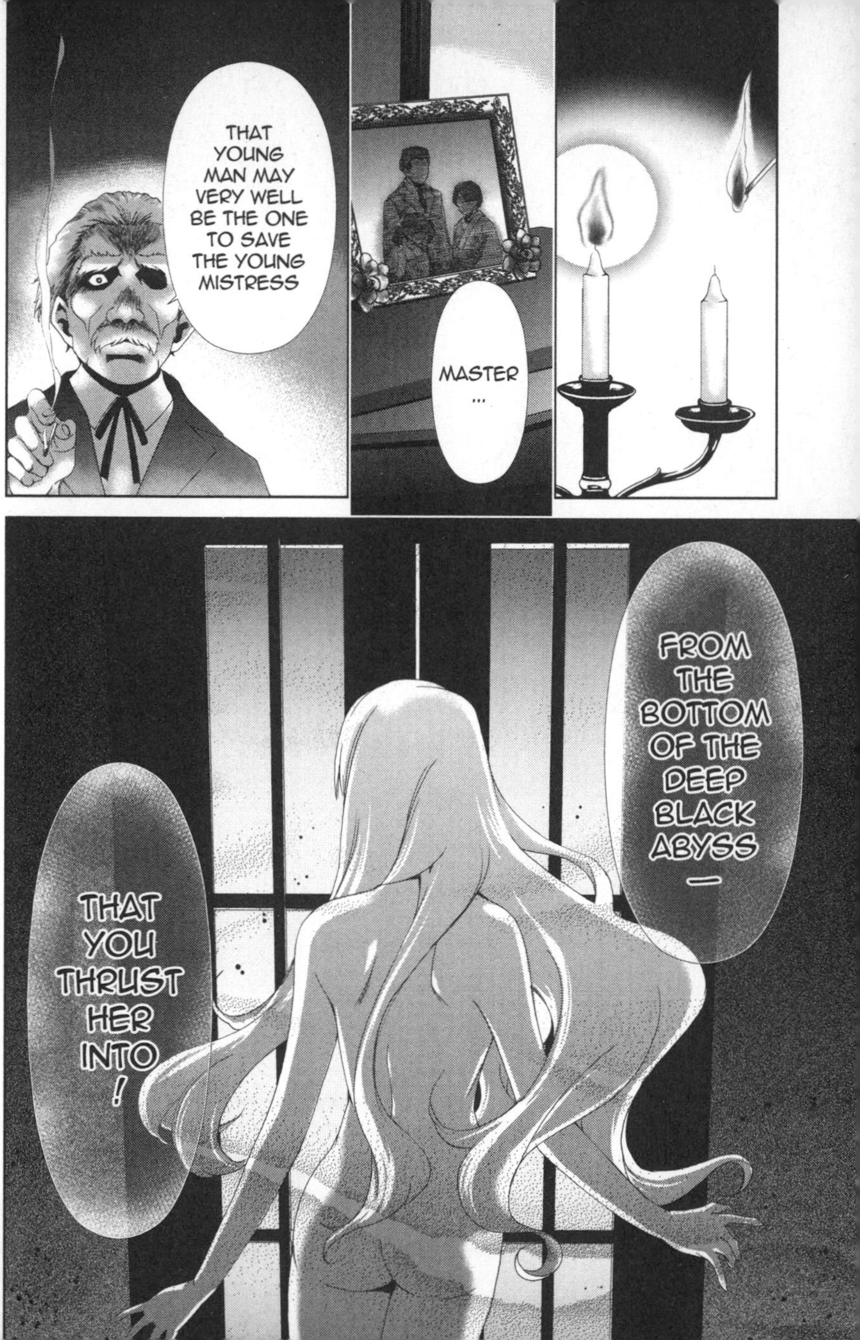
MASTER ...
THAT YOUNG MAN MAY VERY WELL BE THE ONE TO SAVE THE YOUNG MISTRESS
FROM THE BOTTOM OF THE DEEP BLACK ABYSS —
THAT YOU THRUST HER INTO!

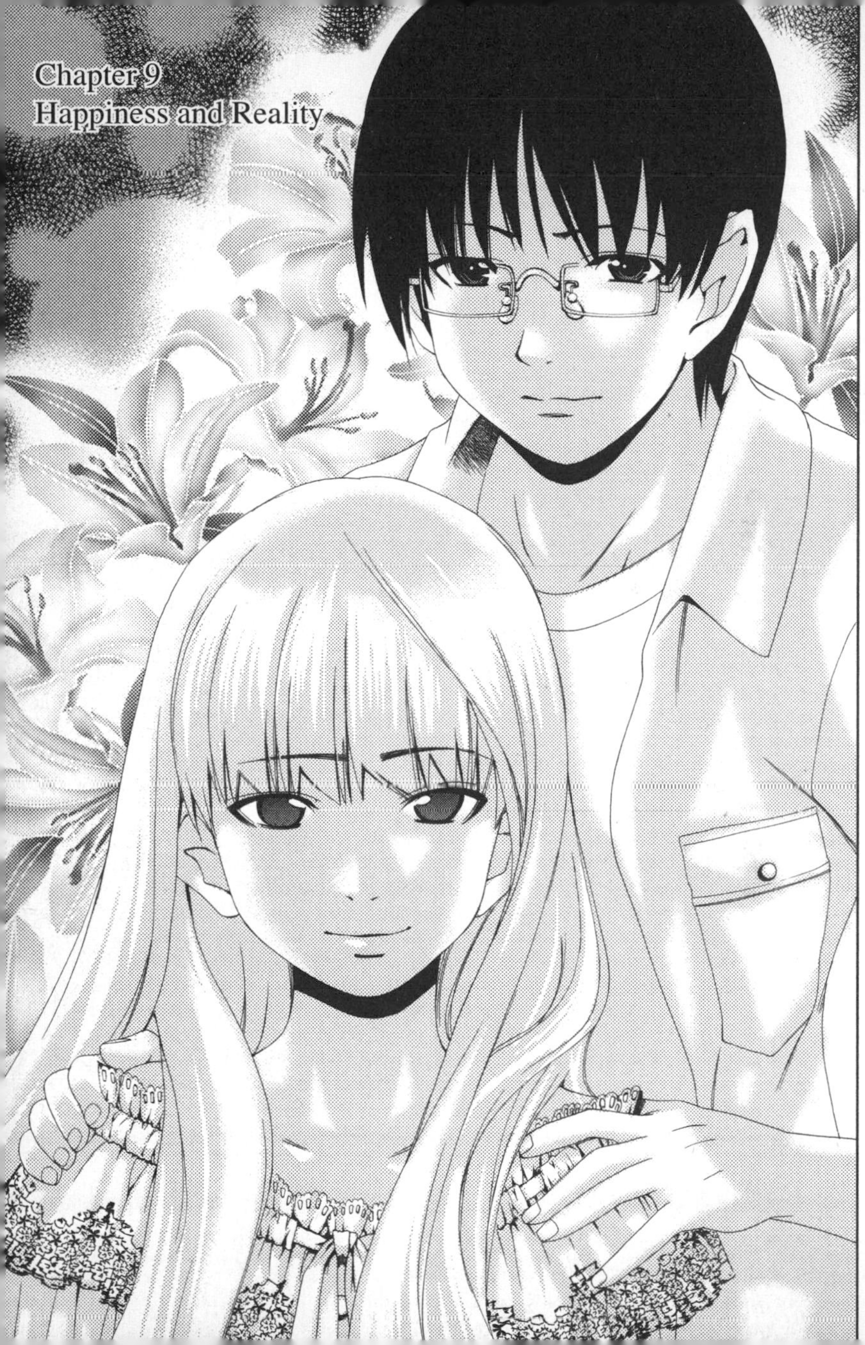
Chapter 9
Happiness and Reality

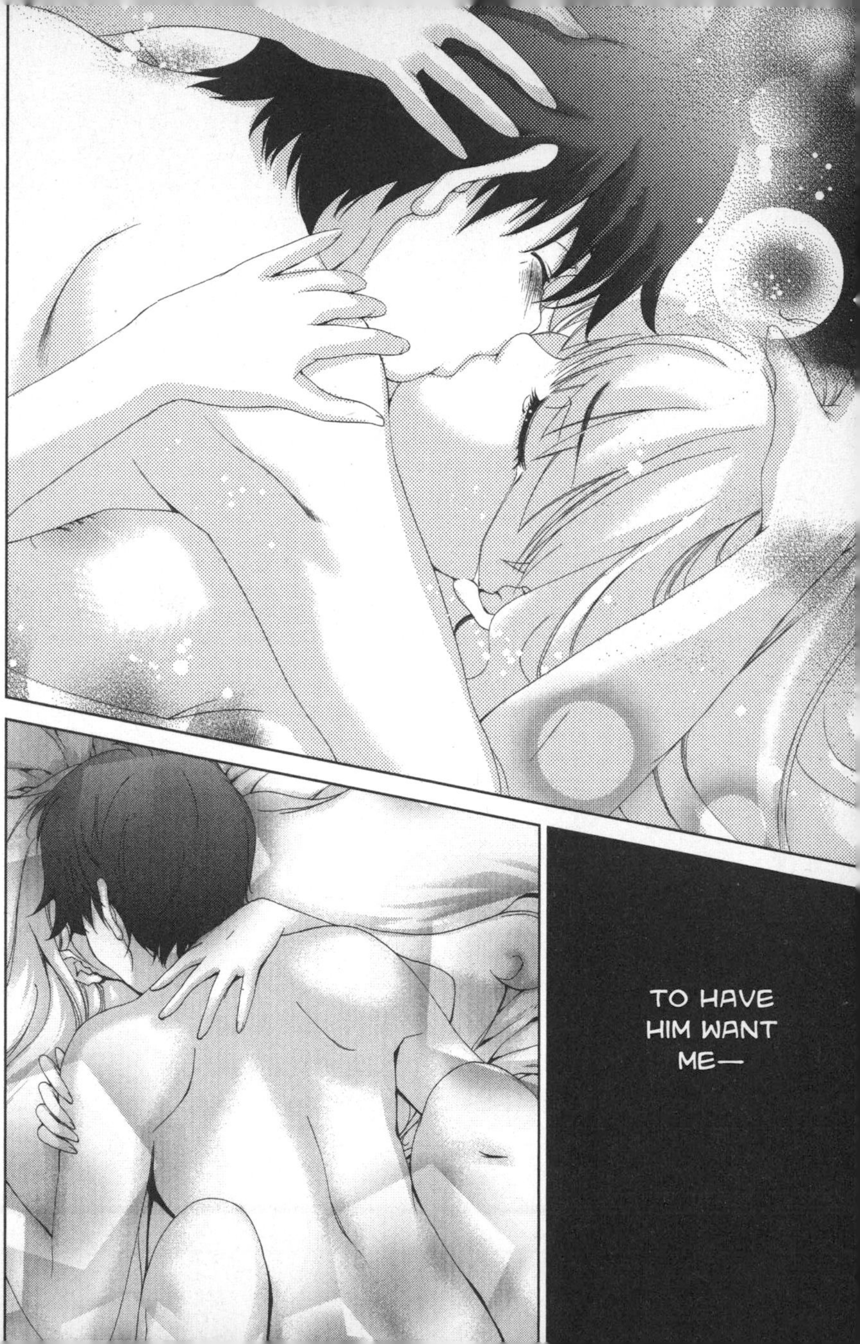
TO HAVE HIM WANT ME—

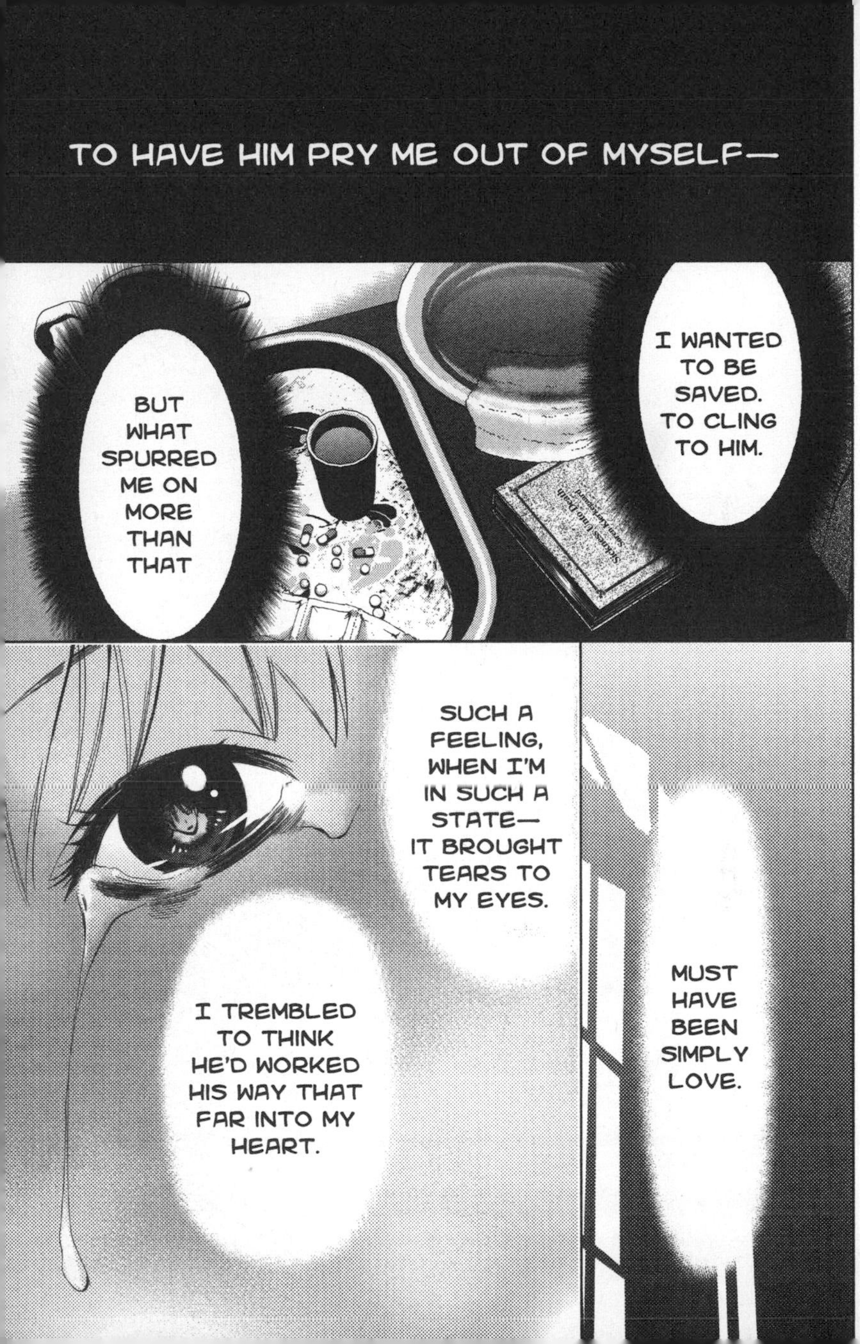
TO HAVE HIM PRY ME OUT OF MYSELF—
I WANTED TO BE SAVED. TO CLING TO HIM.
BUT WHAT SPURRED ME ON MORE THAN THAT
MUST HAVE BEEN SIMPLY LOVE.
SUCH A FEELING, WHEN I'M IN SUCH A STATE— IT BROUGHT TEARS TO MY EYES.
I TREMBLED TO THINK HE'D WORKED HIS WAY THAT FAR INTO MY HEART.

THAT'S PRECISELY WHY I NEEDED TO STOP.

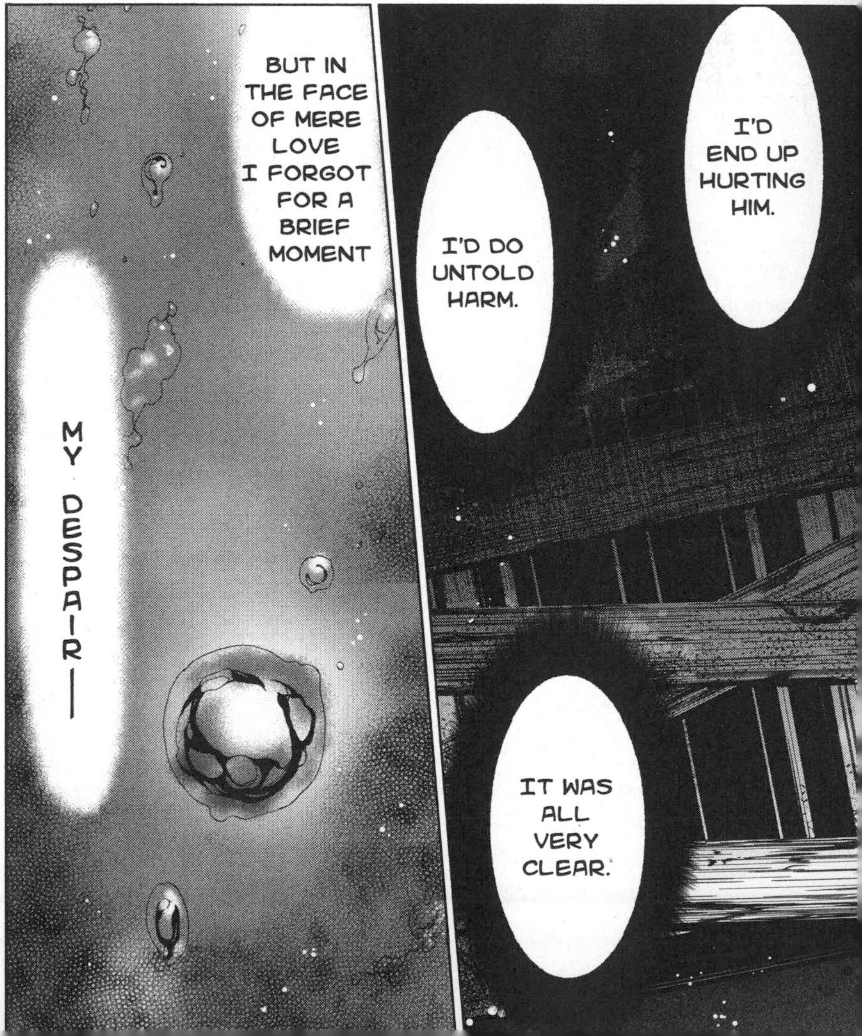
I'D END UP HURTING HIM.
I'D DO UNTOLD HARM.
IT WAS ALL VERY CLEAR.
BUT IN THE FACE OF MERE LOVE I FORGOT FOR A BRIEF MOMENT
MY DESPAIR—

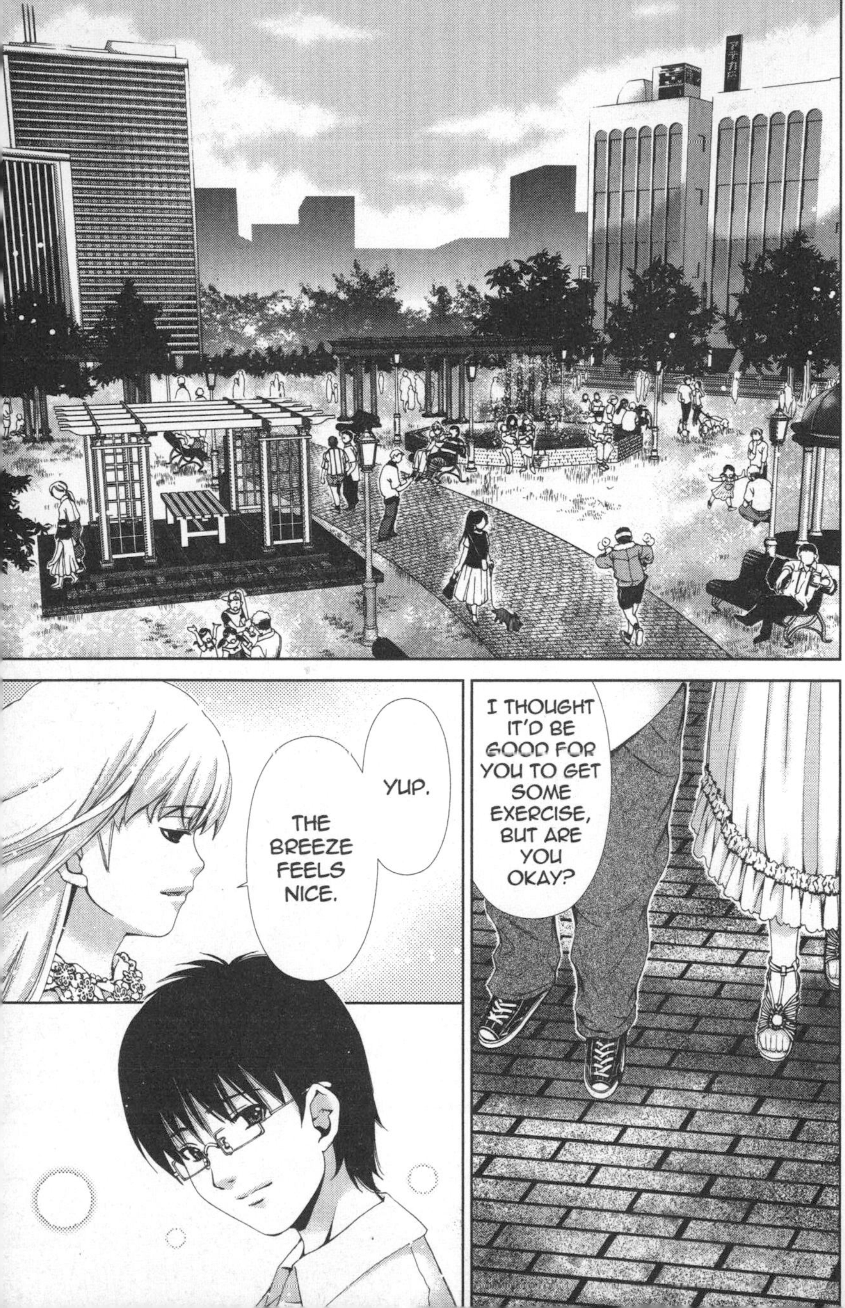
I THOUGHT IT'D BE GOOD FOR YOU TO GET SOME EXERCISE, BUT ARE YOU OKAY?
YUP. THE BREEZE FEELS NICE.

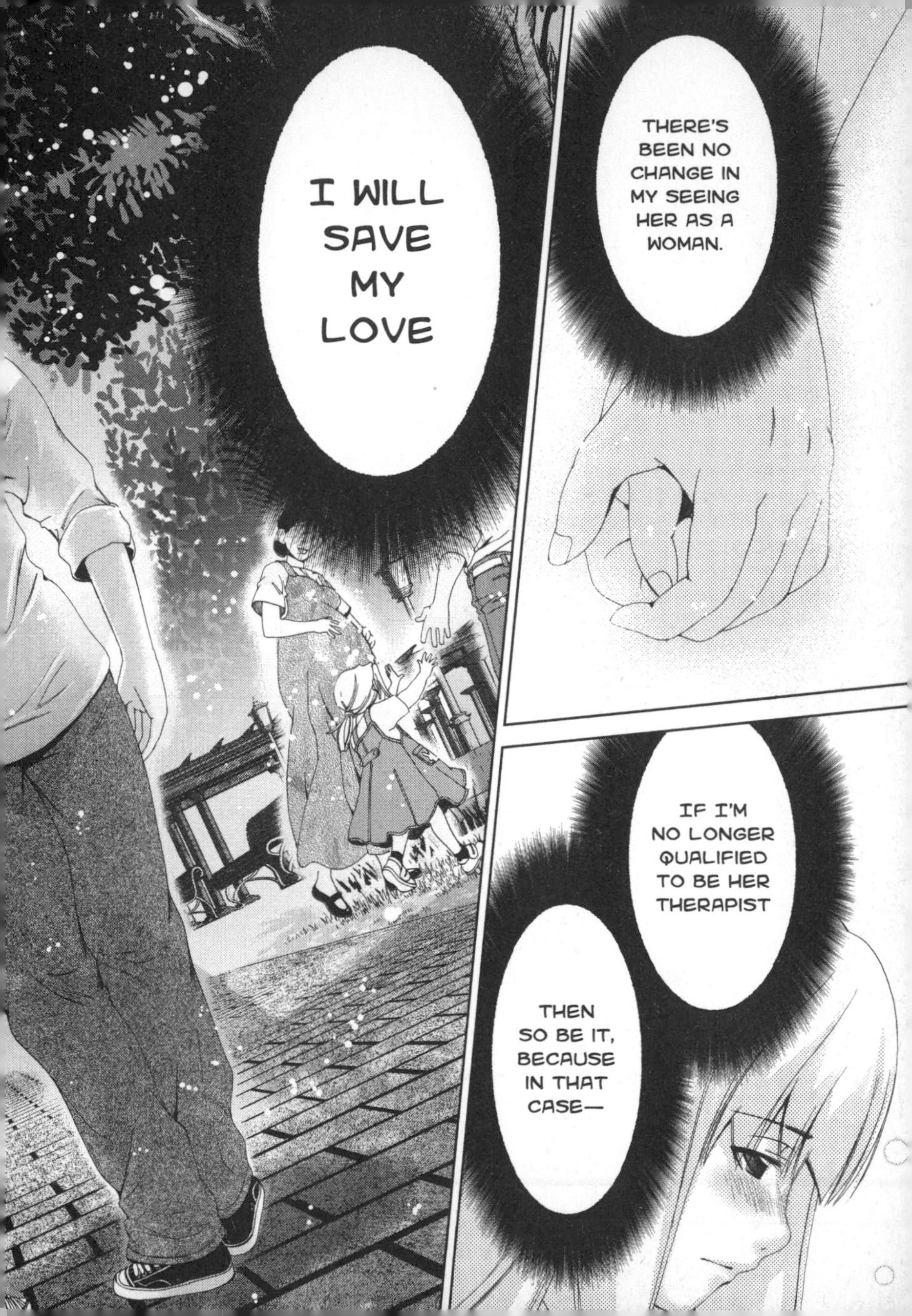
THERE'S BEEN NO CHANGE IN MY SEEING HER AS A WOMAN.
IF I'M NO LONGER QUALIFIED TO BE HER THERAPIST
THEN SO BE IT, BECAUSE IN THAT CASE—
I WILL SAVE MY LOVE

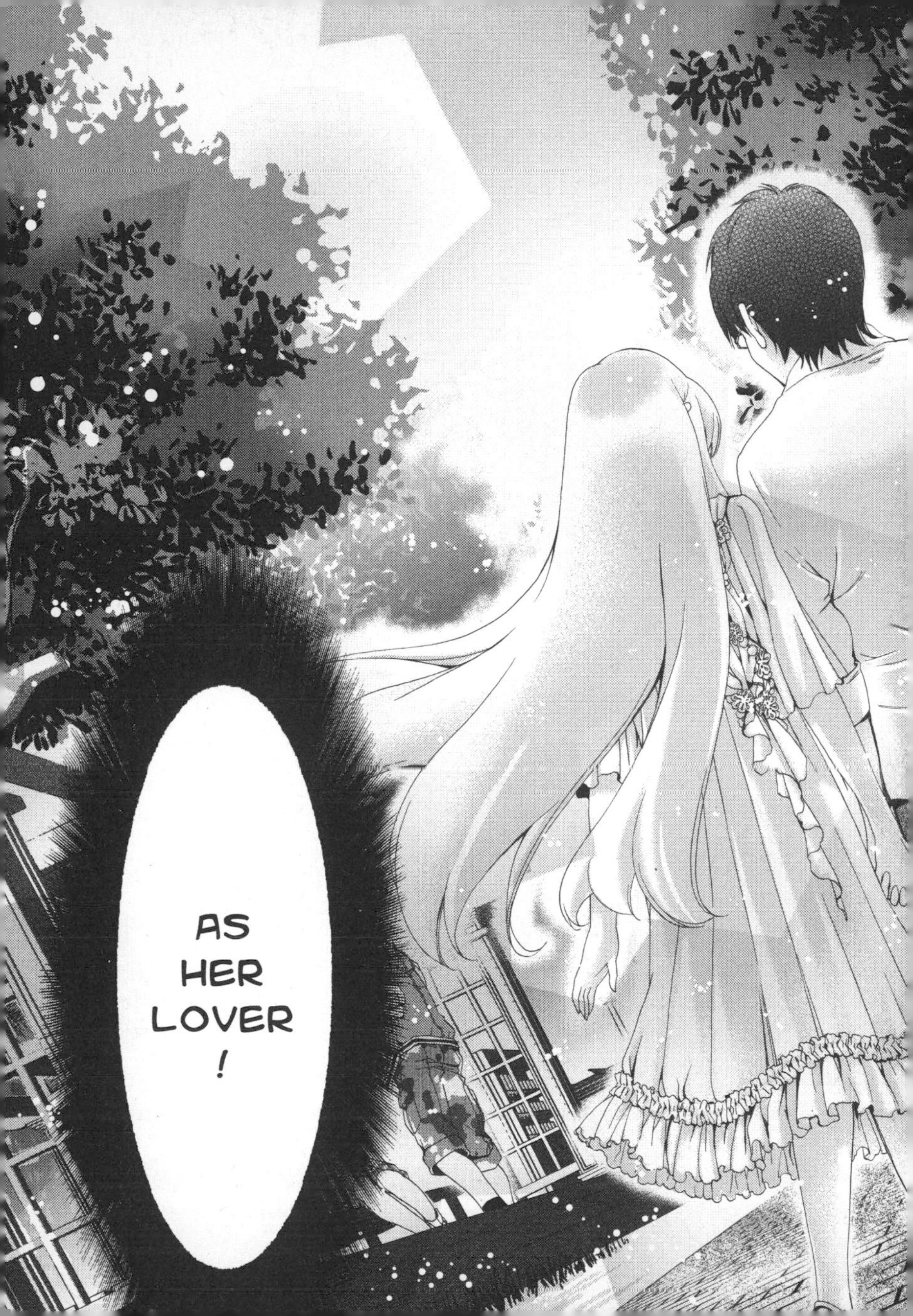
AS HER LOVER!

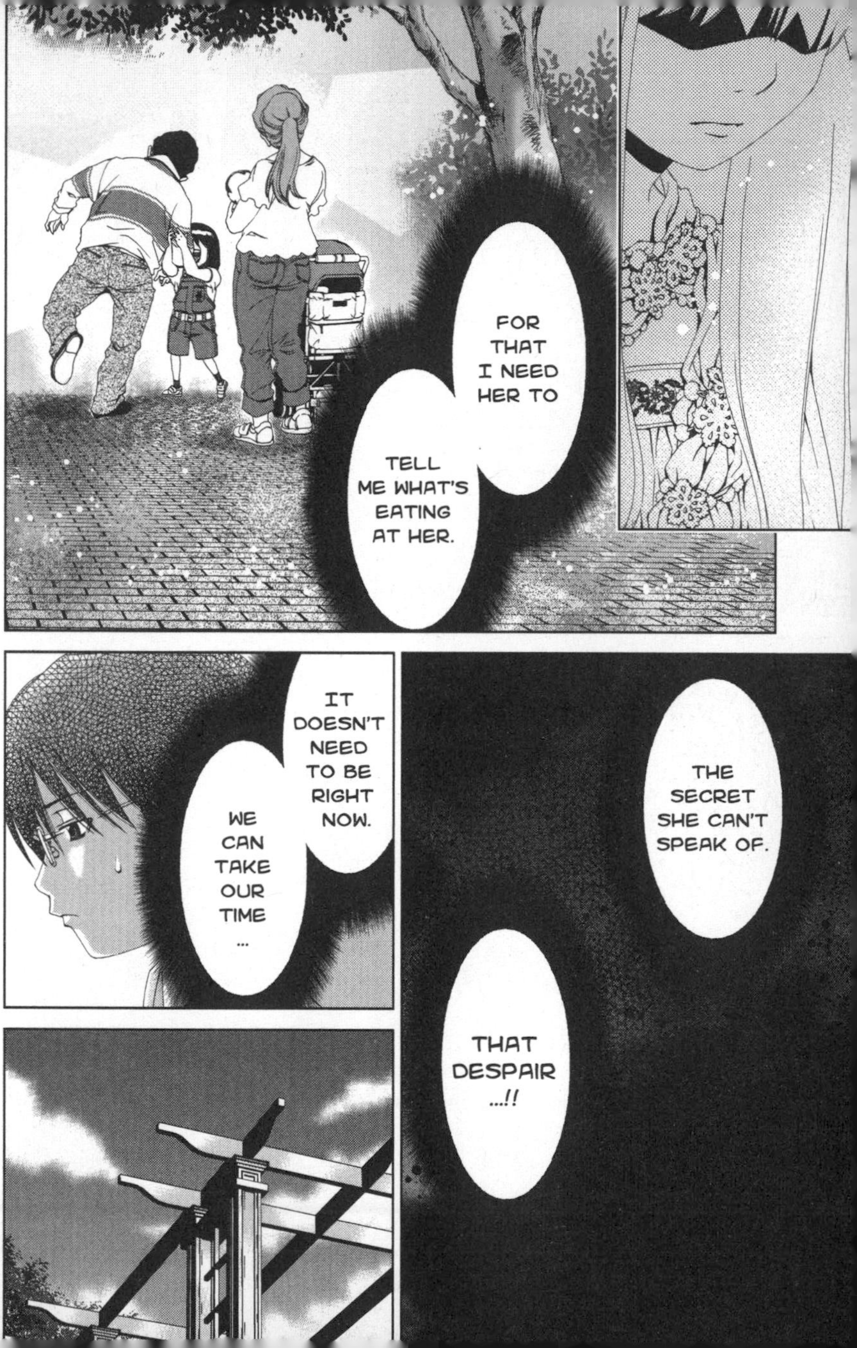
FOR THAT I NEED HER TO
TELL ME WHAT'S EATING AT HER.
THE SECRET SHE CAN'T SPEAK OF.
THAT DESPAIR ...!!
IT DOESN'T NEED TO BE RIGHT NOW.
WE CAN TAKE OUR TIME ...

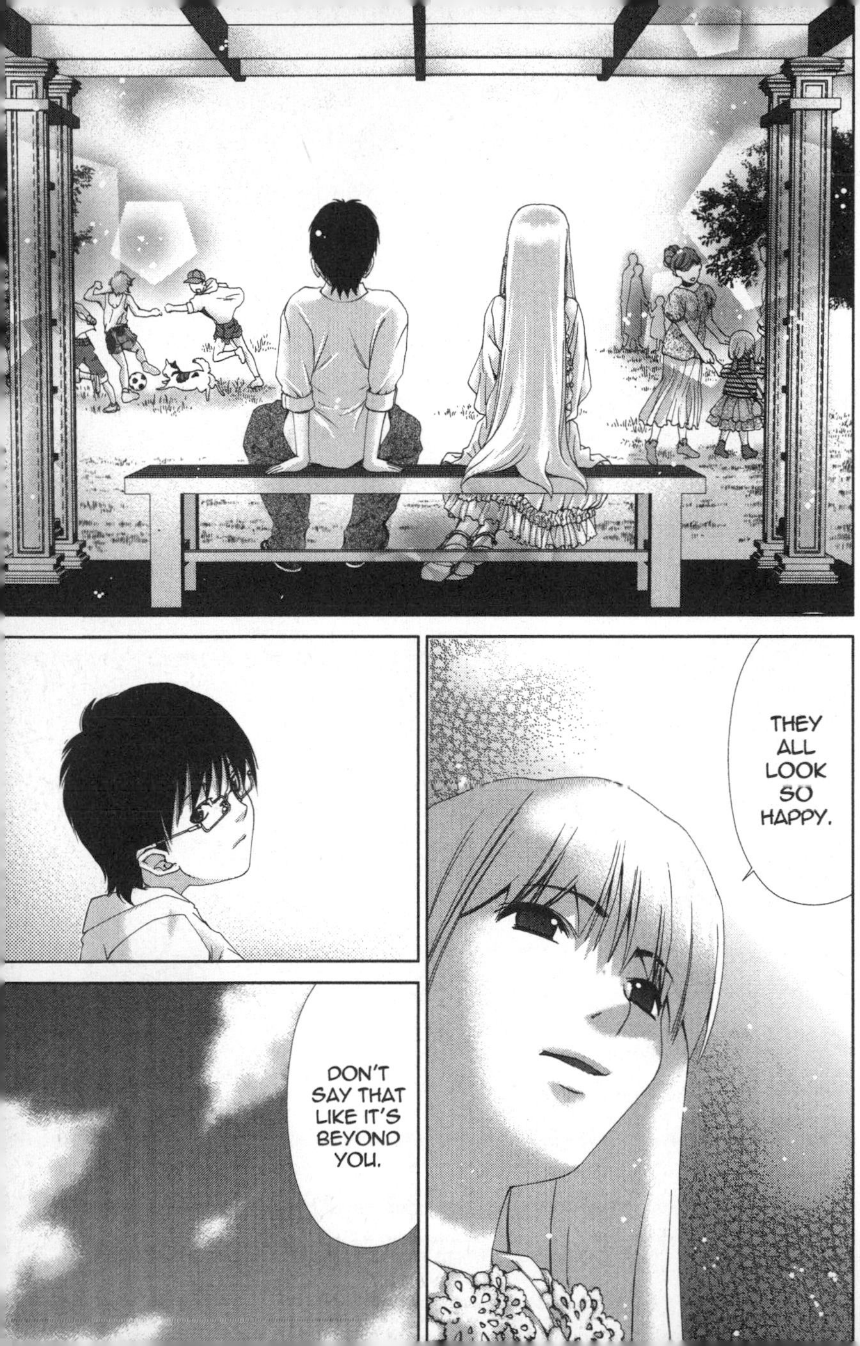
THEY ALL LOOK SO HAPPY.
DON'T SAY THAT LIKE IT'S BEYOND YOU.

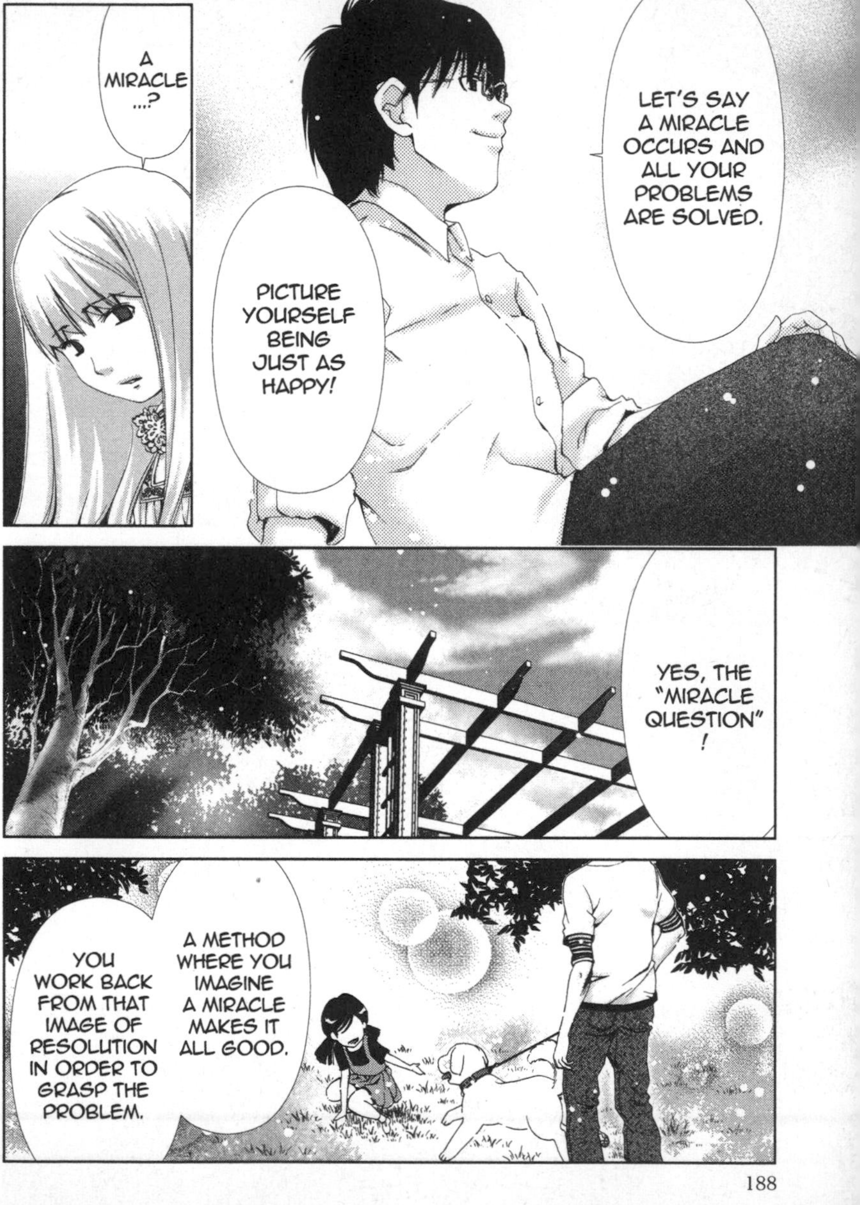
LET'S SAY A MIRACLE OCCURS AND ALL YOUR PROBLEMS ARE SOLVED.
PICTURE YOURSELF BEING JUST AS HAPPY!
A MIRACLE ...?
YES, THE "MIRACLE QUESTION" !
A METHOD WHERE YOU IMAGINE A MIRACLE MAKES IT ALL GOOD.
YOU WORK BACK FROM THAT IMAGE OF RESOLUTION IN ORDER TO GRASP THE PROBLEM.

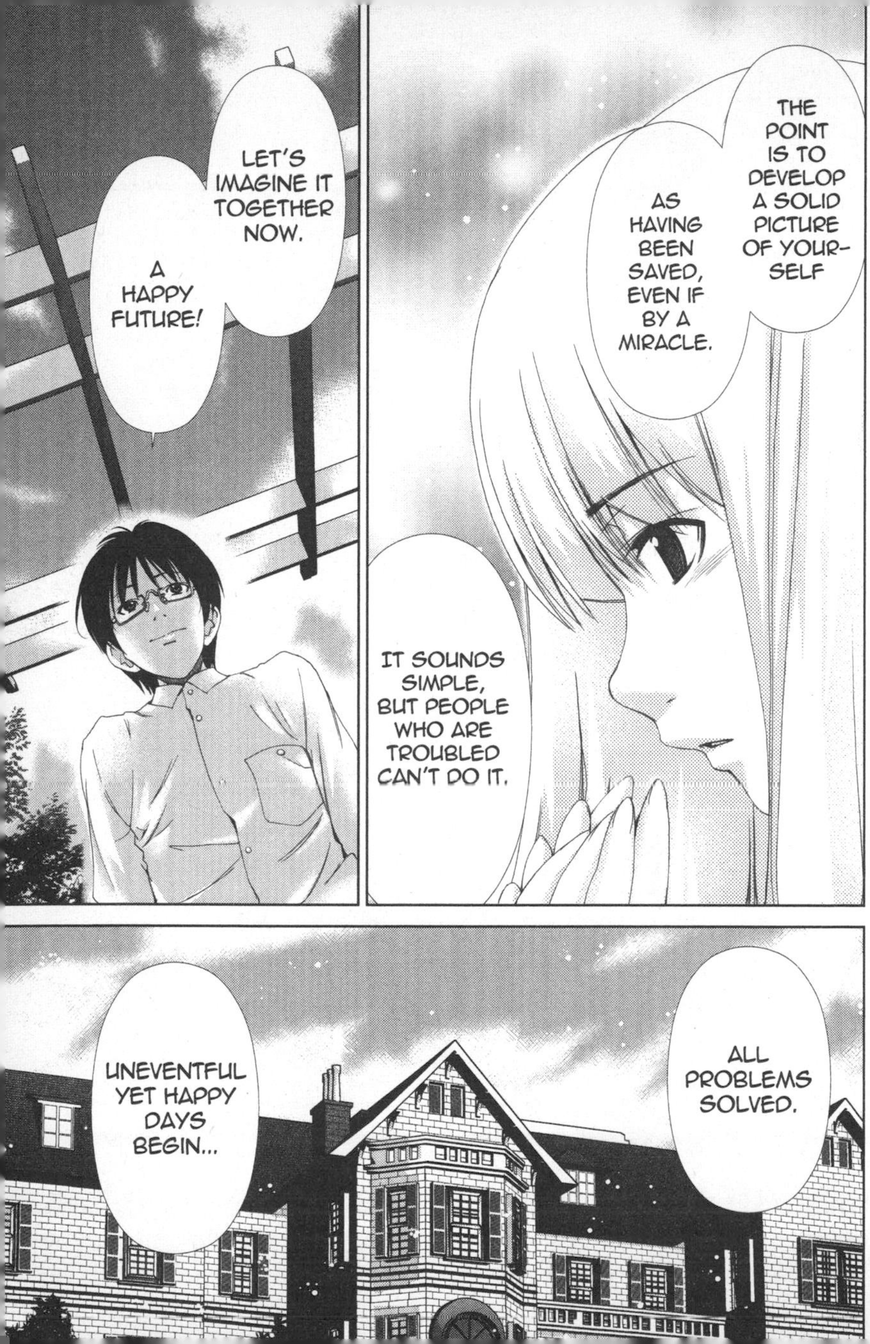
THE POINT IS TO DEVELOP A SOLID PICTURE OF YOUR-SELF
AS HAVING BEEN SAVED, EVEN IF BY A MIRACLE.
IT SOUNDS SIMPLE, BUT PEOPLE WHO ARE TROUBLED CAN'T DO IT.
LET'S IMAGINE IT TOGETHER NOW.
A HAPPY FUTURE!
ALL PROBLEMS SOLVED.
UNEVENTFUL YET HAPPY DAYS BEGIN...

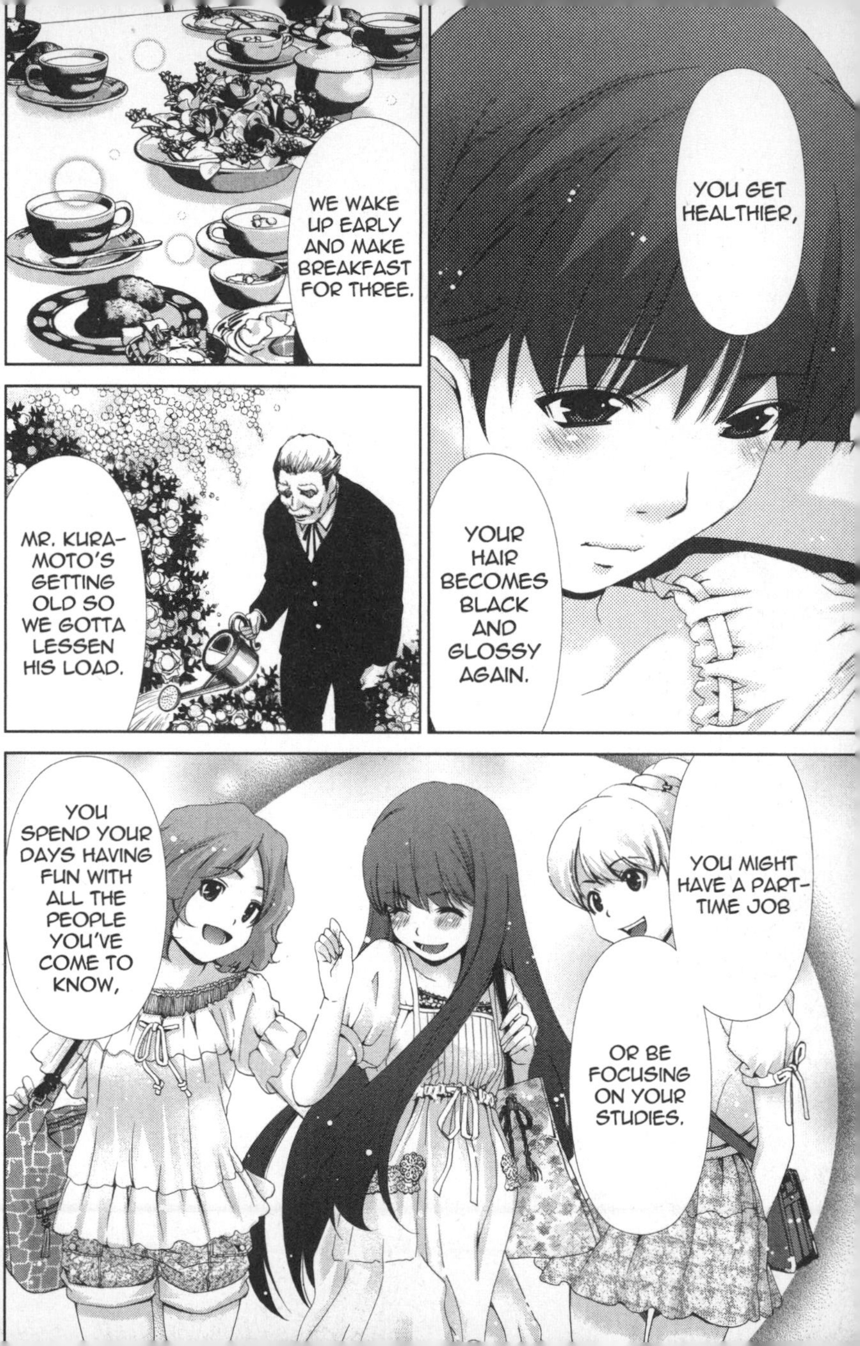
YOU GET HEALTHIER,
YOUR HAIR BECOMES BLACK AND GLOSSY AGAIN.
WE WAKE UP EARLY AND MAKE BREAKFAST FOR THREE.
MR. KURA-MOTO'S GETTING OLD SO WE GOTTA LESSEN HIS LOAD.
YOU MIGHT HAVE A PART-TIME JOB
OR BE FOCUSING ON YOUR STUDIES.
YOU SPEND YOUR DAYS HAVING FUN WITH ALL THE PEOPLE YOU'VE COME TO KNOW,

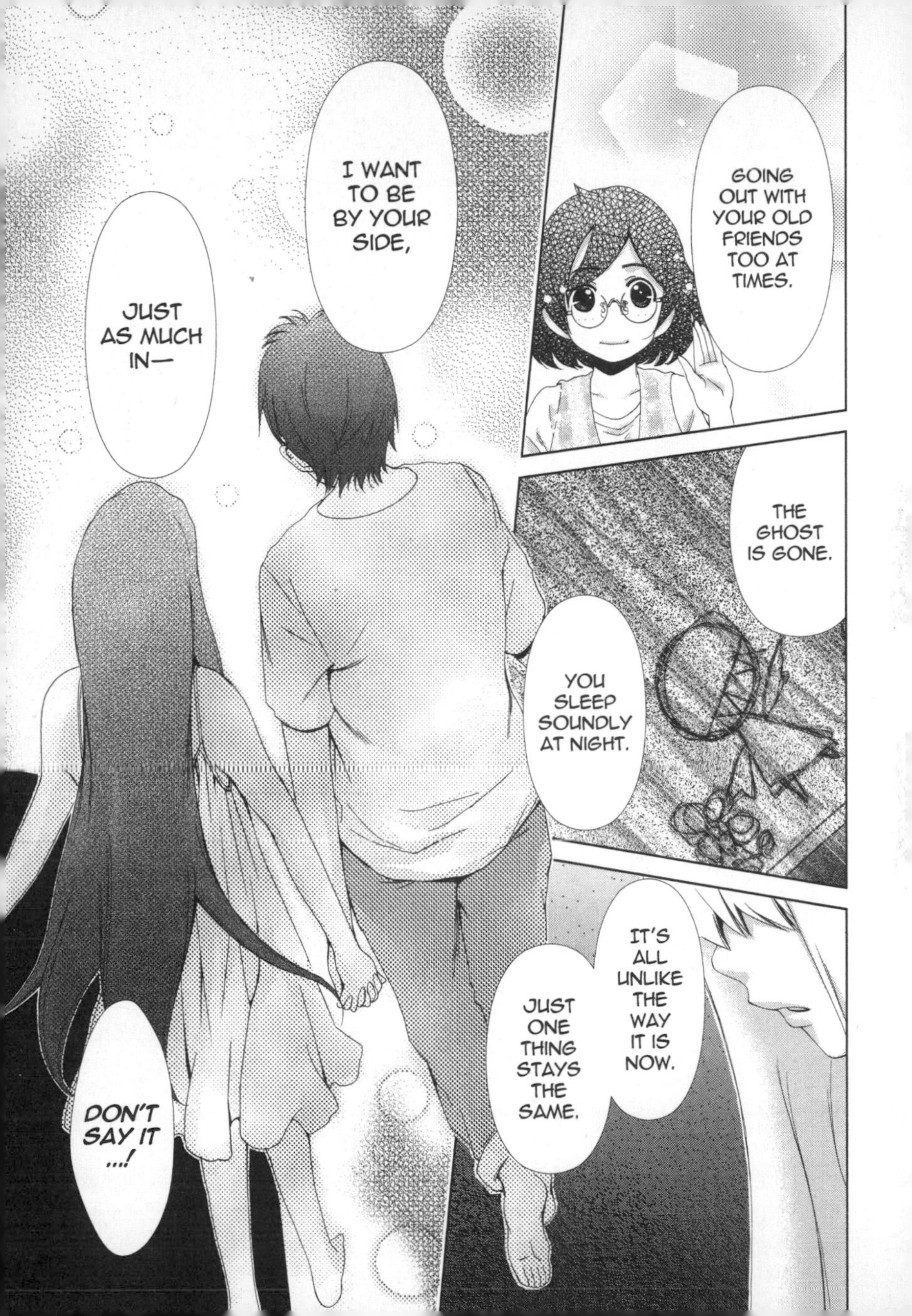

GOING OUT WITH YOUR OLD FRIENDS TOO AT TIMES.
THE GHOST IS GONE.
YOU SLEEP SOUNDLY AT NIGHT.
IT'S ALL UNLIKE THE WAY IT IS NOW.
JUST ONE THING STAYS THE SAME.
I WANT TO BE BY YOUR SIDE,
JUST AS MUCH IN—
DON'T SAY IT ...!

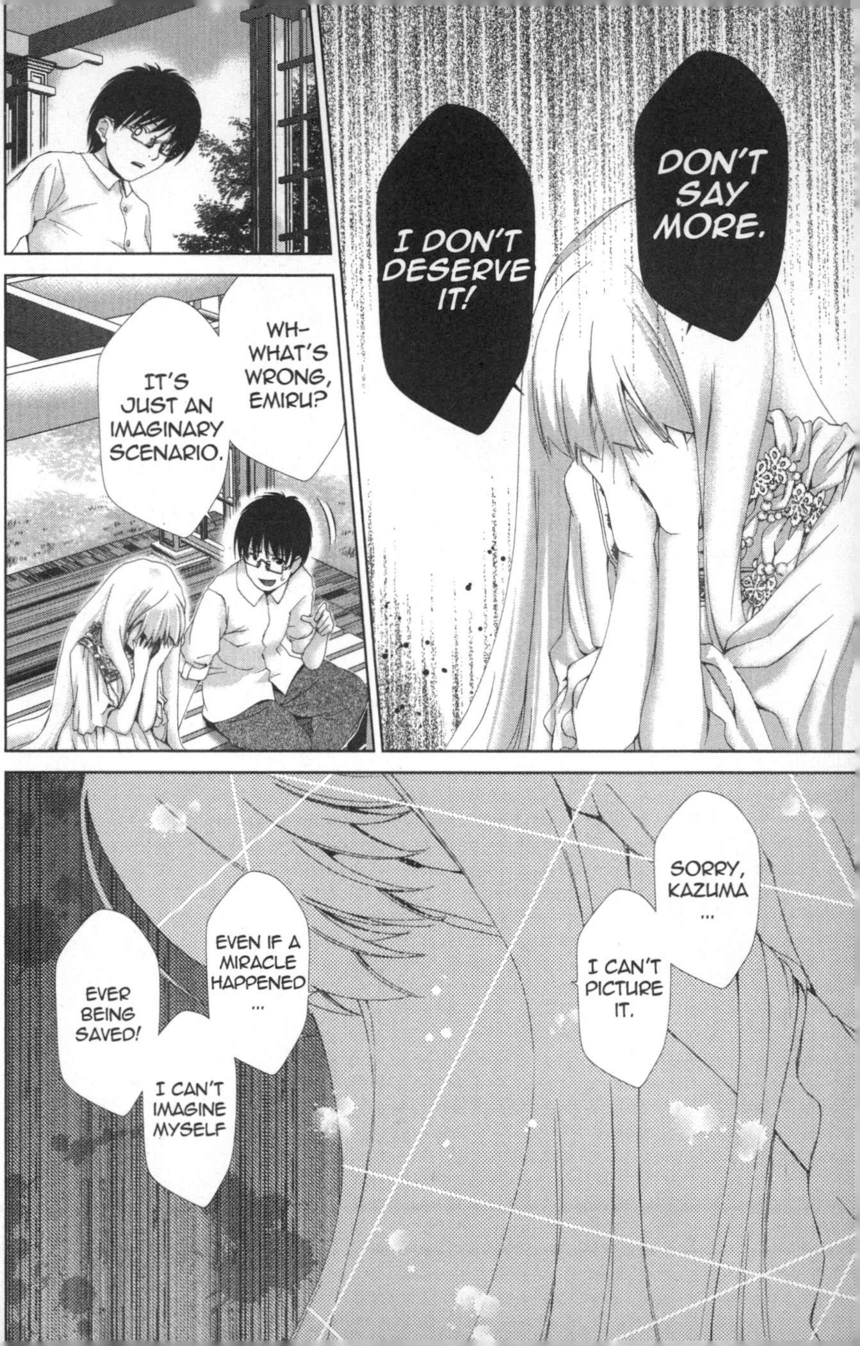
DON'T SAY MORE.
I DON'T DESERVE IT!
WH- WHAT'S WRONG, EMIRU?
IT'S JUST AN IMAGINARY SCENARIO.
SORRY, KAZUMA ...
I CAN'T PICTURE IT.
EVEN IF A MIRACLE HAPPENED ...
I CAN'T IMAGINE MYSELF
EVER BEING SAVED!

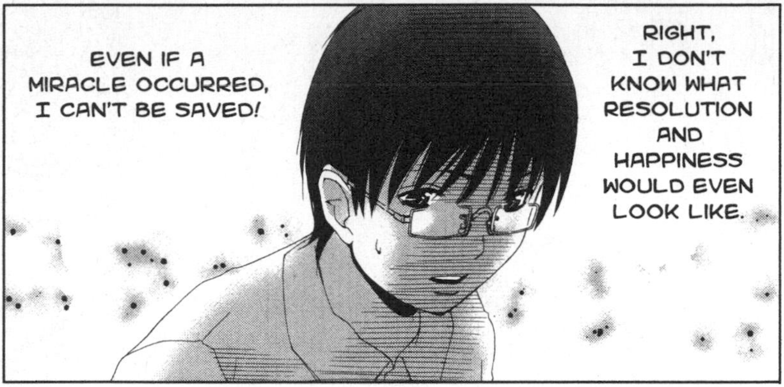
RIGHT, I DON'T KNOW WHAT RESOLUTION AND HAPPINESS WOULD EVEN LOOK LIKE.
EVEN IF A MIRACLE OCCURRED, I CAN'T BE SAVED!

DESPAIR SETS OFF A CHAIN REACTION.

I CAN'T INVOLVE HIM IN THIS ANY FURTHER!

I HAVE TO PUT AN END TO IT —

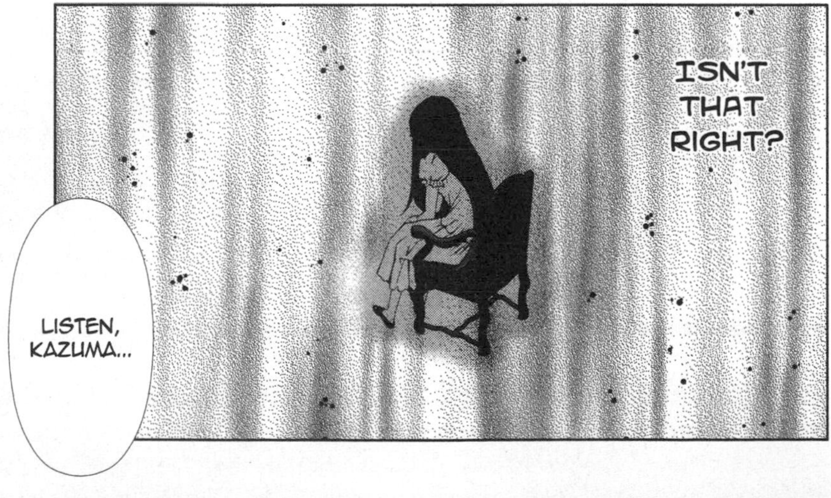
ISN'T THAT RIGHT?
LISTEN, KAZUMA...

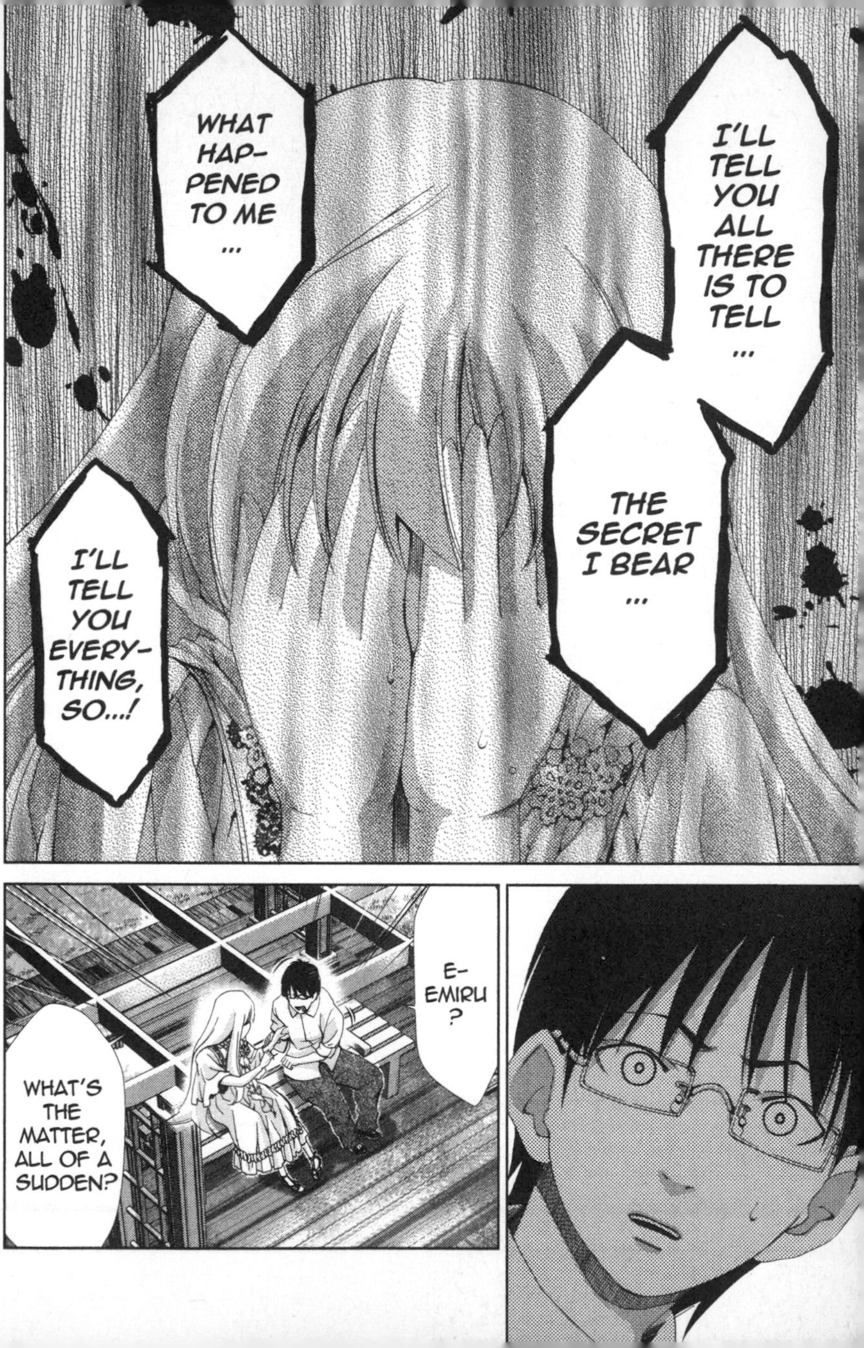
I'LL TELL YOU ALL THERE IS TO TELL ...
WHAT HAP-PENED TO ME ...
THE SECRET I BEAR ...
I'LL TELL YOU EVERY-THING, SO...!
E-EMIRU?
WHAT'S THE MATTER, ALL OF A SUDDEN?

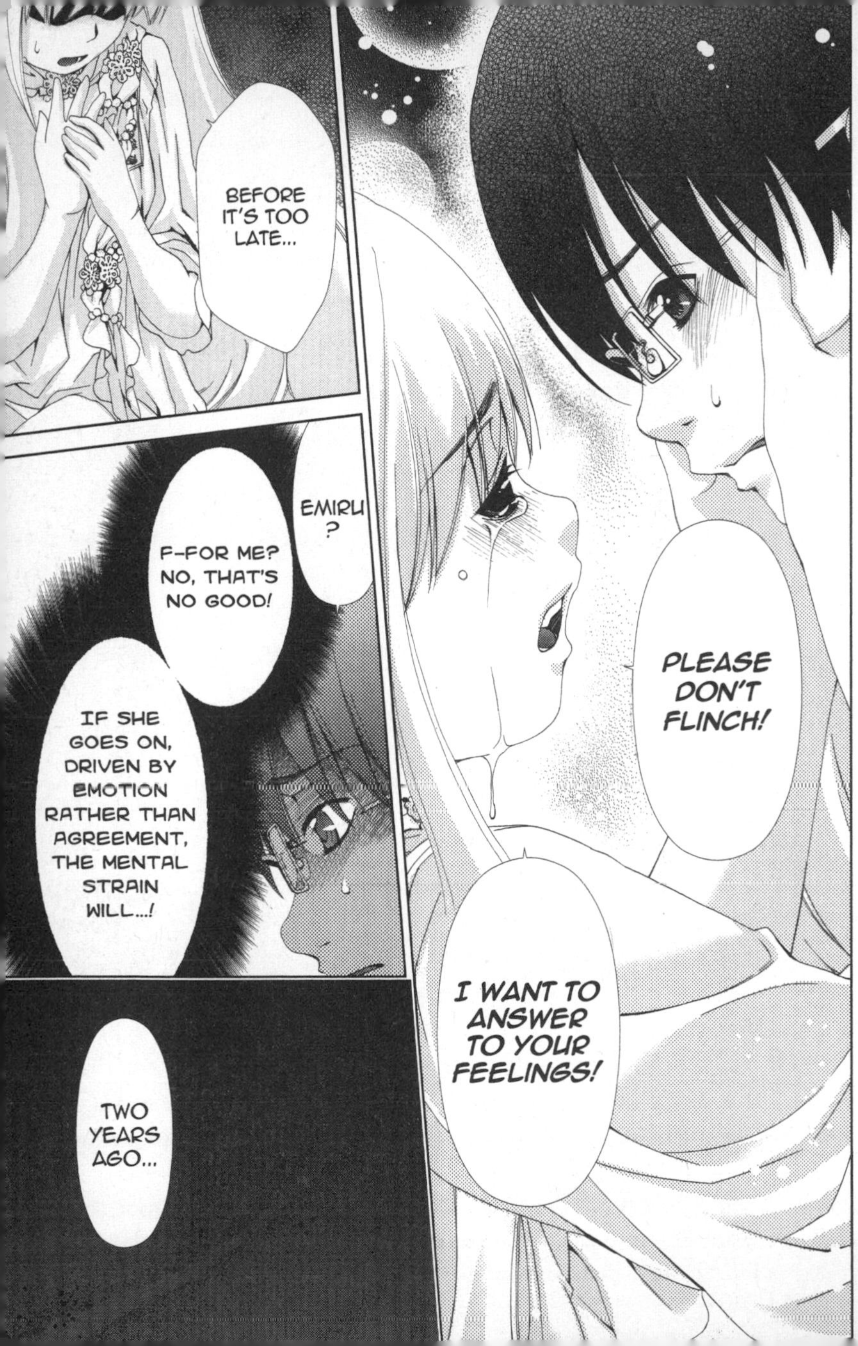
PLEASE DON'T FLINCH!
I WANT TO ANSWER TO YOUR FEELINGS!
BEFORE IT'S TOO LATE...
EMIRU?
F-FOR ME? NO, THAT'S NO GOOD!
IF SHE GOES ON, DRIVEN BY EMOTION RATHER THAN AGREEMENT, THE MENTAL STRAIN WILL...!
TWO YEARS AGO...

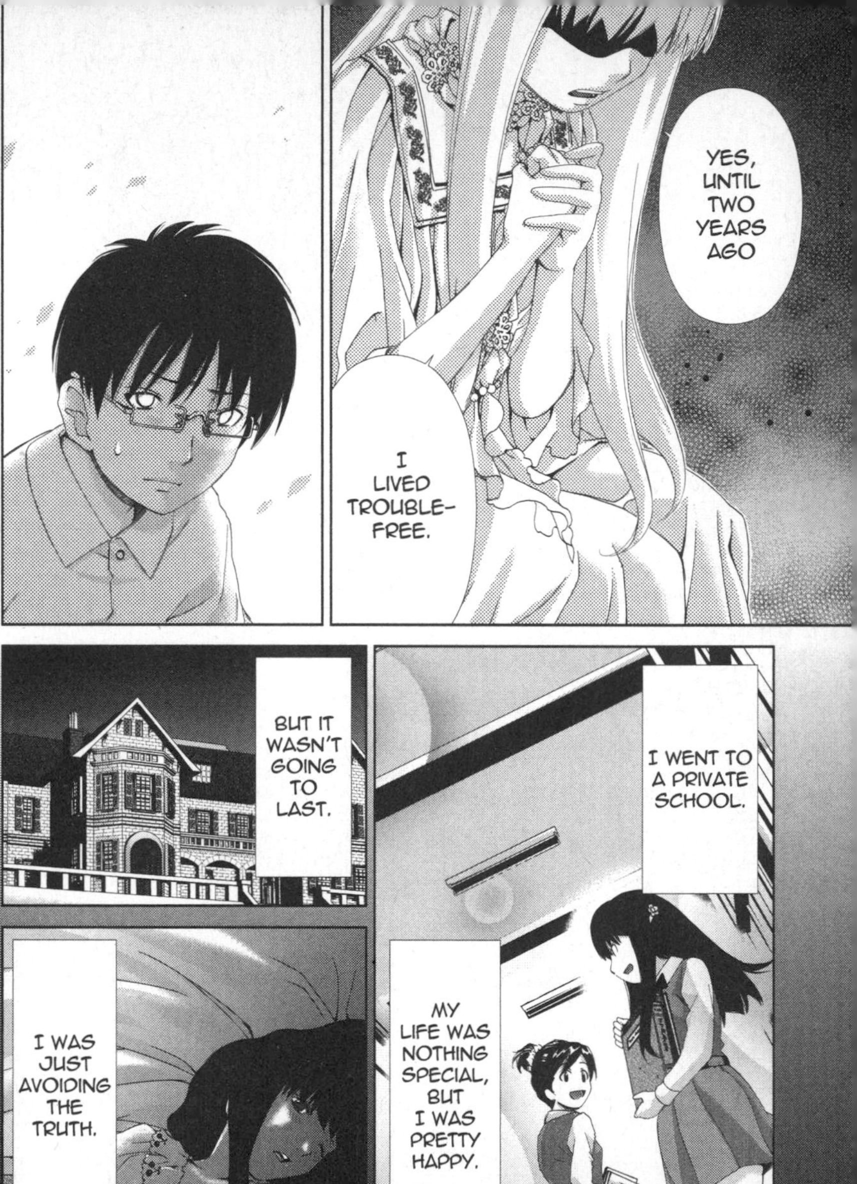
YES, UNTIL TWO YEARS AGO
I LIVED TROUBLE-FREE.
I WENT TO A PRIVATE SCHOOL.
MY LIFE WAS NOTHING SPECIAL, BUT I WAS PRETTY HAPPY.
BUT IT WASN'T GOING TO LAST.
I WAS JUST AVOIDING THE TRUTH.

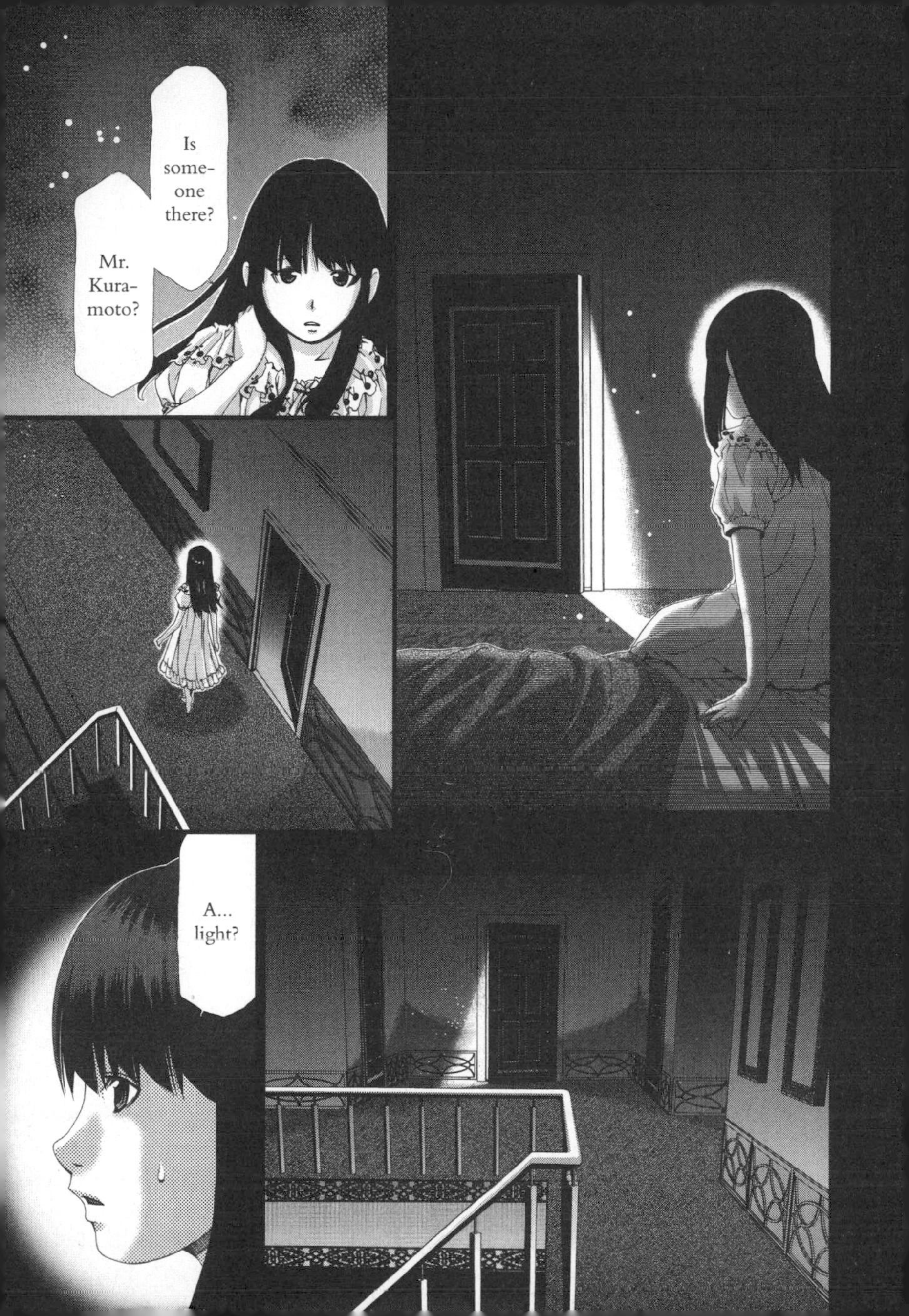
Is someone there?
Mr. Kuramoto?
A... light?

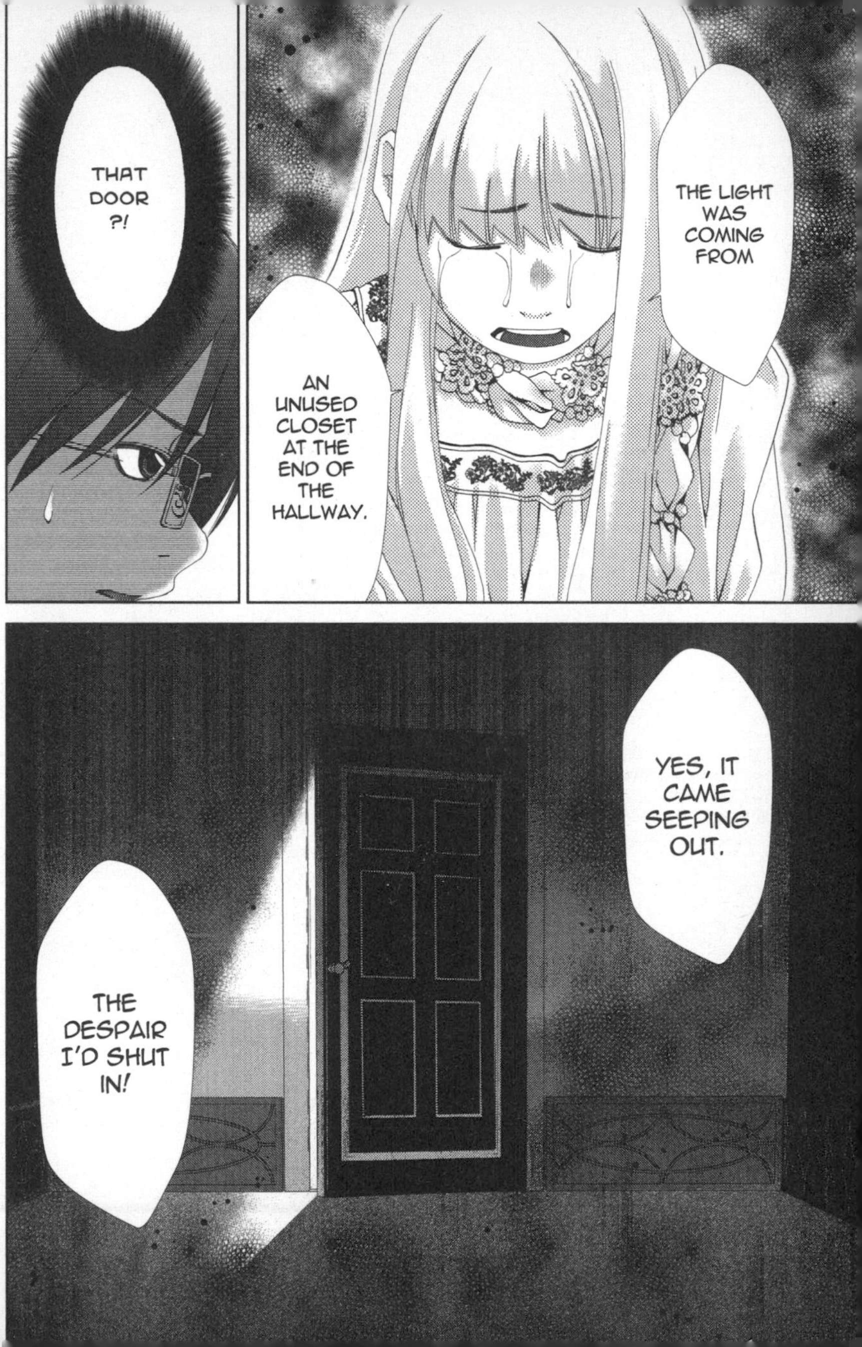
THE LIGHT WAS COMING FROM
AN UNUSED CLOSET AT THE END OF THE HALLWAY.
THAT DOOR ?!
YES, IT CAME SEEPING OUT.
THE DESPAIR I'D SHUT IN!

to be concluded
in *sickness unto death 2*

Production: Risa Cho
        Tomoe Tsutsumi
        Anthony Quintessenza

SHI NI ITARU YAMAI by Hikaru Asada / Takahiro Seguchi
© Hikaru Asada 2010
© Takahiro Seguchi 2010
All rights reserved.
First published in Japan in 2010 by HAKUSENSHA, INC., Tokyo
English language translation rights in the United States of America
and Canada arranged with HAKUSENSHA, INC., Tokyo through
Tuttle-Mori Agency Inc., Tokyo

Translation provided by Vertical, Inc., 2013
Published by Vertical, Inc., New York

Originally published in Japanese as *Shi ni Itaru Yamai 1* by Hakusensha, Inc., 2010
Shi ni Itaru Yamai first serialized in *Young Animal*, Hakusensha, Inc., 2009

This is a work of fiction.

ISBN: 978-1-939130-09-9

Manufactured in Canada

First Edition

Vertical, Inc.
451 Park Avenue South
7th Floor
New York, NY 10016
www.vertical-inc.com